T0345084

Insights in the Economics of Aging

National Bureau
of Economic Research
Conference Report

Insights in the
Economics of Aging

Edited by **David A. Wise**

The University of Chicago Press

Chicago and London

The University of Chicago Press, Chicago 60637
The University of Chicago Press, Ltd., London
© 2017 by the National Bureau of Economic Research
Published 2017
Printed in the United States of America
25 24 23 22 21 20 19 18 17   1 2 3 4 5

ISBN-13: 978-0-226-42667-9   (cloth)
ISBN-13: 978-0-226-42670-9   (e-book)
DOI: 10.7208/chicago/9780226426709.001.0001

Library of Congress Cataloging-in-Publication Data

Names: Wise, David A., editor.
Title: Insights in the economics of aging / edited by David A. Wise.
Other titles: National Bureau of Economic Research conference report.
Description: Chicago ; London : The University of Chicago Press,
    2016– | Series: National Bureau of Economic Research conference
    report
Identifiers: LCCN 2016023995 | ISBN 9780226426679 (cloth : alk.
    paper) | ISBN 9780226426709 (e-book)
Subjects: LCSH: Older people—United States—Economic conditions. |
    Retirees—United States—Economic conditions.
Classification: LCC HQ1064.U5 1547 2016 | DDC 305/.26—dc23
    LC record available at http://lccn.loc.gov/2016023995

Relation of the Directors to the
Work and Publications of the
National Bureau of Economic Research

1. The object of the NBER is to ascertain and present to the economics profession, and to the public more generally, important economic facts and their interpretation in a scientific manner without policy recommendations. The Board of Directors is charged with the responsibility of ensuring that the work of the NBER is carried on in strict conformity with this object.

2. The President shall establish an internal review process to ensure that book manuscripts proposed for publication DO NOT contain policy recommendations. This shall apply both to the proceedings of conferences and to manuscripts by a single author or by one or more co-authors but shall not apply to authors of comments at NBER conferences who are not NBER affiliates.

3. No book manuscript reporting research shall be published by the NBER until the President has sent to each member of the Board a notice that a manuscript is recommended for publication and that in the President's opinion it is suitable for publication in accordance with the above principles of the NBER. Such notification will include a table of contents and an abstract or summary of the manuscript's content, a list of contributors if applicable, and a response form for use by Directors who desire a copy of the manuscript for review. Each manuscript shall contain a summary drawing attention to the nature and treatment of the problem studied and the main conclusions reached.

4. No volume shall be published until forty-five days have elapsed from the above notification of intention to publish it. During this period a copy shall be sent to any Director requesting it, and if any Director objects to publication on the grounds that the manuscript contains policy recommendations, the objection will be presented to the author(s) or editor(s). In case of dispute, all members of the Board shall be notified, and the President shall appoint an ad hoc committee of the Board to decide the matter; thirty days additional shall be granted for this purpose.

5. The President shall present annually to the Board a report describing the internal manuscript review process, any objections made by Directors before publication or by anyone after publication, any disputes about such matters, and how they were handled.

6. Publications of the NBER issued for informational purposes concerning the work of the Bureau, or issued to inform the public of the activities at the Bureau, including but not limited to the NBER Digest and Reporter, shall be consistent with the object stated in paragraph 1. They shall contain a specific disclaimer noting that they have not passed through the review procedures required in this resolution. The Executive Committee of the Board is charged with the review of all such publications from time to time.

7. NBER working papers and manuscripts distributed on the Bureau's web site are not deemed to be publications for the purpose of this resolution, but they shall be consistent with the object stated in paragraph 1. Working papers shall contain a specific disclaimer noting that they have not passed through the review procedures required in this resolution. The NBER's web site shall contain a similar disclaimer. The President shall establish an internal review process to ensure that the working papers and the web site do not contain policy recommendations, and shall report annually to the Board on this process and any concerns raised in connection with it.

8. Unless otherwise determined by the Board or exempted by the terms of paragraphs 6 and 7, a copy of this resolution shall be printed in each NBER publication as described in paragraph 2 above.

Contents

Preface

This volume consists of papers presented at a conference held in Carefree, Arizona, in May 2015. Most of the research was conducted as part of the Program on the Economics of Aging at the National Bureau of Economic Research. The majority of the work was sponsored by the US Department of Health and Human Services, through the National Institute on Aging grants P01-AG005842 and P30-AG012810 to the National Bureau of Economic Research. Any other funding sources are noted in the individual chapters.

Any opinions expressed in this volume are those of the respective authors and do not necessarily reflect the views of the National Bureau of Economic Research or the sponsoring organizations.

Introduction

David A. Wise and Richard Woodbury

This volume marks thirty years since the inception of the NBER program on aging. When the program began, the baby boom generation was in their twenties and thirties, and life expectancy at older ages was nearly three years shorter than it is today. The program was created with a forward-thinking orientation, drawing together economists from multiple subfields of the profession to consider together what would become one of the most important demographic, social, and economic transitions of the twenty-first century. The underlying focus of the program is to study the health and financial well-being of people as they age, and of a population that is increasingly composed of older people.

This is the sixteenth in a series of NBER volumes that highlight economics of aging research. The previous volumes are *The Economics of Aging, Issues in the Economics of Aging, Topics in the Economics of Aging, Studies in the Economics of Aging, Advances in the Economics of Aging, Inquiries in the Economics of Aging, Frontiers in the Economics of Aging, Themes in the Economics of Aging, Perspectives on the Economics of Aging, Analyses in the Economics of Aging, Developments in the Economics of Aging, Research Findings in the Economics of Aging, Explorations in the Economics of Aging, Investigations in the Economics of Aging,* and *Discoveries in the Economics of Aging.*

David A. Wise is the John F. Stambaugh Professor of Political Economy at the Kennedy School of Government at Harvard University. He is the area director of Health and Retirement Programs and director of the Program on the Economics of Aging at the National Bureau of Economic Research. Richard Woodbury is a senior administrator with the Program on the Economics of Aging at the National Bureau of Economic Research.

For acknowledgments, sources of research support, and disclosure of the authors' material financial relationships, if any, please see http://www.nber.org/chapters/c13628.ack.

The demographic backdrop to the research in this volume is substantially different from when the program began thirty years ago. Today, the leading edge of the baby boom generation is entering their seventies. Many are retiring from paid work, yet they are living longer than ever. Their health and financial well-being are shaped by individual decisions people made through the life course, as well as by unanticipated events, economic conditions, medical innovations, and a rapidly evolving landscape of policy incentives and supports. What is most apparent from the mass of research conducted through the program over the years is how integrally related are the multiple dimensions of people's well-being.

As we confront the demographic challenges of a substantially larger population of older people, opportunity lies in three sets of trends, all of which are a focus of continuing research. First, saving in 401(k) and similar plans is now a mainstream aspect of retirement preparation. Though large parts of the population appear to save too little, and access to employment-based saving programs is far from universal, a policy foundation for the accumulation of personal retirement resources is in place, and financial preparation can be improved through saving-related interventions. Second, many, though not all, measures of health are improving, and these improvements can be accelerated through health-related interventions. Third, some of the bounty of longer and healthier lives can reasonably be allocated to prolonging the labor force participation of older workers, among those who are able, helping to pay for higher social security and health care costs, and moderating the macroeconomic challenges we collectively face. But whether people work or retire at one age or another depends significantly on how we structure our public policies and work environments. Each of these issues is being considered in ongoing program research.

The current volume is organized in three sections, corresponding to three aspects of well-being: financial, physical, and emotional. The first four chapters look at factors relating to people's financial circumstances in later life, such as saving, home ownership, and the use of accumulated assets in retirement. Chapter 1 analyzes the effects of pension cash-out at job change on people's long-term financial balance sheets. Chapter 2 considers the trade-offs between allowing liquidity in retirement savings systems versus penalizing preretirement withdrawals. Chapter 3 looks at the implications of housing price risk in influencing people's investments in housing as a financial asset. Chapter 4 is a retrospective analysis of asset holdings and pathways at older ages, looking back from a date near the end of life.

The next five chapters in the volume focus on health and disability. Chapter 5 considers the factors underlying the improvements in disability-free life expectancy in the elderly population. Chapter 6 looks at racial differences in mortality following heart attacks, what causes these differences, and how they are changing. Chapter 7 is a methodological study of the difficulties in measuring disease prevalence in different kinds of data. Chapter 8 analyzes Medicare spending among patients with highly complex combinations of medical conditions. Chapter 9 assesses the impact and pitfalls of a major health intervention experiment in reducing anemia in a very poor region of the world.

The last two chapters in the volume explore issues in mental health, emotional well-being, life satisfaction, or happiness. Chapter 10 focuses specifically on suicide, and the degree to which suicide relates to other measures of physical and mental health. Chapter 11 asks whether retirement makes people more or less happy with their lives.

As with previous volumes, the collection of studies is not intended to cover economics of aging research in a broad or comprehensive way, but rather to highlight selected investigations that are at the cutting edge of the field. Many of the studies are components of longer-term research themes of the NBER program on aging. Through these sixteen volumes, the large majority of this research has been funded by the National Institute on Aging, which has made a long-term commitment to advancing the economics of aging field.

The remainder of this introduction provides an overview of the studies contained in the volume, relying to a significant extent on the authors' own language to summarize their work.

Financial Well-Being

Certainly one aspect of well-being at older ages is financial. Among the resources potentially available to support people in their later years are Social Security, employer-provided pension benefits, financial asset savings, housing wealth, and earnings. Of course the amount and distribution of financial support from these various resource categories varies significantly across households, with a significant number of households relying on Social Security almost entirely.

Notwithstanding the wide variability in financial circumstances across households, one significant trend of the last two decades is the emergence of retirement saving accounts, and particularly employer-sponsored 401(k) plans, as a mainstream component of financial preparation for retirement. How much people save in these plans, however, and how much they withdraw from their accounts before retirement depend on a multitude of factors, including the tax treatment of the plans, employer-matching provisions, plan enrollment protocols, default saving rates, investment allocations, management fees, loan provisions, and early withdrawal penalties. Chapters 1 and 2 consider the particular options, prevalence, and implications of preretirement withdrawals.

In chapter 1, Philip Armour, Michael D. Hurd, and Susann Rohwedder explore "Trends in Pension Cash-Out at Job Change and the Effects on Long-Term Outcomes." Federal tax rules discourage such pension cash-outs, notably by imposing a 10 percent tax penalty on preretirement withdrawals, but the limited evidence available suggests the practice is common. The study reported in chapter 1 takes advantage of long-term longitudinal data in the Health and Retirement Study to update prior findings on pension cash-out behavior, investigate cohort differences, and study the long-term consequences of cash-outs for household finances.

The authors find that pension cash-out is more concentrated among workers who experience economic or health shocks around the time of job separation. The events most likely to trigger cash-outs are issues with mortgages; in particular, over half of those who fell behind on their mortgage cashed out pension accounts. Health was another important factor: more than one-third of those losing their health insurance at job separation engaged in cash-outs, and only a quarter of those whose health worsened did so.

Comparing cash-out behavior across cohorts, the most recent cohort of older workers more often cashed out pension balances and more frequently used the balances for spending or to pay off debt. This is likely due to most of the job separations for this cohort occurring during or in the aftermath of the Great Recession, which brought about economic shocks at higher frequency.

Long-term outcomes for those who cashed out pension balances are worse than for those who did not cash out, but so were their baseline characteristics. Taking this together with the fact that outcomes are largely similar across populations of workers with or without access to pension cash-out, the authors conclude that the worse financial outcomes of workers who cashed out are due to the experience of shocks leading to cash-out behavior rather than due to their having access to the cash-out option.

In a related study reported in chapter 2, John Beshears, James J. Choi, Joshua Hurwitz, David Laibson, and Brigitte C. Madrian consider "Liquidity in Retirement Savings Systems: An International Comparison." Moving beyond the United States experience, this study compares the policy provisions imposed in several different countries, as they relate to preretirement withdrawals. The positive side of greater liquidity, they suggest, is that it allows people to flexibly respond to unexpected preretirement events, such as temporary job loss or medical expenses. The negative side of liquidity is the risk that too much money is withdrawn from the plans and too little saved, particularly if people are subject to self-control problems or planning mistakes.

The six countries analyzed in chapter 2 fall into three groups. Germany, Singapore, and the United Kingdom have the most illiquid systems. In these countries, withdrawals for general consumption in employer-based defined-contribution (DC) plans are banned no matter the level of transitory income.

In Canada and Australia, liquidity in employer-based DC plans is income related. For Canadian households that normally earn US$60,000, for example, DC accounts are completely illiquid unless annual income falls substantially. But for those households that temporarily have very low income, the incentive reverses. In these adverse circumstances, there are actually strong incentives for households to withdraw their DC balances. Hence, the Canadian DC system has the intuitively appealing property that, for a typical household, DC withdrawals are barred when income is near its normal level, but are encouraged when income declines substantially.

The United States stands alone in allowing a high degree of liquidity in its DC system, regardless of income. Penalties for early withdrawals are relatively low (the 10 percent tax penalty), even at normal levels of income, and early withdrawals are slightly subsidized (through lower marginal tax rates) as income falls transitorily. According to the authors, this liquidity generates significant preretirement "leakage" in the United States: for every $1 contributed to the DC accounts of savers under age fifty-five (not counting rollovers), $0.40 simultaneously flows out of the DC system (not counting loans or rollovers).

Chapter 3, by James Banks, Richard Blundell, Zoë Oldfield, and James P. Smith, looks at investments in home equity, focusing on "House Price Volatility and the Housing Ladder." One of the most critical consumption and investment decisions that individuals and families make over their life cycle involves the amount of housing services to consume and whether or not to combine consumption with ownership. Housing is an important component of consumption, both as a large fraction of the household budget and a key ingredient in defining one's lifestyle. But housing, or more particularly housing wealth, can be even more critical as an investment as it is the biggest marketable asset of most households.

The contribution of this chapter is to bring together two key elements of housing consumption and home ownership decisions into an empirical model of housing purchases. The first of these is the housing ladder. Rather than modeling home ownership as a one-time durable purchase, the study models it as a series of purchase decisions, or a housing ladder, where the desired flow of housing services rises with family formation and growing family size over the life cycle. The second is house price risk. In some geographic markets, housing can be a risky asset with unpredictable price volatility, while in other places the market is more stable.

The study analyzes the role of home ownership as a form of insurance against future house price risk as individuals move up the ladder. Both their modeling and empirical findings suggest that in a market with more house price risk, there is an incentive to become a homeowner earlier and, once an owner, to move more rapidly up the housing ladder. The study uses microdata from both the United States and the United Kingdom, and the results are consistent with theory, both across and within the two countries.

In chapter 4, James M. Poterba, Steven F. Venti, and David A. Wise consider "What Determines End-of-Life Assets? A Retrospective View." Many individuals reach the end of life with limited financial assets. The study explores the determinants of asset balances at death by following respondents in the Health and Retirement Study (HRS) "backward" from the last wave prior to their death to the first wave in which they were observed.

Because the prevalence of low wealth among those near the end of life is of particular interest, we begin by describing several potential pathways that can lead a household to have very little wealth in old age. One is by entering retirement with certain assets, and then experiencing unanticipated events that drain financial resources such as widowhood or divorce, an acute health event, the onset of a chronic illness, or a general decline in health. A second pathway to having low assets at the end of life is to enter retirement with assets, but to "outlive" them. A third pathway is simply failing to save adequately before retirement. Our aim is to determine which of these three alternative pathways is most consistent with observed asset trajectories late in life.

In our descriptive analysis, we find little difference between median assets in the first year observed and median assets in the last year observed. For the younger (HRS) cohort, 70 percent of the persons that had less than $50,000 in total assets when last surveyed before death also had fewer than $50,000 in assets when first surveyed. For the older (AHEAD) cohort, 52 percent of the persons that had less than $50,000 in assets when last surveyed before death also had fewer than $50,000 in assets when first surveyed. Low levels of both housing and financial assets are also persistent. Most of those who had substantial assets at the end of life also had substantial asset balances when first observed. The persistence of wealth is confirmed in a series of figures showing median total assets in each survey wave between the wave first observed and the last wave observed before death.

Our regression estimates and simulations reinforce this core finding that in the absence of change in family composition or health status, asset trajectories are relatively flat. However, many people do exhibit asset declines in connection with important medical events or disruptions in family composition. In addition, changes in assets between first and last year observed is strongly, and negatively, related to the respondent's education level. Those with more education exhibit slower asset declines.

Health and Disability

No aspect of well-being is more fundamental than health. As people live longer, it is important whether those increased years of life are characterized by poor health and functional disability, or by good health and functional independence. Health also affects one's ability to work at older ages, and is strongly associated with financial well-being. Health also has societal implications for labor markets, government finances, and health care costs. The second section of the volume explores some of the trends and determinants of health, and how health might be improved through medicine or public health interventions.

Chapter 5, by Michael Chernew, David M. Cutler, Kaushik Ghosh, and Mary Beth Landrum is on "Understanding the Improvement in Disability-Free Life Expectancy in the US Elderly Population." Data on life expectancy is easy to obtain, but data on healthy life expectancy is more difficult. To a great extent, this is because there is no single measure of good or bad health commonly accepted in the literature. In a predecessor to this investigation, and in much of the literature, there is a focus on disabled and nondisabled life expectancy. The predecessor study, for example, shows that between 1992 and 2005, life expectancy increased by 0.7 years while disability-free life expectancy increased by 1.6 years. Thus disabled life expectancy fell by 0.9 years. However, little research has examined why disability-free life expectancy has increased so greatly, and in particular what role medical advances may have played in this.

The study in chapter 5 addresses these issues in three ways. First, the authors calculate disabled and disability-free life expectancy for a longer period of time than has been done previously. This by itself does not change the conclusions materially, but the additional three years does encompass an era of relatively low growth in medical spending, so it is important to note that even with slow medical care cost increases, disability-free life expectancy kept increasing.

Second, the chapter examines which medical conditions are associated with the greatest additions to disability-free life expectancy. The investigators decompose both mortality and disability into fifteen medical conditions, ranging from acute but recoverable diseases such as heart disease and vision impairment, to chronic degenerative conditions such as Alzheimer's disease and Parkinson's disease, and to chronic but nonfatal conditions such as arthritis and diabetes. The central finding is that the vast bulk of the increase in disability-free life expectancy is accounted for by improvements in acute, recoverable conditions, and two in particular: heart disease and vision problems. An estimated 85 percent of the improvement in disability-free life expectancy is attributed to these two conditions.

Third, the chapter considers how much improvements in medical care have contributed to the health improvements associated with heart disease and vision problems. This analysis is the most speculative, but the results suggest that treatment changes are responsible for about half of the overall health improvements observed. Most of the treatment improvements for heart disease are pharmaceutical—cholesterol-lowering agents and anti-hypertensives are the major ones, but some are surgical as well. In the case of vision, the study focuses primarily on increased use of cataract surgery, and finds significant benefits of cataract surgery on both vision and disability trends. People who receive cataract surgery are less likely to experience adverse disability trends than people who do not receive cataract surgery, controlling for the prior year's level of vision impairment.

Chapter 6, by Amitabh Chandra, Tyler Hoppenfeld, and Jonathan Skinner asks "Are Black-White Mortality Rates Converging? Acute Myocardial Infarction in the United States, 1993–2010." There is a vast literature documenting racial disparities in US health care. Some of the literature focuses on how physicians treat patients of different races and ethnicities. A much different source of health disparities arises from the fact that black and white patients go to different providers. One study, for example, documented that nearly half of all black acute myocardial infarction (AMI) patients were admitted to 571 hospitals serving just 7 percent of white AMI patients (see reference in chapter 6). Moreover, the authors estimated that most of the gap between black and white ninety-day mortality was the consequence of the quality of the hospital to which the patient was admitted, and not because of how black and white patients were treated within the hospital.

Chapter 6 explores two trends related to these past findings. First, to what extent (if at all) are the racial differences in which hospitals patients choose converging over time? And second, are differences in the quality of hospitals converging so that provider choice is less relevant to health outcomes? The chapter explores these questions by analyzing hospital admissions for acute myocardial infarction, or AMI, using a sample of more than four million patients.

The study first explores trends in the ninety-day mortality rates of black and white patients with an AMI diagnosis. From 1993 to 1998, black AMI patients experienced risk-adjusted mortality rates 0.4 percentage points greater than white AMI patients, increasing to a gap of 1.6 percentage points from 1999 to 2005, and then attenuating to a gap of 1.0 percentage points from 2006 to 2010. The authors then try to decompose the sources of the gap into "within hospital" and "between hospital" racial variations.

Of the overall racial disparity in risk-adjusted outcomes, the study finds that most was the consequence of "between" hospital differences in quality; black patients were admitted to lower-quality hospitals (where quality was measured by risk-adjusted outcomes for white patients), and these between-hospital disparities have shown little evidence of convergence. At the same time, the "within-hospital" disparities have been growing, not declining. In sum, the study does not find evidence that black patients have sorted or migrated to higher-quality hospitals, or that racial differences in treatment within hospitals have converged.

The authors emphasize that black and white AMI patients going to different hospitals is, in many respects, the consequence of racial segregation in where people live and not a systematic effort to discriminate against black AMI patients. Of greater interest is segmentation of markets not driven by distance alone; for example, black patients who are admitted to lower-quality hospitals when there are higher-quality hospitals nearby. Studying these more granular travel patterns is a topic for future research.

Chapter 7, by Florian Heiss, Daniel McFadden, Joachim Winter, Amelie Wuppermann, and Yaoyao Zhu, is on "Measuring Disease Prevalence in Surveys: A Comparison of Diabetes Self-Reports, Biomarkers, and Linked Insurance Claims." Much of the existing literature on the health-wealth nexus relies on survey data, such as self-reported survey data in the Health and Retirement Study (HRS). Such survey data typically contain self-reported measures of disease prevalence, which are known to suffer from reporting error. Two more recent developments—the collection of biomarkers and the linkage with data from administrative sources such as insurance claims—promise more reliable measures of disease prevalence. The goal of the study in chapter 7 is to systematically compare these three measures of disease prevalence.

The comparison is made between three measures of diabetes that are now integrated into the consolidated Health and Retirement Study database: (a) the commonly used survey measure of diabetes, (b) diabetes as measured by HbA1c levels collected in the HRS biomarker data, and (c) diabetes in the Medicare insurance claims linked to the HRS data. Self-reported diabetes and biomarker data align for a large part of the sample (85 percent). Most of the differences between the two measures is likely explained by the fact that treatment lowers HbA1c levels in some cases even below the 6.5 percent threshold.

When considering the three data sources, roughly 2–3 percent of individuals have diabetes according to HbA1c, but do not report diabetes and do not receive diabetes treatment according to their claims records. Even in the Medicare population there is thus a fraction of individuals who likely have undiagnosed diabetes. Somewhat surprisingly, however, the study does not find that the probability of being undiagnosed is related to socioeconomic status.

Importantly, comparing the three measures of diabetes, as well as taking into account information on treatment, suggests that none of the three measures should be taken as a gold standard. In particular, the results indicate that both the presumably more objective biomarker as well as the claims data suffer from error just as the self-reports contain errors. While the biomarker data can be influenced by treatment and thus may not identify cases as diabetic because their diabetes is well managed, the claims data may falsely classify individuals as diabetics. In addition, individuals who have diabetes but are not treated for it will also be misclassified based on the claims data.

In a final section, the chapter discusses the potential for integrative statistical models that take advantage of the combined information in all three measures. Even in more simplistic integration of the measures, the authors find that adding claims information to combined self-reports and biomarkers reduces undiagnosed diabetes cases from 3.26 percent to 2.4 percent in 2006 and from 4.05 percent to 3.1 percent in 2008, that is, by between one-quarter and one-third. Thus, including all three measures in a major study such as the HRS improves measurement of disease prevalence substantially.

In chapter 8, Thomas MaCurdy and Jay Bhattacharya look at "Challenges in Controlling Medicare Spending: Treating Highly Complex Patients." They point out that any policy offering hope of success in mitigating the unsustainable rise in Medicare expenses must focus its impacts on the highest-cost users of Medicare. The goal of the study, therefore, is to better understand these high-cost users. What the study reveals is that beneficiaries with multiple illnesses cost considerably more than would be predicted by adding up the costs of treatment for each disease/illness condition in isolation. Put differently, increasing the number of comorbidities induces a multiplicative rather than an additive cost structure. Moreover, the patterns of disease/illness combinations are quite diverse with individual combinations populated by small numbers of patients. These empirical findings demonstrate that most Medicare expenditures are associated with small sets of medically complex patients.

Among the more specific quantitative findings of the study, about 52 percent of Medicare spending goes to treat 8 percent of the total service months when beneficiaries are afflicted by four or more major health conditions (e.g., cancer, diabetes, renal failure, chronic heart failure, etc.). During these periods of treatment, beneficiaries suffer from nearly 5.5 million combinations of major health conditions. Around 31 percent of spending goes to treat less than 3 percent of the time when Medicare beneficiaries suffer from six or more major health conditions; during these periods, beneficiaries suffer from nearly 4.2 million combinations of major conditions.

Translated into an annual context for beneficiaries, 18 percent of Medicare beneficiaries are afflicted by four or more major health conditions sometime during the year, and they account for 63 percent of total Medicare spending. These beneficiaries suffer from nearly 7.5 million combinations of major health conditions during the year. About 7 percent of Medicare beneficiaries are afflicted by six or more major health conditions and account for 41 percent of Medicare spending. These beneficiaries alone suffer from more than 6.4 million combinations of major illnesses, with an average of three distinct combinations per Medicare beneficiary with six or more health conditions. Regardless of the perspective used to assess medical complexity, patients are strikingly more expensive to treat and more distinct as the number of comorbidities grows.

These findings have some significant policy implications. First, in the area of reimbursement policy, the findings suggest that risk-adjustment models currently used by Medicare inadequately compensate for complex patients due to a cost structure that assumes linearity in health-condition indicators.

Second, quality-improvement programs such as disease management and care coordination must be formulated to individualize treatments necessary for patients suffering from a wide array of illnesses. Although these forms of medical practice can offer flexibility in dealing with comorbidities, the level of variability in comorbidities documented in this report indicates that care coordination models will be continually challenged with novel clinical situations.

In chapter 9, "Movies, Margins, and Marketing: Encouraging the Adoption of Iron-Fortified Salt," Abhijit Banerjee, Sharon Barnhardt, and Esther Duflo analyze a major experimental intervention designed to reduce anemia in the Bihar region of India. According to the National Family Health Survey, 67 percent of adult women, 34 percent of adult men, and 78 percent of children under the age of three years suffered from some form of anemia in Bihar in 2005–2006. The promise of double-fortified salt to reduce anemia and increase productivity rests on two premises: that households will be willing to buy it and use it, even at a reduced price—or potentially for free—and that it is effective enough, at the levels of fortification that are stable and safe, to make a real difference. The chapter addresses the first question.

A number of experiments were conducted, parts of which provided for the free distribution of fortified salt, parts of which offered shopkeepers the opportunity to stock fortified salt at a subsidized price, and parts of which tested the effectiveness of different forms of social marketing. For example, one marketing approach used a twenty-six-minute "edutainment movie," screened during the intermission of a very popular film. Another hand delivered flyers with information about the product.

The study finds that the basic marketing campaign conducted by the manufacturer at launch was completely ineffective at conveying why this salt should be purchased: two years after the introduction of the product, absent any additional information campaign, no one who bought the salt knew that it helps reduce anemia or reports buying it because it is good for the health of household members. Even when the salt was provided for free, only about half of households actually used it for cooking. And when they could buy it for just below half price, with no other intervention, about 20 percent of households give it a try, but only 10 percent still used it after three years.

Against this backdrop, the chapter also shows the power of a strong communication campaign. In villages where about 20 percent of residents saw the movie, consumption of doubled-fortified salt increased by 5.5 percentage points, an increase of 50 percent over the mean for households who get price subsidies, and more than 10 percent over the mean usage among those who get the salt for free. Eight percent of households who reported buying fortified salt at the end of the experiment period indicate that they bought this salt because it helps fight anemia (although that leaves 92 percent who do so for other reasons), and because it is subsidized (as advertised in the movie).

The chapter also highlights how powerful shopkeepers are in influencing what households do. A small increase in retailer margins resulted in an increase in take-up at least as large as that caused by the movie screening. There is some ambiguity on how this was achieved. The retailers claim that they dropped the final price of the salt (very little). Village households do not report such a decline and instead claim that they bought the salt because it was the only one available. More generally, over half of the buyers report that they just bought whatever the shopkeeper gave them. While the study is informative, there remains substantial work in refining these interventions to be as effective as possible.

Life Satisfaction or Happiness

Extending beyond traditional measures of health, some of the most recent research in the NBER aging program has considered well-being in a more general sense. It has explored issues in mental health, emotional well-being, life satisfaction, and happiness.

In chapter 10, Anne Case and Angus Deaton focus specifically on "Suicide, Age, and Well-Being: An Empirical Investigation." The study juxtaposes suicide rates with other measures of physical and mental well-being, using data from the United States and from other countries to examine patterns of suicide and well-being by age and across space.

Suicide rates, life evaluation, and measures of affect are all plausible measures of the mental health and well-being of populations. Yet in the settings examined in chapter 10, correlations between suicide and measured well-being are at best inconsistent. With a few exceptions, the findings suggest that suicide has little to do with life satisfaction. Differences in suicides between men and women, between Hispanics, blacks, and whites, between age groups of men or of African Americans, between countries or US states, between calendar years, and between days of the week, do not match differences in life evaluation.

Suicide rates in the United States have risen in recent years, though there is no evidence of decreases in subjective well-being (SWB). Marriage and education do indeed bring more life satisfaction and less suicide, though the relative sizes of the effects do not match the effects on SWB, even for men and women separately. For example, when controlling for age, sex, and race, being married comes with higher life evaluation and lower suicide. For men, as one should expect, those who are divorced have lower well-being and higher suicide rates, but the magnitude of the effect on suicide is much larger relative to the effect on life evaluation than is the case for marriage. When looking at widowers, there is more suicide, comparable to the suicide associated with divorce, yet widowed men actually show slightly higher life evaluation.

Women's suicide rates peak in middle age and men's in old age; yet, both men and women show a U-shape in life evaluation. Suicide rates among non-Hispanic blacks fall with age alongside declines in life evaluation. Sixteen percent of suicides happen on Mondays and only 13 percent happen on Saturdays. Yet life evaluation is the same on all days of the week.

Age patterns of suicide are different for men and women and have changed differentially over time. The authors suggest that the most important facts about suicide over the last decade are that for white non-Hispanics, both men and women, (a) suicide is rising overall, which is driven by (b) increasing suicide rates in middle age, offset by (c) falling suicide rates among the elderly. The suicide epidemic in middle age is the tip of an iceberg of mortality and morbidity, especially pain, among middle-age Americans. In Gallup data, "pain yesterday" is now higher in middle age than in old age. The authors do not know what is driving this epidemic, but it is showing up in at least some of the SWB indicators, including low positive affect in middle age, and perhaps even as some of the dip in middle-age life evaluation, the presence of which they find little evidence of prior to the last decade. Their tentative hypothesis is that pain is an underlying fundamental cause, and that it is driving changes in both suicides and SWB.

There are very large variations in suicides across states in the United States (by a factor of more than two) and across counties (by a factor of more than seven). At the county level, but not the state level, suicide rates are lower where life evaluation is higher, but higher where negative affect is lower, and uncorrelated with positive affect. Pain is strongly correlated with suicide, across both states and counties, and is a significant predictor even conditional on standard predictors, such as income, income inequality, and religious denomination.

Finally, across fifty-two countries in the Organisation for Economic Co-operation and Development (OECD), Latin America, and Eastern Europe, suicide rates are neither well nor consistently correlated with well-being measures. In a majority of countries, suicides are higher among the elderly, particularly for men. In countries where life evaluation is high in old age relative to middle age, suicides are relatively low in old age, and vice versa. At least some of this is driven by the extreme negative effects of the transition on the elderly in Eastern Europe.

In chapter 11, Raquel Fonseca, Arie Kapteyn, Jinkook Lee, and Gema Zamarro ask "Does Retirement Make You Happy? A Simultaneous Equations Approach." Labor force participation may affect subjective well-being in different ways and in different contexts. It may relate to the type of job in which retirees were employed before retirement, whether the retirement is perceived as voluntary or forced, whether retirement affects the financial circumstances of the household, or the cultural context of one country or sociodemographic group versus another. With policy reforms that increase pension entitlement ages in many countries, and that induce more workers to continue in the labor force until older ages, the relationship between retirement and subjective well-being is an important one.

The study in chapter 11 aims to improve our understanding of these issues using a simultaneous model that accounts for the interplay of pension incentives, retirement, income, and subjective well-being. By estimating the complete system of equations, the aim is to more accurately evaluate the role of retirement induced through Social Security or pension eligibility in determining the subjective as well as financial well-being of the elderly.

In the raw data, the study finds that being retired is positively correlated with the risk of depression and negatively correlated with life satisfaction. However, after accounting for the reverse causal effects of well-being measures on retirement, the estimated relationships are reversed. In the most flexible specification with forty age dummies, the effect of retirement on either depression or life satisfaction is insignificant. Income does not appear to play much of a role in the determination of depression or life satisfaction, once other factors are accounted for. This also contrasts with the correlations in the raw data, which suggested that higher income leads to higher life satisfaction and to fewer depressive symptoms.

As one would expect, household wealth, being married, and educational attainment are all positively related to life satisfaction and reduce the probability of depression. Health conditions and difficulties with activities of daily living increase the probability of depression and reduce life satisfaction.

The fairly weak effects of retirement on life satisfaction and depression suggest that, at least as far as these variables are concerned, gradual increases in retirement ages will have only moderate effects on population measures of well-being. The authors emphasize, however, that these are average effects and do not account for either individual variations in how retirement affects well-being or, possibly, more systematic variations across sociodemographic groups.

Trends in Pension Cash-Out at Job Change and the Effects on Long-Term Outcomes

Philip Armour, Michael D. Hurd, and
Susann Rohwedder

1.1 Introduction

Promoting financial security in retirement is a major objective of US policies governing employer-provided pensions. To encourage workers and employers to participate, legislation mandates very large tax advantages for private-pension savings. These effectively represent "tax expenditures" to the federal government in the form of forgone tax revenues.

US policymakers have a substantial interest in the results of these large expenditures for promoting financial security in retirement. Is the private-pension system effectively enhancing financial security in retirement? What are the barriers or impediments to achieving economic security for old age among US workers? Which groups of workers are at greatest risk of falling short?

One feature of the US pension system in particular may jeopardize the objective of promoting retirement-income security: the ability of workers to cash out (i.e., withdraw funds from) their private-pension plans upon job separation. Federal rules aim to discourage such preretirement cash-outs. For example, the Tax Reform Act of 1986 introduced a 10 percent tax penalty on withdrawals from tax-advantaged accounts prior to the age of 59.5. Burman et al. 2012 showed that this tax penalty reduced preretirement cash-out of pension balances and increased rollovers into individual retirement

Philip Armour is associate economist at the RAND Corporation and a professor at the Pardee RAND Graduate School. Michael D. Hurd is senior principal researcher at the RAND Corporation and a research associate of the National Bureau of Economic Research. Susann Rohwedder is senior economist at the RAND Corporation, associate director of the RAND Center for the Study of Aging, and a member of the Pardee RAND Graduate School faculty.

For acknowledgments, sources of research support, and disclosure of the authors' material financial relationships, if any, please see http://www.nber.org/chapters/c13635.ack.

accounts that preserve the tax-advantaged status of the pension balances. They also found reductions of cash-outs in response to a 1992 reform that imposed 20 percent tax withholding (without affecting the total tax liability).

These policy changes have reduced, but not eliminated, early withdrawals. As we document below, following workers in their early fifties in 1992 through subsequent job separations, 13.6 percent of those with a defined-contribution (DC) plan cashed out all or part of their plan; among workers with defined-benefit (DB) plans, 18.9 percent cashed out. For later cohorts the percent cashing out was substantially higher, even exceeding a 50 percent increase for the latest cohort in our study.

Several studies have investigated the causes of these early pension withdrawals now subject to withholding. It appears that a significant portion of these are made by households facing liquidity constraints and experiencing financial shocks (Amromin and Smith 2003; Scherpf 2010). Still, according to Butrica, Zedlewski, and Issa (2010), about half of early withdrawals from 401(k) defined-contribution pension accounts and individual retirement accounts (IRAs) could not be attributed to the events observed in the data, possibly indicating "unnecessary loss of retirement savings."

This chapter uses the long panel of data collected in the Health and Retirement Study (HRS), spanning up to twenty years for the earliest cohorts, to add new insights to prior research findings on this topic. Analyses in the current study addressed trends in pension cash-outs among older workers, cohort differences, and retirement-income security metrics at later years or ages and their relations to earlier job and cash-out choices. We did not restrict ourselves to looking at single cash-out actions, but incorporated cumulative measures of pension cash-out decisions. The chapter includes analyses of precipitating events that shed light on determinants of cash-out behavior and how it may have changed over time. We were especially interested in how the Great Recession affected cash-out choices. The HRS data allowed relation of variation in cash-out choices of older workers to a variety of outcomes observed in panel up to twenty years later, including assets, income, and health.

In an antecedent to this chapter, Hurd and Panis (2006) analyzed HRS data on cash-outs and other dispositions of pension entitlements among workers over the age of fifty who left their jobs between 1992 and 2000 (five waves of biennial HRS data). In this study, they found 13 percent of pension entitlements were cashed out, representing 5.3 percent of entitlement dollars. Among plans with a lump sum option, 20 percent were cashed out. However, their study highlighted an issue that had been underappreciated in prior research: whether a lump-sum distribution (LSD) harms retirement preparation depends critically on what the worker does with the money, and whether these cash-outs represent "leakage" from wealth available to finance consumption in retirement. Some LSDs may be rolled into an IRA, some may be annuitized, and some may be cashed out. Only the last of these may

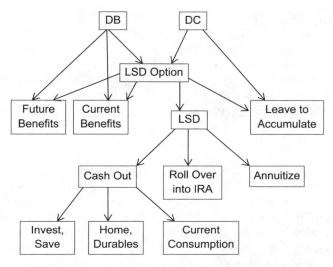

Fig. 1.1   Potential options for the disposition of pension entitlements, as illustrated in Hurd and Panis (2006)

harm retirement preparation, and even then some uses may function as savings. Hurd and Panis use the following graphic to clarify the situation. In the cash-out branch, some of the funds may be invested or saved directly and some may be invested in the home, which is a form of saving. While bringing such funds out of tax-sheltered accounts may not be optimal tax management, it is primarily spending for current consumption among those not facing binding credit constraints that poses the greatest harm to economic preparation for retirement (see figure 1.1).

Hurd and Panis established several facts that are important for understanding the causes and consequences of LSD decisions. Not all plans allow an LSD on job separation. In fact, the availability of LSDs varies dramatically across types of plans: a little over 80 percent of DC-plan participants report an LSD option versus just 42 percent of DB-plan participants.

Besides looking at the fraction of workers who cashed out their pensions, Hurd and Panis examined the implications of cash-outs for aggregate pension balances and net wealth, including nonretirement wealth. They identified two factors that implied a limited overall impact of cash-outs on retirement and total household wealth. First, cashed-out plans had lower average value than other plans, especially among those holding DC plans. Second, over 75 percent of cashed-out funds were either invested or used to pay off debt. Hurd and Panis (2006, 2226) conclude that "among workers that are within roughly ten years of retirement, only a small fraction of pension plan dollars is consumed immediately after job separation and that the vast majority is preserved for retirement income security."

While the Hurd and Panis paper provided a useful perspective up through the year 2000, the demographic and pension landscape has changed considerably with the decreasing importance of DB plans, the increasing pension entitlement of women, and changing trends in marriage and divorce. Furthermore, the Great Recession may have led to more cash-outs, harming particular segments of the population. These changes in the landscape warrant revisiting the Hurd and Panis analysis, which is the objective of this chapter.

1.2   Data

The HRS is a biennial longitudinal survey of persons at least fifty years of age. Since its launch in 1992, the HRS has gathered data on income, work assets, pension plans, health insurance, disability, physical health and functioning, cognitive functioning, and health-care expenditures, among other topics. Periodic additions of cohorts ensure the HRS remains representative of the population at least fifty years of age.

The analyses in this chapter are focused on several key variables. We analyzed self-reported data on employer-provided pensions for HRS respondents. The HRS asks whether respondents own such a pension, and whether it is a defined-benefit (DB) or a defined-contribution (DC) plan. It also asks respondents whether the pension plan allows for a lump-sum distribution. They are asked about the disposition of the pension plan at job separation or retirement: whether it was left with the former employer to accumulate; whether a full or partial LSD was taken; whether DB holders started drawing benefits on separation or chose to await future, larger benefits; whether the pension plan was lost with separation (likely where there is lack of vesting); or whether some other disposition occurred. For those who took an LSD, the survey asks whether the money was rolled into an IRA, converted to an annuity, or cashed out. For those who cashed out their pension plan, the HRS asks whether the money was saved or invested, whether it was used to pay off debt[1] or to purchase durable goods or a home, or whether it was used for nondurable consumption.

This research updates and expands that of Hurd and Panis in several directions. First, more waves of the HRS are now available. Hurd and Panis used five waves of HRS data from 1992 through 2000. Since then, six more waves of HRS surveys—from 2002 through 2012—have been conducted and the data made available for analysis, bringing not only an increase in sample size, but also an expansion in the types of analyses that could be

---

1. Paying off debt is conceptually the same as investing or saving the money when considering net asset levels, but this distinction is recorded in the HRS responses and shows patterns of interest, especially in the context of the Great Recession when the fraction reporting paying off debt was markedly higher.

conducted. In particular, because additional waves of data became available, differences across cohorts (e.g., those born before World War II and postwar "baby boom" cohorts) could be analyzed. A growing number of DC plans is also available for analysis, partly because of the time elapsed since 2000, but perhaps more importantly because DC plans have become increasingly prevalent in the US pension system, so workers in more recent cohorts are more likely to have them.

More recent cohorts are also likely to consist of more women who have earned pension entitlements at work. Their decisions regarding pension wealth may differ from those of men and merit additional analysis. Indeed, within a household, the behavior of both spouses is important in determining use or disposal of pension assets. The incorporation of more waves of HRS data with more female respondents who hold pension wealth promotes the analysis of pension wealth and its use or disposal from a household perspective.

The analysis has been updated to provide insights on the effects of the Great Recession on pension behavior, particularly on cash-outs. The earlier work by Hurd and Panis studied a period of relatively low unemployment and high stock market and housing returns. The years since then, particularly those surrounding the Great Recession that began in 2008, have not been as favorable. Unemployment in 2009 reached 10 percent, more than 2 percentage points higher than it was at any point between 1992 and 2000, and more than double what it was in the late 1990s. Though eventually recovering, the US stock market lost about half its value during the Great Recession, and housing values decreased by more than one-third, representing a large shock to wealth that may have led some workers to cash out their pensions. Indeed, using tax data on preretirement withdrawals, Argento, Bryant, and Sabelhaus (2015) verified that workers substantially increased withdrawal rates between 2004 and 2010, especially after 2007.

The long HRS panel supports analyses of retirement-security outcomes at later years or ages and how they relate to earlier job and cash-out choices. For example, consider a fifty-seven-year-old worker who cashed out a pension between 1992 and 1994. We have been able to observe that worker's subsequent economic position at age seventy-five in 2012, and we could then compare that worker with otherwise similar workers who did not cash out.

By gaining access to more years of data, we were able to analyze and compare a broader array of events precipitating cash-out, including whether different precipitating events led to differences in subsequent events. We could, for example, analyze and compare cash-outs resulting from adverse health changes, unemployment, shocks to household wealth caused by the Great Recession, marital disruption, and extractions to buy real estate during the housing bubble of 2004 to 2008 and the subsequent loss of equity and, possibly, home ownership during the Great Recession.

1.2.1   Changes in the Macroeconomic Environment, 1992–2012

We begin with an overview of the contextual changes occurring over the period 1992–2012. The first half of that period covers the HRS waves available to Hurd and Panis in conducting their analysis, and the second half folds in the years covered by the current work. We specifically focus on labor force participation (LFP) and the recessions that characterized the macroeconomy near the beginning and toward the end of the period of interest.

Labor Force Participation

Using Current Population Survey (CPS) data, we examined trends in LFP by sex. As shown in figure 1.2, between the early 1990s and the early 2010s, LFP among males ages sixty-five to sixty-nine increased substantially, whereas LFP among males forty to fifty-four decreased slightly. Men of intermediate age (fifty-five to sixty-four) increased their LFPs modestly, if at all. The LFPs among older women (figure 1.3), ages fifty-five to sixty-nine, increased at rates matching those of the oldest men in the analysis, although there appears to have been a leveling off following the start of the Great Recession. The LFPs among women in their forties exhibited a slight increase or stasis until around the turn of the century, and a slight downward trend thereafter.

Clearly, the most dramatic trends are the LFP increases among older men and women. These increases reflect trends toward later retirement. In the descriptive analyses, which compare cohorts over eight years, we thus expect to see trends toward relatively fewer separations due to retirement, which may alter the frequency of pension cash-outs.

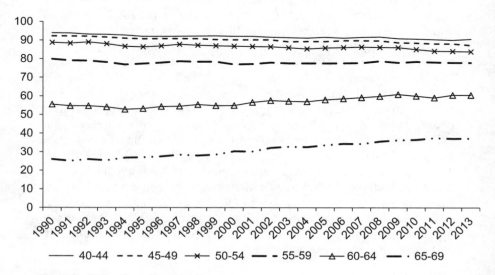

Fig. 1.2   Labor force participation, men

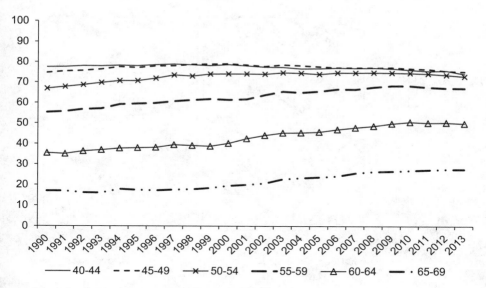

Fig. 1.3   Labor force participation, women

Macroeconomic Conditions

We are here concerned with the recession of 1991 and the Great Recession beginning in 2008. They are of interest because a recession is characterized by unemployment and adverse financial outcomes—loss of income and loss of assets, including the value of stocks and real property. Involuntary job losses could trigger pension cash-out particularly when accompanied by wealth losses.

Recession of 1991.   Unemployment, which had been falling in the late 1980s from around 7.5 percent to 5 percent, turned around with the recession to exceed 7 percent again in 1992 (all figures seasonally adjusted). Stocks simultaneously dropped in value; the Standard & Poor's 500 index lost some 15 percent of its worth in 1991. Value of housing was not so dramatically affected. The Case-Schiller house price index had been falling for several years and bottomed out in 1991. (The Federal Housing Finance Agency's house price index showed no movement, but had just been established.)

Great Recession.   While changes in macroeconomic indexes were noticeable in 1991, they were much more dramatic for the Great Recession that began in 2008 (see figure 1.4). The unemployment rate had been falling for several years to 4.3 percent, or down about 20 percent since 2002. In the second half of 2007 it began rising and continued doing so very rapidly until the end of 2009, when it topped out at more than 10 percent.

The Standard & Poor's 500 index had been rising since 2003, making

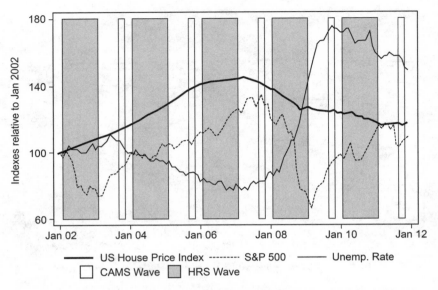

Fig. 1.4   Fluctuations in US house prices, the S&P500, and the unemployment rate

up some losses from 2002 and eventually reaching some 35 percent over the 2002 datum. It then plummeted through 2008, losing more than half its value. The Federal Housing Finance Agency (FHFA)'s US house price index had increased dramatically, by about 40 percent, between 2002 and the middle of 2007. It then began a long downturn that by early 2011, when it leveled off, it had lost almost half of the gain.

1.3   Results

1.3.1   Cohort Comparisons

Table 1.1 defines the cohorts and shows sample sizes. For example, we follow as Group 1 the 5,355 people who entered the HRS with the 1992 wave of data collection. Of these 5,355 persons, 3,871 were working at entry, 2,161 were working with pension coverage, and 1,396 were working and covered by a pension plan allowing a lump-sum distribution (LSD). We follow these groups for eight years, as their participants age from fifty-one to fifty-six up to fifty-nine to sixty-four. Group 4 only entered in 2010, so insufficient time has elapsed for a longitudinal analysis; we use this group for baseline comparisons only.

Baseline Comparisons

Labor Force Status.   Figure 1.5 shows labor force status at age fifty-one to fifty-six, as reported by the respondents in each group. Employment was

Table 1.1   Sample sizes of four groups used in analyses

				Sample size		
	Initial year observed in HRS	Age 51–56	Age 51–56 and working	Age 51–56 and working with pension coverage	Age 51–56 and working with pension coverage allowing LSD option
Group 1	1992	5,355	3,871	2,161	1,396
Group 2	1998	3,209	2,402	1,401	878
Group 3	2004	3,322	2,477	1,417	908
Group 4	2010	4,690	3,172	1,688	1,144

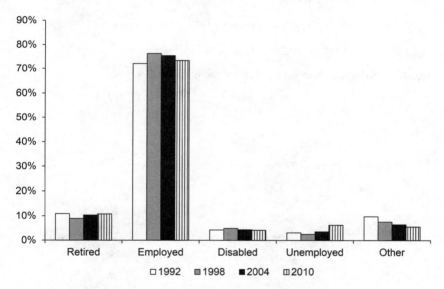

Fig. 1.5   Labor force status at ages fifty-one to fifty-six

lower in 1992 and 2010, and unemployment was higher particularly in 2010, reflecting the Great Recession.

Pension Coverage and Plan Type.   Pension coverage improved modestly over the period of interest (see figure 1.6), increasing a few percentage points to a 60 percent coverage rate in 2010. There was a large change in the *type* of coverage, though. Most respondents who had pensions were covered by defined-benefit (DB) plans versus defined-contribution (DC) plans in 1992. By 1998, that pattern switched around. The trend from DB to DC still continues.

The great majority—over 80 percent—of persons having a DC pension plan are allowed by the plan to cash out via an LSD (see figure 1.7). The like

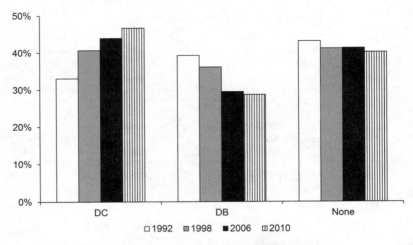

Fig. 1.6   Pension coverage and plan type, conditional on working

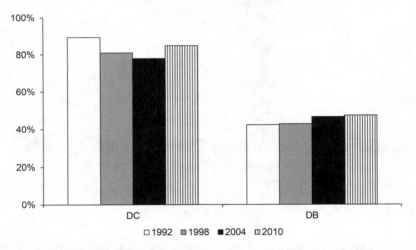

Fig. 1.7   Pension plan allows LSD, conditional on work and pension on job

percentage for DB plans is 47 in 2010, which represents a steady but modest increase since 1992.

Longitudinal Comparisons

Job Separations.   Table 1.2 lists the number of job separations within HRS cohorts between their entry year (1992, 1998, or 2004, when they were fifty-one to fifty-six years old) and eight years later (when they were fifty-nine to sixty-four). These can be separations to another job, to unemployment, to retirement, or to any other employment status category. They also include

Table 1.2   **Number of persons with job separations over eight years**

	All		
Cohort	No. individuals with one or more job separations	No. individuals with any separations from a job with a pension plan	No. individuals with any separations from a job with a pension and cash-out option
1992	2,067	1,204	731
1998	1,386	901	567
2004	1,319	738	528

Note: Separation counts are larger for 1992 because the HRS cohort was larger.

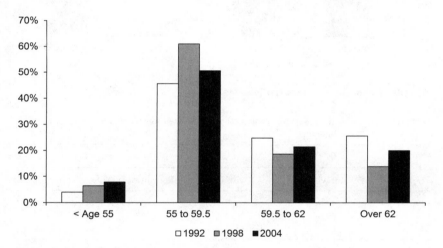

Fig. 1.8   **Age at time of cash-out**

separations by individuals not having a job at entry into the HRS who later take a job and then separate from that job, and they count multiple separations per individual where those occur.

We sought trends in age at separation and in labor force status following job separation among respondents with pensions. Figure 1.8 shows the age at which cash-outs occur. The large cash-outs appear to happen around ages fifty-nine to sixty, the age at which tax penalties for early withdrawals end. There is little evidence of any trend in age.

There were substantial differences by cohort in labor force status after job separation (see figure 1.9). The 2004 cohort (Group 3) was much more likely to be unemployed than the other two cohorts, whereas the 1992 cohort was much more likely to retire after a job separation and thus be less likely to be employed.

Table 1.3 shows the number of job separations over eight years among respondents covered by a pension plan, classified by whether the individual had a DC or DB plan. For example, there were 637 job separations among

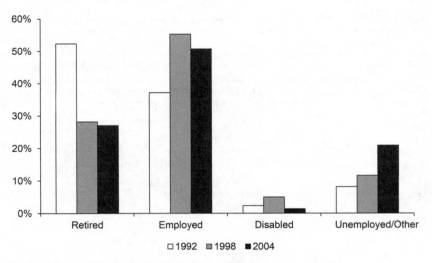

Fig. 1.9   Labor force status after job separation

Table 1.3   Job separations among those with a pension: number and percent by plan type

	Any DC		Any DB	
Cohort	Percent with DC	N with DC	Percent with DB	N with DB
1992	44.8	637	67.9	956
1998	57.4	614	62.5	642
2004	70.1	591	46.6	400

persons with DC plans, and those amounted to 44.8 percent of all job separations involving a pension plan. The table documents sharp increases in the percentage of respondents with pension-plan coverage who have a DC plan, and sharp decreases in the percentage with a DB plan. (Note that some persons have both types of plan, so the row totals exceed 100 percent.)

As the prevalence of DC plans was changing over the period of interest, so was the means of disposition of these plans at job separation (see table 1.4A). Cash-outs increased sharply from less than 14 percent to 24 percent (not conditioned on LSD availability), while rates of rolling plan assets into IRAs remained high, at around 30 to 40 percent. While cash-outs may be the principal worry from the retirement security point of view, IRAs do not necessarily protect savings well. These funds are no longer under the protection of the Employee Retirement Income Security Act (ERISA), and transfers to IRAs may presage spending.

If the analysis is altered to include only those respondents who had DC plans with LSD options, some differences are observed (see table 1.4B).

Table 1.4A   **Pension disposition of DC plans at job separation, by cohort (over eight years each)**

	Cohort		
	1992 (%)	1998 (%)	2004 (%)
Cashed out	13.6	19.0	24.0
Rolled over into IRA	35.1	31.6	40.8
Annuitized	2.4	2.5	2.6
Left with employer	41.5	45.6	32.7
Transferred to new employer	0.0	2.4	2.8
Lost	0.3	1.3	3.9
Other	9.3	5.6	3.2

Note: Not conditioned on cash-out option being available, weighted.

Table 1.4B   **Cohort comparison: Pension disposition of DC plans at job separation (over eight years), conditioned on availability of lump-sum distribution option**

	1992 (%)	1998 (%)	2004 (%)
Cashed out	18.9	26.7	29.1
Rolled over into IRA	49.0	44.5	49.5
Annuitized	3.3	3.5	3.2
Left with employer	26.0	29.3	21.9
Transferred to new employer	0.0	2.2	2.0
Lost	0.0	0.2	3.2
Other	5.7	4.3	2.3

Note: All percentages are weighted; categories are not mutually exclusive. Conditioned on cash-out option being available.

Cash-outs are higher in levels when the LSD option is available, but increase at about the same rate across cohorts. Rollover prevalence does not exhibit consistent trends across cohorts and is higher, but variably so, when the sample is restricted to these having the LSD option. The LSD-available group also shows consistently reduced probabilities of leaving savings with the employer (down 34 to 38 percent).

A like analysis was conducted for respondents with DB plans at job separations. As shown in table 1.5A, the prevalence of cash-outs increased with cohort from 12 percent to 18 percent. There was a much smaller rate of rollover to IRAs than there was for the DC people, but IRA rollover rates did increase across cohorts, from 8 percent to 21 percent. Over half the respondents with DB plans at job separation were drawing benefits from it—an important annuity feature of DB plans—but this had fallen by over 30 percent in the 2004 cohort.

If we restrict the sample to those having DB plans with an LSD option (table 1.5B), cash-out rates are considerable higher but there is no longer an

Table 1.5A   Cohort comparison: Pension disposition of DB plans at job separation
                    (over eight years)

	1992 (%)	1998 (%)	2004 (%)
Cashed out	12.5	12.0	18.0
Rolled over into IRA	8.1	11.2	20.6
Annuitized	0.0	0.0	0.0
Expecting benefits	29.3	28.8	28.7
Drawing benefits	57.3	52.6	36.4
Lost	2.7	1.9	2.9
Other	2.2	3.8	3.2

Note: Not conditioned on cash-out option being available, weighted.

Table 1.5B   Cohort comparison: Pension disposition of DB plans at job separation
                    (over eight years), conditioned on availability of lump-sum
                    distribution option

	1992 (%)	1998 (%)	2004 (%)
Cashed out	37.7	29.2	29.3
Rolled over into IRA	24.5	27.3	33.6
Annuitized	0.0	0.0	0.0
Expecting benefits	19.2	16.7	21.7
Drawing benefits	45.0	43.3	24.5
Lost	0.5	0.4	3.6
Other	1.5	3.7	2.8

Note: All percentages are weighted; categories are not mutually exclusive. Conditioned on cash-out option being available.

increase across cohorts. The IRA rollover rates are higher and they markedly increased across cohorts. Fewer individuals are drawing benefits, though the cross-cohort profile is similar.

The prior work by Hurd and Panis established that among respondents who cash out their pension plan upon job separation, whether it was DB or DC, these pension plans were of lower average value than plans that were rolled over into IRAs or kept with employers. Table 1.5C shows a similar pattern across all cohorts in our analysis. The table has the cumulative distributions of the value of pension plans at job separation classified by whether the plan was cashed out.[2] For example, in 1992 about 49 percent of DC plans that were cashed out had value of less than $5,000, whereas just 20 percent of DC plans that were either left to accumulate or rolled into an IRA had value of less than $5,000. As far as trends in DC cash-outs are concerned,

2. The distributions are restricted to three categories of pension value (in 2000 CPI-U-RS dollars) due to differences in valuation elicitation and top-coding across surveys.

the 1998 and 2004 distributions are almost identical, but both are shifted toward higher values from the 1992 distribution. However, the distributions of DC plans that were not cashed out (three right-side columns) shifted in the same way, leading us to conclude that there was no trend in the cashing out of more valuable plans relative to all plans. With respect to DB plans, the distributions also show that less valuable plans are cashed out, but there is a clear trend toward relatively more cash outs of less valuable plans. For example, in 1992 23 percent of DB plans cashed out had value less than $5,000; in 2004 36 percent had value less than $5,000, even as there was little change in the value of DB plans rolled into IRAs.

If people have been cashing out retirement savings more often and at younger ages, what have they been doing with the money? Patterns of use of cashed-out retirement funds among persons with a DB plan are shown in table 1.6. Use patterns were similar for the 1992 and 1998 cohorts. Somewhat more than half was put into some other form of savings, and the remainder divided between spending and paying off debt. The 2004 cohort (data for 2004 to 2012) cut the percentage of cash-out funds going to other savings by half, doubling the percentage spent on debt and increasing spending by half. These patterns are consistent with a greater rate of negative shocks generated by the Great Recession and experienced by this cohort, which caused them to use the funds for immediate needs, spending and paying down debt.

Table 1.5C   **Cumulative percentage distributions of pension values by whether cashed out at job separation (year 2000$)**

	DC plans					
	Cashed out			Left to accumulate or rolled into IRA		
Pension value	1992	1998	2004	1992	1998	2004
0	0.0	0.0	0.0	0.0	0.0	0.0
5,000	48.7	40.0	35.4	19.7	14.3	15.6
50,000	91.0	78.3	80.5	69.1	56.5	54.0
	DB plans					
	Cashed out			Rolled into IRA		
Pension value	1992	1998	2004	1992	1998	2004
0	0.0	0.0	0.0	0.0	0.0	0.0
5,000	22.8	33.9	36.4	10.8	13.0	11.8
50,000	59.8	64.3	82.9	48.6	58.7	51.3

Table 1.6   Uses of cash-out funds by those with a DB plan

	1992 (%)	1998 (%)	2004 (%)
Spent	24.8	21.9	31.0
Saved	55.9	55.7	29.2
Debt	19.3	18.6	38.3
Durables	0.0	3.7	1.5

Note: All percentages are weighted.

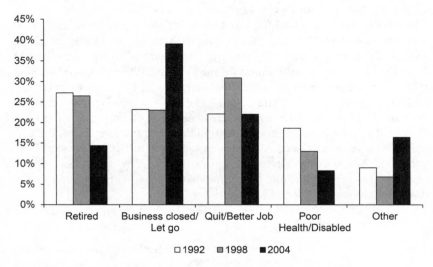

□ 1992   ▨ 1998   ■ 2004

Fig. 1.10   Reason for job separation among DC cash-outs

1.3.2   Precipitating Events of Pension Cash-Outs

Closely related to the question of what cash-out recipients do with the money is why they sought the cash-out. A respondent's use of funds from a cash-out could reflect a specific event that precipitated the transfer. We have a window into this through HRS questions on reasons for job separations. Potential reasons include health shocks, unemployment, other wealth shocks (such as the Great Recession's effects on retirement savings), and family needs such as the effects of divorce or widowing or the need to support children financially. Answers to the HRS question on reasons for job separations are given for those with DC plans in figure 1.10 and for those with DB plans in figure 1.11.

Among individuals separating from a job with a DC plan (figure 1.10), the first three reasons shown—retirement, job loss, or voluntary separation—were all important reasons for separating from a job. However, retirement was less often the reason in the 2004 cohort and job loss—"let go" or "business closed"—was more often the reason. Poor health or disability is less often cited by each cohort than by the preceding one.

Among those separating from a job with a DB plan, retirement was given as the reason by 40 to 55 percent of the respondents, whereas fewer than 20 percent gave any other reason (figure 1.11). Fewer retired in the 1998 and 2004 cohorts, but there was no increase in those responding "business closed/let go" for the 2004 cohort.

We next seek to learn what fraction of respondents cashed out their retirement plans when facing a shock around the time of job separation. The results of this analysis are shown in table 1.7. Among those separating with a pension, the overall fraction that cashed out for any reason was 18.6 percent. Rates were much higher among those affected by some specific shock. In particular, among those who were separating from a job with a pension and

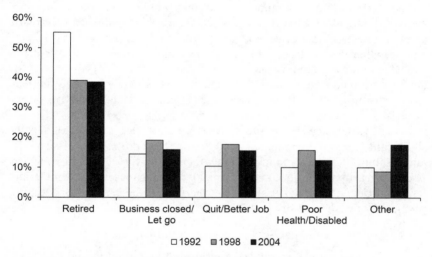

□ 1992   ▥ 1998   ■ 2004

Fig. 1.11   Reason for job separation among DB cash-outs

Table 1.7   Among those separating with a pension, the percent that cashed out, by precipitating events

Shock at (or around time of) job separation	Fraction cashed out (%)
Lost health insurance	36.2
Got divorced	20.7
Became widowed	19.5
Became work-limited	22.1
Health worsens	19.4
Became poor health	26.5
Fell behind on mortgage	54.6
Any mortgage issues	47.2

falling behind on their mortgage, 55 percent cashed out, as did 36 percent of those losing their health insurance at job separation, and 26 percent of those whose health became poor.

1.3.3   Predictors of Pension Cash-Out: DB and DC Plans with Lump-Sum Option

To control for a number of covariates, we estimated several regression models of the relationship between cash-out of pension plans among those separating from jobs and twenty-six right-hand (explanatory) variables, including shocks. Probit estimation was employed on five models. In one model (designated "0") the dependent variable was cash-out of a DB or DC pension. The other models all pertained to cash-out of a DC plan. They differed from each other in whether the value of the DC plan and/or membership in the 2004 cohort (relative to the 1992 cohort) was included.

The analysis identified numerous variables predictive of cash-outs at a statistically significant level (see table 1.8). Being older, living in an area with a higher unemployment rate, and being African American were associated with a higher probability of a pension cash-out. Being wealthier or more educated or having a longer planning horizon, better health (self-reported), health insurance, or a higher DC plan value was associated with lower pension cash-out probability. Generally, these were similarly predictive across models.

Several variables were not predictive of pension cash-out at statistically significant levels (these included gender, subjective probability of survival, and disability). They also included membership in the 2004 cohort, which predicted cash-out but not at a statistically significant level (when the latter was dropped from the analysis, membership in the 1998 cohort became predictive of cash-out with $p < .05$).

1.3.4   Longitudinal Analyses: Consequences of Cash-Outs

By taking advantage of the HRS's longstanding longitudinal panel, we can track respondents who cashed out and compare outcomes (economic status, personal characteristics, survival) with those of participants who did not cash out. Specifically, we focus on the 1992 cohort and follow it for twenty years.

As shown in table 1.9, 25 percent of those who had never separated from a job died by 2012, compared with only 16 percent of those who had ever separated. This difference is at least partially due to the time window over which a job separation could occur: those who died early had fewer chances for job separation.

Among those who had ever separated with a cash-out, over 19 percent died compared with 16 percent among those who separated without a cash out. Most likely this difference is a reflection of a positive correlation between cash-out and economic shocks, and a negative correlation between

Table 1.8 Probit coefficients predicting cash-out of pension plan among separations from jobs with pension coverage with lump-sum option

	Dependent variable				
	DB or DC cash-out		DC cash-out		
	(0)	(1)	(2)	(3)	(4)
Age (continuous)	0.0102*	0.0218***	0.0214***	0.0368***	0.0370***
	(0.00546)	(0.00682)	(0.00702)	(0.00865)	(0.00887)
Group 2	0.0101	0.0721	0.0615	0.201**	0.184**
	(0.0661)	(0.0839)	(0.0877)	(0.0886)	(0.0932)
Group 3	0.0575	0.122	0.102	**Dropped**	**Dropped**
	(0.0712)	(0.0896)	(0.0918)		
Unemployment rate (1–100)	0.0619***	0.0374**	0.0454**	0.0469*	0.0570**
	(0.0143)	(0.0184)	(0.0187)	(0.0253)	(0.0256)
Male	−0.0309	−0.0521	0.00166	−0.0821	−0.0200
	(0.0474)	(0.0604)	(0.0618)	(0.0688)	(0.0715)
Black	0.226***	0.245***	0.275***	0.151	0.180*
	(0.0705)	(0.0881)	(0.0888)	(0.107)	(0.107)
Less than high school	0.0995	0.200**	0.190*	0.279***	0.285***
	(0.0821)	(0.0971)	(0.0993)	(0.0998)	(0.101)
More than high school	−0.119**	−0.191***	−0.159**	−0.209***	−0.169**
	(0.0520)	(0.0661)	(0.0672)	(0.0758)	(0.0773)
Log(total HH wealth)[a]	−0.0477***	−0.131***	−0.101***	−0.141***	−0.100***
	(0.0157)	(0.0217)	(0.0217)	(0.0265)	(0.0258)
Subjective prob(survive to 85) = 0	−0.0951	−0.119	−0.148	−0.0494	−0.0585
	(0.114)	(0.140)	(0.136)	(0.142)	(0.138)
Few months planning horizon	0.0589	0.165*	0.124	0.242**	0.203*
	(0.0789)	(0.0949)	(0.0968)	(0.103)	(0.104)

(continued)

Table 1.8 (continued)

	Dependent variable				
	DB or DC cash-out	DC cash-out			
	(0)	(1)	(2)	(3)	(4)
Five years or more planning horizon	-0.0191	-0.0407	-0.0513	-0.124*	-0.115
	(0.0498)	(0.0648)	(0.0659)	(0.0741)	(0.0761)
Health (increasing in healthiness, 1–5 scale)	-0.0392	-0.0713**	-0.0662**	-0.0630*	-0.0535
	(0.0240)	(0.0299)	(0.0304)	(0.0345)	(0.0349)
Any health insurance	-0.271***	-0.376***	-0.331***	-0.377***	-0.307**
	(0.0875)	(0.104)	(0.106)	(0.125)	(0.125)
Disabled	-0.319*	-0.0814	-0.0414	0.00375	0.0638
	(0.192)	(0.228)	(0.234)	(0.242)	(0.237)
Working	-0.0193	0.0981	0.0429	0.116	0.0589
	(0.0513)	(0.0654)	(0.0672)	(0.0753)	(0.0788)
DC plan value			-0.136***		-0.152***
			(0.0224)		(0.0245)
Missing DC plan value			-1.445***		-1.713***
			(0.237)		(0.257)
Observations	4,910	3,802	3,802	2,890	2,890

[a]Wealth includes net values of primary residence, secondary residence, other real estate, business, stocks and investment funds, bonds, bank accounts, and other savings.

Robust standard errors in parentheses.

***Significant at the 1 percent level.

**Significant at the 5 percent level.

Table 1.9   **Mortality among 1992 workers**

	Percent dead by 2012
Never separated	24.9
Ever separated	15.9
Ever separated with cash-out	19.3

Table 1.10   **Labor force status in 2012**

	Alive in 2012 and had ever worked with pension coverage
Retired	2,443
Working	855
Disabled	2
Unemployed	44
Other	17

cash-out and 1992 socioeconomic status: as will be shown below, those who cashed out were initially less wealthy, had lower incomes and were in worse health, all of which predict greater mortality.

Table 1.10 shows the labor force states in 2012 among those who survived and who worked with pension coverage over the twenty years between 1992 and 2012. Although, of course, most had retired, a nonnegligible fraction was still working.

Table 1.11 shows several measures of health and economic status in 1992 and in 2012 by employment and cash-out status.

Considering wealth, health, household income, and pension income among those who survived to 2012, those who cashed out do look worse off in 2012 compared to those who never separated or separated without cash-out, for either retirees or those still working. However, these individuals were also worse off in 1992, *before they cashed out*. Whether cashing out affects individuals negatively is therefore conflated with the types of people who choose to cash out: selection plays a role in attempts to isolate the effects of cashing out on these well-being measures. Further, as we have seen, cash-out is accompanied by shocks such as losing health insurance and falling behind on mortgages. Those events by themselves would lead to relatively worse outcomes in 2012, even were the individual not to cash out.

To separate the causal effect of cash-out from initial conditions that are correlated with cash-out and from precipitating shocks, we used as a classifying variable the availability of an LSD option in the pension plan. Under the assumption that the availability of an LSD was orthogonal to initial characteristics and to the probability of a shock during the twenty years of observation, the variation by availability shows whether giving an LSD option results in worse outcomes, and when properly used as an instrumental

Table 1.11   Economic measures in 1992 and 2012 conditional on survival to 2012

	Log(wealth)[a]	Household income[b]	Health[c]	Pension income
Retirees in 2012				
1992 measures for those retired in 2012				
Never separated	11.43	70,314	3.83	603
Ever separated	11.24	69,277	3.84	413
Ever separated with cash-out	10.78	53,130	3.47	245
2012 measures for those retired in 2012				
Never separated	11.43	32,665	3.16	3,374
Ever separated	11.38	33,853	3.11	2,410
Ever separated with cash-out	9.94	23,617	2.87	339
Workers in 2012				
1992 measures for those working in 2012				
Never separated	11.14	72,399	3.83	718
Ever separated	11.49	72,376	3.88	504
Ever separated with cash-out	10.98	59,600	3.73	655
2012 measures for those working in 2012				
Never separated	11.65	78,795	3.64	1,438
Ever separated	11.76	55,236	3.63	3,339
Ever separated with cash-out	10.94	45,022	3.49	1,339

[a]For components of wealth, see note to table 1.8.
[b]Includes income from individual earnings, household capital, employer pension or annuity, public pension (including Social Security), Supplemental Security Income, unemployment or workers' compensation benefits, and other government transfers.
[c]Self-reported health status on a five-point scale, where 1 corresponds to "very poor" and 5 corresponds to "excellent."

variable, how large the negative effects of cash-out are. Additionally, we limit our sample to DB plan holders, since the vast majority of DC plan holders report having an LSD option, providing little useful variation in availability of such an option.

We first note (see table 1.12) that about 10.5 percent of workers who apparently did not have an LSD option in their DB plan reported a DB cash-out. However, the classification is by DB LSD status on the 1992 job. Because of subsequent job changes (prior to 2012), a respondent who did not have an LSD option in 1992 could have shifted into a job that had one and on switching out of that job cashed out that pension. Alternatively, individuals may have misreported the availability of such an option, perhaps unaware of this option until job separation. Hurd and Panis (2006) also noted this. Nonetheless, the rates of DB cash-out are over 60 percent higher among the 893 reporting the option, showing that respondent reporting about DB LSD availability does have discriminatory power.

There are several results of interest. First, there is little apparent difference in the survival rates. Second, availability of a DB LSD option does

Table 1.12   Long-term outcomes based on 1992 availability of LSD option in DB plans, among 1992 DB plan holders

	LSD option in 1992		
	No	Yes	
Counts	1,548	893	
Fraction alive in 2012	80.22%	82.54%	Not significant
Conditional on being alive in 2012			
Any nonretirement separation by 2012	26.63%	31.15%	Significant at 10% level
Any retirement separation by 2012	93.80%	90.88%	Significant at 5% level
Both nonretirement and retirement			
separations	23.75%	25.15%	Not significant
Any DB cash-out	10.50%	17.00%	Significant at 0.1% level
Wealth in 2012	511,031	556,601	Not significant
Pension income in 2012	817	263	Not significant
Household income in 2012	35,922	38,302	Not significant

Sample: Fifty-one to sixty-one 1992 HRS Cohort, working in a job with DB pension coverage in 1992.

appear linked with a greater propensity to separate from a job preretirement, marginally significant at the 10 percent level, and a lower propensity to have retired, significant at the 5 percent level, both of which suggest that having a DB LSD option allows for more preretirement job switching. However, there appear to be no resulting statistically significant differences in household wealth or household income among those with a cash-out option; if anything, the averages for these outcomes are slightly higher for those with a DB LSD option. Although average pension income is lower for those with the DB LSD option, this difference is not statistically significant. Thus, this table does not support the view that a cash-out option has led to pension holders being less economically prepared for retirement.

1.4   Conclusions

Among policymakers concerned about economic security in retirement, the practice of cashing out retirement plans at the time of job separation has been a worry. Changes to the tax code have been enacted to discourage such transfers, but the limited evidence previously available suggests that cash-outs continue to pull substantial amounts out of retirement plans, even when households are not facing imminent liquidity challenges. In this chapter we have attempted to add to the literature on pension cash-out practices. Specifically, we draw on long-duration panel data from the Health and Retirement Study to learn what shocks can trigger cash-outs, whether and how cash-out practices are changing, and what might be their long-term consequences.

The events most likely to trigger cash-outs are issues with mortgages; in particular, over half of those who fell behind on their mortgage cashed out pension accounts. Health was another important factor: more than one-third of those losing their health insurance at job separation engaged in cash-outs, and only one-quarter of those whose health turned bad did so.

Trends are of particular interest. To identify them, we took advantage of the HRS entering cohorts in 1992, 1998, and 2004. Most of these analyses showed that cashing out was becoming more frequent. Also, fewer job separations in the 2004 cohort were followed by retirement; among those with DC plans, more separations were due to employer closures and layoffs.

Ultimately, the concerns about economic security in retirement rest on the long-term welfare of the nation's senior citizens. How are these affected by cash-outs? The 1992 HRS cohort has been observed for over twenty years, so some inferences can be drawn. At first glance, those who cashed out do look worse off in 2012 compared to those who never separated or separated without cash-out. However, these individuals were also worse off in 1992, *before they cashed out.* This suggests some confounding of genuine cash-out effects with participants' prior attitudes and behaviors. Further work to isolate these relationships suggests that respondents having access to cashing out have more nonretirement job separations and less retirement than those without this access, but twenty years after reporting the availability of such an option, there are no statistically significant differences in wealth and income between these two groups. This is not the outcome we would have expected because of the literature that has focused on the harmful effects of pension cash-out. Further attention to this topic is warranted.

References

Amromin, G., and P. Smith. 2003. "What Explains Early Withdrawals from Retirement Accounts? Evidence from a Panel of Taxpayers." *National Tax Journal* LVI (3): 595–612.

Argento, Robert, Victoria L. Bryant, and John Sabelhaus. 2015. "Early Withdrawals from Retirement Accounts during the Great Recession." *Contemporary Economic Policy* 33 (1): 1–16. doi: 10.1111/coep.12064.

Burman, L. E., N. B. Coe, M. Dworsky, and W. G. Gale. 2012. "Effects of Public Policies on the Disposition of Pre-Retirement Lump-Sum Distributions: Rational and Behavioral Influences." *National Tax Journal* 65 (4): 863–88.

Butrica, Barbara, Sheila R. Zedlewski, and Philip Issa. 2010. "Understanding Early Withdrawals from Retirement Accounts." Discussion Paper no. 10-02, The Urban Institute. http://www.urban.org/research/publication/understanding-early-with drawals-retirement-accounts.

Hurd, Michael D., and Constantijn Panis. 2006. "The Choice to Cash Out Pension Rights at Job Change or Retirement." *Journal of Public Economics* 90:2213–27.

Scherpf, E. M. 2010. "Three Essays on the Disposition of Employer-Sponsored

Retirement Plan Balances." PhD diss., University of Illinois at Urbana-Champaign.

Comment   James M. Poterba

This chapter presents important new evidence on the circumstances under which US workers make preretirement withdrawals from their retirement saving accounts. "Leakage" is often cited as an important challenge to the provision of retirement security for US workers, but the causes and consequences of early distributions from retirement accounts have received relatively little attention. A number of policy proposals call for new restrictions on preretirement distributions. The impact of these proposals depends critically on the way pension participants respond to such changes; this study presents new information that bears on that issue.

Before turning to the specific findings in this chapter, it is important to note that it is very difficult to measure leakage from the US retirement saving system. Not all funds that are withdrawn from a given retirement plan are lost to the provision of retirement security. Withdrawals from one plan may be rolled to another retirement plan. Alternatively, a plan participant might withdraw assets from a DC plan and transfer the assets to another savings account outside the pension system. While this step might forego the benefits of tax-deferred accumulation, the transferred assets would still be available to support retirement consumption.

A number of recent studies have tried to estimate the rate of leakage from the US defined-contribution pension system. Munnell and Webb (2015) draw on data from the retirement plans administered by Vanguard. They estimate that cash-outs account for about 0.5 percent of the plan assets at the start of each year, hardship withdrawals for 0.3 percent, in-service withdrawals by individuals over the age of 59.5 for 0.2 percent, and loan defaults for 0.2 percent. Taken together, these various components of leakage represent about 1.5 percent of plan assets. If none of these withdrawals were redeployed in other forms of retirement saving, this rate of outflow would represent a substantial drag on aggregate retirement wealth accumulation. Munnell and Webb (2015) estimate that aggregate retirement wealth would fall by about 20 percent if there were no offsetting participant behaviors. One reason for studying leakage is to determine which retirement plan param-

James M. Poterba is the Mitsui Professor of Economics at the Massachusetts Institute of Technology and president and chief executive officer of the National Bureau of Economic Research.

For acknowledgments, sources of research support, and disclosure of the author's material financial relationships, if any, please see http://www.nber.org/chapters/c13636.ack.

eters and public policies may affect it, so that policymakers and employers have a sound basis for designing both plan attributes and the regulatory environment.

One of the "stylized facts" about preretirement distributions is that the likelihood of cashing out at the time of job separation is inversely related to the size of the retirement account balance. Aon-Hewitt (2013), for example, reports that larger account balances are more likely to be left in place, or if withdrawn to be rolled over, than are smaller account balances when workers separate from firms. For accounts valued at between $1,000 and $4,000, 49 percent choose a cash distribution, 31 percent roll over their balance to another retirement account, and 20 percent remain in the DC plan at the time of separation. Among those with $30,000 to $49,000 in their DC account, the respective proportions were 22 percent, 36 percent, and 42 percent. For those with more than $100,000, only 6 percent choose the cash option, while 43 percent choose to roll over their balance and 51 percent choose to remain in the plan. These statistics apply only to the "cash-outs" identified by Munnell and Webb (2015), which appear in their data to account for about one-third of retirement plan leakage. It would be valuable to understand how the likelihood of other leakage events is related to account size.

The most intriguing finding in this chapter is that defined-contribution plan attributes, in particular the provisions that affect the ease of preretirement distributions, have little if any effect on the level of retirement accumulation by participants. This finding is surprising: one might have expected that more generous plan withdrawal provisions would be associated with lower retirement wealth. Mechanically, if the participants in plans with and without generous withdrawal provisions reach retirement with similar pension resources, it must either be the case that the presence of these withdrawal provisions is not correlated with the level of participant withdrawals, or that some aspect of participant behavior, such as contribution levels or the length of the working life, is adjusting in a way that offsets the impact of easier access to retirement plan accumulations. Before discussing the empirical findings in more detail, it is helpful to outline a framework that can guide the analysis. The level of DC plan retirement assets (A) that a plan participant accumulates by retirement age (R) may be written as $A(R)$:

$$(1) \qquad A(R) = \int_0^R \left[C\big(\theta, x(a), z(a)\big) - D\big(\theta, x(a), z(a)\big) \right] e^{r(R-a)} \, da,$$

where C denotes plan contributions and D distributions. Net contributions at age a are $C(a) - D(a)$, but equation (1) permits a richer specification by allowing age-specific flows to depend on θ, a set of retirement plan characteristics that are set by public policy, such as the age at which an employed worker may take a penalty-free distribution, $x(a)$, a set of person-specific traits at age a that include age itself but might also include health status, and $z(a)$, a set of plan-specific traits such as the flexibility of the plan in allowing for distributions prior to retirement age. In this specification, C and D are participant-choice variables.

The vector of plan attributes, $z(a)$, is potentially endogenous, since by choosing which firm to work for, an individual can affect the $z(a)$ vector he faces. This raises the possibility that employee attributes $x(a)$ and plan characteristics $z(a)$ are correlated, which in turn poses a key challenge for empirical work that seeks to determine the effect of changes in the components of z on accumulation $A(R)$. There is very little empirical work on the extent to which plan attributes affect worker decisions about whether to join a particular firm, so it is difficult to assess the magnitude of potential endogeneity bias.

This chapter asks how changes in $\{z(a)\}$, the vector of plan-specific policies under which a worker was employed, and potentially θ, the public policy rules that affect preretirement withdrawals, affect $D(a)$ and ultimately $A(R)$. Equation (1) provides a framework for considering the various links between these plan design features and retirement accumulation, $A(R)$. The first channel to consider, and the most direct link, is between $z(a)$ or θ and plan distributions before retirement age, $D(a)$ for $a < R$. Do plan participants take advantage of opportunities to withdraw assets? A second channel confirms how greater withdrawal levels relate to the level of assets held in DC plans at retirement. This can be studied by comparing $A(R)$ with the set of $\{z(a)\}$ attributes that characterized the plan during an individual's working career. Other choice variables can also be affected by the set of $\{z(a)\}$ variables. For example, participants might be prepared to contribute a higher share of salary to a plan that they know is more flexible with regard to withdrawals. Thus $C(a)$ might be positively affected by more generous $\{z(a)\}$ provisions, offsetting in part or whole the positive effect of these provisions on $D(a)$. Alternatively, if participants have drawn down their retirement wealth by preretirement distributions, they might decide to work longer; R could be a function of $\{z(a)\}$.

This chapter presents important evidence on the relationship between plan attributes and retirement accumulation. A promising next step in this research program would be a decomposition of this relationship into its constituent parts to better understand the full set of saving and labor supply adjustments that are associated with more generous plan withdrawal rules.

One important contribution of this study is a detailed description of the circumstances under which pension plan participants make preretirement withdrawals. In most cases, such withdrawals coincide with periods of financial stress, such as job loss or a health shock that brings substantial out-of-pocket expenses. The prevalence of such circumstances suggests that many of those who take early distributions are not using these funds for discretionary consumption, but rather are funding expenses that were largely nondiscretionary. If this is the case, the alternative to a preretirement plan distribution might have been incurring debt, and the net effect on the individual's net worth at retirement might have been modest if anything at all. The fact that a substantial number of plan participants draw on pension assets during times of financial need suggests that, at least with regard to this aspect of the pension plan, workers are aware of their plan provisions. Mitchell (1988) and many subsequent studies suggest that pension plan participants have limited knowledge of their plan rules.

This chapter's careful analysis of participant distribution behavior raises questions about the design of policies that might affect distributions from retirement plans. There are three broad classes of such policies. First, there are policies that would change the set of allowable provisions in DC plans. For example, the Department of Labor and the Internal Revenue Service could prohibit lump-sum distributions from DC plans when individuals change jobs. Second, either regulatory bodies or employers could try to increase the degree of participant understanding about the linkages between preretirement behavior, such as contribution rates and withdrawal decisions, and retirement accumulation.

Finally, there may be other steps that would address the potentially divergent interests of retirement savers, plan providers, and financial advisers with regard to retaining pension assets within the retirement saving system. Because the cost of administering a retirement plan is increasing in the number of participants, and because the firm's liability is reduced if a former employee withdraws assets from the plan, firms have an incentive to encourage those who leave the firm, whether mid-career or at retirement, to withdraw their funds. The same incentives operate for firms that sponsor defined-benefit (DB) plans, which may encourage participants to choose a lump-sum payout at their retirement rather than a lifetime stream of annuity payments. A worker who quits or who is fired well before retirement may therefore face some pressure to withdraw assets, which raises the likelihood of leakage from the pension system.

Personal financial advisers may similarly face conflicts of interest. Since their earnings are related to the assets they manage or the transactions that they intermediate, when an individual leaves assets in a DC plan, those assets do not generate any revenue for an adviser. When an individual moves assets to an individual retirement account, or when they withdraw assets from the retirement system entirely and reinvest them in a taxable account, the financial adviser's income increases. This can create incentives for advisers to encourage their advisees to withdraw funds from DB and DC plans and to redeploy them in other investment vehicles. As the baby boom cohort reaches retirement, the complex incentives of the various participants in the retirement savings process are likely to come under increased scrutiny. The recent proposal to expand fiduciary standards to retirement advisers is an example of a policy reform that could shift the incentives facing financial advisers as they interact with their clients.

References

Aon-Hewitt. 2013. "Retirement Plan Leakage: Cause for Concern and Action." Presentation to ERISA Industry Committee, April. Accessed July 10, 2015. http://www.eric.org/uploads/doc/meetings-events/AonHewittPresentation _18April2013.pdf.

Mitchell, Olivia S. 1988. "Worker Knowledge of Pension Provisions." *Journal of Labor Economics* 6:28–39.

Munnell, Alicia H., and Anthony Webb. 2015. "The Impact of Leakages from 401(k)s and IRAs." CRR Working Paper no. 2105–2, Center for Retirement Research at Boston College.

2

Liquidity in Retirement Savings Systems
An International Comparison

John Beshears, James J. Choi, Joshua Hurwitz,
David Laibson, and Brigitte C. Madrian

What is the socially optimal level of liquidity in a retirement savings system? Liquid retirement savings are desirable because liquidity enables agents to flexibly respond to preretirement events that raise the marginal utility of consumption, like income shocks.[1] On the other hand, preretirement liquidity is undesirable when it leads to undersaving arising from, for example, planning mistakes or self-control problems.[2]

John Beshears is assistant professor of business administration at Harvard Business School and a faculty research fellow of the National Bureau of Economic Research. James J. Choi is professor of finance at Yale University and a research associate of the National Bureau of Economic Research. Joshua Hurwitz is a PhD candidate in economics at Harvard University. David Laibson is department chair, Harvard College Professor, and the Robert I. Goldman Professor of Economics at Harvard University, and a research associate of the National Bureau of Economic Research. Brigitte C. Madrian is the Aetna Professor of Public Policy and Corporate Management at the Harvard Kennedy School and a research associate and co-director of the Household Finance Working Group at the National Bureau of Economic Research.

An earlier version of this chapter was published as: Beshears, John, James J. Choi, Joshua Hurwitz, David Laibson, and Brigitte C. Madrian. 2015. "Liquidity in Retirement Savings Systems: An International Comparison." *American Economic Review* 105(5): 420–25. We thank Susanne Schwarz for helpful research assistance. We are grateful for suggestions from Sumit Agarwal, Julie Agnew, Keith Ambachtsheer, Bob Baldwin, James Banks, Hazel Bateman, Richard Blundell, Christopher Carroll, Jeremy Duffield, Manuel Garcia-Huitron, Alexandre Laurin, Raimond Maurer, Daniel McFadden, Olivia Mitchell, Jessica Pan, John Piggott, Eduard Ponds, Mark Rozanic, and Wenlan Qian. This research was supported by the Pershing Square Fund for Research on the Foundations of Human Behavior and NIA grant awards R01AG021650, P01AG005842, and P30AG034532. The content is the sole responsibility of the authors and does not represent the official views of NIA, NIH, or the NBER. The authors have been compensated to present academic research at events hosted by financial institutions that administer retirement savings plans. See the authors' websites for a list of outside activities. For acknowledgments, sources of research support, and disclosure of the authors' material financial relationships, if any, please see http://www.nber.org/chapters/c13633.ack.

1. For example, see Carroll (1992, 1997).
2. See Laibson (1997), Gul and Pesendorfer (2001), and Fudenberg and Levine (2006).

This chapter compares the liquidity that six developed economies have built into their employer-based defined-contribution (DC) retirement savings systems.[3] We find that all of them, with the sole exception of the United States, have made their DC systems largely *illiquid* before age fifty-five.

In the United States, employer-sponsored DC account balances can be moved to an individual retirement account (i.e., a "rollover" IRA) once the individual no longer works for the employer, which provides considerable scope for liquidation before the withdrawal-eligibility age of 59.5. Pre-eligibility IRA withdrawals may be made for any reason by paying a 10 percent tax penalty, and certain classes of pre-eligibility IRA withdrawals are exempt from this penalty.[4]

Liquidity generates significant preretirement "leakage" in the United States: for every $1 contributed to the DC accounts of savers under age fifty-five (not counting rollovers), $0.40 simultaneously flows out of the DC system (not counting loans or rollovers).[5] This amount of leakage may or may not be socially optimal, an issue that is beyond the scope of the current chapter.[6]

2.1   Analytic Framework

We focus on the five highest-GDP-developed countries that have English as an official language: the United States, the United Kingdom, Canada, Australia, and Singapore.[7] We also analyze Germany, the largest developed economy with a substantial pool of DC savings that does not have English as an official language.[8]

We analyze employer-based DC plans instead of defined-benefit (DB) plans for three reasons. First, DC plans are gaining assets relative to DB plans in almost all countries around the world, including the six that we study. Second, DC plans already have more than half of retirement wealth

3. For an extensive set of international pension comparisons, see Garcia-Huitron and Ponds (2015).

4. For example, no penalty is charged on withdrawals made for (a) permanent and total disability; (b) unreimbursed medical expenses exceeding 10 percent of adjusted gross income; (c) buying, building, or rebuilding a home if the withdrawal does not exceed $10,000 and the account holder has not owned a home in the past two years; (d) higher education costs; (e) tax payments resulting from an IRS levy; (f) health insurance premiums if unemployed for more than twelve weeks; (g) a series of substantially equal periodic payments made over one's life expectancy; (h) distributions to an alternate payee under a qualified domestic relation order; or (i) recovery from designated natural disasters.

5. See Argento, Bryant, and Sabelhaus (2015).

6. However, see Laibson, Repetto, and Tobacman (1998), Amador, Werning, and Angeletos (2006), Beshears, Choi, Harris, et al. (2015), and Beshears, Choi, Clayton, et al. (2015).

7. South Africa is coded as economically developing and is omitted.

8. Since 2002, DC arrangements have been permitted in three of the five types of occupational schemes in Germany. German savers had also set up over 14 million Riester plans as of 2011 (Börsch-Supan, Coppola, and Reil-Held 2012). The DC saving in Japan is still in its infancy.

in three of the countries that we study: Australia, Singapore, and the United States.[9] Third, in most circumstances, DC assets are at least as liquid as DB assets, so DC assets are the relevant margin for a household considering liquidating retirement wealth to augment preretirement consumption.

There are many ways to measure liquidity, including the actual quantity of liquidations or the marginal price of liquidations. We use the marginal price because statistics on actual liquidations are difficult to obtain. Even if such statistics were readily available, it is unclear how they should be compared across countries. For example, should liquidations be normalized by DC balances, retirement assets, total assets, or gross domestic product (GDP)? Also, from an economic perspective, the most natural object to study is the marginal price because it summarizes the incentives that consumers face.

Accordingly, we compute the marginal rate of transformation (MRT) between withdrawal-funded consumption at ages when the household is "*pre*eligible" for withdrawals and withdrawal-funded consumption at ages when the household is "eligible" to make withdrawals (in all countries that we study, eligibility age begins no earlier than fifty-five and no later than sixty-three):[10]

$$(1) \qquad \mathrm{MRT} = \frac{1 - \tau(pre, y)}{\left[1 - \tau(\mathrm{eligible}, Y)\right] \times R^n}.$$

We apply this definition to "general" consumption, which means consumption for any purpose (as opposed to targeted consumption—such as paying a medical bill or buying a home). In this equation, $\tau(pre, y)$ is the marginal tax rate (accounting for penalties and phase-outs of means-tested benefits) on a \$1 withdrawal from the DC plan when (a) the household is young enough to be at a preeligible withdrawal age *and* (b) the household's

9. In 2013, the Social Security trust fund contained \$2.8 trillion, and other retirement plan assets totaled \$23.0 trillion, summing to \$25.8 trillion. The DC plans (including the federal government's Thrift Savings Plan and state and local DC plans) had assets of approximately \$13.2 trillion, more than half of the \$25.8 trillion total. (Sources: Social Security Trust Fund, Investment Company Institute, Thrift Savings Plan, and authors' calculations.)

10. Singaporeans turning fifty-five after 2012 may only withdraw S\$5,000 of their Central Provident Fund (CPF) balances plus amounts exceeding the Minimum Sum and Medisave Minimum Sum between age fifty-five and the drawdown age (currently sixty-four). The remainder is paid out as an annuity beginning at the drawdown age.

In Germany, access to vested occupational pension benefits is typically linked to eligibility for state-provided pension benefits. Benefits can only commence when the member provides a pension approval certificate (i.e., proof that she receives state-provided pension benefits). The early state retirement age for the long-term insured is currently sixty-three.

We do not model provisions allowing for early access to small balances upon job separation. For example, employers in Canada (Ontario) may allow (or require) separated employees to withdraw balances of less than 20 percent of the Year's Maximum Pensionable Earnings (YMPE) (as defined under the Canada Pension Plan) applicable to their termination year. Employers in Germany may enforce the liquidation of balances below a restrictive minimum threshold if the separating employee does not transfer her pension rights to a new employer. Superannuation fund members in Australia may access balances of less than AU\$200 from previous employers.

employment income, y, in the withdrawal year is less than or equal to the household's permanent income, Y. Likewise, τ(eligible, Y) is the marginal tax rate on a $1 withdrawal from the DC plan when (a) the household is old enough to be eligible to make withdrawals *and* (b) household earnings in the withdrawal year equal permanent income, Y. Because we are studying a situation in which the household may have a liquidity need at a preeligible age, we calculate how the MRT varies as we change y. We assume permanent income is Y = US$60,000, which is approximately the median household income in each of the six countries. For simplicity, we set the gross real interest rate, R, to 1 (i.e., we set the net real interest rate to zero). Cross-country comparisons are not affected by this interest rate assumption.

We need to make additional demographic assumptions to pin down the household's marginal tax rate. We assume the household is a one-earner married couple with no dependents that rents housing, takes the standard income tax deduction, and is not disabled. In the preeligible withdrawal state, the earner is any age strictly under fifty-five; in the eligible withdrawal state, the earner is at least sixty-five years old.

In some situations, withdrawals are completely prohibited in the preeligible state. We treat such a ban as a 100 percent marginal tax rate—that is, $\tau(pre, y) = 1$. High values of the MRT are associated with high levels of liquidity (early withdrawals are potentially encouraged), and low values of the MRT are associated with low levels of liquidity (early withdrawals are discouraged or completely banned).

2.2   DC Liquidity across Six Countries

We are now ready to describe the MRT as a function of labor income during the preeligible withdrawal year, y, country by country. More detailed analysis and a description of our methodology are provided in the appendix.

2.2.1   Germany, Singapore, and the United Kingdom

In Germany, Singapore, and the United Kingdom, early withdrawals from retirement accounts are banned for general consumption: MRT = 0 for all y.[11] Only disabled[12] or terminally ill individuals may receive payments (an allowance that exists in all six countries). Although Singapore's DC assets are completely illiquid with respect to general (untargeted) consumption, Singapore has targeted DC accounts for medical expenses, a home purchase

11. We do not consider the Supplementary Retirement Scheme in Singapore, a voluntary DC plan designed to complement the CPF. More details can be found in the appendix.

12. In Germany, *if* the occupational pension plan covers disability, any payments during disability will be contingent on providing an official pension approval certificate from the social insurance system. If the employee is temporarily disabled, the payment of state-provided pension benefits will be discontinued and the employee will lose the pension approval certificate once s/he returns to work.

(which must be repaid with interest if the home is sold), and education (which must be repaid with interest in twelve years).[13]

2.2.2 Canada and Australia

In Canada[14] and Australia, the MRT = 0 under normal circumstances,[15] but DC balances become liquid in the event of adverse transitory labor income shocks.

Canada (Ontario). Employer-based DC plan balances cannot be accessed before the eligibility age unless a household's expected income in the twelve-month period following the application for withdrawal falls below US$32,428.[16] Therefore, MRT = 0 at our hypothetical household's normal level of income: US$60,000. Once income in the preeligible withdrawal year falls below US$32,428, the MRT jumps from 0 to 1.11. The MRT increases with further declines in income, y, because the marginal tax rate in the pre-eligible year falls while the marginal tax rate in the eligible year is held fixed. Means-tested benefit programs generate (local) non-monotonicities in the marginal tax rate that feed through to the MRT. As income approaches zero, the MRT plateaus at a peak value of 1.50 (see figure 2.1). Hence, the Canadian DC system has the intuitively appealing property that, for a typical household, DC withdrawals are barred when income is near its normal level but are encouraged (MRT > 1) when income declines substantially.

Australia. In Australia, the MRT = 0 as long as the household remains employed, no matter how low income falls. However, if the household receives income support from the government for at least twenty-six weeks (e.g., unemployment benefits), the household becomes eligible for DC with-

---

13. See Agarwal, Pan, and Qian (2014) for a discussion of spending that occurs in Singapore once participants can access part of their balance at age fifty-five.

14. Our analysis for Canada considers Registered Pension Plans, which require employer contributions and are subject to both federal tax jurisdiction and federal or provincial pension legislation. Group Registered Retirement Savings Plans, on the other hand, do not require employer contributions and are not subject to pension legislation. Legally, these plans may allow for withdrawals at any age, but sponsoring employers can and typically do place restrictions on early access, at least until separation from employment. A more detailed analysis of these plans can be found in the appendix.

15. There are some additional withdrawal provisions in these two countries, which are limited to a specific need (such as outstanding medical expenses, mortgage payments, etc.) or group (such as temporary residents permanently leaving Australia) and are explained in the appendix.

16. We assume that the preeligible household accesses DC funds transferred to a "locked-in retirement account." Withdrawals may be made from a locked-in account under the "low expected income" financial hardship provision if total expected income in the twelve-month period following the application for withdrawal falls far enough below two-thirds of the YMPE to permit a withdrawal of at least C$500. The maximum eligible withdrawal amount is (50 percent × YMPE)—(75 percent × Expected Income During the Next 12 Months). Therefore, withdrawals of at least C$500 may be made when expected income falls to C$33,400, or about US$32,427 using the 2013 annual exchange rate: (50 percent × C$51,100)—(75 percent × C$33,400) = C$500. Due to the C$500 minimum withdrawal requirement, we calculate the MRT in this case based on the effective marginal tax rate on the last dollar of a C$501 pension withdrawal.

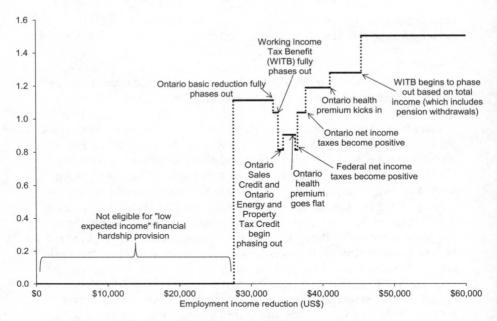

Fig. 2.1   Marginal rate of transformation (MRT) for Canada

Note: This figure reports the MRT for a household in Ontario, Canada, with assets from a DC registered pension plan that has been rolled over to a locked-in retirement account. For more details see the appendix.

drawals.[17] Hence, Australia also has a rising MRT as income in the preeligible year declines if low income in the preeligible year is due to a long unemployment or underemployment spell and the household receives government benefits as a result (see figure 2.2).

2.2.3   United States

In contrast, even at a normal level of income, the US DC system is liquid. Workers can roll over balances from a previous employer's DC plan into an IRA and then liquidate those balances under any circumstances with a maximum tax penalty of 10 percent. For instance, if our hypothetical household

---

17. The severe financial hardship provision that allows early access in this case restricts the withdrawals to AU$10,000 (with a minimum of AU$1,000) to cover reasonable and immediate family living expenses, such as general outstanding bills, insurance premiums, or mortgage payments. These withdrawals must be approved by the plan trustee. Given the AU$1,000 minimum withdrawal requirement in this case, we calculate the MRT based on the effective marginal tax rate on the last dollar of a AU$1,001 pension withdrawal. In Australia, withdrawals are also possible during temporary disability. In this case, withdrawals must typically be taken as an income stream throughout the period of disability (whereas a single lump sum may be taken for permanent disability).

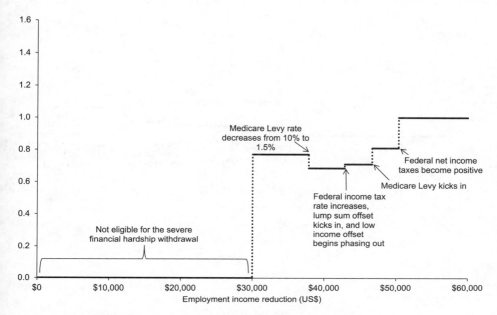

Fig. 2.2   Marginal rate of transformation (MRT) for Australia

Notes: This figure reports the MRT for a household in New South Wales, Australia, with DC assets in a superannuation fund. We assume that the reduction in employment income is due entirely to an unemployment spell. Hence, an *x* percent reduction in income is engendered by *x* percent of fifty-two weeks of unemployment. We also assume that the household receives unemployment benefits throughout the unemployment spell. For more details see the appendix.

lived in Texas, its MRT with preeligible income equal to permanent income would be

(2)
$$MRT = \frac{1 - \tau(pre, y)}{1 - \tau(\text{eligible}, Y)}$$

$$= \frac{1 - 0.1 - 0.15}{1 - 0.15} = 0.88.$$

As preeligible income falls below its normal level, the MRT tends to rise (as in Canada and Australia) due to falling marginal tax rates in the preeligible withdrawal year. As preeligible income approaches zero, the MRT eventually exceeds one (see figure 2.3). Hence, like the Canadian and Australian systems, the US MRT increases as income falls transitorily, but the rise is much more muted in the United States: the MRT increases from 0 to 1.50 in Canada, from 0 to 1 in Australia, and from 0.88 to 1.06 in the United States.

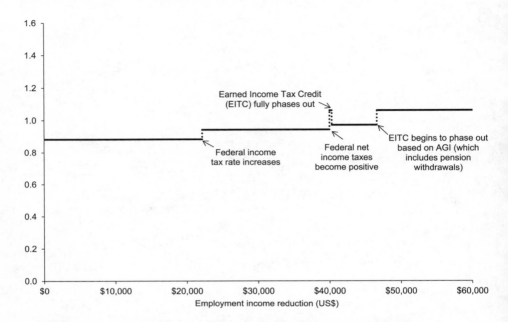

Fig. 2.3   Marginal rate of transformation (MRT) for the United States

Note: This figure reports the MRT for a household in Texas with some DC assets that have been or can be rolled over to an IRA. For more details see the appendix.

2.3   Conclusions

The six countries that we study fall into three groups. In Germany, Singapore, and the United Kingdom, withdrawals for general consumption in employer-based DC plans are banned, no matter the level of transitory income.

By contrast, in Canada and Australia, liquidity in employer-based DC plans is sharply state-contingent. For a household that normally earns US$60,000, DC accounts are completely illiquid unless annual income falls substantially, at which point the DC assets may be accessed. For example, Canadian workers who temporarily have very low income face strong incentives to *withdraw* their DC balances (MRT = 1.50).

The United States stands alone with respect to the high degree of liquidity in its DC system. Penalties for early withdrawals are relatively low, even at normal levels of income, and early withdrawals are slightly subsidized as income falls transitorily.

Explaining these cross-country differences in employer-based DC plans is beyond the scope of the current chapter. Nevertheless, we list four (mutually compatible) hypotheses for future research.

First, the differences in liquidity across DC regimes might matter little for welfare because the benefits of illiquidity (e.g., addressing a self-control problem) and the benefits of flexibility (e.g., liquidity during financial emergencies) are approximately equal in magnitude. Under this first hypothesis, differences across countries are welfare-neutral, so it is not surprising to see wide variation. See Beshears, Choi, Clayton, et al. (2015) for analysis that points in this direction.

The second hypothesis is akin to the first. If a country's DC system was designed to only be a minor supplement to a larger retirement income system, then its liquidity properties would have little welfare consequence. Thus, wide variation in these properties could ensue. The US DC system was first conceived as a top-up for DB pension plans. Only by historical "accident" did it instead become a substitute for DB plans over time, as DB plans lost appeal because of their nonportability and (employer) balance sheet risk. The United States was not intended to have a highly liquid workplace pension system, but this is what resulted from the unforeseen atrophy of the DB leg of the retirement savings system. The German DC system was also designed as a top-up to a DB system, but unlike in the United States, it is essentially illiquid before retirement.

Third, cross-country differences might reflect different ideological preferences. If a country's citizens have a relatively strong preference for economic freedom (potentially as an end in itself), this would tilt the retirement savings system toward more flexible institutions.

Finally, variation in the employer-based DC plans might result from other cross-country differences, like the strength of the social safety net. Liquid DC accounts are particularly useful if other sources of income support (e.g., unemployment benefits) are not sufficient during periods of financial duress. However, if this were the explanatory mechanism for the US DC system's liquidity, we would expect to see US liquidity being made contingent on the presence of an income/expenditure shock (e.g., withdrawals that are only liquid during an unemployment spell or coincident with a large health shock). Instead, US households are able to access their balances under any circumstances by paying no more than a 10 percent penalty.

Appendix

Methodology

In our analysis we consider households in the most populated regions of the six countries that we study: the United States (California and Texas), Canada (Ontario), Australia (New South Wales), the United Kingdom (London), Singapore (Singapore), and Germany (Berlin). We focus on the early withdrawal rules of the primary employer-based defined-contribution

(DC) schemes in these countries, as well as personal DC schemes that are largely funded by rollovers from employer-based plans (such as individual retirement accounts in the United States). Within this set of DC schemes, we consider all tax-advantaged DC retirement plans except those that accept only after-tax contributions (such as Roth 401[k] plans in the United States). Whereas all six countries permit early benefit access for disability or terminal illness, we focus on the degree of early access to retirement savings permitted in response to a general liquidity need at various levels of household income.

We calculate the marginal rate of transformation (MRT) between consumption of $1 (for general spending) funded by a withdrawal from the DC account prior to the retirement-eligibility age and consumption of $1 funded by a withdrawal from the account after the retirement-eligibility age. This calculation requires knowledge of the rules regarding pension eligibility and tax treatment of pension withdrawals and income in each country. To understand each country's pension rules, we analyzed governmental sources, including pension legislation and agency websites, as well as industry reports and academic literature. To verify our tax calculations, we used professional software for the United States and Canada (TurboTax) and free software provided by the government for Australia (E-tax). Since early access to DC retirement savings is fully restricted for our purposes in the United Kingdom, Singapore, and Germany, we did not need to conduct a tax analysis for these countries.

To standardize our tax calculations across countries, we assume the household is a one-earner married couple that files jointly, takes the standard income tax deduction, has no dependents, rents its housing, and is not disabled. These assumptions minimize differences in marginal tax rates across age and income states driven purely by state-dependent tax credits and deductions. We also assume that both partners are less than age fifty-five in the preeligible state and at least age sixty-five in the eligible state. These age restrictions ensure a change in eligibility status across the two states in all six countries, although the age threshold for the latter state could be set as low as age fifty-five (depending on the country) with no change in results.

Finally, we assume in our baseline scenario that the household has an annual gross income equivalent of US$60,000 for all countries. By comparison, median household income was US$60,190 in California and US$51,704 in Texas in 2013 (United States Census Bureau 2013). In Singapore, the average annualized 2012–2013 income for households residing in four-room flats (32.6 percent of resident households) was US$71,002 for the third income quintile, while the average for those residing in five-room and executive flats (25.5 percent of resident households) was US$82,166 for the third income quintile (Department of Statistics Singapore 2014a, 2014b).[18]

18. The income data reported in this section are converted to 2013 US$ using historical exchange rates from the Federal Reserve Bank of St. Louis FRED Economic Data and CPI data from the Bureau of Labor Statistics.

In London, 2009 median household income was £33,430, or roughly US$57,209 in 2013 dollars (Greater London Authority 2010). In Ontario, 2012 median income for "all census families" was US$74,890, or roughly US$75,600 in 2013 dollars (Statistics Canada 2014a). This estimate excludes about 16 percent of the population classified as "persons not in census families," who had 2012 median income of about US$24,000 (in 2013 dollars). In 2012, *median net* household income in Berlin was about US$25,800 in 2013 dollars (Office for Statistics Berlin-Brandenburg 2013), whereas *average gross* household income in Berlin and New Länder was about US$49,265 (German Federal Statistical Office [Destatis] 2013). Finally, annualized 2011–2012 median income in New South Wales was US$77,769, or about US$79,700 in 2013 dollars (Australian Bureau of Statistics 2013). The deviation between the median household income in each country and our assumption of US$60,000 does not affect any of the MRT calculations.

The remainder of this appendix presents profiles of each country that we study, including general information on each country's DC retirement schemes, a summary of the eligibility rules that apply to our analysis, and a detailed presentation of our MRT calculations.

United States

In the United States, about half of private-sector workers participate in an employer-sponsored retirement plan, of whom more than two-thirds are covered by a DC plan, primarily a traditional 401(k) plan (Munnell 2014). In 2013, private-employer-sponsored DC plans held $4.9 trillion in assets (34 percent of total private retirement assets) and individual retirement accounts (IRAs) held $6.5 trillion in assets (45 percent of total private retirement assets). The IRAs are personal DC accounts that are not linked to an employer; however, incoming flows to IRAs are dominated by rollovers from employer-sponsored plans (Copeland 2014). There has been a significant increase in DC plan participation in the public sector over the last decade, although the vast majority of public pension assets still reside in defined-benefit (DB) plans (Beshears et al. 2011).

Contributions to traditional 401(k) plans and IRAs are tax deductible, and investments grow tax deferred until withdrawal. Distributions are taxed as ordinary income, and withdrawals before age 59.5 incur an additional 10 percent federal tax penalty.[19] There are, however, many circumstances under which the tax penalty for early withdrawals from 401(k) plans is waived, including (a) the account holder has a job separation at or after age fifty-five; (b) the account holder suffers permanent and total disability; (c) the account holder has unreimbursed medical expenses exceeding 10 percent of adjusted gross income (AGI); (d) the withdrawal is used to make back tax payments resulting from an IRS levy; (e) the withdrawals

19. Throughout this appendix, we refer to the effective income tax rates applicable to pension withdrawals rather than the withholding tax rates.

take the form of a series of substantially equal periodic payments made over one's life expectancy; (f) the withdrawal is a refund of excess contributions; (g) the withdrawals are distributions to an alternate payee under a Qualified Domestic Relations Order; (h) temporary relief granted to victims of designated natural disasters; (i) the withdrawals are used to pay inheritances to beneficiaries after the death of the account holder; and (j) the withdrawals are used to make certain distributions to qualifying military reservists (Internal Revenue Service 2014).

Traditional IRAs carry the same early withdrawal rules except they do not allow penalty-free withdrawals upon job separation at or after age fifty-five. They do, however, permit penalty-free withdrawals of up to $10,000 at any age to buy, build, or rebuild a home if the account owner has not owned a home in the previous two years. They also allow for penalty-free withdrawals to pay for higher education costs and health insurance premiums (conditional on receiving unemployment benefits for at least twelve consecutive weeks). All other IRA withdrawals before age 59.5, which may be made at any time and for any reason, are subject to the 10 percent tax penalty.

Employers sponsoring 401(k) plans may permit loans or distributions (hardship or nonhardship related) while the account holder is still working for the employer, although they are not legally required to do so. In-service distributions made before age 59.5 are subject to the 10 percent tax penalty; loans are not subject to the tax penalty unless the recipient defaults on repayment. Loans are restricted to the lesser of 50 percent of the vested account balance or $50,000, and are generally repayable over five years at an interest rate determined by the employer.

For our analysis of the United States, we assume that both the preeligible household and the eligible household take distributions from an IRA containing funds rolled over from a 401(k) plan linked to a previous employer. The results would be the same if we assumed that the household was permitted to take an in-service distribution from its current 401(k) plan. In practice, some employers do not allow in-service withdrawals, and of those that do, many place restrictions on their use. As noted earlier, the total amount of assets held in IRAs in the United States exceeds that in employer-sponsored plans by over 30 percent; it is a relevant withdrawal margin for most households with retirement assets because all 401(k) accounts at previous employers can be rolled over into an IRA.

In calculating the effective marginal tax rate on pension withdrawals, we use the *tax rate schedules* published in the IRS Tax Guide for Individuals to determine the federal income tax liability (Internal Revenue Service 2013b).[20] In practice, the IRS *tax tables* provided in the same document determine the actual income tax paid on a given level of taxable income.

---

20. Our tax calculations for the United States apply for the 2013 tax year, which coincides with the 2013 calendar year.

These tables provide discrete tax amounts that apply to taxable incomes within a certain range, as opposed to a rate that is assessed on each dollar of taxable income. For instance, according to the tax tables, taxable income between $10,000 and $10,049 is subject to a tax of $1,003. For our calculations, we apply the underlying marginal tax rate (10 percent in this example) from the tax schedule to each dollar of taxable income within this range, so that the tax on $10,000 of taxable income is $1,000.00 and the tax on $10,049 of taxable income is $1,004.90. Similarly, we phase out the Earned Income Tax Credit (EITC) linearly, as opposed to adhering to the discrete amounts provided in the EITC table (Internal Revenue Service 2013a). This ensures that there are no large jumps in the figures we plot below.

We perform separate calculations for the two most populated states: California and Texas. Both of these states are unique in that California is one of only two states to our knowledge that levies its own tax penalty on early distributions (2.5 percent) in addition to the 10 percent federal penalty,[21] while Texas is one of seven states with no state income tax (two additional states do not tax *wage* income) (Intuit TurboTax 2014). Texas (figure 2.3) is illustrative in that it allows us to focus solely on the incentives built into the federal tax system. California (figure 2A.1), on the other hand, illustrates the combined effect of both federal and state income taxes, along with both federal and state penalties for preeligible pension withdrawals.

The figures we show plot the MRT between the withdrawal-funded consumption of preeligible and eligible households for different levels of preeligible household income. Our baseline scenario is when both the preeligible and the eligible household have incomes of US$60,000. This corresponds to the left-most point on the x-axis in all of the figures that follow. We place the figure for Texas in the body of the chapter—figure 2.3—and we place the figure for California in this appendix: figure 2A.1. The MRT is 0.88 in Texas and 0.85 in California. That is, the preeligible household in these states can consume 88 percent (Texas) and 85 percent (California) of what the eligible household can consume out of a marginal $1 withdrawal from its retirement account. In no other country that we study does the MRT of the primary employer-based DC scheme exceed zero (with a zero income shock).[22]

The x-axis in the figures measures the magnitude of the negative transitory labor income shock experienced by the preeligible household. As we move to the right, this negative income shock increases from US$0 (the far left) to US$60,000 (the far right), at which point the preeligible household has no income. In both Texas and California, the MRT is either flat or increasing with the size of the income shock with one exception: the region where AGI is between US$13,350 and US$19,680, which is where the EITC (a refund-

---

21. Nebraska imposes a tax penalty on early withdrawals equal to a specified percentage (29.6 percent in 2014) of the federal tax penalty (Nebraska Department of Revenue 2014).

22. As discussed in the next section, the only potential exception to this finding is group RRSPs in Canada, which are not subject to pension legislation.

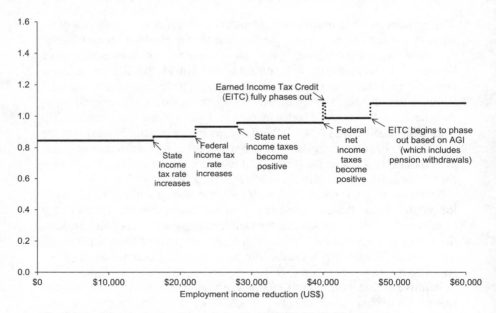

Fig. 2A.1   Marginal rate of transformation (MRT) for California

Note: This figure reports the MRT for a household in California with some DC assets that have been or can be rolled over to an IRA.

able tax credit for lower-income workers) phases out. When AGI, which includes pension withdrawals, is less than US$13,350, the EITC is determined solely based on employment income, which excludes pension withdrawals. Once AGI exceeds this threshold, it becomes the income measure used to determine the EITC, and pension withdrawals reduce the amount of the credit. In general the MRTs are similar across the two states, although a progressive state income tax in California and the lack of a state income tax in Texas makes the MRT greater at lower levels of income in California, despite the 2.5 percent tax penalty on early withdrawals. The MRT in both states hovers close to or above 1.0 once income falls below US$19,680 (corresponding to an income reduction of US$40,320) and increases to 1.06 in Texas and 1.08 in California when income falls to $0 (corresponding to an income reduction of US$60,000).

Canada

About one-third of the Canadian labor force, or 40 percent of employed workers, are covered by workplace pensions, or Registered Pension Plans (RPPs) (Ambachtsheer 2009; Government of Canada Office of the Chief Actuary 2014). Among these covered private (public)-sector workers, about 48 percent (94 percent) are covered by DB plans, and about 52 percent (6 percent) are covered by DC or other plans. Participation in these plans is often mandatory, and employer contributions are required. Similar to traditional 401(k) plans in the United States, employee and employer contributions to DC RPPs are tax deductible, investment earnings grow tax deferred, and distributions are taxed as ordinary income. The RPPs must comply with the provisions of the federal Income Tax Act to receive tax benefits, but the minimum standards for design, funding, communications, and administration for most plans are established by provincial legislation (Van Riesen 2009).[23] For this analysis, we have focused on the provincial legislation of Ontario, established under the Pension Benefits Act.[24] Ontario's RPP membership accounts for more than 35 percent of total RPP membership in Canada (Statistics Canada 2014b).

In Ontario, vested funds in DC RPPs may in general not be accessed until age fifty-five, ten years before the normal retirement age. Vested RPP participants who separate from employment may generally (a) leave their balances in the plan until becoming eligible or deciding to receive a benefit;[25] (b) transfer their balances to a new employer's plan; (c) purchase a life annuity that commences no earlier than the plan's eligible retirement age; or (d) transfer their balances to a locked-in retirement account (LIRA) or a life income fund (LIF). The LIRAs are accounts that allow for continued tax-deferred growth but do not accept contributions or permit withdrawals (except under the conditions described below). By age seventy-one, funds in a LIRA must be transferred to a LIF or used to purchase an annuity. The LIFs are income funds that provide a regular stream of retirement income once the original pension plan eligibility age has been reached. They have both a minimum withdrawal percentage and a maximum withdrawal percentage that increase with age.

Since December 21, 2010, Ontario has permitted LIRA holders to withdraw up to 50 percent of their LIRA balances upon transfer to a LIF, as long as the holder is at least fifty-five years old and the distribution is made within sixty days of the transfer. Those with less than C$21,000 (in 2014) across all of their locked-in accounts may also withdraw all of these balances if at least age fifty-five.

There are several financial and nonfinancial hardship provisions that allow early distributions from LIRAs before age fifty-five (Financial Services Commission of Ontario 2014). These distributions are also taxed as ordinary income. The financial hardship provisions allow for early distributions if (a) the account owner has low expected income; (b) the distributions

---

23. A minority of RPPs are regulated under federal pension legislation.

24. The Pension Benefits Act is available at: http://www.e-laws.gov.on.ca/html/statutes/english/elaws_statutes_90p08_e.htm.

25. Currently, DC RPP members cannot receive retirement income directly from the plan. However, Bill 120 (legislated in 2010) amends the Pension Benefits Act to allow members to establish a variable account within the DC RPP to receive income directly from the plan. This amendment has not yet been proclaimed.

are used to pay for outstanding medical expenses, including renovations to a principal residence for medical reasons; (c) the distributions are used to pay for first and last month's rent payments for the account owner's principal residence; or (d) the account owner is in arrears of rent or in default on a mortgage. These withdrawals may be made from an account only once a year (unless for outstanding medical expenses) as a lump sum that is limited to a minimum amount of C$500 and a maximum amount that is set as a percentage of the Year's Maximum Pensionable Earnings (YMPE).[26] The nonfinancial hardship provisions allow early distributions in cases of (a) terminal illness that reduces life expectancy to two years or less; (b) emigration from Canada as a nonresident for at least twenty-four months; or (c) excess transfers to LIRAs exceeding federal Income Tax Act limits. Under the first two conditions, the entire balance may be accessed; under the third condition, only the amount of the excess transfer may be accessed.

Finally, effective July 1, 2012, a new provision was added to the Pension Benefits Act allowing separated vested DC RPP members with account balances that are less than 20 percent of the YMPE in the year they separated from employment to withdraw all of these funds at any age. The funds may be accessed as a lump sum at any time or transferred to a RRSP (described below) within the first ninety days of receiving the option. Employers are not required to offer this withdrawal option; they are also allowed to make these withdrawals mandatory (Financial Services Commission of Ontario 2013).

Another DC savings option in Canada is the Registered Retirement Savings Plan (RRSP), an individual retirement account that may be opened privately through a financial institution ("individual RRSP") or offered through an employer ("group RRSP"). The RRSPs must be registered with the Canada Revenue Agency (and thus are subject to the federal Income Tax Act[27]) but are *not* subject to pension legislation (Van Riesen 2009). As such, these plans are less regulated than RPPs. Unlike RPPs, group RRSPs are typically voluntary, do not require employer contributions, allow for distributions at any age, and do not require any benefits to be taken as an income stream. However, employers can and typically do place restrictions on early access to these funds, at least until separation from employment. Under the Income Tax Act, employers may not make direct contributions to group RRSPs; instead, they must increase an employee's gross salary by a set amount and then transfer this amount into the employee's RRSP account (Frenken 1995). These contributions are included in the employee's taxable income and are subject to payroll taxes, unlike contributions to RPPs. The employee may later deduct these contributions up to the RRSP deduction limit (18 percent of the previous year's earnings up to C$23,820 in 2013).

---

26. The YMPE is defined under the Canada Pension Plan, a contributory public pension plan covering workers in all Canadian provinces except Quebec. The YMPE was C$51,100 in 2013.

27. For provisions in the Income Tax Act pertaining to RRSPs, see Canada Revenue Agency, "IC 72–22R9," available at http://www.cra-arc.gc.ca/E/pub/tp/ic72–22r9/ic72–22r9-e.html.

This limit is reduced by employer and employee contributions to RPPs; however, the difference between the maximum limit and actual contributions in any year can be carried forward to increase the contribution limit in future years. Withdrawals from RRSPs are subject to ordinary income taxes. Tax- and interest-free loans may be taken from RRSPs for first-time home purchases under the Home Buyer's Plan (repayable over fifteen years beginning two years after the withdrawal) or to finance education or training under the Lifelong Learning Plan (repayable over ten years beginning five years after the withdrawal).

For this analysis, we focus on DC RPPs, since they are subject to Ontario's pension legislation, are typically mandatory, and require employer contributions. Unfortunately, Statistics Canada's Pension Plans in Canada database, the best-known source of pension data in the country, provides plan and membership data on RPPs but not on group RRSPs (Baldwin 2015). This makes it difficult to quantify the relative importance of the two systems. In 2012, there were about 1.63 million members in RPPs with DC components (Statistics Canada 2014c). A recent government estimate suggests that in the same year there were about 1.50 million separate participants (those who do not participate in a RPP) in group RRSPs and/or Deferred Profit Sharing Plans (DPSPs) (Government of Canada Office of the Chief Actuary 2014).[28] Data comparing assets are even harder to come by. One source is Canadian Institutional Investment Network (2013), which summarizes survey data from nearly 400 firms with employer-sponsored DC plans. Among the surveyed organizations, 27 percent offer only a DC RPP, 15 percent offer only a group RRSP, and 59 percent offer both.[29] Assets under management in the average surveyed DC RPP were over five times the amount of assets in the average group RRSP. If group RRSPs were considered to be part of the primary employer-based DC scheme in Canada, these plans would be the only caveat to our finding that the United States is the sole country where the MRT does not equal zero at higher levels of income.

One feature relevant to our analysis of RPPs in Ontario is the "low expected income" financial hardship withdrawal provision that allows individuals of any age to make a withdrawal from a LIRA, which typically contains funds rolled over from RPPs. Under this provision, individuals can access their LIRA for any purpose if their total expected (self-reported) income in the next twelve months is less than two-thirds of the YMPE (C\$51,100 × 2/3 = C\$34,067 in 2013) (Financial Services Commission of Ontario 2014). Withdrawals are limited to the difference between 50 percent of the YMPE and 75 percent of total expected income in the next twelve months (with a

---

28. The DPSPs, in which an employer allocates a share of firm profits to employees in a trust account, are also not subject to pension legislation and may allow an employee to withdraw all or part of her account while still in active employment (Service Canada 2014).

29. Of the employers sponsoring a group RRSP, 58 percent made a contribution to the plan (whereas employer contributions are mandatory for RPPs).

minimum withdrawal amount of C$500).[30] We assume that the preeligible household accesses funds previously rolled over from a DC RPP to a LIRA using this financial hardship withdrawal provision. For the eligible household, we assume that the household transfers rolled over DC RPP funds within a LIRA to a LIF and then exercises the option to access part of this transfer as an immediate lump sum. Figure 2.1 presents our calculations under these assumptions.

Figure 2.1 shows the MRT between the withdrawal-funded consumption of preeligible and eligible households in Canada for different assumptions about preeligible household income relative to our prespecified benchmark.[31] In contrast to the United States, the MRT in our baseline scenario (income of US$60,000) is zero: preeligible households cannot access their balances at all outside of the limited exceptions noted above. Given the relatively stringent eligibility requirements for the low expected income withdrawal provision, the MRT remains zero as the size of the negative income shock increases until household income in the preeligible state falls below US$32,428. At this point, the MRT jumps to 1.11 and remains above 1.0 at most lower levels of income as well. Reductions in income generally result in a higher MRT, although this pattern is not monotonic for several reasons. Similar to the EITC in the United States, the Working Income Tax Benefit (WITB) for lower-income workers phases out based on total income (which includes pension withdrawals) between the range of US$14,572 and US$26,203, creating an implicit tax on pension withdrawals. Similarly, the phasing out of the Ontario basic income tax reduction, the Ontario Sales Credit, and the Ontario Energy and Property Tax Credit at lower levels of income create additional taxes on withdrawals. Finally, the Ontario health premium is levied at a 6 percent rate on income between US$18,932 and US$23,785, but then changes to a flat amount (C$300) for income between US$23,786 and US$32,247 (at which point the household is no longer eligible for a withdrawal). This shift removes the health premium's impact on the effective marginal tax rate on pension withdrawals within the higher income range. The Canadian MRT reaches its peak of 1.50 when income falls below US$14,572. Note that this MRT is substantially higher than the maximum US MRT.

30. Given these restrictions, withdrawals can only be made when expected income in the twelve months following application falls to C$33,400: (50% × C$51,100) – (75% × C$33,400) = C$500.

31. Our tax calculations for Ontario apply for the 2013 tax year, which coincides with the 2013 calendar year. We convert from C$ to US$ using the average daily exchange rate over this period (1.03 C$ to 1 US$). Since the "low expected income" withdrawal provision requires minimum withdrawals of at least C$500, we calculate the MRT based on the effective marginal tax rate on the last dollar of a C$501 pension withdrawal.

Australia

Over 90 percent of employed Australians save for retirement in a superannuation fund ("super"), which is a tax-advantaged private retirement plan with mandatory employer contributions (Agnew 2013).[32] Employees may also make voluntary income tax-deductible or after-tax contributions to their super. The vast majority of active employees participating in employer-sponsored retirement plans are members of DC or hybrid plans.

For this analysis, we assume that the household has a super funded solely from income tax-deductible contributions (which include employer contributions).[33] These contributions are not taxed as ordinary income. Instead, the contributions are taxed (when contributed) at a rate of 15 percent (30 percent if income exceeds AU$300,000)(Australian Taxation Office 2014).[34] Eligible distributions from supers are tax free after age sixty and predominantly taken as lump sums or account-based pensions (Chomik and Piggott 2012). Super members may access their balances when they reach the preservation age (currently fifty-five, increasing to sixty for those born after June 30, 1964) if retired from the labor force, or when they reach age sixty-five, regardless of work status.[35] There are also several exceptions allowing earlier access (detailed in the next paragraph). Lump-sum withdrawals made before the preservation age are taxed at the lower of the individual's marginal tax rate and 20 percent (plus the Medicare levy). Lump-sum withdrawals made between the preservation age and age sixty are tax free up to an inflation-indexed lifetime cap (AU$180,000 in 2013), and excess lump sums

32. The Superannuation Guarantee program that mandates private retirement provision commenced in 1992 (Bateman and Piggott 1999). It complements the first pillar of retirement savings, which unlike the public earnings-based schemes in many countries, is a means-tested "age pension" that phases out at higher levels of assets and retirement income. Generally, an employer must make mandatory super contributions for all employees age eighteen and over earning AU$450 or more per month (regardless of whether the employee is a full-time, part-time, or casual worker). An employer must also make contributions for employees under age eighteen who earn AU$450 or more per month and work at least thirty hours per week. The current employer contribution rate is 9.5 percent, increasing to 12 percent by 2025.

33. We do not consider after-tax contributions, which are made by less than 20 percent of employees (Australian Bureau of Statistics 2009). Unlike withdrawals of tax-deductible contributions, withdrawals of after-tax contributions are never taxable. Withdrawals from accounts containing both tax-deductible and after-tax contributions are taxed based on the proportion of each component in the account (i.e., withdrawals may not be taken solely from the after-tax component).

34. About 10 percent of super members, nearly all of which are public servants, participate in "untaxed" DB super schemes. Unlike in the funded DC arrangement that we consider, employer contributions in these schemes are not made until a benefit becomes payable and no contributions or earnings tax is paid. As a consequence, benefit payments are taxed at a higher rate. The majority of these plans are closed to new entrants.

35. Individuals who have reached the preservation age can access their super without retiring if using a "transition to retirement income" drawdown stream. Those who switch jobs after age sixty may also access accounts from previous employers.

above this cap are taxed at the lower of the individual's marginal tax rate and 15 percent (plus the Medicare levy). Annuities received before age sixty are taxed at the individual's marginal rate (plus the Medicare levy), minus a 15 percent tax offset if the individual has reached the preservation age.

Exceptions that permit access to super before the preservation age include (a) becoming disabled or terminally ill (if temporarily disabled, an individual may usually only receive an annuity for as long as she is unable to work; if permanently disabled, an individual may take an annuity or lump sum[36]; and if terminally ill, an individual may take a *tax-free* lump sum), (b) qualifying under "compassionate grounds" as determined by the Department of Human Services, (c) qualifying under severe financial hardship as determined by the plan trustee, (d) payment to a beneficiary following the death of an account owner,[37] (e) temporary residents permanently leaving Australia,[38] or (f) cashing out a balance of less than AU$200 following a job change.

Qualifying early withdrawals under the "compassionate grounds" exception are generally restricted to medical treatment or transport, mortgage assistance, disability-related home or vehicle modifications, palliative care, and funeral expenses for a dependent (Australian Department of Human Services 2014a). The severe financial hardship early withdrawal provision is limited to individuals under age fifty-five and thirty-nine weeks who receive government income support payments for at least twenty-six consecutive weeks.[39] This provision allows withdrawals of between AU$1,000 and AU$10,000 to cover reasonable and immediate family living expenses. Eligible expenses include general outstanding bills, outstanding insurance premiums, necessary motor vehicle repairs, education expenses, outstanding medical bills, minimum outstanding mortgage payments, and essential household goods. These withdrawals must be approved by the plan trustee.

For this analysis, we assume that the preeligible household is able to exploit this financial hardship provision after becoming unemployed and receiving Newstart Allowance, Australia's version of unemployment benefits, for at least twenty-six weeks (when annual employment income has been halved). In 2014, the maximum Newstart Allowance benefit for a married couple is AU$931 per fortnight (or AU$465.50 per week) (Australian Department of Human Services 2014b). This amount is reduced in accor-

---

36. For withdrawals on account of permanent disability before age sixty, a 15 percent tax offset applies if the payment is received as an annuity.

37. If the beneficiary is a dependent of the deceased account owner, the inheritance is tax free if taken as a lump sum. If taken as an income stream, the payments are tax free if either the deceased account holder or the beneficiary is at least sixty years old; if both are under sixty years old, the payments are taxable as ordinary income minus a 15 percent tax offset. If the beneficiary is not a dependent, the inheritance may only be taken as a lump sum and is taxed at the lower of the individual's marginal tax rate and 15 percent (plus the Medicare levy).

38. These payments are receivable as lump sums and taxed at 38 percent, regardless of age.

39. A similar provision is also available to individuals who are at least age fifty-five and thirty-nine weeks if they are not gainfully employed and have received income support payments for at least thirty-nine cumulative weeks since turning fifty-five.

dance with an asset test and an income test that considers income earned during the benefit receipt period (there is no look-back period). We assume that each reduction in employment income displayed on the x-axis of figure 2.2 corresponds to a period of unemployment in which the preeligible household receives the maximum Newstart Allowance benefit in the background. For instance, when employment income falls to US$45,000, or three-fourths of the starting amount, we assume that the household accrues [$(1 - \frac{3}{4}) \times 52$ weeks $\times$ (AU$465.50)] in Newstart Allowance benefits. The eligible household, being at least age sixty-five, is able to make tax-free withdrawals from the super for any reason.

Under these assumptions, the MRT in Australia starts at zero in the baseline scenario and remains so until employment income has been halved (US$30,000), at which point the MRT jumps to 0.77.[40] The MRT increases as employment income falls with the exception of a slight dip resulting from a change in the Medicare levy from a 1.5 percent rate on total income to a 10 percent rate on income within a lower threshold. The MRT increases to 1.0 once employment income reaches US$9,664 and the household's marginal tax rate falls to 0 percent. Had we barred this household from receiving income support payments, early super access at lower levels of income would be prohibited, and the MRT would remain zero across the income distribution.

United Kingdom

In 2012, about 47 percent of workers in the United Kingdom participated in an employer-sponsored retirement plan, split between DB occupational plans (28 percent), DC occupational plans (7.0 percent), group personal pension plans (6.7 percent), group stakeholder pension plans (3.5 percent), and unknown pension plans (1.3 percent) (United Kingdom Office for National Statistics 2013). Additionally, 7 percent of people age sixteen to sixty-four voluntarily contributed to an individual personal pension account.[41] Group personal pension plans are individual, tax-advantaged DC accounts

40. Our tax calculations for Australia apply for the 2014 tax year, which extends from July 2013 to June 2014. We convert from AU$ to US$ using the average daily exchange rate over this period (1.09 AU$ to 1 US$). Since the severe financial hardship withdrawal provision that we consider requires a minimum withdrawal of AU$1,000, we calculate the MRT based on the effective marginal tax rate on the last dollar of a AU$1,001 pension withdrawal.

41. There are two pillars of public retirement provision in the United Kingdom: the Basic State Pension, a flat benefit based on years of contributions, and the State Second Pension, an earnings-based scheme that replaced the State Earnings-Related Pension Scheme in 2002. The 1986 Social Security Act made it possible for employers offering occupational DC plans and employees opening individual personal pension accounts to "contract out" of the public earnings-based scheme beginning in 1988 (Liu 1999). By meeting minimum standards, these plans could substitute for the second layer of public provision. Since 2012, only DB plans have been eligible to contract out. For people reaching the state pension age after April 2016, the Basic State Pension and State Second Pension will be consolidated into a single-tier system and contracting out will no longer be an option (Towers Watson 2014).

that are linked to an employer. Group stakeholder pension plans are similar to group personal pension plans, but they have minimum standards set by the government, including limited management fees and the ability to switch providers at no charge. Contributions to all of these plans are tax relieved, investment earnings grow tax deferred, and distributions are taxed as ordinary income.[42]

Beginning in 2012 and following a phased-in schedule extending through 2017, employers will be required to automatically enroll most employees into a qualifying tax-registered occupational plan (DB or DC) or a DC employer-sponsored personal plan (The Pensions Regulator 2014). Employers may choose to enroll employees in the National Employment Savings Trust (NEST), a centralized DC plan established by the government that carries no initial charges or administrative fees for employers and a simple charging structure for employees.

Funds in occupational and personal pensions may not be legally accessed until age fifty-five at the earliest (rising to age fifty-seven by 2028), except under the circumstances described in the next paragraph. Beginning at age fifty-five, 25 percent of plan balances may be accessed as a tax-free lump sum; the remaining 75 percent may be received through (a) a life annuity, (b) a "capped drawdown" approach, (c) a "flexible drawdown" approach, or (d) a lump sum. The first three options are taxed as regular income; lump sums are taxed at a 55 percent rate. Exceptions to the 55 percent tax include lump sums from combined pension accounts holding £30,000 or less, lump sums from individual workplace pensions holding £10,000 or less, and lump sums from up to three personal pension plan accounts holding £10,000 or less, if the account holder is at least sixty years old. The capped drawdown approach sets a maximum annual withdrawal limit equal to 150 percent of an equivalent single life annuity. The flexible drawdown approach, which may only be utilized by individuals with at least £12,000 in guaranteed annual pension income, allows withdrawals with no maximum limit. Beginning in April 2015, individuals will be able to access the remaining 75 percent of their balances (after receiving the first 25 percent as a tax-free lump sum) as a lump sum subject to ordinary income tax rates.

The only exceptions to the age fifty-five eligibility requirement are for those who qualify under "ill health" or a "protected pension age." To qualify under the ill health exception, an individual must have a mental or physical illness that renders her incapable of carrying out her job until she reaches the eligible retirement age (as determined by a physician). The standard

42. There are two types of tax relief arrangements for pension contributions: net pay and relief at source. Under the net pay arrangement, employee contributions are fully tax deductible from income up to the contribution limit. Under the relief at source arrangement, contributions are taxed at the employee's marginal rate, but the provider adds tax relief directly to the employee's pension account at the "basic" marginal tax rate. The employee can later claim additional relief when filing income taxes if she is subject to a higher marginal tax rate than the basic rate.

tax rules apply to withdrawals under this condition unless life expectancy is reduced to less than one year, in which case all withdrawals are tax free. The protected pension age provision applies to certain individuals who were exempt from the normal minimum pension age increase (from fifty to fifty-five) in April 2010.

In contrast to the countries discussed so far, the MRT equals zero at all levels of income for our representative household in the United Kingdom: under no circumstances may DC retirement funds be accessed early to service a general liquidity need.

Singapore

In Singapore, the vast majority of retirement savings are made through the Central Provident Fund (CPF), a compulsory savings plan with three separate accounts: the Special Account (used for retirement savings and investment), the Ordinary Account (used to buy a home, finance education, pay for CPF insurance, invest, or transfer funds to the Special Account), and the Medisave Account (used for medical expenses and approved medical insurance). The Ordinary Account may be accessed throughout the working life to finance education at qualifying institutions (limited to 40 percent of the balance) or to buy a home and service its mortgage payments. Funds used for education must be repaid (with interest) within twelve years of completing or leaving a course of study; funds used for home purchases must only be repaid upon sale of the home.[43] The Medisave Account is also completely liquid throughout the working life for approved medical expenses or insurance and does not require repayment. Funds in the Special Account may not be accessed until age fifty-five, at the earliest. All contributions, investment earnings, and eligible withdrawals are tax free.

Required contributions to the CPF currently total 36 percent of covered wages (consisting of 20 percent employee contributions and 16 percent employer contributions) until the employee reaches age fifty, at which point both the employee and employer contribution rates begin to decline. The Ordinary Account receives a greater share of contributions than the Special Account and Medisave Account combined throughout most of the working career. Savings in the Ordinary Account earn a minimum credited return of 2.5 percent, and savings in the Special Account and Medisave Account earn a minimum credited return of 4 percent. The first S$60,000 of combined balances (with up to S$20,000 coming from the Ordinary Account) receive an additional 1 percent return. The CPF members may also choose to self-invest their Ordinary Account and/or Special Account savings in a range of investments, forgoing the guaranteed floor on returns.[44]

Upon reaching age fifty-five, the Ordinary and Special Accounts are con-

---

43. In reality, these housing loans typically span the life cycle since households can continue to draw CPF funds for subsequent home purchases.

44. Members must satisfy a minimum balance requirement of S$20,000 (S$40,000) in the Ordinary (Special) Account to be eligible to self-invest funds from this account.

solidated to form the Retirement Account, up to the legislated Minimum Sum (S$148,000 in 2013). Any excess balances in the Ordinary and Special Accounts above the Minimum Sum may then be withdrawn, conditional on also first securing the Medisave Minimum Sum (S$40,500 in 2013). Excess balances in the Medisave Account above the Medisave Minimum Sum may also be withdrawn if the regular Minimum Sum has been met. For those who are unable to meet the minimum sums, the maximum withdrawal permitted from the Retirement Account at age fifty-five is S$5,000.[45] These withdrawals may be made at any time between age fifty-five and the drawdown age (currently sixty-four, increasing to sixty-five in 2018). Savings in the Retirement Account are guaranteed an interest rate of at least 4 percent. Beginning at the drawdown age, funds from the Retirement Account are used to pay monthly income for life (i.e., an annuity).[46]

Other than for the purposes specified above, the only exceptions for accessing CPF funds before age fifty-five are for leaving Singapore residence permanently or suffering from a permanent disability or terminal illness. If terminally ill, an individual may take a full lump sum of the Ordinary and Special Accounts; if permanently disabled but not terminally ill, an individual may only withdraw balances exceeding a certain amount (known

45. These withdrawal provisions apply to CPF members turning fifty-five after 2012. Those who turned fifty-five between 1987 and 2009 were able to withdrawal 50 percent of their total account balances at age fifty-five regardless of whether they met the minimum sum requirements (Agarwal, Pan, and Qian 2014). This percentage declined by 10 percent each subsequent year (i.e., 40 percent for those turning fifty-five in 2009, 30 percent for those turning fifty-five in 2010, etc.) until January 1, 2013, when the current rules became active.

46. The CPF members born after 1957 are automatically placed on "CPF LIFE," a mandatory annuity scheme, if they have at least S$40,000 in their Retirement Account at age fifty-five or at least S$60,000 in their Retirement Account at the drawdown age. Those who are not placed on CPF LIFE (and do not choose to opt in) receive phased withdrawal payments from the Retirement Account over about twenty years (or until the balance is exhausted) beginning at the drawdown age. Members in the CPF LIFE scheme may choose from one of two plans ("CPF LIFE Standard" or "CPF LIFE Basic"), which differ based on the size of the monthly payments (higher under the Standard plan) relative to the bequest (higher under the Basic plan). The Standard plan commits funds from the Retirement Account worth up to half the Minimum Sum to an annuity premium at age fifty-five; the remainder of the Retirement Account is committed to the annuity one to two months before the drawdown age. Beginning at the drawdown age, the annuity begins to pay a monthly income for life. Any unused annuity premiums are refunded to heirs as a bequest after the member's death. The Basic plan commits a small amount of funds (about 10 percent) from the Retirement Account to an annuity premium at age fifty-five; a second annuity premium worth a small portion of the money accrued in the Retirement Account after age fifty-five is paid one to two months before the drawdown age. Beginning at the drawdown age, remaining funds in the Retirement Account are used to pay a monthly income until the member turns ninety. At age ninety, the annuity contract begins to make monthly payments for life. The annuity payments are structured to preserve an equivalent benefit level to the Retirement Account payments. Any unused funds in the Retirement Account and unused annuity premiums are refunded to heirs as a bequest after the member's death. For details on the origin of the CPF LIFE scheme and pricing of the original annuity options, see Fong, Mitchell, and Koh (2011). For a description of the scheme in its current form, see the CPF LIFE member brochure available at http://mycpf.cpf.gov.sg/NR/rdonlyres /09EA0C05-C8E9-4705-9D91-E8BD1D12CF1E/0/LIFEBrochure.pdf.

as the Reduced Minimum Sum because it is below the regular Minimum Sum), which then immediately begins to provide monthly annuitized payouts. There is also a voluntary DC scheme in Singapore, the Supplementary Retirement Scheme (SRS), which is operated by three Singaporean banks. It was established in 2001 as a means for individuals to fund retirement savings in addition to their CPF savings and began allowing voluntary employer contributions in 2008 (Kok et al. 2013). However, few employers take advantage of the SRS as a supplementary retirement system for Singaporean citizens and permanent residents. It has received some limited use by employers to offer notional CPF contributions to foreign employees, who are not eligible to participate in the CPF, but the majority of employers who grant these contributions do so in cash payments (that are paid as salary and not as contributions to the SRS). Unlike the CPF, distributions from the SRS are taxable as income and can be made at any age. Only 50 percent of withdrawals made after the drawdown age are taxable, whereas 100 percent of withdrawals made before the drawdown age are taxable and are also subject to a 5 percent tax penalty (Island Revenue Authority of Singapore 2014).

For this analysis, we focus on the liquidity features of the CPF, since it is a mandatory plan and by far the dominant employer-based DC plan in Singapore. While the CPF is liquid throughout the working life to finance medical needs, education, and home purchases, there is no provision for early access for general liquidity needs (such as a decline in income). Thus, as in the United Kingdom, the MRT in Singapore equals zero across the income spectrum. (In addition, the special account is completely illiquid.)

Germany

Historically, Germany's statutory public pension insurance system guaranteed a generous net standard replacement rate of around 70 percent for a worker with average lifetime earnings and forty-five years of creditable service. Occupational and private pensions were largely supplemental and accounted for a small portion of retiree income (Berner 2006a; Börsch-Supan and Wilke 2004). However, in response to rising contribution rates required to fund the statutory system for a rapidly aging population, the Riester Reform of 2001 was legislated to stabilize the contribution rate and improve the balance of intergenerational risk sharing. To offset the reduction in future benefit levels prompted by these changes, the reform also introduced a series of new regulations, tax incentives, and subsidies aimed at increasing voluntary savings through occupational and personal plans.

Since 2002, German employees have had the legal right to request access to employer-based retirement benefits. These benefits can be funded internally through *Direktzusage* (a direct pension commitment through book reserves) or externally through one of four methods: *Unterstützungskasse* (support funds), *Direktversicherung* (direct insurance), *Pensionsfonds* (pension funds), and *Pensionskasse* (pension insurance funds). The current occupational pension landscape is made up predominantly of DB plans, but pension experts foresee a significant increase in DC activity in the future (Allianz Global Investors 2009). However, "pure DC" schemes do not exist under German law. Occupational DC schemes must provide a guarantee of minimum benefits, typically the sum of nominal paid-in contributions (Federal Financial Supervisory Authority of Germany 2014). They also involve no investment choice on the part of the employee. Since 2002, these DC schemes with minimum benefits have been permitted in the three fully funded vehicles: pension funds, pension insurance funds, and direct insurance. These plans allow tax-advantaged contributions and tax-deferred growth; benefits are taxed as income.

These plans are mostly illiquid during the accumulation phase, with access typically linked to eligibility for state-provided pension benefits.[47] The earliest retirement age for old-age pension benefits under the state system is sixty-three for the long-term insured (Börsch-Supan and Juerges 2011). In some cases, plans allow for disability benefits, which are also typically linked to state-provided benefits. Upon an employee's termination from employment, a sponsoring employer may also choose to cash out the employee's balances if they are below a restrictive minimum threshold and the employee does not transfer her pension rights to a new employer. Early distributions for other purposes, such as temporarily low income, are prohibited (Mackenzie 2010).

The most significant growth in DC coverage has been through private pensions known as Riester pensions, which were introduced with the 2001 reforms (Börsch-Supan, Coppola, and Reil-Held 2012).[48] Since 2006, these plans have outpaced occupational pensions as the main instrument for funded pension provision. Similar to occupational DC plans, they require a guarantee of nominal contributions. Government-matching subsidies are provided on contributions of up to 4 percent of gross earnings,[49] which are also tax deductible up to a limit. Additional subsidies are provided for each child. Like occupational DC schemes, Riester pensions are mostly illiquid, but unlike occupational DC schemes, Riester pensions do allow for early withdrawals of up to 100 percent of the accumulated balance for the pur-

47. German occupational pensions are regulated under the Betriebsrentengesetz (BetrAVG), available at http://www.gesetze-im-internet.de/bundesrecht/betravg/gesamt.pdf.

48. Here we refer to "Riester pensions" as personal investment accounts that are not linked to an employer and qualify for the Riester incentives (subsidy and tax relief). These plans must comply with the conditions set forth in the Certification of Retirement Pension Contracts Act ("AltZertG") in order to receive certification for the Riester incentives (United States General Accounting Office 2003). Certain employer-sponsored plans are also eligible to receive the Riester incentives but are not subject to the same certification requirements (Berner 2006b).

49. The full subsidy is receivable when total contributions, *including the subsidy*, equal 4 percent of gross earnings (Berner 2006b). Therefore, the required employee contribution to receive the full subsidy (a flat lump-sum benefit) scales down as a percentage of gross earnings at lower levels of income.

chase of owner-occupied housing. Otherwise, account holders are barred from making withdrawals before age sixty-two (age sixty for contracts concluded before 2012). They do retain the right to cancel a contract before the eligibility age, but then must repay all government subsidies and tax relief received to date (United States General Accounting Office 2003). Therefore, Riester pensions are usually not canceled before retirement (Kissling 2011). Benefits are taxable as income and typically received as an annuity, although a lump sum of up to 30 percent of account value is permitted (Hagen and Kleinlein 2012). Since occupational *and* private DC balances in Germany are inaccessible before the eligibility age for general liquidity needs, the MRT equals zero across all levels of household income, as in the United Kingdom and Singapore.

References

Agarwal, Sumit, Jessica Pan, and Wenlan Qian. 2014. "Age of Decision: Pension Savings Withdrawal and Consumption and Debt Response." Unpublished Manuscript, National University of Singapore.

Agnew, Julie. 2013. "Australia's Retirement System: Strengths, Weaknesses, and Reforms." Issue in Brief no. 13–5, Center for Retirement Research at Boston College.

Allianz Global Investors. 2009. "Defining the Direction of Defined Contribution in Europe: Results of an Expert Survey." International Pension Papers no. 4. http://www.slideshare.net/AllianzKnowledge/defined-contribution-in-europe -the-direction.

Amador, Manuel, Iván Werning, and George-Marios Angeletos. 2006. "Commitment vs. Flexibility." *Econometrica* 74 (2): 365–96.

Ambachtsheer, Keith. 2009. "Pension Reform: How Canada Can Lead the World." C. D. Howe Institute Benefactors Lecture, Toronto, November 18. https://www .cdhowe.org/pdf/BenefactorsLecture_09.pdf.

Argento, Robert, Victoria L. Bryant, and John Sabelhaus. 2015. "Early Withdrawals from Retirement Accounts during the Great Recession." *Contemporary Economic Policy* 33 (1): 1–16.

Australian Bureau of Statistics. 2009. "Employment Arrangements, Retirement and Superannuation, Australia, Apr to Jul 2007 (Re-issue)." Cat. 6361.0. http://www.abs.gov.au/ausstats/abs@.nsf/Latestproducts/6361.0Main%20 Features2Apr%20to%20Jul%202007%20(Re-issue)?opendocument&tabname =Summary&prodno=6361.0&issue=Apr%20to%20Jul%202007%20(Re-issue) &num=&view=.

———. 2013. "Household Income and Income Distribution, Australia 2011–12— Detailed Tables." Table 1.2A. Version from December 19, 2013. http://www.abs .gov.au/AUSSTATS/abs@.nsf/DetailsPage/6523.02011-12.

Australian Department of Human Services. 2014a. "Early Release of Superannuation." Version from November 17, 2014. http://www.humanservices.gov.au /customer/services/centrelink/early-release-of-superannuation.

———. 2014b. "Newstart Allowance." Version from December 22, 2014. http://www .humanservices.gov.au/customer/services/centrelink/newstart-allowance.

Australian Taxation Office. 2014. "Super." Version from July 16, 2014. https://www
.ato.gov.au/Individuals/Super/.
Baldwin, Bob. 2015. "The Economic Impact on Plan Members of the Shift from DB
to DC in Workplace Pension Plans." Working Paper, 19 Canadian Lab. & Emp.
L.J. 23 (2015). http://heinonline.org/HOL/LandingPage?handle=hein.journals
/canlemj19&div=5&id=&page=.
Bateman, Hazel, and John Piggott. 1999. "Mandating Retirement Provision: The
Australian Experience." *Geneva Papers on Risk and Insurance* 24 (1): 95–113.
Berner, Frank. 2006a. "Beyond the Distinction between Public and Private: Hybrid
Welfare Production in German Old-Age Security." Regina—Arbeitspapier 22.
http://www.ssoar.info/ssoar/handle/document/42555.
———. 2006b. "Riester Pensions in Germany: Do They Substitute or Supplement
Public Pensions? Positions in the Debate on the New Public Policy on Private
Pensions." Regina—Arbeitspapier 21.
Beshears, John, James J. Choi, Christopher Clayton, Christopher Harris, David
Laibson, and Brigitte C. Madrian. 2015. "Optimal Illiquidity." Unpublished
Manuscript, Harvard University.
Beshears, John, James J. Choi, Christopher Harris, David Laibson, Brigitte C.
Madrian, and Jung Sakong. 2015. "The Demand for Savings Commitments: Is
Less Liquidity More Attractive?" Unpublished Manuscript, Harvard University.
Beshears, John, James J. Choi, David Laibson, and Brigitte C. Madrian. 2011.
"Behavioral Economics Perspectives on Public Sector Pension Plans." *Journal of
Pension Economics and Finance* 10 (2): 315–36.
Börsch-Supan, Axel H., Michela Coppola, and Anette Reil-Held. 2012. "Riester
Pensions in Germany: Design, Dynamics, Targeting Success and Crowding-In."
NBER Working Paper no. 18014, Cambridge, MA.
Börsch-Supan, Axel H., and Hendrik Juerges. 2011. "Disability, Pension Reform,
and Early Retirement in Germany." NBER Working Paper no. 17079, Cam-
bridge, MA.
Börsch-Supan, Axel H., and Christina B. Wilke. 2004. "The German Pension Sys-
tem: How It Was, How It Will Be." NBER Working Paper no. 10525, Cambridge,
MA.
Canadian Institutional Investment Network. 2013. "2013 CAP Benchmark Report:
Understanding Results to Create Desired Outcomes." https://ssl.grsaccess.com
/GRSAsset/media/24057/gwl-2013-cap-benchmark-report-en.pdf.
Carroll, Christopher D. 1992. "The Buffer-Stock Theory of Saving: Some Macroeconomic Evidence." *Brookings Papers on Economic Activity* 1992 (2): 61–156.
———. 1997. "Buffer-Stock Saving and the Life Cycle/Permanent Income Hypoth-
esis." *Quarterly Journal of Economics* 112 (1): 1–55.
Chomik, Rafal, and John Piggott. 2012. "Pensions, Ageing and Retirement in Aus-
tralia: Long-Term Projections and Policies." *Australian Economic Review* 45 (3):
350–61.
Copeland, Craig. 2014. "Individual Retirement Account Balances, Contributions,
and Rollovers, 2012; With Longitudinal Results 2010–2012: The EBRI IRA
Database." Issue Brief no. 399, Employee Benefit Research Institute Center for
Research on Retirement Income.
Department of Statistics Singapore. 2014a. "Key Household Income Trends, 2013."
Table 2. http://www.singstat.gov.sg/docs/default-source/default-document-library
/publications/publications_and_papers/household_income_and_expenditure/pp
-s20.pdf.
———. 2014b. "Report on the Household Expenditure Survey, 2012/13." Table
27B. http://www.singstat.gov.sg/docs/default-source/default-document-library

/publications/publications_and_papers/household_income_and_expenditure
/hes1213.pdf.

Federal Financial Supervisory Authority of Germany. 2014. "Occupational Pension Schemes—Frequently Asked Questions." http://www.bafin.de/EN/Con sumers/FAQs/BetrieblicheAltersversorgung/betrieblichealtersversorgung_node .html.

Financial Services Commission of Ontario. 2013. "Payment of a Small Amount under Section 50(1) of the Pension Benefits Act." Version from September 25, 2013. http://www.fsco.gov.on.ca/en/pensions/legislative/pages/smallamount.aspx.

———. 2014. "Pension Forms." Version from October 17, 2014. http://www.fsco .gov.on.ca/en/pensions/Forms/Pages/default.aspx#unlocking.

Fong, Joelle H. Y., Olivia S. Mitchell, and Benedict S. K. Koh. 2011. "Longevity Risk Management in Singapore's National Pension System." *Journal of Risk and Insurance* 78 (4): 961–81.

Frenken, Hubert. 1995. "Tax Assistance for Pensions and RRSPs." *Perspectives on Labor and Income* 7 (4): 9–13.

Fudenberg, Drew, and David K. Levine. 2006. "A Dual-Self Model of Impulse Control." *American Economic Review* 96 (5): 1449–76.

Garcia-Huitron, Manuel, and Eduard Ponds. 2015. "Worldwide Diversity in Funded Pension Plans: Four Role Models in Choice and Participation." Working Paper, Tilburg University and Network for Studies on Pensions, Aging and Retirement (NETSPAR).

German Federal Statistical Office (Destatis). 2013. "Income, Receipts and Expenditure of Households in Germany." https://www.destatis.de/EN/FactsFigures /SocietyState/IncomeConsumptionLivingConditions/IncomeReceipts Expenditure/Tables/IncomeExpenditure_D.html.

Government of Canada Office of the Chief Actuary. 2014. "Registered Pension Plan (RPP) and Retirement Savings Coverage (Canada)." Version from October 28, 2014. http://www.osfi-bsif.gc.ca/eng/oca-bac/fs-fr/Pages/fs_rpp_2014.aspx.

Greater London Authority. 2010. "Focus on London 2010: Income and Spending at Home." https://londondatastore-upload.s3.amazonaws.com/fol/FocusOn London2010-income-and-spending.pdf.

Gul, Faruk, and Wolfgang Pesendorfer. 2001. "Temptation and Self-Control." *Econometrica* 69 (6): 1403–35.

Hagen, Kornelia, and Axel Kleinlein. 2012. "Ten Years of the Riester Pension Scheme: No Reason to Celebrate." *DIW Economic Bulletin* 2 (2012): 3–13.

Internal Revenue Service. 2013a. "Earned Income Credit (EIC): For Use In Preparing 2013 Returns." Publication 596. http://www.irs.gov/pub/irs-prior/p596—2013 .pdf.

———. 2013b. "Tax Guide 2013: For Individuals." Publication 17. http://www.irs .gov/pub/irs-pdf/p17.pdf.

———. 2014. "401(k) Resource Guide—Plan Sponsors—General Distribution Rules." Version from December 17, 2014. http://www.irs.gov/Retirement-Plans /Plan-Sponsor/401(k)-Resource-Guide-Plan-Sponsors-General-Distribution -Rules.

Intuit TurboTax. 2014. "States Without an Income Tax." Version from March 20, 2014. https://ttlc.intuit.com/questions/1901267-states-without-an-income-tax.

Island Revenue Authority of Singapore. 2014. "Tax on SRS Withdrawal." Version from February 26, 2014. http://www.iras.gov.sg/irasHome/page04.aspx?id=1170.

Kissling, Sandra. 2011. "Lessons Learnt From the German Riester Pension Scheme and Their Possible Application to India." Discussion Papers on Social Protection, Deutsche Gesellschaft für Internationale Zusammenarbeit.

Kok, Marcus, Mark Whatley, Danny Quant, and David Richardson. 2013. "Employer-Sponsored Retirement Schemes in Singapore: The Need for Change." Singapore Actuarial Society. http://www.actuaries.org.sg/files/library/committee _reports/Employer-Sponsored%20Retirement%20Schemes%2027Jun2013.pdf.

Laibson, David. 1997. "Golden Eggs and Hyperbolic Discounting." *Quarterly Journal of Economics* 112 (2): 443–77.

Laibson, David, Andrea Repetto, and Jeremy Tobacman. 1998. "Self-Control and Saving for Retirement." *Brookings Papers on Economic Activity* 1998 (1): 91–196.

Liu, Lillian. 1999. "Retirement Income Security in the United Kingdom." *Social Security Bulletin* 62 (1): 23–46.

Mackenzie, George A. (Sandy). 2010. *The Decline of the Traditional Pension: A Comparative Study of Threats to Retirement Security*. New York: Cambridge University Press.

Munnell, Alicia. 2014. "401(k)/IRA Holdings in 2013: An Update from the SCF." Issue in Brief no. 14–15, Center for Retirement Research at Boston College.

Nebraska Department of Revenue. 2014. "2014 Nebraska Individual Income Tax Booklet." http://www.revenue.nebraska.gov/tax/14forms/f_1040n_booklet.pdf.

Office for Statistics Berlin-Brandenburg. 2013. "Mittleres Haushaltsnettoeinkommen 2012 in Berlin bei 1650 EUR, in Brandenburg bei 1750 EUR." Pressemitteilung 8(21): 1–3.

Service Canada. 2014. "Digest of Benefit Entitlement Principles: Chapter 5—Earnings." Version from January 21, 2014. http://www.servicecanada.gc.ca/eng/ei /digest/5_15_0.shtml.

Statistics Canada. 2014a. "Median Total Income, by Family Type, by Province and Territory (All Census Families)." CANSIM Table 111–0009. Version from July 23, 2014. http://www.statcan.gc.ca/tables-tableaux/sum-som/l01/cst01/famil108a -eng.htm.

———. 2014b. "Registered Pension Plan (RPP) Members, by Area of Employment, Sector and Type of Plan (by Province)." CANSIM Table 280–0008. Version from August 28, 2014. http://www.statcan.gc.ca/tables-tableaux/sum-som/l01/cst01 /famil119g-eng.htm.

———. 2014c. "Registered Pension Plans (RPPs) and Members, by Type of Plan and Sector (Total Public and Private Sectors)." CANSIM Table 280–0016. Version from August 28, 2014. http://www.statcan.gc.ca/tables-tableaux/sum-som /l01/cst01/famil120a-eng.htm.

The Pensions Regulator. 2014. "Detailed Guidance for Employers No. 2. Getting Ready: First Steps to Prepare for the New Employer Duties." http://www.the pensionsregulator.gov.uk/docs/detailed-guidance-2.pdf.

Towers Watson. 2014. "U.K.: New Basic State Pension to Replace Contracting Out of DB Plans." http://www.towerswatson.com/en/Insights/Newsletters /Global/global-news-briefs/2014/05/uk-new-basic-state-pension-to-replace -contracting-out-of-db-plans.

United Kingdom Office for National Statistics. 2013. "Pension Trends—Chapter 7: Private Pension Scheme Membership, 2013 Edition." http://www.ons.gov.uk/ons /dcp171766_314955.pdf.

United States Census Bureau. 2013. "American Community Survey 1-Year Estimates." American FactFinder: Table S1903. http://factfinder.census.gov/faces/nav /jsf/pages/searchresults.xhtml?ref=geo&refresh=t&tab=map&src=bkmk.

United States General Accounting Office. 2003. "Social Security Reform: Information on Using a Voluntary Approach to Individual Accounts." GAO Report no. 03–309, Washington, DC.

Van Riesen, Gretchen. 2009. "The Pension Tangle: Achieving Greater Uniformity of Pension Legislation and Regulation in Canada." C.D. Howe Institute Commentary 294.

Comment   Daniel McFadden

Defined-contribution (DC) tax-qualified savings plans became broadly available in the United States after the Revenue Act of 1978, in which Section 401(K) estabished that firms offering these plans had to make them available equitably to all employees. Justifications for DC plans such as 401(k)s and for individual retirement accounts (IRAs) were that they would increase overall savings, and encourage retirement savings to supplement Social Security and keep middle-class retirees out of poverty. A question, then and now, is whether these plans do in fact increase total savings, or just divert savings into tax-qualified channels. The same question, writ smaller, can be asked about taxable early withdrawals from DC plans. First, does making DC plans more liquid induce higher withdrawals? If so, where do these withdrawals go? To a tax-qualified rollover individual retirement account (IRA)? To non-tax-qualified investments that achieve better or more diversified returns? To essential consumption in emergencies? To discretionary consumption such as vacations, cars, and boats? Second, does increased liquidity induce higher contribution rates, offsetting increased withdrawals, or does it instead reduce incentives for after-tax precautionary savings? Overall, does making tax-qualified plans more liquid increase consumers' lifetime welfare, or just pander to present bias that is in the end harmful?

Table 2C.1 shows that tax-qualified defined contribution (DC) and IRA savings plans are major components of retirement savings of individuals in the United States. Individuals age 59.5 and older are eligible to take taxable distributions from their tax-qualified assets without penalty, but below this age are *preeligible*, subject to a 10 percent early withdrawal penalty (paid to the IRS) unless the distribution qualifies as meeting IRS plus employer-specified hardship conditions. Argento, Bryant, and Sabelhaus (2013) use IRS data to estimate early withdrawals, penalized and not penalized, in 2010, with the results shown in table 2C.2. Collecting their results, gross contributions to tax-qualified savings plans by preeligible individuals were about 6.6 percent of their tax-qualified plan balances, but taxable distributions were 2.9 percent of these balances, leading to a net contribution rate

Daniel McFadden is the Presidential Professor of Health Economics at the University of Southern California. He has joint appointments at the USC Sol Price School of Public Policy and the Department of Economics at USC Dornsife College. He is also a research associate of the National Bureau of Economic Research.

For acknowledgments, sources of research support, and disclosure of the author's material financial relationships, if any, please see http://www.nber.org/chapters/c13634.ack.

Table 2C.1   US retirement assets, trillions of dollars (year-end)

	Other plans	DC plans	IRAs	DC + IRA	Total	Tax-qualified pct. of total
1995	4.0	1.7	1.3	3.0	7.0	42.9
2000	6.1	2.9	2.6	5.5	11.6	47.4
2005	7.6	3.6	3.4	7.0	14.6	47.9
2010	8.6	4.5	5.0	9.6	18.2	52.6
2013	10.6	5.9	5.6[a]	11.5	23.0	49.8

Source: Investment Company Institute (2014). **Other plans** include private-sector DB plans; federal, state, and local pension plans; and all fixed and variable annuity reserves at life insurance companies less annuities held by IRAs, 403(b) plans, 457 plans, and private pension funds. Federal pension plans include US Treasury security holdings of the civil service retirement and disability fund, the military retirement fund, the judicial retirement funds, the Railroad Retirement Board, and the foreign service retirement and disability fund, Federal Employees Retirement System Thrift Savings Plan. The **DC plans** include 401(k), 403(b), 457, and Keogh plans, and other DC plans without 401(k) features. **IRAs** include traditional, Roth, and employer-sponsored IRAs (SEP IRAs, SAR-SEP IRAs, and SIMPLE IRAs). See also Bricker et al. (2012), SCF (2015), U.S. Treasury (2010), and VanDerhel et al. (2012).
[a]Estimates.

Table 2C.2   Distributions from retirement accounts (2010)

Distributions from DC and IRA retirement accounts (2010)	All returns		Age < 55		Age 55+	
	Millions of returns	Billions of dollars	Millions of returns	Billions of dollars	Millions of returns	Billions of dollars
DC and IRA account balances		9,600.0		3,596.6[a]		6,003.0
Gross contributions	—			$238.4[a]		—
Gross distributions	38.5	1,281.2	12.4	241.0	26.1	1,040.0
Nontaxable distributions	18.0	466.7	6.4	134.3	11.6	332.4
Direct rollovers	4.0	292.4	2.3	92.5	1.7	199.8
Indirect rollovers	0.5	37.5	0.3	10.9	0.2	26.6
Other nontaxable	10.9	110.5	1.9	20.2	9.0	90.2
Taxable distributions	32.5	804.4	8.1	104.3	24.4	700.0
Nonpenalized	29.3	746.6	5.2	57.1	24.1	689.6
Penalized	5.7	57.7	4.9	47.3	0.8	10.5
Taxable as % of balances		8.4		2.9[a]		11.7
Taxable as % of gross distributions	*84.4*	*62.8*	*65.3*	*43.3*	*93.5*	*67.3*
Penalized as % of taxable	*17.5*	*7.2*	*60.5*	*45.3*	*3.3*	*1.5*
Contributions as % of balances	—			6.6[a]		—

Source: Argento, Bryant, and Sabelhaus (2013).
[a]Approximations derived from their statistics.

of about 3.7 percent. Thus, there is considerable leakage from the DC retirement accounts of preeligible individuals. The immediate policy questions are whether the high leakage rates in the US system lower net retirement savings substantially, and if so whether this harms US consumers and the public welfare system (e.g., Medicaid) that acts as a insurer of last resort to retirees if they exhaust their resources.

In their chapter, Beshears, Choi, Hurwitz, Laibson, and Madrian (hereafter BCHLM) carefully measure effective marginal tax rates on early withdrawals from tax-qualified defined-contribution (DC) savings plans (like 401[k]s) in six developed countries. For this comparison, the authors define a *marginal rate of transformation*

$$\text{MRT} = \frac{\text{net increase in consumption from preeligible withdrawal of US\$1 from a DC plan}}{\text{net increase in consumption from eligible withdrawal of US\$1 from a DC plan}}$$

$$= \frac{1 - \left(\text{pre\_eligible marginal tax rate at current income including early withdrawal penalty}\right)}{\left[1 - \left(\text{age\_eligible marginal tax rate at permanent income}\right)\right] \cdot \left[\text{interest factor}\right]}$$

$$= \frac{1 - \left[0.1 + 0.15\right]}{1 - 0.15}$$

in the United States for nonhardship preeligible withdrawal, \$US60K permanent income. BCHLM calculate these MRTs for a nonhardship withdrawal from a tax-qualified plan by a consumer with a permanent income of US\$60K and an interest factor of 1; table 2C.3 gives their results, along with parallel results for an individual with a permanent income of US\$30K. They conclude that tax-qualified savings are far more liquid in the United States than in comparable developed countries.

To motivate the BCHLM focus on their MRT and clarify its definition and application, consider the transactions through available channels that an individual can use to move resources between a preeligible age *t* and an age, say sixty, when this person is eligible for withdrawals without penalty from tax-qualified accounts. These transactions can include additions to or withdrawals from tax-qualified and ordinary savings plans, adjustments to direct investments in health and human capital (through education and health maintenance), and in physical capital (through housing maintenance, business investment and reinvestment, and real estate). In addition to shifting consumption between ages *t* and sixty, transactions may be combined to improve the rate of return between these ages, for example, by diverting funds from ordinary savings into education that increases future income. Legal, contractual, and tax rules constrain the transactions, determining

Table 2C.3   **MRT for nonhardship withdrawals**

Country	MRT at US\$60K	MRT at US\$30K
Australia	0	0
Canada	0	1.11
Germany	0	0
Singapore	0	0
United Kingdom	0	0
United States	0.88	0.88

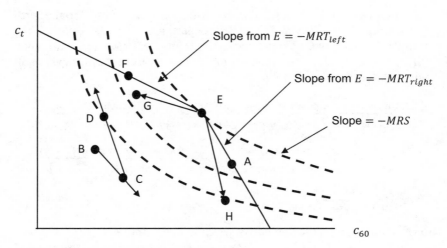

Fig. 2C.1   Intertemporal transactions

their liquidity. Each possible transaction can be characterized by its after-tax rate of transformation (MRT) between resources available at t and at age sixty. From the status quo at age t, there will be a minimum MRT_{right} among the available transactions that shift consumption forward to age sixty, and a maximum MRT_{left} among those that shift consumption backward to age t. The familiar Fisher diagram in figure 2C.1 shows possible points A to H where the consumer may be located. From status quo point E, the transactions feasible ex post define a frontier (and associated MRT) extending through points F and A. There are additional points and transactions that are not efficient, such as the transactions from E to G or to H. Another is point B that is dominated by the point D reached by the feasible transaction from B to C followed by the feasible transaction from C to D. The figure also shows the consumer's indifference curves between consumption at ages t and sixty, with slopes characterized by marginal rates of substitution $MRS \equiv m_t / m_{60} \cdot \rho_{t,60}$, where m_t and m_{60} denote the marginal utilities of consumption at these respective ages, and $\rho_{t,60}$ denotes the rate of impatience between these ages (including or excluding the influence of present bias).

Placed at the point E, the consumer will stay due to the stability condition $MRT_{left} \leq MRS \leq MRT_{right}$. Conversely, placed at the point A, the consumer has MRT > MRS if a move toward E is feasible, and will choose this transaction. The BCHLM MRT for withdrawals from tax-qualified savings is operative when the consumer is at a point like A, prefers to move consumption toward age t, and there is no other available transaction in this direction that has a larger MRT. The figure illustrates that it is important to consider the full set of transactions available to the consumer, ex ante at the times life-planning decisions are made and ex post after realization of life events, and it is important to distinguish between transactions that move the consumer along the ex post intertemporal frontier from transactions inside the frontier that increase or reduce efficiency. Liquidity determines the availability of ex post transactions, and is a consideration in ex ante planning where there are trade-offs between liquidity and expected return, not only for savings channels, but also for direct investments such as education, businesses, and real estate.

Risk is important in assessing the benefits and costs of liquidity; otherwise, transactions costs are the only barrier to holding assets in illiquid form (see Cannon and Tonks 2013). The marginal utility of future consumption is uncertain because of uncertain survival and future needs, and the marginal utility of current consumption is influenced by factors imperfectly observed by an employer or policymaker such as meeting emergency needs of children or parents, or moving expenses associated with job changes for family members. On the outcomes side, future wage and salary income, payouts from defined-benefit plans such as Social Security, and rates of return on tax-qualified and ordinary savings and on direct investments, are all uncertain. Then the individual faces a portfolio problem of allocating assets across savings and direct investment channels as well as the intertemporal allocation problem of setting savings targets to balance consumption at ages t and sixty. The focus on expected returns in the BCHLM definition of MRT obscures the role of risk and its impact on retirement savings portfolio management. Some risk effects could be modeled within their framework by assuming temporally separable CARA utility functions and risks that have a multivariate normal distribution across transaction channels. This leads to expected utilities of certainty-equivalent expected returns that depend on the degree of risk aversion, overall market risk, and "market βs," and permit a CAPM analysis of the consumer's portfolio decisions. However, liquidity constraints, bankruptcy risk, and providers of last resort make the consumer's problem more complex than the usual CAPM setup.

The MRT defined by BCHLM is for nonhardship withdrawals where preeligible withdrawal penalties apply. In the United States, hardship withdrawals are also important. Table 2C.2 shows that in 2010, hardship withdrawals were 54.7 percent of all preeligible taxable withdrawals. Hardship withdrawals are allowed to varying degrees in every country; table 2C.4 gives an overview of the authors' findings. Analysis of the effects of hardship exemptions, particularly with varying categories across countries, would seem to require modeling (stochastic) needs and consumption in each category, with category-specific MRTs rather than a blended MRT for the average mix of penalized and hardship preeligible withdrawals. It may help that some hardship categories, such as education, new home purchase, and house emergency repairs, are investments rather than current consumption, so the impact of a withdrawal is confined to an assessment of the expected

Table 2C.4   **Categories of allowed preeligible hardship withdrawals**

	Australia	Canada	Germany	Singapore	United Kingdom	United States
Health	Y	Y	Y	Y	Y	—
Permanent and total disability	—	—	—	—	—	Y
Medical expenses > 10% of AGI	—	—	—	—	—	Y
Terminal illness	Y	Y	Y	Y	Y	Y
Higher education	N	—	—	Y	N	Y
Housing investment	N	N	—	Y	N	Y
Unemployment	Y	N	N	N	N	N
Health insurance premiums	—	—	—	—	—	Y
Income loss	N	Y	N	N	N	N
IRS tax levy	—	—	—	—	—	Y
Annuity	—	—	—	—	—	Y
Natural disaster	—	—	—	—	—	Y
Domestic dissolution	—	—	—	—	—	Y

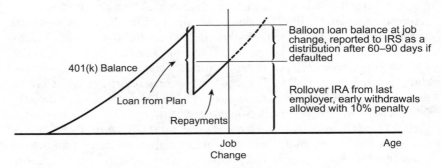

Fig. 2C.2   Withdrawal paths from DC plans

returns, the risks of these investments relative to DC-plan assets, and the benefits of diversification. A daunting but potentially very useful research effort would be to disaggregate consumption along the lines of the hardship categories allowed in the various countries, and draw conclusions on the effective liquidity and consumer welfare benefits offered by DC plans with different hardship categories.

A peculiarity of tax-qualified savings plans in the United States is that taxable withdrawals from 401(k)s are substantially restricted by IRS and employer policies, but at the time of a job change, individuals can elect to roll over their 401(k) balances into IRAs that are essentially unrestricted. Figure 2C.2 shows the 401(k) balances of a typical individual over time, and can be used to identify points in lifetime savings plans where policy interventions are likely to be effective. The pictured individual has an accumulating balance in a 401(k) plan, and at a point in time takes a loan from his plan. This is allowed by many employers, subject to IRS rules. Lu et al. (2015) study borrowing from DC plans using data on a sample of more than 900,000 participants in 882 plans over the period 2004–2009. They state that loans from 401(k)s can vary from a lower limit (often US$1K) up to the minimum of half the 401(k) balance and US$50K. Some employers allow only one loan at a time; others allow multiple loans up to these limits. Loan repayment periods are set by tax rules, typically five years, with interest rates set by the employer, and are collected by deductions from the employee's after-tax salary. Lu et al. find that over a five-year period, about 40 percent of DC-plan holders have taken a loan at some point from their DC assets, and in any given month, about 20 percent have a loan outstanding. Thus, gross loan rates and balances are fairly high. However, individuals do not have an opportunity to default on loan repayments and trigger a taxable distribution as long as they remain on their job.[1] Consequently, *net* withdrawal rates will be near zero as long as loans cannot default. (There are second-order effects on expected retirement balances if interest rates on 401[k] loans are different than the rate of return on the assets remaining in the 401[k] account, or if 401[k] loan repayments reduce other after-tax saving.)

However, the event of a job termination (quit or separation, transiting to unemployment or to a new job) triggers several critical consequences. First, any outstanding loan balance is converted to a balloon balance that is immediately due. Any part of this balance not repaid in sixty days is reported to the IRS as a taxable distribution, subject to the US early withdrawal penalty. (Of course, if the individual has a balloon loan balance upon retirement, and at that point they are age eligible, then this is an eligible distribution, that is not penalized but is nevertheless a net reduction in tax-qualified assets available from that point in time on.) Second, upon a job change, an individual can elect to roll over their 401(k) plan balances into an IRA, or may be forced out of their 401(k) if their plan balance is below an employer-set threshold. After establishing a rollover IRA, they can take taxable distributions from this plan at will, subject to the 10 percent early withdrawal penalty if they are preeligible and do not meet IRS rules for a hardship withdrawal.

How important are these preeligibility leakages from DC savings? Because they are largely triggered by job changes, a first question is how often individuals change jobs and have needs and opportunities associated with these changes. Table 2C.5 gives the distribution of job durations in the most recent job, up to 2008, in the cohort of workers ages eighteen to forty-four in 1978. For most individuals, turnovers are frequent and job durations are short, giving ample opportunities to withdraw DC assets.

Thus, only about 26 percent of workers remain in one job long enough to substantially restrict their opportunities for early withdrawals from DC

---

1. There are "deemed distributions" from loan defaults associated with temporary layoffs, long-term disability, maternity leave, or other leaves of absence that are not connected to a job termination. LMUK estimate that 8 percent of total 401(k) loan defaults are of this type.

Table 2C.5   **Distribution of job durations**

Years in job	<1	1–2	3–4	5–9	10–19	20+
Percent in 2008	22.9	13.0	16.9	20.2	16.8	10.3

Source: www.bls.gov/news.release/pdf/nlsoy.pdf.

plans. For the same NLSY cohorts, table 2C.6 gives the distribution of numbers of jobs held between 1978 and 2008, broken down by educational attainment and gender. There is substantial "mover-stayer" heterogeneity, but the overall number of job changes is high in all the socioeconomic groups. The table also indicates that the share of available weeks employed is always less than 90 percent. This reflects both unemployment and time out of the labor force, but is an indication that financial shocks due to not working are an important feature of lifetime income profiles. Since such shocks are strongly correlated with job terminations, there will be for many individuals a "perfect storm" in which balloon balances on 401(k) loans and the withdrawal opportunities from rollover IRA accounts coincide with negative income shocks that trigger income replacement needs.

Argento, Bryant, and Sabelhaus (2013) found US$104.3 billion in preeligible taxable withdrawals in 2010, of which about US$6 billion is estimated by LMUY to arise from unrepaid 401(k) balloon loan balances incurred at the time of a job change.

The disposition of preeligible gross withdrawals from tax-qualified savings plans is pictured in figure 2C.3. These can be rolled over directly or indirectly to IRA or similar tax-qualified accounts, or can be taken as taxable nonhardship withdrawals with penalty and directed to discretionary consumption or after-tax investments such as business and real estate, or when they qualify can be taken as hardship withdrawals that either go to qualifying consumption categories such as mortgage assistance when unemployed or into investment categories such as education or home repair/remodeling.

Clearly, if net withdrawals go to current consumption, overall retirement savings fall. Discretionary consumption may be influenced by present bias, but essential consumption may be desirable for the consumer even if there is no present bias. The impact of investments in health capital, education, or housing, all of which will qualify as hardship withdrawals under some circumstances, or investment in real estate, a business, or in permanent reduction in after-tax debt (e.g., credit card debt), have more complex consequences, depending on the comparative expected return on investment (ROI) inside and outside the tax-qualified account, and the relative risks of investments inside and outside DC plans.

The distribution of IRA withdrawals from nonretirees in 2013 is given in table 2C.7, with categories that correspond roughly to figure 2C.3. About

Table 2C.6   Number of jobs over thirty years

	0 or 1 job (%)	2 to 4 jobs (%)	5 to 7 jobs (%)	8 to 10 jobs (%)	11 to 14 jobs (%)	15 or more jobs (%)	Number of jobs held (%)	Percent of weeks employed
Men								
Less than HS graduate	0.8	10.0	18.4	20.7	21.8	28.4	11.6	84.0
High school graduate	0.7	7.4	11.6	16.0	26.1	38.2	13.3	70.7
Some college	1.0	12.6	21.0	20.4	18.4	26.6	11	83.4
Bachelor's degree up	0.6	10.4	20.6	17.3	18.1	33.1	12	86.3
Women	0.6	7.2	16.8	25.8	27.1	22.6	11.2	87.9
Less than HS graduate	1.4	10.2	20.2	21.0	23.2	24.1	11	71.2
High school graduate	5.8	13.5	19.6	18.2	23.1	19.7	9.9	45.8
Some college	1.0	13.8	25.5	20.1	19.8	19.8	10.1	68.8
Bachelor's degree up	0.6	9.3	18.3	20.7	26.5	24.6	11.4	73.5
	0.8	5.2	15.4	23.4	24.7	30.5	12.2	79.7

Source: www.bls.gov/news.release/pdf/nlsoy.pdf.

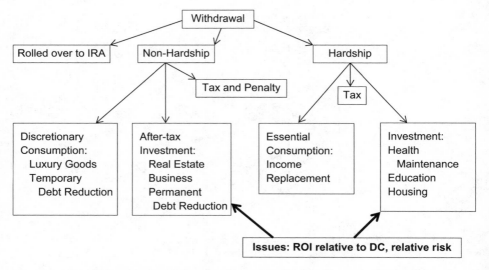

Fig. 2C.3   Disposition of preeligible gross withdrawals from tax-qualified plans

Table 2C.7   IRA withdrawals of nonretirees

Use of IRA withdrawal	Percent
Living expenses	**19**
Car, boat, other big ticket item (except housing)	**12**
Emergency	17
Home purchase, remodel, repair	19
Health	9
Education	7
Rolled over to another retirement account	24
Not specified/other	**8**

Sources: Investment Company Institute (2014, table 7.23) and Vanguard (2014).

31 percent of gross distributions go to discretionary consumption; the remainder may be justified as meeting essential short-term needs or as financing productive alternative investments.

In conclusion, we can look forward to answers in the future from BCHLM, informed by international comparisons, and perhaps data on comprehensive household accounts and dynamic portfolio rebalancing, savings, and dissaving, on whether liquidity in DC plans induces more contributions, what happens to withdrawals from DC plans, and to what extent a benevolently paternalistic planner would conclude that liberal withdrawal policies promote lifetime welfare rather than just undoing the protection against present bias that these plans were in part designed to suppress.

References

Argento, R., V. Bryant, and J. Sabelhaus. 2013. "Early Withdrawals from Retirement Accounts during the Great Recession." FEDS Working Paper no. 2013-22, Washington, DC, Federal Reserve Board. http://www.federalreserve.gov/pubs/feds/2013/201322/201322abs.html.

Bricker, J., A. Kennickell, K. Moore, and J. Sabelhaus. 2012. "Changes in U.S. Family Finances from 2007 to 2010: Evidence from the Survey of Consumer Finances." *Federal Reserve Bulletin* 98.

Cannon, Edmund, and Ian Tonks. 2013. "The Value and Risk of Defined Contribution Pension Schemes: International Evidence." *Journal of Risk and Insurance* 80: 95–119.

Investment Company Institute. 2014. *Factbook*. Investment Company Institute.

Lu, T., O. Mitchell, S. Utkus, and J. Young. 2015. "Borrowing from the Future: 401(K) Plan Loans and Loan Defaults." NBER Working Paper no. 21102. Cambridge, MA: National Bureau of Economic Research.

Survey of Consumer Finances. 2015. *Chartbook*. http://www.federalreserve.gov/econresdata/scf/scfindex.htm.

U.S. Treasury. 2010. *Statistical Trends in Retirement Plans*. Inspector General for Tax Administration.

VanDerhel, J., S. Holden, L. Aloriso, and S. Bass. 2012. *401(K) Plan Asset Allocation, Account Balances, and Loan Activity in 2011*. Employee Benefit Research Institute.

Vanguard. 2014. *How America Saves*.

3

House Price Volatility and the Housing Ladder

James Banks, Richard Blundell, Zoë Oldfield,
and James P. Smith

One of the most critical consumption and investment decisions that individuals and families make over their life cycle involves the amount of housing services to consume and whether or not to combine consumption with ownership. Housing is an important component of consumption, but not simply because it absorbs a large fraction of the household budget—which it does. Where we live and how much we decide to spend on housing is a key ingredient to the amenities and lifestyle we have chosen for our families and ourselves. But housing, or more particularly housing wealth, can be even more critical as an investment as it is typically by far the biggest marketable asset in the household portfolio for most people.

The contribution of this chapter is to bring together two key elements of housing consumption and home ownership decisions into an empirical model of housing outcomes. The first of these is the housing ladder. Rather

James Banks is professor of economics at the University of Manchester and deputy research director of the Institute for Fiscal Studies (IFS). Richard Blundell holds the David Ricardo Chair of Political Economy at University College London and is the research director of the Institute for Fiscal Studies (IFS), where he is also director of the ESRC Centre for the Microeconomic Analysis of Public Policy. Zoë Oldfield is the data manager at the Institute for Fiscal Studies. James P. Smith holds the Distinguished Chair in Labor Markets and Demographic Studies at the RAND Corporation.

The authors gratefully acknowledge the financial support of the Economic and Social Research Council through the research grant RES-000-22-0513. Blundell would like to thank the ESRC Centre for the Microeconomic Analysis of Public Policy at IFS. James Smith's research was supported by grants from the National Institute on Aging (R37AG025529) and benefited from the expert programming assistance of David Rumpel and Iva Maclennan. This chapter was presented at the biannual NBER Conference on the Economics of Aging at Carefree, Arizona, in May 2015. We would like to thank our discussant Steven Venti and participants in the meeting for very helpful comments. The usual disclaimer applies. For acknowledgments, sources of research support, and disclosure of the authors' material financial relationships, if any, please see http://www.nber.org/chapters/c13647.ack.

than modeling home ownership as a one-time durable purchase, we model it as a series of purchase decisions, or a housing ladder, where the desired flow of housing services rises with family formation and growing family size over the life cycle. The second is the acknowledgement of the role of future house price risk. In some geographic markets housing can be a risky asset with high levels of unpredictable price volatility, while in other places the prospect of capital gains or losses in housing are understandably not the subject of much social conversation.

Our contribution is to focus on the importance of ownership as a hedge against future house price risk as individuals move up the ladder. We use a stylized model to show that increasing house price risk acts as an incentive to become a homeowner earlier in the life cycle and, once an owner, to move more rapidly up the housing ladder. Increases in volatility are shown to increase ownership and to increase the quantity of housing wealth conditional on ownership in earlier periods of the life cycle. We then establish that these relationships hold empirically using panel data on families in different geographic markets in Britain and in the United States.

Housing needs change over the life cycle and the decision of when to buy the first property and at what point to move up the ladder is a key life-cycle decision. For example, Ortalo-Magne and Rady (2004, 2006) note the importance of new entrants at the bottom of the ladder for the determination of housing transactions along the whole ladder. Ermisch and Pevalin (2004) document the importance of childbearing and family formation decisions on housing choices. We follow this lead by allowing the demand for housing consumption and movements up the ladder to depend directly on the demographic profile of the family. We then add to this the enhanced incentive to own and to move up the ladder created by more volatile house prices.

The idea that home ownership can be seen as a hedge against uncertainty in the price of housing services has many precedents. For example, Sinai and Souleles (2005) use this observation to carefully show the increased demand for ownership when rental price uncertainty is higher. Our contribution instead is to focus on the importance of ownership and the quantity of housing owned as a hedge against future house price risk as individuals move up the ladder. We examine the impact of volatility on both ownership and on measures of the quantity of housing wealth conditional on ownership. Both are shown to rise with increased house price volatility.

In contrast to other risky assets in which risk-averse individuals can simply choose to avoid them, everyone must consume housing, and the vast majority of people desire to and eventually do end up owning their own home. In addition, for most individuals the demand for housing will rise over the life cycle as family size increases. The combination of these factors results in an insurance role for housing wealth in early adult life that drives the predictions we investigate in our empirical analysis.

Using panel data from the United Kingdom and the United States, we test the implications of the ladder and price volatility on the decision on when to become a homeowner, how much housing to consume, and whether to refinance out of housing equity. In the presence of volatility in house prices, housing has three roles—investment, consumption, and insurance—against price fluctuations for future movements up the housing ladder. A simple theoretical discussion illustrates these effects, and the predictions for home ownership and housing wealth accumulation are drawn out.

Because housing price volatility is spatially variable, we test the importance of the role of volatility in housing decisions empirically using comparable panel data from the United States and the United Kingdom. There are significant differences in housing price variability between and within these two countries. But in addition there are also differences in the tax treatment of mortgage debt, the nature of mortgage arrangements, and even the level of geographic mobility of younger households. Consequently a test relying on between-country differences is unlikely to isolate the effects of interest. In our analysis we show that while the international differences are indeed in accordance with the predictions of our model, the model also performs well when estimated from within-country variation in each of the countries we consider, despite their rather wide institutional differences.

The analysis in this chapter is in five sections. Section 3.1 documents a critical and salient fact—a steep housing ladder with age that is coincident with changing demographics over the life cycle that are common across the two countries. Section 3.2 shows the large spatial dispersion in house price volatility within and between the United Kingdom and the United States. Section 3.3 then discusses the implications of housing price variability for housing choices in a simple life-cycle framework. In section 3.4 the model predictions concerning the age of initial home ownership, the decision to refinance, the shape of housing wealth and the number of rooms, and the decision in the United Kingdom to obtain an endowment mortgage are put to the test. In the final section we summarize our conclusions.

3.1   The Housing Ladder

Even without credit constraints or income uncertainty, individuals would not choose to consume the same flow of housing services at all times in their lives. People may start by moving out of the parental home into a small rented or purchased apartment or flat of their own. When they marry they may know that two may well live more cheaply than one, but they generally do not want to live in smaller places and often may want to own a bigger but still modest first home. Children then appear on the scene and eventually will age into rooms of their own—all of which requires a bigger, if not better, home.

A simple way of illustrating this point is to examine how the size of homes

Table 3.1   Number of rooms by age of head of household

	Age of head of household						
	< 25 years	25–34	35–44	45–54	55–64	65+	All
United States							
Owners and renters	3.89	4.97	5.99	6.40	6.16	5.34	5.61
Owners only	5.22	6.16	6.82	6.89	6.56	5.99	6.48
United Kingdom							
Owners and renters	3.04	3.69	4.45	4.98	4.89	4.07	4.40
Owners only	4.36	3.92	4.69	5.24	5.17	4.54	4.78

Note: Pooled data from the PSID and BHPS. The US data excludes bathrooms, and the UK data excludes kitchens and bathrooms.

people live in changes with age. Table 3.1 shows the age profile of mean number of rooms of household heads for owners and renters alike in the United States and the United Kingdom using the Panel Study of Income Dynamics (PSID) in the United States and the British Household Panel Study (BHPS).[1] Note that the number of rooms in the British data excludes kitchens and bathrooms, while in the American data they exclude only bathrooms, and so the number of rooms is not strictly comparable across the two countries.

In both countries there is a strong increase in size of house as the head of household grows older, flattening out around the age of fifty, but rising steeply from the twenties to the forties. The general shape of the ladder is similar in the two countries.[2] It is important to note that the steep part of the ladder is not simply the consequence of changing tenure status from renter to owner, although that transition certainly plays an important role. While owned homes are always larger than rented ones on average, the steep early ladder characterizes both rented and owned properties.[3]

Another way of seeing this transition is to examine the increase in home size at the time of purchase among new and repeat buyers as shown in table 3.2. New buyers are defined as those who were previously renters in the prior wave of PSID or BHPS so that, especially at young ages, this often will be their first owned home. Repeat buyers were previously also homeowners so

1. A detailed data description is provided in appendix A.
2. In the United Kingdom there is little evidence of cohort effects during the early part of the adult life cycle for the period 1968–1998 (Banks, Blundell, and Smith 2003). This suggests the rise would be the same whether we look at individual date-of-birth cohorts or pool across cohorts as in the tables here. In the United States there is some evidence of the number of rooms plateauing out at higher values among more recent cohorts.
3. The profiles in table 3.1 show some evidence of "downsizing" at older ages as children move out and the parents transit into retirement. While this downsizing may be important, especially for retired American households (see Venti and Wise 2001; Banks et al. 2012), it is not the focus of this chapter, which concentrates instead on the implications of the steps up the ladder earlier in life. A full analysis would need to take into account the possible effects of cohort differences among those at older ages on these profiles.

Table 3.2   Changes in rooms for movers, by type of buyer

	Age of head of benefit unit						
	< 25	25–34	35–44	45–54	55–64	65+	All
	United States						
First-time buyers—before	3.86	4.66	4.95	4.87	4.99	4.01	4.70
First-time buyers—after	5.51	6.61	6.24	5.91	5.72	4.63	5.98
First time—difference	1.62	1.45	1.28	1.05	0.71	0.61	1.27
Repeat buyers—before	4.84	5.91	6.56	6.87	6.56	5.92	6.32
Repeat buyers—after	5.49	6.72	7.27	6.94	5.99	5.48	6.66
Repeat—difference	0.65	0.81	0.71	0.07	−0.57	−0.43	0.30
	United Kingdom						
First-time buyers—before	—	3.31	3.83	4.25	4.13	3.98	3.79
First-time buyers—after	—	3.83	4.43	4.95	4.49	3.97	4.29
First time—difference	—	0.52	0.60	0.70	0.36	−0.01	0.50
Repeat buyers—before	—	3.63	4.38	4.98	5.23	4.98	4.59
Repeat buyers—after	—	4.54	5.26	5.45	4.99	4.05	4.99
Repeat—difference	—	0.91	0.88	0.47	−0.24	−0.93	0.40

Note: Pooled PSID and BHPS data from 1990 to 1999 and 1991 to 2003, respectively. First-time buyers restricted to those previously living in rented accommodation. Cell sizes too small in the United Kingdom for age < 25.

that this change now reflects changes in the size of owner-occupied housing. In the United States, while the transition from renter to owner involves a larger increment in house size, people are also clearly trading up in the early part of the life cycle when they purchase their second and subsequent homes. This effect is even stronger in the United Kingdom—on average, first-time buyers purchase houses that are bigger comparable to their rented house, but bigger movements up the ladder, defined in terms of increments to number of rooms, tend to take place for repeat buyers.

We view the shape of the ladder as demographically determined as individuals marry, form families with children growing, and eventually complete their family building with the by now older children leaving home to go off on their own. Figures 3.1A and 3.1B plot the cumulative distribution of individuals who have completed their fertility by age.[4] The steepness of this cumulative distribution mimics closely the overall shape of the housing ladder—a steep incline during the twenties and thirties with a flattening out during the forties. In fact, between ages twenty-five and the late thirties, this cumulative distribution of completed fertility is almost linear, with each year of age increasing the fraction that has finished childbearing by 5 percentage

4. Completed family size is computed by taking individuals age fifty or older and assuming they will not have any more children. We then look back through their fertility history and find the age at which their final child was born, and call this age the age of completed family size.

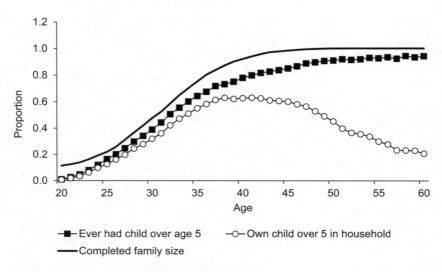

Fig. 3.1A   The demographic ladder, United States

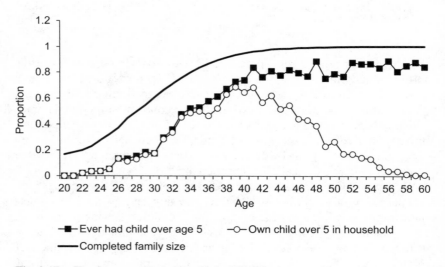

Fig. 3.1B   The demographic ladder, United Kingdom

points. For example, around age thirty-one, half of all American individuals have completed their fertility with three out of every four doing so by age thirty-six. The shape and level of the profile corresponds extremely closely to that observed in the United Kingdom over the same ages.

Children turning five years old may be at a critical stage for housing decisions since parents may choose places to live with the quality of schools in mind and may want to stay longer in the same place. This could be another indicator of reaching the top of the housing ladder and arrival in the "family home." With this in mind, figures 3.1A and 3.1B also plot the cumulative fraction of individuals who ever had a child at least five years old. Not surprisingly, compared to the cumulative completed fertility, this figure is shifted out to the right so that, if age five is taken as the marker, reaching the top of the ladder takes place for the median family in the mid- to late thirties. Nevertheless, as with the completed family-size profile, the proportion rises steeply over the life cycle up to age forty in parallel to the sharp rise in the number of rooms demonstrated over the same ages. Finally, figures 3.1A and 3.1B also plot the proportion with their own children ages five or over currently in the household, as a measure of contemporaneous housing needs. Again the similarities between the United States and the United Kingdom are striking—in both countries after age forty there is a sharp decline in young children at home, an indication of an eventual demographic rationale for downsizing in later life.

3.2   House Price Volatility

Figure 3.2 shows real indices of country-wide average house prices for the United States and United Kingdom over the period 1974 to 1998 with both series normalized to take a value of 1 in 1980. Immediately apparent is the much larger volatility of housing prices in the United Kingdom, with real prices rising by 50 percent over the period 1980 to 1989 and then falling back to their previous value by 1992. Over the period as a whole, however, real returns were similar across the two countries.

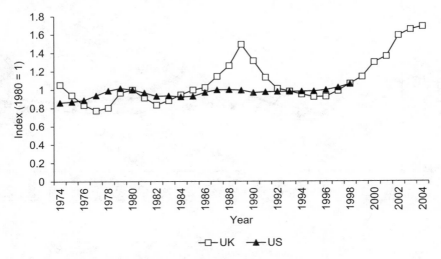

Fig. 3.2   Comparison of UK and US house prices

Although such difference will be instructive when looking at differences in housing choices across the two countries, the majority of our testing will rely instead on within-country differences in house price volatility over time in each of the two countries. The United Kingdom and the United States indexes both hide considerable differences across regions with some places and times being much more volatile in housing prices than others. In figures 3.3A and 3.3B, we present house prices from regional subindices, grouped to show house price trends in the more and less volatile areas.

The variation across American states in housing price volatility is large. Using the standard deviation in real prices (relative to a 1980 base) as the index, Massachusetts ranks at the top with price swings between peak and trough over this period of more than 2 to 1. At the other extreme lies South Carolina, where the peak price exceeds the trough by only 15 percent. The most volatile states are concentrated in New England and along the Northeastern seaboard (Massachusetts, New York, New Jersey, Rhode Island, Connecticut, New Hampshire, and Maine) and in California and Hawaii. While we will use a continuous measure of volatility in our analyses below, for descriptive purposes now we label these the volatile states.

To exploit regional and time-series differences in volatility in house prices, we construct indices of volatility by computing the standard deviation of the change in the log real house price index over the previous five years for each of the fifty US states and twelve UK regions for which we have house price indices. These indices, which measure percent volatility over the sample, are plotted in figures 3.4A and 3.4B, grouped by the same two "volatile" and

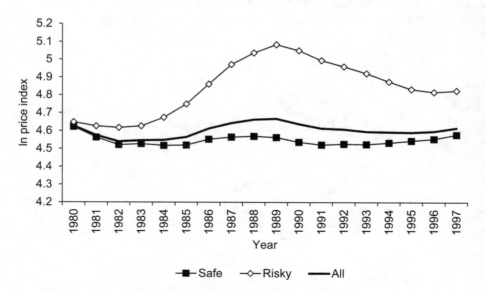

Fig. 3.3A   US mean house price index by area, 1980–1997

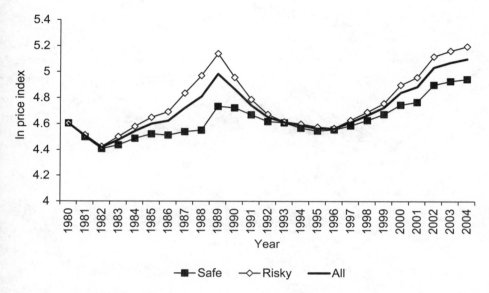

Fig. 3.3B   UK mean house price index by area, 1980–2000

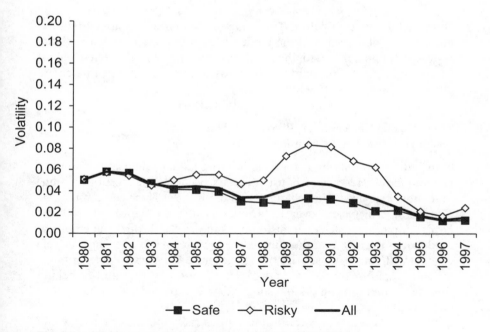

Fig. 3.4A   Regional volatility indices by area (US, 1980–1997)

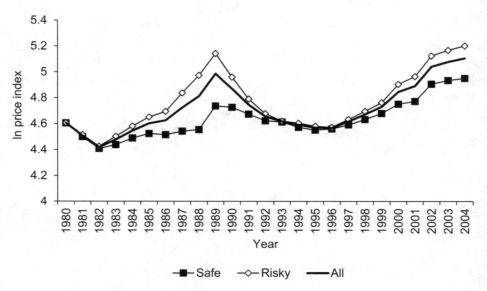

Fig. 3.4B   Regional volatility indices by area (UK, 1980–2000)

"nonvolatile" areas as before. Two things are important to note. First, the higher levels of volatility in the United Kingdom (even in the nonvolatile regions) are apparent. Second, in both countries it will be the state/regional level volatility index, not an average across groups of regions, that enters our empirical specifications.

3.3   Housing Choices in the Presence of House Price Risk and the Housing Ladder

In order to think about how the housing ladder might affect housing demand in the presence of house price risk, we use the concept of a minimum housing "need" that changes with family size. This need can then be thought of as increasing over the life cycle as individuals form into couples, have children, and reach their maximum family size. Central to our empirical modeling is the idea that these increasing housing needs over the life cycle interact with future house price risks to generate an insurance role for housing consumption early in life.[5] In this section, we discuss the intuition behind this idea before moving on to testing the predictions of such a framework empirically.

In a standard model without house price risk, housing demand would

5. In a related framework, Ortalo-Magne and Rady (2006) have looked at the theoretical predictions of an equilibrium model of home ownership when house prices are volatile.

increase with wealth but would also adjust to reflect the minimum necessary level of consumption. In such a framework one could write housing demands in each period as a function of adjusted lifetime wealth (i.e., the present discounted value of lifetime wealth *net* of the discounted sum of minimum necessary levels of housing over the lifetime[6]), the real user cost of housing services, and the minimum level of housing needs in that period. Any future change in household demographic composition would simply act through its effect on adjusted wealth. While the consumption of housing services may involve the purchase of a house and an asset accumulation decision, the assumption of perfect credit markets and certainty would yield this aspect of housing consumption unimportant in such a setting. We need to generalize this model in order to incorporate house price risk and consider the additional role of housing as a durable asset.

For ease of exposition we will assume the life-cycle profile can be represented by the following sequence of three discrete life stages: at (Demographic) stage $D = 1$ the individual is living with his or her parents, at stage $D = 2$ he or she partners to form an independent family unit, and at stage $D = 3$ the couple has had children and completed its family size. This is a simplified demographic profile but effectively represents the upside of the housing "ladder" that we wish to capture in our model.[7] For further simplicity we will assume that the leaving home decision $D = 1 \rightarrow D = 2$ simply concerns a decision over whether to rent or own in light of the possible increase in family size associated with the arrival of children between $D = 2$ and $D = 3$.

Without price uncertainty the rent/own decision will be driven by transaction costs of ownership as well as the desire for mobility, the potential tax advantage of a mortgage, and any down payment rules or constraints on the multiples of income that may be borrowed. For a household that expects to remain in their house for a reasonable length of time, for example, at $D = 3$ (the top stage of the demographic ladder), owning is the most efficient way of achieving a desired level (and type) of housing service—with idiosyncratic tastes a renter can never commit to stay long enough to make it in the landlord's interest to invest in the renter's idiosyncratic tastes. Hence we will assume for simplicity that all households will be owner-occupiers at $D = 3$ and that this is known to them at $D = 2$.[8]

Before turning to the introduction of house price risk, there are two

6. This wealth variable contains the current value of assets and the future stream of discounted income flows. Housing equity and other assets will be added in our discussion of uncertainty below.

7. We ignore here older stages of the life cycle where the possibility of downsizing comes into play (e.g., see Venti and Wise 2001; Banks et al. 2012).

8. To the extent that this probability is less than 1 then any insurance motive will be dampened, but as long as the positive probability of home ownership at $D = 3$ is not zero, the insurance motive will still exist. Since our empirical tests are simply for the presence of an insurance effect of house price risk on housing choices at $D = 2$, all they formally require is that this probability is not zero.

aspects of the supply of housing services that are relevant to our discussion. First, a more inelastic supply will induce a larger sensitivity of house prices to changes in demand and, in particular, to fluctuations in incomes of young first-time buyers. The second aspect relates to the rental market—imperfections and/or regulation of the private rental market may make it difficult for the young to use rental housing as the step between leaving the parental home and acquiring a house.

The introduction of house price uncertainty into the model adds an important distinction between ownership and renting that will enhance the desire to accumulate housing wealth and thus the need to become an owner earlier in the life cycle—house price risk generates an incentive to accumulate housing equity at $D = 2$ before the family is complete. At first sight this may seem a puzzle since accumulation of a risky asset might normally be expected to decrease with the level of price volatility for a household with risk-averse preferences. That usual result does not hold because of the vital insurance role played by housing in early life in our framework. We argue this intuitively below, but to back up this intuition in appendix B we simulate the predictions of a simple three-period model with constant relative risk-aversion preferences that allows us to demonstrate more formally the effects on housing consumption profiles of changing volatility, the changing steepness of the housing ladder, and changing degrees of risk aversion.

At $D = 2$ there are two choices: how much housing to consume, and whether to own or to rent. If house prices are variable and uncertain then, given the expected increase demand as the household moves up the demographic ladder from $D = 2$ to $D = 3$, housing equity will be an important source of insurance against future house price risk. Indeed, in the absence of a financial instrument that could insure this house price risk (which may well be defined at a very local level), holding housing early in life may be the only insurance mechanism. The larger the uncertainty in house prices and the steeper the increase in minimum housing needs over the life cycle, the more important is the insurance aspect of housing equity.

Thus the key mechanism for these effects is the insurance role of housing in period 2. If prices turn out to fall or stay the same then ownership will not, ex post, dominate renting. Indeed, if house prices fall there will be some loss to ownership. However, because of the strongly declining marginal utility of consumption associated with housing consumption in period 3 approaching the minimum necessary requirement, insuring the risk of house price rises is more important than avoiding the risk of a house price fall. To achieve this, the consumer needs to hold an asset whose return is correlated with (local) housing prices. If such an asset is not available on the financial market, the insurance can only be achieved by purchasing the asset itself. Consequently, other things equal, the higher the level of house price uncertainty the higher the incentive to become an owner-occupier. In this context increasing minimum housing requirements or increases in risk aversion are acting in a similar way to an increase in volatility. By a straightforward exten-sion of these arguments, individuals will also stay away from endowment mortgages and refinancing of housing equity for nonhousing consumption or investment purposes.[9]

In summary, the decision to accumulate housing equity early in the life cycle will be an increasing function of house price volatility for risk-averse households who expect an increase in family size. In the absence of an equity market in local housing assets, this demand for housing equity also enhances the decision to own.[10]

Some housing price insurance against mid-life house price risk could be provided by inheritances from parents of which housing wealth is frequently the most important part. But this insurance is limited by a number of fac-tors. First, not all parents are homeowners themselves, especially since their homeowner decisions were made in a distant past when home ownership was much less common. Second, inheritances are typically split among all the siblings, making this type of insurance partial at best. Parents may also not live in the same type of housing price volatility area as their children, which would also diminish the insurance value of this mechanism. Finally, the timing of the inheritance is relevant. Inheritances received when adult children are in the early stages of the adult-housing ladder have lost their insurance value, while those received after the peak of the ladder may have liquidity problems in creating an insurance value.

One further extension that needs to be discussed, since we endeavor to control for it in the empirical analysis that follows, is geographic mobility. If individuals anticipate residing in less volatile areas in period 3, then their demand for insurance is reduced (and the insurance value of their housing equity in period 2 will be reduced also to the extent that house prices are not perfectly correlated across regions). It is expected volatility at $D = 3$ (from the point of view of $D = 2$) that drives the insurance motive. In the case of

9. Borrowing constraints add further refinements to the model. They typically take two forms: a down payment constraint and a multiple-income (or debt-to-income) constraint. The down payment is proportional to the house price. The multiple-income constraint restricts the mortgage to be a multiple of current income. With such constraints in place, the potential downside of a house price rise between $D = 2$ and $D = 3$ for a nonowner enhances the insurance value of ownership at $D = 2$. If house prices rise relative to incomes then the capital gain reduces the mortgage requirement and makes it more likely that the earnings-to-mortgage debt can be met. Such borrowing constraints add to the insurance value of ownership since an unexpected price increase at $D = 3$ considerably relieves the down payment constraint.

10. An additional reason for ownership is given by rental price risk. As Sinai and Souleles (2005) point out, house ownership insures housing consumption from rental price risk (although it may not alleviate cyclical fluctuations in housing costs when variable-rate mortgages are the predominant form of finance for housing purchases). Our focus here is specifically on the hous-ing ladder where we show house price risk enhances the probability of ownership and the speed with which an individual moves up the ladder. At this stage of the life cycle where expected duration of stay in rental housing is relatively short, rental price risk may be less relevant than for lifetime renters. In addition, young agents can avoid rental price risk by living with their parents until they are ready to buy a home. This is relatively common pathway in Britain.

individuals in $D = 2$ anticipating moving to a safe area at $D = 3$, both these factors are likely to play a reduced role, although they could still be important to some extent.

3.4   The Empirical Relationship between Housing Choices and Risk

On the basis of our discussions in the previous section, and the numerical model solutions presented in appendix B, there are three principal predictions that we will test empirically in this chapter: (a) other things being equal, individuals should buy homes earlier in more volatile areas; (b) young homeowners are less likely to consume capital gains on housing through refinancing in more volatile areas; and (c) young homeowners will consume "more" housing in more volatile areas than their counterparts in less volatile areas. In the following subsections we deal with each of the above predictions in turn.

3.4.1   Age of Home Ownership

In the presence of a housing ladder, individuals living in places with more volatile housing prices need to self-insure by buying their first home at a younger age. In the final column of table 3.3, we list for both the United Kingdom and the United States the proportion of individuals who are homeowners, by age, for a typical year—1994. These patterns do not depend critically on the year chosen. The data are also presented separately for the volatile and nonvolatile areas in both countries. While average rates of home ownership are similar, there are striking differences by age between the two

Table 3.3	Proportion of individuals who are homeowners in 1994		
Age	Volatile regions	Nonvolatile regions	All
United Kingdom			
20–29	0.336	0.397	0.357
30–39	0.717	0.755	0.731
40–49	0.799	0.784	0.794
50–59	0.801	0.723	0.775
60–69	0.754	0.667	0.723
70+	0.602	0.547	0.583
All	0.652	0.641	0.648
United States			
20–29	0.187	0.273	0.253
30–39	0.528	0.612	0.590
40–49	0.691	0.748	0.736
50–59	0.825	0.830	0.828
60–69	0.784	0.875	0.850
70+	0.683	0.723	0.714
All	*0.583*	*0.649*	*0.633*

Source: Data are from the 1994 BHPS and PSID.

countries. Home ownership rates among young households are far higher in the United Kingdom than in the United States, with differences of 10 percentage points for householders between ages twenty and twenty-nine and 13 percentage points those between ages thirty and thirty-nine. However, through middle age, home-ownership rates converge so quickly that US rates actually exceed those in the United Kingdom among older households.

Since prices are far more variable in the United Kingdom, these cross-country differences in home-ownership rates are consistent with our theoretical implication that ownership should occur at a younger age in more price-volatile housing markets. However, when we compare home-ownership rates between the volatile and nonvolatile areas within each country, the challenge to our theory becomes more apparent. In both countries, owning a home is somewhat less common among younger households in the volatile market.

However, there are other significant differences between these two markets in each country that will presumably strongly affect the decision to own. Tables 3.4A and 3.4B list some of the more salient ones. Perhaps,

Table 3.4A   **Differences across broad regions, United States (twenty-one to thirty-five-year-olds)**

	Nonvolatile	Volatile
Fraction of population (1999)	0.78	0.22
Owns home	0.43	0.33
Rents	0.37	0.44
Ever had a child	0.58	0.47
Years of education	13.04	13.58
Log income in 1995$	9.90	10.07
Mean PSID house value	83,777	155,989
Mean PSID annual rent	4,116	6,025

Source: PSID and BHPS.

Table 3.4B   **Differences across broad regions, United Kingdom (twenty-one to thirty-five-year-olds)**

	Nonvolatile	Volatile
Fraction of population (2000)	0.34	0.66
Owns home	0.53	0.50
Rents	0.24	0.27
Has a child	0.45	0.50
Education—low	0.48	0.48
Education—medium	0.24	0.25
Education—high	0.28	0.28
Ln income (in £2000)	9.50	9.55
Mean BHPS house value (£)	80,455	103,405
Mean BHPS weekly rent (£)	64.00	85.70

Source: PSID and BHPS.

most important, housing prices are much higher in the volatile markets. For example, the average price of a home in the more volatile states is almost twice that in the less volatile ones, which should certainly discourage home ownership among the young. While rental prices are also higher in the more volatile states, the percentage difference is 46 percent compared to 68 percent for housing prices. Young individuals living in the volatile states also have more education, more household income, and are less likely to be married and to have children. All of these factors are obviously relevant to the housing tenure decision, so the final verdict on the theory requires multivariate modeling.

In our multivariate analysis, we estimate a probit model of whether or not one is a homeowner using a sample of individuals who are between the ages of twenty-one and thirty-five. Results are similar if one uses a somewhat younger or somewhat older age band that corresponds to the rising part of the housing ladder. In addition to our measure of housing price volatility described above, this model includes several relevant demographic attributes—a quadratic in age, indicator variables for whether one is married and whether one has children, the log income of the tax unit in which the individual participates, and measures capturing years of schooling. We measure area and age-specific housing prices by using the PSID and BHPS to compute mean housing prices and mean rents in each state/region for owners and renters respectively, within broad age groups. These prices as well as benefit unit income are entered in logs.

The critical variable for testing our theory concerns housing price variability, which varies across space and time. We construct a five-year moving window of the standard deviation of the year-to-year differences in the log real housing prices in a region[11] as described in the previous section. Since our US housing price series starts in 1974, this means that our PSID analysis starts with the 1980 PSID and extends to the 1997 PSID. Since fewer historical years are available in the BHPS, the analysis there covers the years 1991–2003.

We stop our analysis at these times for several reasons. First, after the 1997 wave the PSID switched its periodicity from one year to two years, making it not strictly comparable to the BHPS, especially for the type of time-series price volatility analysis we are conducting in this chapter. Second, the signature event after this period would be the housing price collapse in both countries associated with the Great Recession. But the magnitude of this event is an order of magnitude more unique and larger than the house price volatility risk we are trying to model in this chapter.

As noted earlier, expected capital gains are likely to be an important component of the demand for a risky asset like housing. Expected capital gains reduce the user cost, reflecting the risk-return trade-off. To construct an

11. For each of the fifty US states and the twelve UK regions.

expected gains variable, we use the change in the regionally varying log real house price index over the previous five years—precisely the same five-year moving window for house prices we use in constructing the house price risk variable.

There may well be other attributes of states or regions that create an incentive to own homes and that may be correlated with housing price volatility. To control for the possibility that the variability in housing prices across regions and states may simply be capturing unmeasured differences across states and regions, we estimated all models with and without state and region effects. Putting in these geographic-level fixed effects means that only attributes of geographic areas that are changing over time can affect our results. We see this as much less likely. A linear time trend is added to our models so our time-series variation is relative to a common linear trend.

The results are displayed in tables 3.5A and 3.5B, which list marginal effects and standard errors of all variables obtained from probit models. In both countries we find positive income effects (slightly higher in the UK) and education effects (a possible proxy for permanent income) on home ownership. Not surprisingly, marriage in both countries encourages home ownership and children do likewise. In the United States and the United Kingdom, we also have statistically significant negative price-level effects on the probability of owning a home. We also find a positive impact of expected capital gains, although this is not uniformly significant across all model specifications.

In both countries high area-specific rents also discourage home owner-

Table 3.5A   **Probability of home ownership, United States**

	(1)		(2)	
	dF/dx	Std. err.	dF/dx	Std. err.
Price volatility index	0.1873	0.0945	0.4061	0.1084
Age	0.0448	0.0061	0.0478	0.0061
Age squared	−0.0004	0.0001	−0.0005	0.0001
Married	0.2727	0.0045	0.2698	0.0045
Ever have a child	0.0628	0.0039	0.0671	0.0039
Education	0.0105	0.0009	0.0104	0.0009
Ln income	0.2057	0.0026	0.2070	0.0026
Ln housing prices	−0.0561	0.0051	−0.0365	0.0069
Exp. capital gains	0.0360	0.0538	0.1069	0.0554
Ln rental prices	−0.0476	0.0057	0.0151	0.0069
Move A-B	−0.1513	0.0155	−0.1139	0.0157
Move B-A	−0.1114	0.0173	−0.1341	0.0174
Trend	0.0022	0.0004	0.0009	0.0004
State dummies	No		Yes	

Note: Ages twenty-one to thirty-five. Models also control for city size, missing values, trend, number of waves in panel, and a constant term.

Table 3.5B   Probability of home ownership, United Kingdom

	(1)		(2)	
	dF/dx	Std. err.	dF/dx	Std. err.
Price volatility	0.3361	0.1212	0.3629	0.1226
Age	0.1107	0.0127	0.1093	0.0127
Age squared	–0.0014	0.0002	–0.0014	0.0002
Married	0.4623	0.0065	0.4623	0.0065
Has children	0.0349	0.0089	0.0352	0.0089
Educ.—low	–0.0874	0.0086	–0.0866	0.0087
Educ.—medium	0.0066	0.0097	0.0070	0.0097
Ln income	0.2992	0.0061	0.2989	0.0061
Ln house prices	–0.1084	0.0203	–0.1080	0.0222
Exp. capital gains	0.1648	0.0928	0.1595	0.0968
Ln rental prices	–0.1025	0.0174	–0.0963	0.0186
Move A–B	–0.0808	0.0302	–0.0802	0.0302
Move B–A	–0.1558	0.0279	–0.1559	0.0280
Regional dummies	No		Yes	

Note: Ages twenty-one to thirty-five. Models include controls for living in a big city, number of waves observed in panel, trend, and a constant term.

ship. While this may at first blush seem counterintuitive, it is important to remember that there are three options open to young persons in terms of their housing choices—owner, renter, or living with others—especially parents. When we estimated models for whether one was a renter, higher rental prices discouraged both renting and home owning.

The coefficients on the price-volatility variables form the basis of the fundamental test of our central prediction. In both the United States and the United Kingdom, we estimate statistically significant positive effects of price volatility indicating that as predicted individuals choose to own homes at a younger age in the more housing price volatile areas. When state/region dummy variables are included, these estimated effects are remarkably similar in the two countries so that on the margin Britons appear to react more in moving into home ownership at a younger age only because volatility on average is so much higher there.

3.4.2   The Decision to Refinance

As discussed above, our key hypothesis is that households in areas where housing prices are volatile should self-insure at young ages by holding more housing. However, if they were to buy a house and then refinance and use the proceeds to finance consumption or to purchase risky assets, this would simply undo the safety housing provides. As such, we would expect less of such behavior in volatile areas and we test this prediction in this section. Although imperfect, our two data sets provide some measure of the extent to which individuals engage in such activities. With regard to the United

Table 3.6A   **Probability of refinancing a US home**

	(1)		(2)	
	dF/dx	Std. err.	dF/dx	Std. err.
Price volatility index	−0.5654	0.1268	−0.3715	0.1485
Age	−0.0081	0.0094	−0.0072	0.0093
Age squared	0.0001	0.0002	0.0001	0.0002
Married	−0.0042	0.0065	−0.0025	0.0065
Ever have a child	0.0181	0.0054	0.0170	0.0054
Education	−0.0081	0.0011	−0.0079	0.0012
Ln income	−0.0183	0.0035	−0.0153	0.0036
Ln house equity $t-1$	0.0367	0.0022	0.0384	0.0022
Exp. capital gains	0.1626	0.0696	0.2228	0.0740
Move A–B	0.0012	0.0344	0.0177	0.0337
Move B–A	0.0239	0.0330	0.0182	0.0328
State dummies	No		Yes	

Note: Ages twenty-one to thirty-five. Models also include controls for city size and missing value dummies.

States, PSID data contain no direct questions in each year on refinancing, so we define an indicator of refinancing to take the value 1 if an individual's mortgage is observed to have risen by a specified amount between waves.[12] The problem with this measure is that individuals could well be using the extra finance to improve their home, which would not unravel the housing as price insurance mechanism, thus making it an imperfect measure for our purposes.

This prediction can, however, be directly addressed in the United Kingdom using BHPS data, where individuals are asked specific questions about whether they refinanced their housing equity between waves, and if so the purposes for which the resulting money was used. With such detailed questions we are able to construct a more precise indicator in the United Kingdom that takes the value 1 only if individuals refinance between waves and do not increase the quantity or quality of housing as a result.

Our results are summarized in tables 3.6A and 3.6B. In addition to the nonprice variables that were part of the home-ownership model, we included a measure of home equity in the previous year to capture the amount available for refinancing. In both countries, using both measures of refinancing, the predictions of the theory are borne out—individuals in more risky areas are less likely to refinance, conditional on other characteristics and their initial level of net housing equity.

12. In practice, small rises could simply be a result of measurement error, so we choose a variety of thresholds above which we assert a change in mortgage can be interpreted as a refinance. The specification in table 3.6A uses a definition of mortgage rising by at least 30 percent or $5,000, whichever is the greater.

Table 3.6B   **Probability of refinancing a UK home**

	(1)		(2)	
	dF/dx	Std. err.	dF/dx	Std. err.
Price volatility	−0.1726	0.0885	−0.2093	0.0876
Age	0.0071	0.0071	0.0071	0.0071
Age squared	−0.0001	0.0001	−0.0001	0.0001
Married	−0.0115	0.0069	−0.0116	0.0069
Has children	0.0124	0.0036	0.0128	0.0036
Educ.—low	0.0148	0.0043	0.0145	0.0043
Educ.—medium	0.0112	0.0049	0.0110	0.0049
Ln income	0.0083	0.0031	0.0074	0.0031
Ln equity $t-1$	0.0056	0.0017	0.0050	0.0017
Exp. capital gains	0.2262	0.0661	0.1434	0.0759
Regional dummies	No		Yes	

Note: Ages twenty-one to thirty-five. Models include controls for living in a big city, number of waves observed in panel, trend, tax unit composition change between waves $t-1$ and t.

3.4.3   Increased Consumption of Housing

As pointed out in section 3.2, one can insure against future housing price volatility in period $D = 3$ not only by purchasing a house in period $D = 2$, but also by consuming more owned housing than one might otherwise want given the objective demographic circumstances. Moreover, in the presence of borrowing constraints there is a possibility that, if prices rise more quickly than income, debt-to-income restrictions may prevent individuals being able to purchase a larger home at $D = 3$. With this possibility on the horizon, individuals already more likely to be an owner-occupier as a result of the increased volatility would also choose to increase their consumption of housing. In the case of prices rising, the capital gain will be higher and can be used as down payment on the final home in order to offset the debt-to-income restriction. Indeed, in the United Kingdom the two conditions are often linked (since on a secured loan the consequences of default to the lender are reduced with a higher down payment) such that individuals with higher down payments can borrow a higher multiple of income.

In order to measure the consumption of housing for the purposes of testing this prediction, we use two variables—the number of rooms in the house and the gross value of the house.[13] Neither is perfect since the former omits

13. With increasing availability of appropriate panel data on wealth, there has been renewed interest in the study of housing wealth dynamics and its implications for other economic factors. Flavin and Yamashita (2002) look at the effect on households' optimal financial-asset holding of integrating housing (i.e., both housing wealth and the associated consumption demand for housing services) into the portfolio model. In a more empirical study, Banks, Blundell, and

Table 3.7A   **Number of rooms in the United States**

	(1)		(2)	
	Coeff.	Std. err.	Coeff.	Std. err.
Price volatility index	0.0593	0.6931	0.5800	0.7514
Age	0.3916	0.0495	0.3585	0.0468
Age squared	−0 0041	0.0008	−0.0036	0.0008
Married	1.6815	0.0765	1.5641	0.0699
Ever have a child	0.7385	0.0317	0.7569	0.0302
Education	0.1309	0.0064	0.1235	0.0061
Ln income	1.5806	0.0519	1.4971	0.0488
Ln housing prices	−0.5104	0.0368	−0.3232	0.0490
Exp. capital gains	0.9832	0.3889	1.2084	0.3766
Move A–B	−1.0676	0.1376	−0.6873	0.1295
Move B–A	−0.3129	0.1482	−0.4833	0.1419
Mills ratio	2.7749	0.1186	2.6086	0.1087
State dummies	No		Yes	

Note: Ages twenty-one to thirty-five. Models also include controls for city, trend, missing value dummies, number of waves observed in panel, and a constant term. Selection equation is reported in table 3.5A. Rental price omitted from rooms equation.

possible quality effects (such as variation in the size and quality of a room, which varies much more in the United States than in the United Kingdom), and the latter may be contaminated by unmeasured price variation leading to uncontrolled-for demand effects. Nevertheless, each provides a useful complementary test for the predictions of the model. For each of these measures of housing consumption, we use a standard Heckman-type selectivity model to evaluate the predictions for homeowners only, using the probits reported in tables 3.5A and 3.5B as the selection equations and omitting the rental price from the continuous part of the model.

Tables 3.7A and 3.7B report the results of estimating selection models for the number of rooms occupied by young homeowners. These estimates show significant positive effects of volatility on house size, but only in the United Kingdom—other things equal, young British homeowners in risky areas tend to consume more rooms than their counterparts in safer areas in order to partially insure themselves against housing price risk. The effects are positive in the United States as well, but not statistically significant at conventional test levels. It is possible that the much larger variation in size and quality of rooms in the United States make it a weaker test there.

Smith (2003) show that housing wealth differentials between the United States and the United Kingdom offset to some extent the differences in financial wealth observed between the two countries. But in spite of recognition of the dual importance of housing as both consumption and investment, the implications of the often-considerable housing price uncertainty for the life-cycle path of housing wealth are not well understood.

Table 3.7B   Number of rooms in the United Kingdom

	(1)		(2)	
	Coeff.	Std. err.	Coeff.	Std. err.
Price volatility	4.2949	0.6503	4.1218	0.6474
Age	0.2886	0.0766	0.2874	0.0760
Age squared	−0.0023	0.0013	−0.0023	0.0013
Married	2.2813	0.1268	2.2594	0.1258
Has children	0.9393	0.0470	0.9377	0.0465
Educ.—low	−0.5862	0.0471	−0.5909	0.0467
Educ.—medium	−0.1119	0.0501	−0.1172	0.0496
Ln income	1.3262	0.0721	1.3193	0.0716
Ln house price	−1.2942	0.0817	−1.3970	0.1084
Exp. capital gains	2.0882	0.4611	2.3989	0.5026
Move A–B	−0.2887	0.1768	−0.2973	0.1749
Move B–A	−0.8030	0.1788	−0.7649	0.1773
Mills ratio	2.6704	0.1556	2.6425	0.1544
Regional dummies	No		Yes	

Note: Ages twenty-one to thirty-five. Model also includes controls for city size, trend, number of waves observed in panel, and a constant term. Selection equation is reported in table 3.5B. Rental price omitted from rooms equation.

Other estimated parameters accord with a priori intuition. The number of rooms increases with income, education, whether an individual is married, and with the presence of children, and decreases with the average price of housing per room in the area. The magnitude of the demographic effects (marriage and children) and the income effects are similar in the two countries. Finally, those individuals moving from risky to safe areas have a reduced number of rooms, as would be predicted by their insurance motive being reduced, although not by enough to offset the volatility effect altogether.

In tables 3.8A and 3.8B we repeat this analysis using gross house value as our measure of housing consumption. Again in both countries, as predicted by our theory, individuals in risky areas choose to have higher housing wealth than those living in safe areas. This effect is reduced for those observed to move from risky to safe areas during the period of our data. Thus, those individuals who end up moving out of the risky housing-price areas appear to insure less in the sense that they do not overconsume housing when they are young. Once again, the principal demographic variables enter with the expected signs and in about the same magnitude in both countries—home values increase with marriage, children, and age (at least until middle age). Similarly, income and education effects are positive in both countries, although our estimated current income elasticity is much higher in the United States than in the United Kingdom.

Table 3.8A **Gross housing wealth in the United States**

	(1)		(2)	
	Coeff.	Std. err.	Coeff.	Std. err.
Price volatility index	2.5190	0.3510	1.7861	0.3787
Age	0.3266	0.0253	0.3045	0.0241
Age squared	−0.0044	0.0004	−0.0041	0.0004
Married	0.8253	0.0393	0.6766	0.0375
Ever have a child	0.1031	0.0161	0.0888	0.0154
Education	0.1002	0.0032	0.0956	0.0031
Ln income	1.0191	0.0266	0.9176	0.0257
Ln housing prices	0.3990	0.0187	0.3220	0.0248
Exp. capital gains	0.1532	0.1971	0.2007	0.1901
Move A–B	−0.4946	0.0703	−0.4152	0.0678
Move B–A	−0.1506	0.0754	−0.1286	0.0736
Mills ratio	1.3505	0.0613	1.1134	0.0590
State dummies	No		Yes	

Note: Ages twenty-one to thirty-five. Models also include controls for city size, missing value dummies, number of waves observed in panel, and a constant term. Selection equation is reported in table 3.5A. Rental price omitted from rooms equation.

Table 3.8B **Gross housing wealth in the United Kingdom**

	(1)		(2)	
	Coeff.	Std. err.	Coeff.	Std. err.
Price volatility	1.3034	0.2337	1.1828	0.2298
Age	0.1891	0.0276	0.1860	0.0270
Age squared	−0.0023	0.0005	−0.0023	0.0005
Married	0.8706	0.0467	0.8530	0.0458
Has children	0.2426	0.0169	0.2419	0.0165
Educ.—low	−0.2377	0.017	−0.2409	0.0166
Educ.—medium	−0.0448	0.0181	−0.0484	0.0177
Ln income	0.5862	0.0258	0.5794	0.0253
Ln house prices	0.5118	0.0295	0.4291	0.0385
Exp. capital gains	0.7693	0.1659	1.0163	0.1785
Move A–B	−0.087	0.0637	−0.0911	0.0623
Move B–A	−0.2896	0.0646	−0.2653	0.0633
Mills ratio	0.9565	0.0556	0.9347	0.0545
Regional dummies	No		Yes	

Note: Ages twenty-one to thirty-five. Models also include controls for city size, trend, number of waves observed in panel, and a constant term. Selection equation is reported in table 3.5B. Rental price omitted from rooms equation.

The models estimated in tables 3.7A and B and 3.8A and B are based on two alternative and imperfect measures of housing consumption. However, the general similarity of the estimated models across both specifications, and in particular the similar estimated effects of our measure of housing price variability on housing consumption in both countries, lends support to the predictions of our model.

3.4.4   Endowment Mortgages

Over the period covered by our data, one relatively common financial instrument used to finance house purchases in Britain was an endowment mortgage. During the life of the mortgage, the borrower makes only interest payments on the loan, leaving the principal to be repaid at the end of the term of the mortgage. In addition to the interest, the borrower pays into a saving scheme, which is designed to mature and repay at least the value of the capital sum borrowed at the end of the period of the loan. Throughout the 1980s and 1990s these schemes were common, with the most common type of saving scheme being an endowment policy—essentially term life insurance with the accumulating fund invested in the stock market.

While the relative attractiveness of such a mortgage product is not so clearly different across volatile and less volatile areas from the perspective of our main story (after all, the homeowner retains the housing wealth and hence gets the insurance against the future house price risk regardless of how that housing purchase is financed), one might still expect some differences simply due to background risk effects. These endowment funds were typically quite large and unavoidable for anyone who was unable to use a repayment mortgage (typically those without the liquidity to finance a substantial down payment). One might argue that the future house price risk that is the main object of interest in this chapter acts like a large background risk that would discourage individuals from taking on a substantial further risk elsewhere in their portfolio. As such, households who live in volatile areas should be less likely to choose this type of mortgage.[14] These predictions are borne out using the same empirical framework as the tests presented above. In table 3.9, we report results obtained from probit models with the dependent variable being whether individuals finance their house purchase with an endowment mortgage as opposed to some other method. Since mortgage arrangements typically do not change over the term of the mortgage (and in the case of endowment policies the penalties for early termination are high), we are able to use homeowners of all ages for this test, thus also implicitly

---

14. One complication in testing this prediction is that, particularly in the 1980s (and early 1990s), there is some evidence that misselling of this type of mortgage took place by mortgage providers. In particular, there is the possibility that consumers were not fully informed of the nature of other choices of mortgage arrangements available or about the risky nature of the endowment policy. Assuming such effects were constant across regions, however, we might still expect those living in more volatile regions to be less likely to take out such mortgages.

Table 3.9   **Probability of holding endowment mortgage, homeowners in the United Kingdom only**

	(1)		(2)	
	dF/dx	Std. err.	dF/dx	Std. err.
Price volatility	−5.0454	0.1097	−5.0143	0.1120
Age	0.0202	0.0018	0.0203	0.0018
Age squared	−0.0003	2.07E–05	−0.0003	2.08E–05
Married	0.0395	0.0089	0.0392	0.0089
Has children	0.0438	0.0066	0.0442	0.0066
Education—low	0.0430	0.0070	0.0440	0.0070
Education—medium	0.0200	0.0081	0.0201	0.0081
Ln income	0.0072	0.0052	0.0072	0.0053
Exp. capital gains	0.7835	0.0924	0.8017	0.0927
Move A–B	0.1121	0.0452	0.1143	0.0450
Move B–A	−0.0531	0.0479	−0.0590	0.0479
Regional dummies	No		Yes	

Note: All ages. Models also include number of waves observed in panel, city trend.

increasing the period over which effects are apparent. Whether or not we include region dummies, British families who live in more volatile housing price areas are less likely to take out an endowment mortgage. This estimated effect is statistically significant.

3.5   Conclusions

Typically, risk-averse individuals will avoid risky assets as volatility increases. In this chapter we show that owner-occupied housing is an exception to this rule. The consumption role of housing wealth, coupled with increasing necessary levels of housing over the life cycle due to demographic changes, and the fact that individuals will typically prefer to own rather than rent, mean that individuals will expect to be consuming a risky commodity—owner-occupied housing—in middle age. Since housing is a necessity, the utility consequences of this risk might be expected to be relatively large. In the absence of suitable financial products to insure this risk, this will lead individuals to invest in housing early in the life cycle as a way of insuring future price fluctuations. Not only does this lead to higher owner-occupation rates, it also leads to more housing wealth and less propensity to realize capital gains on housing through refinancing to fund nonhousing consumption.

Using microdata from two countries we have constructed tests of these predictions and all are borne out empirically. Cross-country differences between the United States and the United Kingdom correspond to the cross-country differences in volatility—the United Kingdom is more volatile and

UK households own earlier, and have more of their portfolio in housing. Because this may be driven by other differences between countries, we use within-country tests that rely on time-series and cross-sectional variation in volatility within and across states (in the United States) or regions (in the United Kingdom), and we continue to find empirical support for the predictions of the theory.

Appendix A
Data Sources

In 1968 the PSID started collecting information on a sample of roughly 5,000 (original) families. Of these, about 3,000 were representative of the US population as a whole (the core sample), and about 2,000 were low-income families (the Census Bureau's Survey of Economic Opportunities [SEO] sample). Thereafter, both the original families and their split-offs (children of the original family forming a family of their own) have been followed, giving a total of around 35,000 individuals. Panel members were interviewed each year until 1997, when a two-year periodicity rule was established. All original members of the 1968 households and their progeny are considered sample members and thus are part of the panel even if they move out of the original household. The US models presented in this chapter include the SEO over-sample, although they were also estimated using only the core sample and our results regarding the effects of housing price volatility were not affected.

In each wave of the panel, the PSID asks detailed questions on individual and household income, family size and composition, schooling, education, age, and marital status. State of residence is available yearly and individuals are followed to new locations if they move. Unlike many other prominent American wealth surveys, the PSID is representative of the complete age distribution. Yearly housing tenure questions determine whether individuals currently own, rent, or live with others. Questions on housing ownership, value, and mortgage were asked in each calendar year wave of the PSID.[15] Renters are asked the amount of rent they pay and both owners and renters are asked the total number of rooms in the residence.

In addition to the PSID, housing-price data were obtained from the Office of Federal Housing Enterprise Oversight (OFHEO) House Price Index. These data contain quarterly and yearly price indexes for the value of single-family homes in the United States in the individual states and the District

---

15. Mortgages are not available in the PSID for years 1973, 1974, 1975, and 1982.

of Columbia.[16] These data use repeat transactions for the same houses to obtain a quality constant index and is available for all years starting in 1974. All yearly housing prices by state are reported relative to those that prevailed in 1980. By 1995 there were almost seven million repeat transactions in the data so that the number of observations for each state is reasonably large. No demographic data are available with this index.

For the United Kingdom, we use the British Household Panel Survey (BHPS). The BHPS has been running annually since 1991 and, like the PSID, is also representative of the complete age distribution. The wave 1 sample consisted of some 5,500 households and 10,300 individuals, and continuing representativeness of the survey is maintained by following panel members wherever they move in the United Kingdom and also by including in the panel the new members of households formed by original panel members. The BHPS contains annual information on individual and household income and employment as well as a complete set of demographic variables. Like the PSID, data are collected annually on primary housing wealth and on secondary housing wealth.[17]

In addition to the BHPS, regional house price data were obtained from the Nationwide Building Society House Price series, which is a quarterly regional house price series going back to 1974. Rather than use a repeat sales index, the prices are adjusted for changes in the mix of sales to approximate a composition constant index, and are also seasonally adjusted.

Throughout the chapter we take care to define the unit of analysis as the benefit unit (i.e., singles or couples with dependent children) such that young individuals at the beginning of the life cycle living in shared accommodation or with other family members are not lost from the analysis as subsidiary adults in households headed by other individuals. This is particularly important for older independent children who are still residing with parents and who would show up in middle-aged households in a conventional head of household-based analysis. In both countries, housing wealth is allocated to the home-owning benefit unit only. Hence a twenty-five-year-old living with his or her parents in an owned property is not defined as an owner (unless the property is owned jointly with the parents) and is assigned zero housing wealth.

We use several housing wealth concepts in this chapter. The current value of the house is derived in both the PSID and BHPS by asking respondents to report the current market value of their home, while housing equity is constructed by subtracting from the current house value the outstanding mortgage.

---

16. For details on this data see Calhoun (1996). The paper is available on the OFHEO website.
17. Housing wealth and mortgages are not available in 1992.

Appendix B

Numerical Simulation of a Simple Model of Ownership and Housing Equity in the Presence of House Price Risk and a Housing Ladder

The integration of housing price risk into a single theoretical framework is complex and even algebraic closed-form solutions will only be possible under certain (restrictive) forms of preferences. Ideally, however, we want to use relatively flexible preferences for consumption and housing to generate predictions relating to the effects of houseprice risk. In this appendix we use numerical methods in order to offer insight into the predictions of the model using a very simple set of specifications for preferences, the steepness of the housing ladder, and the time-series process for the underlying uncertainty.[18]

For the purpose of our simulations, we assume that individuals maximize expected discounted lifetime utility, with the utility functions for an individual in each of the decision periods being given by:

$$(1) \qquad u_t = \frac{1}{1-\gamma}\Big[\big(q_t - \overline{q}_t\big)^\alpha c_t^{1-\alpha}\Big]^{1/(1-\gamma)},$$

where q_t is the consumption of housing services in period t and all other consumption is summarized by c_t. To accord with our discussions of section 3.3, these preferences are characterized by having a necessary level of housing consumption, $\overline{q}_t$, in each period to capture the housing ladder, but they also take the CRRA form to allow us to look at the impact of varying risk aversion on the predictions of the model.

We solve the numerical model with three periods, aimed at capturing the phases of the life cycle discussed in section 3.3, rather than calendar years, quarters, or even months. When building a numerical solution algorithm, the choice of units and parameter values forces one to think carefully about the relative length of periods. In taking numerical methods to our model we essentially need to think of periods of unequal length in order to capture the sense in which period 2 (the middle rung on the housing ladder) is a transition to a more permanent state of completed family size and a "permanent" family home. A convenient way in which to do this is to introduce factors δ_2 and δ_3, with $0 < \delta_t \le 1$, $t = 2,3$ and $\delta_2 \le \delta_3$, which describe the flow of consumption services q_t from housing stock H_t, so that $q_t = \delta_t H_t$.

---

18. Ultimately, many other extensions could be looked at with this approach, such as the sensitivity of predictions to rental premia, the cost of mortgage borrowing, the extension of the model to a greater number of time periods, or the differences in predictions that emerge as we allow income uncertainty (with differing degrees of correlation between income and house price shocks). But we leave these extensions for further work since, at this stage, we want to make the model as simple as possible while still remaining sufficiently general to examine the specific predictions on which the empirical analyses in this chapter are based.

We choose a stylized model in which the only uncertainty is in house prices. In accordance with our earlier discussions, we assume that in period 1 everyone is a renter and in period 3 everyone is an owner. The key decision is whether to own in period 2 or wait until period 3. We show that increasing house price uncertainty increases the payoff to ownership in the second period. This payoff is larger the larger the degree of risk aversion and the stronger the gradient in the housing ladder. As we are only interested in the relative payoff of ownership we normalize on first-period utility and examine relative payoff in periods 2 and 3. The budget constraint for periods 2 and 3 under each option is given by:

(2a) [Owner at $t = 2$]: $y_2 + y_3 + (p_3 - p_2)H_2 = c_2 + c_3 + p_2\delta_2H_2 + p_2\delta_2H_2$

(2b) [Renter at $t = 2$]: $y_2 + y_3 = c_2 + c_3 + \tau p_2\delta_2H_2 + p_3\delta_3H_3$

depending on which tenure is chosen, where y_t are discounted incomes, p_t are discounted prices, c_t are discounted consumptions, and τ is the rental premium.

Implicit in this set up is that an individual can borrow or save at the same (safe) rate of interest equal to the discount rate. Finally, we introduce house price uncertainty in period 3 by allowing p_3 to take the value $p_2(1 + \pi)$ with probability .5 and $p_2(1 - \pi)$ with probability .5. We can then vary the variance of housing price uncertainty by solving the model for different values of π.[19]

We solve the model by backward induction with a relatively straightforward numerical method that involves a discrete grid search across all possible paths for housing consumption in each period, q, consumption in each period, c, and the owner/renter decision in period 2. For the purposes of the solution, baseline values are set at: $\tau = 1$, $\alpha = 0.3$, $\delta_2 = 0.5$, $\delta_3 = 1$, $\bar{q}_2 = 0$, $y_3 = 200$, and $y_2 = 0.5y_3$. The later equality equates the flow of income across the two periods given the choice of δ_2 and δ_3. The model is then solved under varying degrees of uncertainty for various values of the necessary level of housing in period 3 (which we shall refer to as D) ranging from $D = 10$ to $D = 40$, and for various values of the risk-aversion parameter, γ.

Figure 3A.1A shows the difference between the expected utility of renting and owning in period 2, expressed as a fraction of the utility of renting, as the variance of housing prices increases and as the minimum level of housing required in period 3, that is, the steepness of the housing ladder, increases. The figure shows that increases in the minimum level of housing demand in period 3 result in an increase in the relative utility of owning in period 2 for all positive levels of volatility. Similarly, for all levels of the minimum housing requirement in period 3, increasing price volatility results in a stronger

---

19. In this discussion we abstract from expected capital gains. However, our empirical model will allow for a capital gains term that will reflect the risk-return trade-off. Holding the riskless return constant, an expected capital gain will reduce the user cost of housing and make ownership more attractive.

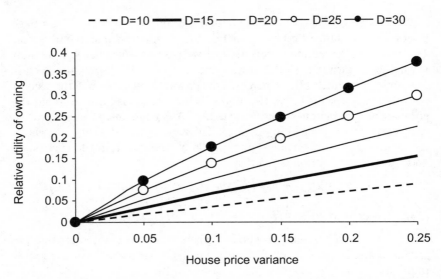

Fig. 3A.1A   Relative utility of owner occupation when young by variance of house prices and steepness of housing ladder

preference for owning: increasing house price risk reduces expected utility for both renters or owners in period 2, but the impact is stronger on the rental option. Consequently there is a gain in expected utility terms from owner-ship in period 2 and this gain increases with risk. Figure 3A.1B presents a complementary analysis, but where we hold the housing ladder constant and vary the degree of risk aversion in preferences. As risk aversion increases, the slopes of the profiles with respect to volatility steepen.

In addition to the home-ownership predictions, the model should also have predictions for the quantity of housing consumed as discussed in section 3.3. Figures 3A.2A and 3A.2B show the predictions for housing consumption in period 2 as the housing ladder steepens and as risk aversion increases. Figure 3A.2A shows that, for any level of the minimum housing requirement in period 3, as volatility increases the quantity of housing demanded in period 2 increases—individuals buy more insurance as risk accumulates.[20] If volatility is significant, a steeper housing ladder results in more housing consumption in period 2. This implies that not only will individuals be more likely to purchase a house in period 2, they will also be more

20. Varying the minimum housing requirement and keeping lifetime resources constant also generates a wealth effect. This is not important for our empirical tests since we will be examining demand for housing as volatility varies for a given steepness of the housing ladder. As a result we abstract from this wealth effect in this figure by normalizing the housing demand to its zero-volatility value in the two figures.

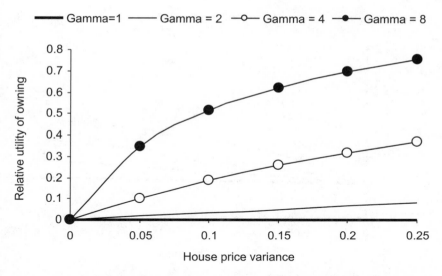

Fig. 3A.1B Relative utility of owner occupation when young by variance of house prices and degree of risk aversion

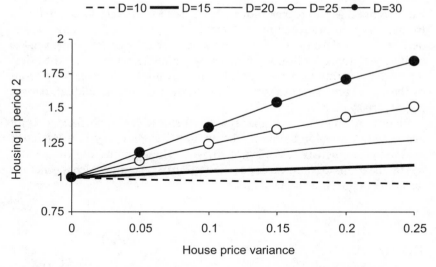

Fig. 3A.2A Consumption of housing when young by variance of house prices and steepness of housing ladder

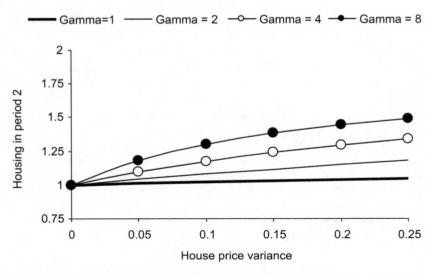

Fig. 3A.2B   Consumption of housing when young by variance of house prices and degree of risk aversion

likely to purchase a "bigger" house. Note that for the very lowest value of the minimum housing requirement ($D = 10$) the quantity of housing actually declines with volatility. At such a low value of the minimum (and given the relative preference for housing implied by our choice of a of 0.3) the housing ladder constraint is not effectively binding and therefore the predictions of the model are in accordance with the standard case: individuals choose less of a risky activity.

Figure 3A.2B presents similar results by risk-aversion coefficient. Once again, as risk aversion increases, the quantity demanded of housing in the second period increases. While not shown in these graphs, our model also has implications for nonhousing consumption in period 2, which is generally declining in housing price volatility.

References

Banks, James, Richard Blundell, Zoe Oldfield, and James P. Smith. 2012. "Housing Mobility and Downsizing at Older Ages in Britain and the USA." *Economica* 79 (313): 1–26.
Banks, James, Richard Blundell, and James P. Smith. 2003. "Wealth Portfolios in the US and the UK." In *Perspectives on the Economics of Aging*, edited by David A. Wise, 205–46. Chicago: University of Chicago Press.
Calhoun, Charles A. 1996. "OFHEO House Price Indexes: HPI Technical Description." Office of Federal Housing Enterprise Oversight, Washington, DC. http://

www.fhfa.gov/PolicyProgramsResearch/Research/PaperDocuments/1996-03
_HPI_TechDescription_N508.pdf.
Ermisch, John, and David J. Pevalin. 2004. "Early Childbearing and Housing
Choices." *Journal of Housing Economics* 13:170–94.
Flavin, Marjorie, and Takashi Yamashita. 2002. "Owner-Occupied Housing and the
Composition of Household Portfolio over the Life Cycle." *American Economic
Review* 92:345–62.
Ortalo-Magne, Francois, and Sven Rady. 2004. "Bargaining over Residential Real
Estate: Evidence from England." *Journal of Housing Economics* 56:192–216.
———. 2006. "Housing Market Dynamics: On the Contribution of Income Shocks
and Credit Constraints." *Review of Economic Studies* 73:459–85.
Sinai, Todd, and Nicholas S. Souleles. 2005. "Owner-Occupied Housing as a Hedge
against Rent Risk." *Quarterly Journal of Economics* 120 (2): 763–89.
Venti, Steven F., and David A. Wise. 2001. "Aging and Housing Equity: Another
Look." In *Perspectives on the Economics of Aging*, edited by David A. Wise, 127–
80. Chicago: University of Chicago Press.

Comment   Steven F. Venti

Housing is the dominant component of wealth and housing services are the dominant component of consumption for most young households. These facts alone suggest that volatile house prices can have enormous consequences for household behavior and welfare. Unlike most other risky assets, housing investments are also indivisible, illiquid, and difficult to diversify. Given these differences, it is not surprising that many of the standard predictions of financial models may not apply to housing. One such prediction is that house price risk should make ownership less attractive. This prediction is challenged by the central finding of this chapter, which concludes: "Typically, risk-adverse individuals will avoid risky assets as volatility increases. In this chapter we show that owner-occupied housing is an exception to this rule." This chapter provides compelling evidence that young households correctly perceive the price risk associated with home ownership and are able to hedge this risk by "buying-in" to the housing market earlier in the life cycle. Results supporting the dominance of the hedging motive are found for five indicators of housing demand and these results are strikingly similar across countries. The authors have done an excellent job establishing the "fact" that housing demand responds positively to price volatility, so in my comments I will try to offer some additional insights into the origins, identification, and limitations of hedging behavior from a finance perspective.

Steven F. Venti holds the DeWalt H. Ankeny '21 and Marie Ankeny Professorship in Economic Policy and is professor of economics at Dartmouth College, and he is a research associate of the National Bureau of Economic Research.
For acknowledgments, sources of research support, and disclosure of the author's material financial relationships, if any, please see http://www.nber.org/chapters/c13648.ack.

Price volatility provides households with two competing incentives. From an investment perspective, risk-adverse households should hold lower levels of all volatile assets—including housing—unless compensated by higher returns. However, households who anticipate that they will need to "buy up" in the future have an incentive to buy more housing (and buy it earlier) to hedge against future price risk. This latter incentive arises because households make a series of decisions over the life cycle that is described by the "housing ladder." These housing decisions are, more or less, forecastable: most households anticipate that at some point in the future they will have to sell their current home and buy another. This exposes the household to house price risk. If a household plans to move up the ladder, then getting into the housing market—both buying earlier and buying a larger quantity of housing—insures the household against price risk because the price of the current house (to be sold) is likely to be positively correlated with the price of the future house (to be purchased). The strength of this correlation is a measure of the benefit of the hedge. Sinai and Souleles (2005) show that in the United States about 80 percent of all moves are in the same metropolitan statistical area (MSA), so the correlation is likely to be quite high. Sinai and Souleles (2013) go further to show that even if moves are not local, households tend to move between markets with correlated housing prices. They also show that the likelihood of home ownership is greater if the covariance between prices in the current and future (postmove) housing markets is high. If current and future house prices are not correlated, then households face two independent risks—the sale price of the current house and the purchase price of the future house—and the hedging motive will not exist.

Most financial analyses of risky assets make a distinction between two types of risk: market (or systematic) risk and firm-specific (or idiosyncratic) risk. For most securities, firm-specific risk can be eliminated through diversification, so only market risk is priced by the market. Thus investors holding a well-diversified portfolio avoid market risk (or require a higher expected return to hold assets with higher market risk), but are oblivious to firm-specific risk. The risk properties of housing are quite different from those of conventional risky assets. Total price volatility can be split into three components: national market volatility, regional or local market volatility, and house-specific volatility. The comovement of the return on housing with national housing market returns is analogous to the comovement of security returns with market returns in conventional asset-pricing models. This source of volatility cannot be eliminated through diversification. The risk associated with regional volatility—the component of risk that is the focus of this chapter—is also nearly impossible to shed through diversification because people rarely own homes in multiple regions. The idiosyncratic risk component in housing (the component of the return on housing that is unrelated to national or regional returns) is likely to be quite large. In a recent paper Droes and Hassink (2013), using data for the Netherlands, find that house-specific risk accounts for 90 percent of total price risk.[1] For most risky assets, this component is diversified away by holding large portfolios. However, most homeowners own only one house and that house is often the largest asset in their portfolio, so again there is little opportunity for diversification. Although investors can limit risk exposure to most risky assets through diversification, this is not the case for housing, giving rise to the hedge that is the focus of this chapter.

The evidence this chapter provides in support of this hedge is the positive estimated effect of house price volatility on various indicators of housing demand. In my view, the empirical challenge is to distinguish the effect of price volatility from other closely related factors that affect demand. If housing is viewed as an investment then the *expected return on housing* is a key factor. If housing is viewed as a consumption good then the *level of house prices* is a key factor. The ability to separate out the effects of each of these factors will depend on the strength of the association between volatility, the level of prices, and the return on housing. These linkages are pursued in this chapter. This can be seen in figures 3.3A and 3.3B that show the log of the price index in "safe" (low volatility) and "risky" (high volatility) regions, yielding the obvious conclusion that regions with high price volatility also tend to have high price levels. I have made similar figures using more recent data for the United States, both to assess the strength of the association between the key variables and to determine whether these associations persist after the end of their sample period. Their analysis for the United States spanned 1980 to 1997, was based on annual data, and used five years of prices to construct the volatility index. My analysis for the United States, shown in the top panel of figure 3C.1, spans 1997 to 2014, uses quarterly data, and bases the volatility index on eight quarters of data.[2] Despite the differences, the figure in the chapter and my figure are remarkably similar. Both show that volatile regions are also pricier. The middle panel of figure 3C.1 shows the level of volatility in "safe" and "risky" regions. The pattern of volatility in the high volatility states is particularly striking. After rising through 2005, the level of prices was essentially flat (and volatility near zero) from the beginning of 2006 and mid-2007, before declining steadily through 2012. Despite these fluctuations, price volatility in the risky states was always greater than volatility in the safe states.

As noted above, from an investment perspective the *expected return* on

---

1. An implication of their finding is that price volatility, as measured by a regional price index, severely underestimates house price risk. It is perhaps surprising that, despite the relative small contribution of regional price variation to total price risk, the estimates in this chapter find that regional price volatility has a strong effect on ownership.

2. We both define regions to be the fifty states and the District of Columbia. My definition of safe states includes the ten states with the lowest standard deviation of the log price in the trailing eight quarters. Risky states include the ten states with the highest standard deviation.

housing (or the expected change in house prices) is a key variable. The bottom panel of figure 3C.1 shows the mean annual *return* in safe and risky regions. Until the Great Recession, the return on housing was quite a bit higher in risky regions than in safe regions. This is likely to have been true over most of the period considered in this chapter as well. Over the 1997 to 2014 period the annual return on housing was 1.69 percent in risky states and 0.38 percent in the safe states. This period of time is highly unusual and includes a burst of extreme price volatility. Nonetheless, the results suggest that the return on housing is also greater in regions with high price volatility.

The figures strongly suggest that volatility, prices, and returns are all closely related. This empirical evidence showing a strong association is also supported by conventional financial theory. In a standard capital asset pricing model (CAPM) equilibrium, expected returns will be a linear function of nondiversifiable risk. Investors will only hold more volatile assets if they are compensated through higher returns.[3] Thus, one challenge for the empirical work in this chapter is to separate out the effect of volatility from both the level of prices and the expected return on housing. Models for five indicators of housing demand are estimated. Each controls for the level of prices, but only one of the five models controls for the expected return. In the one set of estimates that includes the expected return variable, the estimated effect of the expected return on ownership is large, but only marginally statistically significant. Failure to include this variable in the other models makes the interpretation of the coefficient on volatility ambiguous. It would be useful to see results that control for both the price level and the expected return in all specifications.

When I began to write up my discussion of this chapter I would invariably begin with something like: "Recent housing market collapses in the United States and, to a lesser extent on the United Kingdom, demonstrate how volatile house prices can be." But the Great Recession that began in 2007 is a poor choice to motivate the hedging behavior described in this chapter. The behavior described in this chapter hedges future price *increases*: households buy early to protect themselves against rising prices. But price volatility works in both directions. *Decreases* in house prices—as experienced in both the United States and the United Kingdom in the recent past—confront households with a completely different set of concerns. Many households held mortgages in excess of home values and foreclosures were widespread. For younger households that did not yet own a home the collapse of the housing market was a reminder that home ownership is probably the

---

3. Han (2013) does not expect a strong positive association between housing-price risk and the expected return. She argues that, if owning a home is a hedge against price risk, then owners will require lower returns to housing in high-volatility areas. This distorts the tight link between risk and return that one might expect to observe if housing were purely a financial asset. However, Case, Cotter, and Gabriel (2011) find evidence of a strong positive association between price risk and expected return for housing in a CAPM framework.

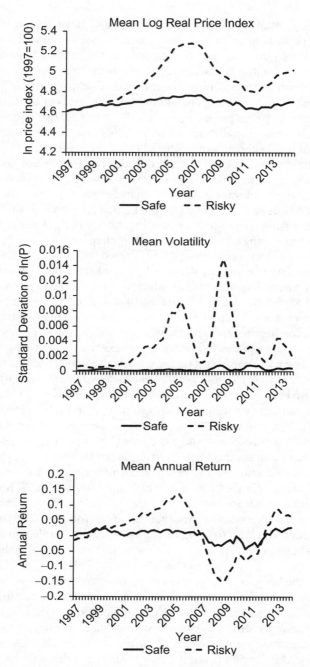

Fig. 3C.1   Price index, volatility, and expected return in high (risky) and low (safe) volatility states

most consequential investment decision they will make in their lifetime. In general, if households anticipate future house price *decreases*, then they are better off *waiting* to buy—just the opposite of the hedging behavior that is central to this chapter. If prices decline modestly, then homeowners suffer a financial loss (and a larger loss the earlier they get in), although they may still be able to match housing consumption to the needs of the housing ladder. However, extreme price declines resulting in negative equity, default, or foreclosure may actually prevent households from moving up the ladder and discourage ownership altogether. Thus the nature of house price risk seems to have changed over the last decade. The salience of recent price declines may make the hedging incentives that were prevalent prior to the Great Recession irrelevant today. The chapter uses data for 1980–1997 for the United States and 1991–2003 for the United Kingdom. It would be useful, in future work, to see if the recent experience in the United States has tempered the hedging effect observed in this chapter.

The strong association between house price volatility and several measures of housing demand for younger households is offered as evidence of hedging behavior. I agree with this interpretation for the two time intervals they consider for the United States and the United Kingdom. However, confidence in this interpretation of the empirical results can be strengthened by estimating the same specifications for subsamples of households for whom the hedging incentive is weak or nonexistent. For these subsamples, we expect a negative coefficient on the volatility variable since the traditional investment incentive to avoid risk is not offset by the incentive to hedge. If the estimated coefficient is positive, then the explanation for the positive association between volatility and housing demand must be something other than the hedging motive. The most obvious subsamples for this test are households without children and older households—both groups for whom the usual demographic incentive to upsize in the future do not apply. Hedging incentives are also likely to be less relevant for high-wealth households who hold more balanced wealth portfolios than low-wealth households. For these households the share of housing in total wealth is lower, so house price risk is better diversified. Another test of the robustness of the hedging interpretation would be to estimate the same models for declining housing markets where, as discussed above, there is no benefit to hedge by "buying in" early.

Finally, the hedging behavior described in this chapter arises because the usual mechanisms for hedging asset risk do not work for housing. In particular, homeowners cannot diversify regional house price risk by owning homes in many regions. The strength of the hedging behavior underscores the strong desire by homeowners to hedge price risk. But the self-hedge described in this chapter is not the only mechanism that can enable households to limit their exposure to house price volatility. One alternative mechanism is the use of publicly traded financial instruments designed to hedge exactly the type of risk considered in this chapter (see Case, Shiller, and Weiss 1993). In the United States, futures and options on the S&P Case-Shiller Home Price Index for ten MSA-level indices and the national index are traded on the CME. Another innovation is the availability of shared equity and shared ownership products in Australia and the United Kingdom (see Whitehead and Yates 2010). These products allow homeowners to diversify across regions by allowing the equity in a house to be shared by many owners. Caplin et al. (1997, 2007) discuss related proposals for housing partnerships and shared equity mortgages in the United States. An ongoing puzzle is why—given the need for households to limit their exposure to house price risk—that neither house price derivatives nor shared equity and similar arrangements have met with much success in the market. The findings of this chapter may provide a resolution to this puzzle. Households have little need for innovations marketed to help households limit risk exposure because they do a pretty good job of hedging house price volatility on their own.

References

Caplin, A., J. Carr, F. Pollock, and Z. Tong. 2007. *Shared-Equity Mortgages, Housing Affordability and Homeownership*, Washington, DC: Fannie Mae Foundation.

Caplin, A., S. Chan, C. Freeman, and J. Tracy. 1997. *Housing Partnerships: A New Approach to a Market at a Crossroads*. Cambridge, MA: MIT Press.

Case, Karl, John Cotter, and Stuart Gabriel. 2011. "Housing Risk and Return: Evidence from a Housing Asset-Pricing Model." *Journal of Portfolio Management* 35:89–109.

Case, Karl, Robert Shiller, and Andrew Weiss. 1993. "Index-Based Futures and Options Markets in Real Estate." *Journal of Portfolio Management* 19 (2): 83–92.

Droes, Martijn, and Wolter Hassink. 2013. "House Price Risk and the Hedging Benefits of Home Ownership." *Journal of Housing Economics* 22:92–99.

Han, Lu. 2013. "Understanding the Puzzling Risk-Return Relationship for Housing." *Review of Financial Studies* 26 (4): 877–928.

Sinai, Todd, and Nicholas Souleles. 2005. "Owner-Occupied Housing as a Hedge Against Rent Risk." *Quarterly Journal of Economics* 120 (2): 763–89.

———. 2013. "Can Owning a Home Hedge the Risk of Moving?" *American Economic Journal: Economic Policy* 5 (2): 282–312.

Whitehead, Christine, and Susan Yates. 2010. "Is There a Role for Shared Equity Products in Twenty-First Century Housing? Experience in Australia and the UK." In *The Blackwell Companion to the Economics of Housing: The Housing Wealth of Nations*, edited by S. J. Smith and B. A. Searle. Oxford: Wiley-Blackwell.

4

What Determines
End-of-Life Assets?
A Retrospective View

James M. Poterba, Steven F. Venti, and David A. Wise

Many individuals reach the end of life with limited financial assets. This chapter explores the determinants of asset balances at death by following respondents in the Health and Retirement Study (HRS) "backward" from the last wave prior to their death to the first wave in which they were observed. We first document the relationship between the assets in an individual's last year observed (LYO) before death and assets in the first year observed (FYO). We then estimate the effect of individual attributes, in particular health status and education, and changes in these attributes on the relationship between assets when first and last observed.

There is particular interest in the factors that lead some individuals to have very low wealth levels near the end of life. There are several pathways that can lead to this outcome. One is for an individual or household to enter retirement with modest or substantial assets, and then to experience

James M. Poterba is the Mitsui Professor of Economics at the Massachusetts Institute of Technology and president and chief executive officer of the National Bureau of Economic Research. Steven F. Venti holds the DeWalt H. Ankeny '21 and Marie Ankeny Professorship in Economic Policy and is professor of economics at Dartmouth College, and he is a research associate of the National Bureau of Economic Research. David A. Wise is the John F. Stambaugh Professor of Political Economy at the Kennedy School of Government at Harvard University. He is the area director of Health and Retirement Programs and director of the Program on the Economics of Aging at the National Bureau of Economic Research.

We are grateful to Brigitte Madrian for very helpful comments. This research was supported by the US Social Security Administration through grant no. RRC08098400–06 to the National Bureau of Economic Research as part of the SSA Retirement Research Consortium. Funding was also provided through grant no. P01 AG005842 from the National Institute on Aging. Poterba is a trustee of the College Retirement Equity Fund (CREF), a provider of retirement income services. The findings and conclusions expressed are solely those of the authors and do not represent the views of SSA, any agency of the federal government, TIAA-CREF, or the NBER. For acknowledgments, sources of research support, and disclosure of the authors' material financial relationships, if any, please see http://www.nber.org/chapters/c13629.ack.

unanticipated events that drain financial resources. For some individuals, the death of a spouse or divorce may result in a decline in wealth. For others, the costs associated with a health event such as a stroke or the onset of a chronic illness may lead to substantial reductions in assets. For still others, a decline in wealth may accompany a general decline in health, a pattern that is documented in Poterba, Venti, and Wise (2010) and a number of other studies.

A second pathway to low assets at death is to enter retirement with some accumulated assets, but to "outlive" them without extraordinary expenditures at any point during retirement. This explanation is most likely to apply to those in households in which one or both individuals lived longer than they expected to.

A third pathway to low assets at death is beginning the retirement period with low assets, the result of low or no saving before retirement. Individuals in households that enter retirement with very limited wealth are unlikely to have substantial wealth when they are last observed. For these individuals, low wealth at the end of life is not a manifestation of economic choices or events during retirement, but rather of events in the preretirement period.

Our aim is to assess these three alternative pathways in light of data on observed asset trajectories late in life. We motivate our analysis with a series of figures that follow the path of assets between the year when an individual is first, and the year when she is last, observed. These figures summarize the widely varying data on household balance sheets by presenting median assets. They are shown for individuals ages fifty-one to sixty-one in 1992 (the original HRS cohort) and those ages seventy and older in 1993 (the original AHEAD [Asset and Health Dynamics among the Oldest Old] cohort). We show separate figures to disaggregate the sample by education level and by family status. The figures generally show little difference between median assets when first and when last observed for those in the younger cohort, and only a modest decline in assets for those in the older cohort.

We then estimate regression models relating the change in assets between the first and last year when an individual is observed and various individual attributes, some fixed and some time varying. Simulations based on these estimates show relatively flat asset trajectories by age for those who do not experience a change in family composition or in health status. However, many individuals exhibit substantial asset declines in connection with important medical events or disruptions in family composition. The rate at which assets decline between the years when an individual is first and last observed is negatively related to the individual's education level.

This analysis is closely related to the findings we report (Poterba, Venti, and Wise 2012), which summarizes individuals' asset holdings in the last survey wave preceding their deaths. Banerjee (2015) presents similar findings. Rather than tracking all HRS respondents who die before 2012, as we do, he focuses on the HRS respondents who die between 2010 and 2012.

His results confirm the prevalence of low levels of assets in the years prior to death. Our findings in this chapter are also related to a much broader literature, surveyed by DeNardi, French, and Jones (2015), that seeks to identify factors affecting wealth accumulation and decumulation in retirement. Numerous studies have used the HRS to consider the effect of health and family disruptions on wealth. Coile and Milligan (2009), French et al. (2006), Lee and Kim (2007), Smith (1999, 2004, 2005), and Wu (2003), among others, estimate the effect of new health events on wealth or on other measures of socioeconomic status. These studies find that health events are an important source of variation in wealth. In related work, Sevak, Weir, and Willis (2003/2004), Johnson, Mermin, and Uccello (2006), and Coile and Milligan (2009) show that widowhood is associated with large reductions in wealth.

This chapter is divided into four sections. Section 4.1 describes the data used in the analysis. Section 4.2 shows how asset balances in the LYO compare to balances in the FYO. Section 4.3 presents the regression results that explore the individual attributes that are associated with changes in assets between the FYO and LYO. Section 4.4 summarizes our results and discusses future directions for research.

4.1 Data Description

Our analysis is based on two cohorts from the HRS—the original HRS cohort whose members were first surveyed in 1992 when they were between the ages of fifty-one and sixty-one, and the original Asset and Health Dynamics among the Oldest Old (AHEAD) cohort whose members were over the age of seventy when first surveyed in 1993. In both cohorts, we drop "age-ineligible" spouses (not age fifty-one to sixty-one in the HRS and not age seventy or older in the AHEAD). We also drop respondents who leave the sample for reasons other than death and we drop the 1992 wave of the HRS because of incomplete data for some variables. With one exception, respondents are surveyed biennially so we are able to use data for ten waves: 1994, 1996, 1998, 2000, 2002, 2004, 2006, 2008, 2010 and 2012 for the HRS cohort and 1993, 1995, 1998, 2000, 2002, 2004, 2006, 2008, 2010 and 2012 for the AHEAD cohort. We choose to use the 1993 AHEAD wave, despite concerns about understatement of wealth in that wave that have been raised by Rohwedder, Haider, and Hurd (2006), to maximize the sample size of our subsequent cohorts. In the figures we present below, the 1993 observations for the AHEAD sample do not seem substantially different from the 1995 values, which supports for including this sample wave.

For each respondent, there is a last year observed (LYO). If an individual is last observed prior to 2012, then the data for the LYO pertain to the last year observed prior to death. If the LYO is 2012, then the data are for a respondent who was alive when last observed. Respondents are surveyed approximately every two years, so for those who die within our sample period, the date at which assets are measured in the LYO may be as much as two years prior to the date of death. On average, it will be about one year prior to death. Because medical expenditures are often substantial in the last six months of life, asset balances observed in the last wave before death may overestimate assets at the time of death.

In principle, we could obtain more precise estimates of assets at the time of death from "exit interviews" administered to a surviving spouse, child, or other knowledgeable person after the death of a respondent. These exit interviews obtain information on the finances of the deceased in the period between the last core interview and the time of death. We have not used these data because exit interviews were not obtained for approximately 20 percent of deceased persons and key components of wealth are missing for many of the remaining 80 percent. Marshall, McGarry, and Skinner (2011), who study late-life medical expenses, use the exit interviews, imputing medical expenditures when necessary but also relying on the core interviews to obtain components of wealth. Since much of our analysis is based on a relatively small subsample of deceased persons, retaining as many of these observations as possible is a high priority. While in principle we could impute components of wealth for the missing and incomplete exit interviews, this approach could be unreliable given the small samples we are studying and the fact that mortality is correlated with individual attributes, making selection a substantial concern.

We define "assets" inclusive of home equity and the net value of other real estate, business assets, and financial assets. Individual retirement accounts and Keogh balances are included in financial assets, but assets in 401(k) plans are not included—401(k) assets were not collected for the AHEAD cohort and the data are incomplete in some years (in particular, 1994 to 1998) for the HRS cohort. This is not an important concern for members of the older AHEAD cohort because they were unlikely to have participated in 401(k) plans. These plans were first authorized in 1982 and did not become widespread until the late 1980s and early 1990s. They were largely unavailable to members of the AHEAD cohort who were age seventy or older in 1993. Members of the HRS cohort were more likely to work for an employer offering a 401(k) plan. Many 401(k) balances are rolled over into IRA accounts, especially when employees change employers. The portion of 401(k) balances not rolled over into an IRA at retirement is excluded from our measure of assets, as well as the capitalized value of annuity income from Social Security and defined-benefit (DB) pensions. The income from both Social Security and DB pensions is included in our definition of household income. All income streams and asset balances have been converted to 2012 dollars using the Consumer Price Index for All Urban Consumers (CPI-U).

Our unit of observation is the person, but the asset balance associated with each person is drawn from the household-asset balance. Some results are presented separately by family status pattern, distinguishing those who were continuously single, continuously married, or married to single. More details on how family status groups are defined, as well as on other aspects of the data are presented below.

4.2   Background and Descriptive Information

We begin by summarizing the distributions of assets when respondents are last observed and when they are first observed. As noted above, the interval between the first and last observation for a person can be as short as two years or as long as nineteen years. The tables below only consider the distribution of assets for deceased persons for whom the number of years between the LYO and the FYO is eight or more. Each table, and each associated figure, presents results separately for the HRS and AHEAD cohorts. To provide further insight on the financial circumstances of those with very low asset levels, we also report the joint distribution of assets in the LYO and annuity income in the LYO.

After summarizing the distributions, we provide additional detail on the prevalence of zero and negative asset balances when individuals are last observed and we present figures that provide more detail on asset trajectories by age, family status, and level of education. The tables focus exclusively on individuals who died within our sample period, but the figures include those who were still alive when last observed.

4.2.1   Summary Tabulations

Tables 4.1A and 4.1B show assets in the first year observed conditional on assets in the last year observed for all individuals who died during the sample period. We exclude all persons for whom the interval between the FYO and the LYO is fewer than eight years; for very short periods between FYO and LYO, a high correlation between the two is almost mechanical. Each table includes three panels. The top panel shows total nonannuity assets (defined to include housing wealth, financial assets, other real estate and business assets), the middle panel shows housing equity (including the net value of other real estate), and the bottom panel shows net financial assets (all nonhousing wealth). Table 4.1A considers all persons between the ages of fifty-one and sixty-one in 1992 (the HRS cohort), and table 4.1B considers all persons over the age of seventy in 1993 (the AHEAD cohort).

We first consider the results for total assets in the top panel of each table. The last column of each of these panels shows that a large fraction of persons die with minimal nonannuity assets. Among persons age fifty-one to sixty-one in 1992, 14.9 percent had nonannuity asset balances that were zero (or negative) just prior to death. Another 23 percent had positive asset balances of less than $50,000. Of persons age seventy and older in 1993,

Table 4.1A   Percentage of persons in each asset interval when first observed by asset interval in last wave prior to death, persons age fifty-one to sixty-one in 1992 (row percents)

Total assets

Total asset interval in LYO	Total asset interval in first year observed (1994)						Percent in each LYO interval
	≤ $0	$1–$50,000	$50,001–$100,000	$100,001–$250,000	$250,001–500,000	> $500,001	
≤ $0	**48.2**	30.8	7.5	7.5	3.8	2.3	14.9
$1–$50,000	21.4	**42.8**	16.8	16.1	2.4	0.5	23.0
$50,001–$100,000	2.0	20.8	**36.5**	34.7	4.0	2.1	9.4
$100,001–$250,000	1.5	9.5	20.8	**43.0**	20.3	4.9	20.9
$250,001–500,000	0.4	1.5	7.8	31.3	**43.8**	15.2	12.5
> $500,001	0.5	1.5	2.3	13.3	30.2	**52.1**	19.3
Percent in each FYO interval	12.8	18.9	14.2	23.6	17.0	13.6	

Housing equity

Housing equity interval in LYO	Housing equity interval in first year observed (1994)						Percent in each LYO interval
	≤ $0	$1–$50,000	$50,001–$100,000	$100,001–$250,000	$250,001–500,000	> $500,001	
≤ $0	**56.6**	16.6	10.3	12.8	2.7	1.0	28.4
$1–$50,000	18.9	**47.9**	21.7	8.0	2.3	1.2	14.6
$50,001–$100,000	3.2	20.3	**49.0**	23.1	4.4	0.0	15.0
$100,001–$250,000	5.1	9.5	24.5	**50.4**	8.3	2.3	25.4
$250,001–500,000	1.2	5.4	9.1	55.7	**20.3**	8.4	9.5
> $500,001	5.2	0.6	5.4	28.3	30.3	**30.2**	7.2
Percent in each FYO interval	21.1	17.7	20.9	28.3	8.0	4.0	

Financial assets

Financial asset interval in LYO	Financial asset interval in first year observed (1994)						Percent in each LYO interval
	≤ $0	$1–$50,000	$50,001–$100,000	$100,001–$250,000	$250,001–500,000	> $500,001	
≤ $0	**54.7**	34.6	4.8	3.3	1.7	0.7	27.7
$1–$50,000	24.8	**50.5**	11.9	9.4	2.3	1.1	36.4
$50,001–$100,000	4.8	46.1	**20.0**	18.2	8.0	2.9	6.8
$100,001–$250,000	1.4	20.7	17.1	**40.6**	13.2	7.1	11.1
$250,001–500,000	0.0	13.5	8.2	33.7	**35.3**	9.3	7.5
> $500,001	0.0	3.0	4.3	20.1	29.7	**42.9**	10.4
Percent in each FYO interval	24.7	34.8	10.0	14.7	9.1	6.8	

Note: Calculations exclude persons alive when last observed and persons for whom fewer than eight years elapsed between FYO and LYO.

13.3 percent had zero or negative nonannuity assets just prior to death and another 25.4 percent had positive balances below $50,000. The cell entries in each table show that for a large proportion of persons, nonannuity assets at death are similar in magnitude to the comparable assets when first observed. For example, for persons in the HRS cohort, 48.2 percent of those with zero

Table 4.1B   **Percentage of persons in each asset interval when first observed by asset interval in last wave prior to death, persons age seventy or older in 1993 (row percents)**

Total assets

Total asset interval in LYO	Total asset interval in first year observed (1993)						Percent in each LYO interval
	≤ $0	$1–$50,000	$50,001–$100,000	$100,001–$250,000	$250,001–500,000	> $500,001	
≤ $0	**28.7**	28.4	13.5	20.9	6.8	1.7	13.3
$1–$50,000	10.0	**39.0**	17.9	22.4	6.4	4.4	25.4
$50,001–$100,000	2.6	15.4	**30.7**	36.9	9.7	4.7	10.8
$100,001–$250,000	1.2	5.9	13.1	**49.2**	23.2	7.5	18.0
$250,001–500,000	0.5	2.5	2.9	31.8	**40.4**	21.9	15.6
> $500,001	0.0	1.2	1.2	15.3	30.6	**51.8**	17.1
Percent in each FYO interval	6.9	17.0	12.7	28.8	19.3	15.4	

Housing equity

Housing equity interval in LYO	Housing equity interval in first year observed (1993)						Percent in each LYO interval
	≤ $0	$1–$50,000	$50,001–$100,000	$100,001–$250,000	$250,001–500,000	> $500,001	
≤ $0	**37.6**	11.7	16.0	25.0	6.7	3.0	47.4
$1–$50,000	6.7	**39.9**	27.9	17.7	6.4	1.4	8.1
$50,001–$100,000	4.4	14.4	**45.1**	30.6	4.4	1.1	12.4
$100,001–$250,000	2.2	2.9	14.8	**65.7**	11.3	3.2	19.4
$250,001–500,000	3.8	0.6	3.6	41.6	**39.5**	10.9	8.6
> $500,001	0.0	0.0	1.4	16.9	27.6	**54.2**	4.1
Percent in each FYO interval	19.6	11.2	18.7	34.1	10.9	5.5	

Financial assets

Financial asset interval in LYO	Financial asset interval in first year observed (1993)						Percent in each LYO interval
	≤ $0	$1–$50,000	$50,001–$100,000	$100,001–$250,000	$250,001–500,000	> $500,001	
≤ $0	**42.2**	42.4	6.9	5.5	1.9	1.1	19.1
$1–$50,000	19.0	**55.3**	12.1	9.0	3.1	1.5	38.8
$50,001–$100,000	4.7	33.7	**21.6**	23.6	10.3	6.0	9.0
$100,001–$250,000	6.6	32.5	15.3	**28.1**	13.0	4.5	13.5
$250,001–500,000	2.9	26.2	9.7	29.6	**18.9**	12.7	9.1
> $500,001	5.2	13.8	11.8	18.4	22.5	**28.3**	10.5
Percent in each FYO interval	17.6	40.8	12.2	15.1	8.3	6.1	

Note: Calculations exclude persons alive when last observed and persons for whom fewer than eight years elapsed between FYO and LYO.

or negative wealth when last observed had zero or negative wealth when first observed in 1994. A larger subset of this group, 79 percent, had less than $50,000 when first observed. Of those with greater than $500,000 when last observed, 52.1 percent had $500,000 or more when first observed and 82.3 percent had greater than $250,000 when first observed. Similar patterns can be seen in table 4.1B for persons age seventy and older in 1993. These tables suggest that for most individuals, nonannuity assets at death are not so different from nonannuity assets when first observed. This is true both for those who were between fifty-one and sixty-one in 1992 and those who were age seventy or older in 1993. A large fraction of persons with meager assets at death also had limited assets when first observed. Most of those with substantial assets at death also had substantial assets when first observed.

These comparisons are more striking if estimates along the diagonal (in bold) are combined with the estimates to the left and to the right of the diagonal element. For example, of HRS persons with assets in the $1–$50,000 interval in the LYO, 42.8 percent were in the same interval in the FYO, but 81 (= 21.4 + 42.8 + 16.8) percent are in this interval or in the intervals to the left and right of this interval, that is, 81 percent had assets of less than $100,000 in the FYO. Thus, of persons who had positive assets of less than $50,000 in the LYO, only 19 percent had assets more than $100,000 in the FYO. A similar calculation reveals that of the persons who had zero (or negative) assets when last observed, only 16.5 percent had more than $100,000 in assets when first observed.

The bottom two panels of each table show the distributions of housing and financial assets, respectively. For both the HRS and the AHEAD cohorts, the relationship between housing equity in the LYO and the FYO are very similar to the relationship for total assets. The same is true for financial assets. Persons with low housing wealth in the LYO also tend to have low housing wealth when first observed. For example, of those in the HRS cohort who had housing assets in the $1–$50,000 interval in the LYO, 88.5 percent had housing wealth less than $100,000 when first observed. For the AHEAD cohort, the comparable statistic is 74.5 percent. The corresponding values for persons with positive financial wealth of less than $50,000 in the LYO are 87.2 percent for the HRS cohort, and 86.4 percent for the AHEAD cohort. The factors that lead some individuals with less than $100,000 in financial assets when first observed to report significantly higher assets when last observed warrants further exploration.

The row percentages in tables 4.1A and 4.1B show the probability of being in a given asset interval in the FYO given the level of assets in the LYO. Tables 4.2A and 4.2B present the same underlying data in a different way, by reporting the probability of being in a given asset interval in the last year observed conditional on the level of assets in the first year observed. As in the previous tables, results are only shown for those for whom the interval between the FYO and the LYO is eight or more years. The results once again suggest a great deal of persistence: those who have substantial assets when first observed also tend to have substantial assets when last observed prior to death. For both age groups, over 55 percent of those with zero or negative total assets in the FYO also have zero or negative total assets in the LYO. For the younger age cohort, 73.8 percent of persons in the top total asset interval

Table 4.2A **Percentage of persons in each asset interval in last wave prior to death by total asset interval when first observed, persons age fifty-one to sixty-one in 1992 (column percents)**

Total assets

Total asset interval in LYO	Total asset interval in first year observed (1994)						Percent in each LYO interval
	≤ $0	$1–$50,000	$50,001–$100,000	$100,001–$250,000	$250,001–500,000	> $500,001	
≤ $0	**56.3**	24.3	7.9	4.8	3.3	2.5	14.9
$1–$50,000	38.7	**52.3**	27.3	15.7	3.3	0.8	23.0
$50,001–$100,000	1.5	10.4	**24.1**	13.8	2.2	1.5	9.4
$100,001–$250,000	2.5	10.6	30.7	**38.2**	24.9	7.6	20.9
$250,001–500,000	0.4	1.0	6.9	16.6	**32.2**	13.9	12.5
> $500,001	0.7	1.6	3.1	10.9	34.2	**73.8**	19.3
Percent in each FYO interval	12.8	18.9	14.2	23.6	17.0	13.6	

Housing equity

Housing equity interval in LYO	Housing equity interval in first year observed (1994)						Percent in each LYO interval
	≤ $0	$1–$50,000	$50,001–$100,000	$100,001–$250,000	$250,001–500,000	> $500,001	
≤ $0	**76.2**	26.6	14.0	12.8	9.6	7.1	28.4
$1–$50,000	13.1	**39.5**	15.2	4.1	4.3	4.5	14.6
$50,001–$100,000	2.3	17.2	**35.1**	12.2	8.3	0.0	15.0
$100,001–$250,000	6.1	13.6	29.7	**45.1**	26.5	14.7	25.4
$250,001–500,000	0.5	2.9	4.1	18.6	**24.1**	19.8	9.5
> $500,001	1.8	0.2	1.9	7.2	27.2	**54.0**	7.2
Percent in each FYO interval	21.1	17.7	20.9	28.3	8.0	4.0	

Financial assets

Financial asset interval in LYO	Financial asset interval in first year observed (1994)						Percent in each LYO interval
	≤ $0	$1–$50,000	$50,001–$100,000	$100,001–$250,000	$250,001–500,000	> $500,001	
≤ $0	**61.5**	27.6	13.4	6.3	5.3	3.1	27.7
$1–$50,000	36.6	**52.9**	43.3	23.3	9.3	5.8	36.4
$50,001–$100,000	1.3	9.0	**13.6**	8.4	6.0	2.9	6.8
$100,001–$250,000	0.6	6.6	19.0	**30.6**	16.1	11.7	11.1
$250,001–500,000	0.0	2.9	6.2	17.2	**29.3**	10.4	7.5
> $500,001	0.0	0.9	4.5	14.2	34.1	**66.2**	10.4
Percent in each FYO interval	24.7	34.8	10.0	14.7	9.1	6.8	

Note: Calculations exclude persons alive when last observed and persons for whom fewer than eight years elapsed between FYO and LYO.

Table 4.2B   **Percentage of persons in each asset interval in last wave prior to death by total asset interval when first observed, persons age seventy or older in 1993 (column percents)**

Total assets

Total asset interval in LYO	Total asset interval in first year observed (1993)						Percent in each LYO interval
	≤ $0	$1–$50,000	$50,001–$100,000	$100,001–$250,000	$250,001–500,000	> $500,001	
≤ $0	**55.2**	22.2	14.2	9.7	4.7	1.4	13.3
$1–$50,000	36.7	**58.3**	36.0	19.7	8.5	7.2	25.4
$50,001–$100,000	4.0	9.8	**26.1**	13.8	5.4	3.3	10.8
$100,001–$250,000	3.1	6.3	18.6	**30.7**	21.6	8.7	18.0
$250,001–500,000	1.1	2.3	3.6	17.2	**32.7**	22.2	15.6
> $500,001	0.0	1.2	1.6	9.0	27.1	**57.3**	17.1
Percent in each FYO interval	6.9	17.0	12.7	28.8	19.3	15.4	

Housing equity

Housing equity interval in LYO	Housing equity interval in first year observed (1993)						Percent in each LYO interval
	≤ $0	$1–$50,000	$50,001–$100,000	$100,001–$250,000	$250,001–500,000	> $500,001	
≤ $0	**90.7**	49.7	40.6	34.8	29.0	26.3	
$1–$50,000	2.8	**29.0**	12.2	4.2	4.8	2.1	8.1
$50,001–$100,000	2.8	15.9	**29.9**	11.1	5.0	2.6	12.4
$100,001–$250,000	2.2	5.0	15.4	**37.4**	20.0	11.2	19.4
$250,001–500,000	1.6	0.5	1.7	10.4	**30.9**	17.0	8.6
> $500,001	0.0	0.0	0.3	2.1	10.4	**40.9**	4.1
Percent in each FYO interval	19.6	11.2	18.7	34.1	10.9	5.5	

Financial assets

Financial asset interval in LYO	Financial asset interval in first year observed (1993)						Percent in each LYO interval
	≤ $0	$1–$50,000	$50,001–$100,000	$100,001–$250,000	$250,001–500,000	> $500,001	
≤ $0	**45.9**	19.8	10.9	7.0	4.4	3.5	19.1
$1–$50,000	42.0	**52.7**	38.6	23.1	14.4	9.7	38.8
$50,001–$100,000	2.4	7.4	**16.0**	14.1	11.1	8.9	9.0
$100,001–$250,000	5.1	10.7	17.0	**25.1**	21.1	9.9	13.5
$250,001–500,000	1.5	5.9	7.3	17.9	**20.7**	19.1	9.1
> $500,001	3.1	3.5	10.2	12.8	28.3	**48.9**	10.5
Percent in each FYO interval	17.6	40.8	12.2	15.1	8.3	6.1	

Note: Calculations exclude persons alive when last observed and persons for whom fewer than eight years elapsed between FYO and LYO.

(> $500,000) in the FYO are also in the top total asset interval in the LYO. In the older cohort, persistence in the top total asset interval is somewhat lower: only 57.3 percent of those in this interval when first observed were also there when last observed.

The relationships between assets when first and last observed are similar for housing wealth and for financial wealth. In the HRS cohort, 76.2 percent of persons with zero or negative housing wealth in the FYO had zero or negative housing wealth in the LYO. For the AHEAD cohort, this statistic is 90.7 percent. For persons in the $250–500,000 housing wealth interval in the FYO, only 24.1 percent of the HRS sample, and 30.9 percent of the AHEAD sample, had housing wealth in this interval when last observed, and most had less.

Financial assets also tend to decline between the first and last years observed. In the HRS cohort, 61.5 percent of persons with zero or negative financial assets in the FYO also had zero or negative assets in the LYO. Only 29.3 percent of persons with assets in the $250–500,000 interval had assets in this interval in the LYO; 34.1 percent had more and 36.7 percent less. For the AHEAD cohort, 45.9 percent of those with zero or negative financial assets in the FYO also has zero or negative assets in the LYO, and only 20.7 percent of those with assets in $250–500,000 interval in the FYO had assets in this interval in the LYO. For this group, 28.3 percent had more and 51.0 percent had less financial assets in the LYO. The data suggest a general tendency for both housing wealth and financial wealth to decline modestly between the FYO and the LYO for both the HRS and the AHEAD cohorts.

To provide a simple way to visualize the mobility patterns across the asset intervals in tables 4.2A and 4.2B, figures 4.1A and 4.1B show the percentage of individuals who are in each FYO interval who moved to a higher interval, dropped to a lower interval, or stayed in the same interval when they were last observed. For both the lowest and the highest interval the chart is of limited interest, but for individuals whose asset holdings place them in one of the four middle categories, the graph shows the pattern of mobility. The contrast between the two figures illustrates the greater likelihood of individuals in the AHEAD sample, who are older than those in the HRS sample, moving to a lower asset interval when last observed than when first observed. Both figures illustrate that for those in the lowest asset category when first observed, the probability of being observed at a similarly low level of assets when last observed is very high.

To highlight those individuals who reach the end of life with very few assets, table 4.3 provides further information on asset trajectories for those who have positive, zero, and negative asset balances in the LYO before death. Negative asset balances just prior to death are common, particularly for those in the younger cohort. The primary source of negative wealth is consumer debt, which typically consists of credit card debt, medical debt, or life insurance policy loans. A substantial fraction of the individuals who died with negative assets died before the Great Recession, and the house-price decline in 2008 and 2009 may have increased the number of older individuals with negative asset positions.

Table 4.3 shows that the members of the older cohort are much less

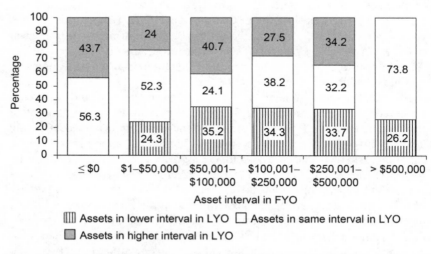

Fig. 4.1A   Percentage of persons with assets in LYO that were more/same/less than assets in FYO, by asset interval in FYO, persons age fifty-one to sixty-one in 1992

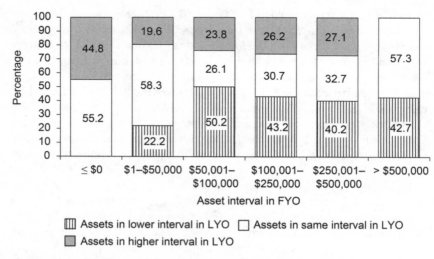

Fig. 4.1B   Percentage of persons with assets in LYO that were more/same/less than assets in FYO, by asset interval in FYO, persons age seventy or older in 1993

Table 4.3 **Summary of asset balances in the LYO, noting zero and negative assets balances, for the HRS and AHEAD cohorts**

Assets in last year observed	Percent of persons	Mean assets in LYO	Median assets in LYO	Percent with negative consumer debt	Percent with negative housing debt	Percent with zero home equity
		Persons age 51 to 61 in 1992				
<$0	7.0	–$25,661	–$6,375	95.3	8.7	82.9
$0	7.9	$0	$0	0.0	0.0	100.0
>$0	85.1	$474,840	$153,770	26.3	0.3	17.2
		Persons age 70 or older in 1993				
<$0	1.8	–$8,615	–$2,310	97.0	3.0	97.0
$0	11.5	$0	$0	0.0	0.0	100.0
>$0	86.7	$357,845	$145,900	6.3	0.2	41.6

Note: A small number of persons hold negative positions in financial assets. Calculations exclude persons alive when last observed and persons for whom fewer than eight years elapsed between FYO and LYO.

likely than those in the younger cohort to have negative asset balances in the LYO—1.8 percent versus 7.0 percent. A substantial proportion in both cohorts, 7.9 percent for HRS and 11.5 percent for AHEAD, also have zero balances. The table also reports mean assets for those with negative, and with positive, net assets. For the 7 percent of the HRS sample that appears to have negative net assets when last observed, the average net assets, –$25,661, is substantially lower than the median (–$6,375). For the older AHEAD sample, only 1.8 percent of sample shows negative net assets when last observed, and the mean and median are much closer to zero.

For individuals who report very low levels of nonannuity assets, their economic well-being depends critically on their annuity income and their access to insurance that can provide support in the event of medical or other emergencies. We provide some information on the income profile for these individuals by cross-tabulating their annuity income in the last year observed by their total nonannuity assets in the same year. Both assets and income are in 2012 dollars (see table 4.4).

The results suggest that among individuals with zero or negative total assets in the year last observed, 36.8 percent have less than $10,000 of annuity income and 85.1 percent have less than $20,000 of annuity income. By comparison, only 6.9 percent of those with more than $500,000 in total assets have annuity income of less than $10,000, and 25.6 percent have an annual annuity income of more than $40,000.

4.2.2 Asset Trajectories

To provide more information on the evolution of assets between the year first observed and the year last observed, we present figures with the median nonannuity assets in each survey wave for respondents stratified by their last year observed. The LYO for each profile is easily identified by the most

Table 4.4   Percentage of persons in each annuity income interval in last wave prior to death by total asset interval in last wave prior to death, persons age seventy or older in 1993 (row percents sum to 100)

Total asset interval in LYO	Annuity income interval in LYO					Percent in LYO interval
	< $10,000	$10,000–$20,000	$20,000–$30,000	$30,000–$40,000	> $40,000	
≤ $0	36.8	48.3	9.4	3.3	2.1	13.3
$1–$50,000	23.5	48.1	18.4	5.7	4.2	25.4
$50,001–$100,000	16.5	46.6	22.5	9.3	5.1	10.8
$100,001–$250,000	9.8	41.2	24.3	16.0	8.6	18.0
$250,001–500,000	6.2	30.6	31.8	14.1	17.3	15.6
> $500,001	6.9	27.4	23.2	16.9	25.6	17.1

Note: Calculations exclude persons alive when last observed and persons for whom fewer than eight years elapsed between FYO and LYO.

recent year for which assets are graphed. Thus the top profile in each panel shows median assets in 2012 and all prior years for all persons whose LYO is 2012. Another profile shows assets in 2010 and all prior years for all persons whose LYO is 2010, and so forth. Our analysis is "backward looking" in the sense that we classify respondents by the last time we observe them, and then examine their survey responses in earlier years.

The top two panels in figure 4.2 show the assets in each year by the LYO for persons who were age fifty-one to fifty-five and age fifty-six to sixty-one in 1992. We draw attention to several features of the data. First, for persons last observed before 2012 (these persons were all deceased after the LYO) the median asset profiles indicate little change in median assets between 1994 and the LYO. Second, for persons last observed before 2012, there appears to be no relationship between assets and mortality, as indicated by the absence of vertical gaps between the profiles. The median assets for those who died earlier are comparable to the median assets for those who died later. While a "mortality gradient," with lower mortality rates for those with higher income and wealth, has been widely documented, our focus on medians by LYO group may confound this relationship. Moreover, a strong relationship between assets and mortality emerges if the group still living in 2012 (the uppermost profile) is considered. Persons who die after 2012 have much more wealth, both when first observed in 1994 and when last observed in 2012, than persons who died prior to 2012. For the group still living in 2012, there is some evidence of asset decline over the sample period, but it is difficult to disentangle age-related drawdown of assets from year-related changes in asset values as contributory factors for this pattern. In both figures the decline in assets coincides with the Great Recession of 2007–2008.

The bottom two panels of figure 4.2 show median asset profiles for two

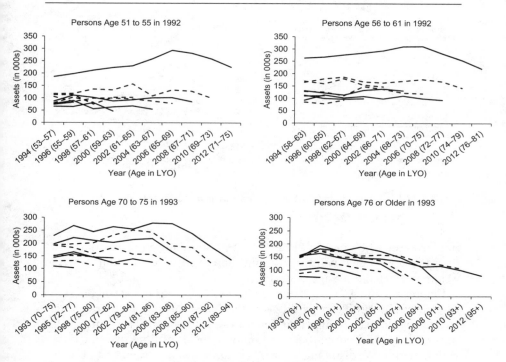

Fig. 4.2   Median assets (in 000s) in each year by last year observed

older age groups from the AHEAD cohort. Relative to the groups from the HRS cohort, these profiles show stronger evidence of asset decline approaching end of life, but again the decline coincides with the Great Recession. There is also some evidence of a positive asset-mortality relationship for both older groups. There is, however, one notable exception to this pattern: for those age seventy-six and older, the group still living in 2012 does not appear to be wealthier than several of the groups that predeceased them.

Figure 4.3 is based on the same data as figure 4.2, but it combines all persons in the top two panels of figure 4.2 and all persons in the bottom two panels of figure 4.2, and then distinguishes persons by level of education. The black lines pertain to persons with more than a high school education and the gray lines are for those with less than a high school education. There is a very substantial difference in the initial nonannuity wealth of the two education groups. Among those ages fifty-one to sixty-one in 1992 with less than a high school degree, those who are still living in 2012 clearly have more wealth than those who died before 2012, but among those who died before 2012 there appears to be little relationship between age of death and wealth in 1994. For this group, wealth at death is approximately the same as wealth in 1994. For those with more than a high school education, the pattern is

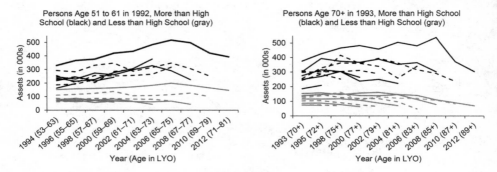

Fig. 4.3   Median assets (in 000s) in each year by last year observed and level of education

similar: those who were alive in 2012 had substantially more wealth in 1994 than those who died before 2012, but there is little relationship between wealth in 1994 and the age of death.

Figures 4.2 and 4.3 do not distinguish married from single persons, even though wealth profiles may differ by marital status and may be strongly affected by changes in this status. Figure 4.4 shows separate asset profiles for persons that experienced different family status transitions over the observation period. We distinguish persons who were single when first observed in the HRS or AHEAD and single when last observed (1→1), persons who were in a two-person household when first observed but single when last observed (2→1), and persons who were in a two-person household when first observed and in a two-person household when last observed (2→2). A fourth group—persons single when first observed and in a two-person household when last observed—was too small for meaningful analysis. The top two panels show data for persons age fifty-one to sixty-one in 1992; the left panel shows data for the 1→1 and the 2→2 groups and the right panel shows data for persons in the 2→1 group. The 1→1 group has the lowest level of assets and for this group there is little difference between assets in 1994 and assets when last observed. The 2→2 group has the highest level of assets and for this group assets in the LYO tend to be larger than assets in 1994. The assets of the 2→1 group are the most dispersed in the LYO and in most but not all cases the level of assets in the LYO tends to be similar to that when first observed.

Profiles for the persons who were over the age of seventy in 1993 are shown in the bottom two panels of figure 4.4. The left panel shows profiles for the 1→1 group, for which assets tend to decline with age. The data show a pronounced relationship between wealth and mortality, with those with more wealth in 1993 living longer. The 2→2 group also shows a substantial wealth-mortality relationship. The profiles show that for persons who

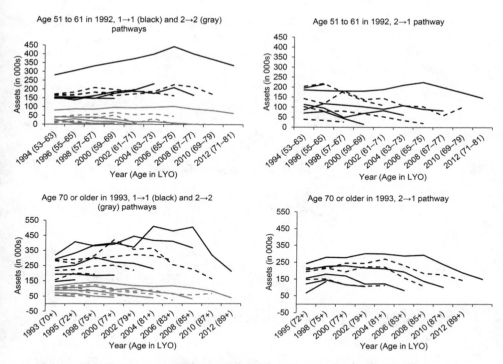

Fig. 4.4   Median assets (in 000s) in each year by last year observed and family status pathway

remain married until their death, median assets in the year last observed are similar to median assets in 1993 for those with an LYO of 2006 or earlier. For those with an LYO of 2008, 2010, or 2012, the profiles for the 2→2 group show a substantial increase in wealth until about six years before the LYO and then a decline. The median asset profiles for the 2→1 group exhibit a strong wealth-mortality relationship, and for all LYO groups, assets when last observed are lower than assets in 1993.

4.3   Regression Estimates

To complement the tabular and graphical analysis of asset profiles, we estimate regression models that describe the relationship between assets when first and last observed. We do this using data on individuals in both the HRS and AHEAD samples. To motivate our estimating equation, figures 4.5A and 4.5B plot the relationship between assets in the first and last year observed for persons between the ages of fifty-one and sixty-one in 1992. There are many outliers in the data; many are probably reporting errors.

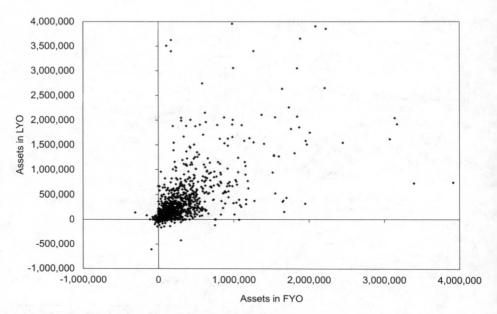

Fig. 4.5A   Assets in LYO by assets in FYO, with axis truncated at $4,000,000

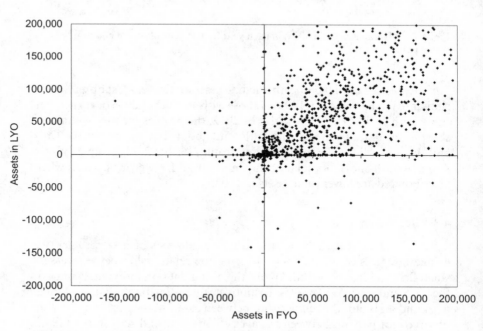

Fig. 4.5B   Assets in LYO by assets in FYO, with axis truncated at $200,000

In figure 4.5A, asset balances are truncated at \$4,000,000. In figure 4.5B, the truncation is at \$200,000. The figures show that there are many negative asset balances in both the FYO and in the LYO.

To minimize the effect of outliers, we estimate regression models in which the dependent variable is the natural logarithm of net worth. The presence of zero and negative asset balances poses an obvious problem for such a specification. We experimented with various transformations of the data that would enable us to use the negative values, but ultimately settled on carrying out our estimation using only the observations with positive values of assets in both the FYO and the LYO. These are the observations in the upper-right quadrants of both figures. For the sample ages fifty-one to sixty-one in 1992, this restriction limits us to 77 percent of the individuals who have data on assets holdings in both the first and last year observed. For the older AHEAD sample, it limits us to 81 percent of the sample. It is difficult to assess the effect of these exclusions on our results. One simple test is to estimate models based on asset *levels* and to compare results for the full sample to results from the subsample that conditions on positive values of assets in both the FYO and the LYO.

Table 4.5 shows the results of estimating a bivariate regression specification relating assets in the last year observed to assets in the first year observed, using a trimmed data sample.

$$\text{Assets}_{LYO} = \alpha + \beta \text{Assets}_{FYO} + \varepsilon.$$

In table 4.5, and in all subsequent tables, we first estimate the regression model for the full sample and we order the residuals. Then, we delete the observations corresponding to the top and bottom 3 percent of the residuals, and we reestimate the equation. The resulting estimates are presented in the table.

The estimate of the coefficient on assets when first observed (β) changes very little when the negative and zero asset values are excluded. The intercept term for the level of assets, not surprisingly, is affected by this sample limitation. This finding gives us some confidence that a model specified in logs may not be appreciably affected by the exclusion of observations with zero or negative asset balances.

To estimate the effect of personal attributes, in particular health, family status, and education on assets when last observed, conditional on assets when first observed, we postulate a simple log-log model linking assets in the LYO and the FYO, and allow for log-linear relationships between assets in the LYO and the other covariates. The log-log specification for assets in the FYO implies that a 1 percent change in assets in the FYO will lead to a constant percentage change in assets in the LYO. The log-linear specification implies that a unit change in each of the covariates leads to a constant percentage change in assets in the LYO. The specification is:

$$LN(\text{Assets}_{LYO}) = \alpha + \beta LN(\text{Assets}_{LYO}) + d_1(\text{Years Since FYO})$$
$$+ d_2(\text{Age in FYO}) + h_1(\text{Cancer}) + h_2(\text{Heart Problems})$$
$$+ h_3(\text{Stroke}) + h_4(\text{Lung Disease})$$
$$+ h_5(\text{Psychological Problems}) + h_6(\text{Diabetes})$$
$$+ e_1(\text{High School}) + e_2(\text{Some College})$$
$$+ e_3(\text{College or More}) + p_1(\text{Path:2 to 2})$$
$$+ p_1(\text{Path:1 to 1}) + \mu$$

We describe the covariates included in this equation in more detail when we discuss the estimates below. Note that this regression framework is focused on the conditional mean of the natural log of assets when last observed, in contrast with the figures in the last section, which emphasized conditional medians.

Estimates of this equation are shown in table 4.6 for persons age fifty-one to sixty-one in 1992 and persons age seventy and older in 1993. For each age group, we present three specifications. The first includes only the log of assets in the FYO, the second also includes other covariates, and the third includes the other covariates and year effects. The year effects are included to absorb changes in wealth that may result from economy-wide shocks, such as the financial crisis and associated drop in house and stock prices in 2008.

The estimates are based only on individuals who are known to be deceased by the end of the sample. Those who are still alive when last observed in the 2012 wave of the HRS and those who left the sample but are not known to be deceased, are excluded. In the specification with no covariates, the estimates of α indicate the log of assets in the LYO if a person had one dollar of assets in the FYO. The estimates of β indicate the fraction of the log of assets in the FYO that are carried over to the LYO. In the specifications

| Table 4.5 | Estimates of the relationship between the level of assets in the LYO and the level of assets in the FYO for the full and restricted samples, for persons age fifty-one to sixty-one in 1992, persons age seventy and older in 1993 |

	β	t-statistic	α	t-statistic
Persons 51 to 61 in 1992				
Full sample	1.085	85.2	11,677	2.3
Positive asset subsample	1.097	69.1	21,601	3.0
Persons 70 and older in 1993				
Full sample	0.964	92.0	18,714	5.4
Positive asset subsample	0.956	73.7	35,293	7.4

Table 4.6   Personal attributes associated with the change in assets between first and last year observed (dependent variable is log of assets in last year observed)

Variable	Age 51 to 61 in 1992						Age 70 or older in 1993					
	Coefficient	t-stat	Coefficient	t-stat	Coefficient	t-stat	Coefficient	t-stat	Coefficient	t-stat	Coefficient	t-stat
Log(assets in FYO)	0.947	54.98	0.873	46.24	0.873	46.71	0.912	73.89	0.856	64.14	0.855	64.15
Years since FYO			0.006	0.93					-0.032	-6.00		
Age in FYO			0.006	0.73	0.007	0.84			-0.008	-2.07	-0.008	-2.06
Health in FYO			0.003	2.70	0.003	2.85			0.002	2.73	0.002	2.34
Cancer			-0.023	-0.39	-0.031	-0.52			0.052	0.93	0.064	1.14
Heart problems			-0.050	-0.81	-0.041	-0.67			0.092	1.89	0.063	1.29
Stroke			-0.284	-3.85	-0.270	-3.65			-0.069	-1.34	-0.072	-1.41
Lung disease			-0.224	-3.17	-0.212	-3.02			-0.002	-0.02	-0.006	-0.10
Psychological problems			-0.253	-3.49	-0.266	-3.68			-0.214	-3.77	-0.240	-4.23
Diabetes			0.008	0.12	0.014	0.21			-0.176	-2.53	-0.134	-1.91
High school degree			0.196	3.01	0.191	2.95			0.127	2.69	0.134	2.82
Some college			0.252	3.25	0.241	3.11			0.289	4.98	0.262	4.53
College or more			0.413	4.80	0.396	4.60			0.406	6.20	0.397	6.08
2→2 pathway			0.298	3.59	-0.042	-0.44			0.394	6.71	0.056	0.98
1→1 pathway			-0.048	-0.50	0.285	3.45			0.058	1.02	0.386	6.58
1998					0.025	0.23					-0.065	-1.00
2000					-0.159	-1.48					-0.062	-0.93
2002					0.139	1.22					-0.048	-0.66
2004					0.096	0.86					-0.204	-2.64
2006					0.150	1.35					-0.533	-6.47
2008					0.049	0.46					-0.301	-3.59
2010					0.007	0.07					-0.350	-3.47
Constant	0.594	2.87	1.014	4.34	1.035	4.36	0.842	5.73	1.415	8.43	1.364	8.10
R^2	0.7019		0.7201		0.7215		0.606		0.6232		0.6245	
N	1,286		1,285		1,285		3,549		3,550		3,548	

Notes: Sample excludes all persons who were alive when last observed. The variable "age in LYO" is the number of years over the age of fifty-three in the LYO for the age fifty-one to sixty-one group and the number of years over the age of seventy for the age seventy or older group.

without covariates, the coefficient on assets in the FYO (β) is lower for the seventy and older group than for the fifty-one to sixty-one group, a finding that is consistent with the patterns observed in figures 4.1 to 4.3.

In the specifications with covariates, the variable *Years since FYO* is the number of years elapsed between the FYO and the LYO. The variable *Age in FYO* is the number of years over the age of fifty-three in the FYO for the fifty-one to sixty-one age group and the number of years over the age of seventy for the age seventy or older group. The next seven variables are intended to capture the effect of health on the change in assets between the FYO and the LYO. The first variable, *Health in FYO*, is the value of a per-centile health index in the FYO. This index, described in Poterba, Venti, and Wise (2013), is constructed from twenty-seven health-related questions in the HRS and is scaled to range from 1 (lowest) to 100 (highest). The next six variables are indicator variables for the onset of particular health conditions between the FYO and the LYO. For married persons, these variables are set to 1 if the health condition is reported for either partner. There are three indicator variables for level of education (less than a high school degree is the excluded category) and two indicator variables for family status pathway (the 2→1 category is excluded).

The estimates of the coefficients on the health-related variables suggest important links between health shocks and the late-life evolution of assets. For both age groups, the overall level of health in the FYO has a statisti-cally significant effect on assets when last observed. For the younger group, the coefficient of 0.003 implies that an improvement in health that moves an individual up by 10 percentiles in the FYO is associated with an increase of approximately 3 percent in assets in the LYO. For the younger group, a stroke, the onset of lung disease, and the onset of psychological problems are all associated with substantial reductions (approximately 25 percent) in assets in the LYO. For the older group, the onset of psychological prob-lems and of diabetes are both associated with declines in assets in the last year observed. The relationship between education and assets in the LYO is strong, even conditional on assets in the FYO. The education estimates for the younger and older groups are similar, with the effect of having received a college degree larger than the effect of having attended some college, which in turn is larger than the estimated effect of a high school degree. On average, persons in the 2→2 family status pathway group have assets in LYO that are 30 to 40 percent higher than those of persons in other pathways.

The final set of estimates for each age group adds year effects for the last year observed (1996 is the excluded year). The variable *Years since FYO* is deleted from this specification to allow estimation of the full set of age effects. The estimates of the coefficients on the covariates are essentially unchanged when the year effects are added. This suggests that the covariate estimates are not picking up macro shocks associated with the financial crisis. For the younger group, for most years we cannot reject the null hypothesis that the coefficient on the year effect is zero. For the older group, the estimates for 2004 through 2010 are all negative and we can reject the null hypothesis of zero coefficients. The magnitudes are large: older persons last observed in these years held between 20 to 50 percent less assets than individuals with similar characteristics who were last observed in 1996.

Table 4.7 shows separate estimates of the regression model by family status pathway for persons fifty-one to sixty-one in 1992 and table 4.8 shows estimates by family status pathway for persons seventy and older in 1993. Both tables show results with and without covariates, excluding year effects. The sample size for the 2→1 pathway group for the HRS (fifty-one to sixty-one) group is quite small and many of the estimates are not significantly different from zero. For the 2→2 group the indicator variables for the onset of lung disease, psychological problems, and stroke have the greatest negative effect on assets in LYO given assets in FYO. For the 1→1 group the most consequential conditions for assets in the LYO are psychological problems, heart problems, and stroke. The general health index level when first observed is associated with higher LYO assets in both the 1→1 and the 2→1 groups, but not for the 2→2 group. This may be because married couples are more financially resilient in the face of health challenges, because one spouse can take actions, such as providing care at older ages or increasing labor supply at younger ages, to offset the adverse financial effects of a health shock. For the 2→2 and the 1→1 groups the education estimates are large; for the 2→2 group they are also precisely measured.

Table 4.8 shows estimates by family status pathway for the age seventy and older group. The sample sizes are much larger than the sample sizes for the fifty-one to sixty-one group. The general level of health is statistically significant in only one of the three family status pathways, although the magnitude of the estimated effect is quite large: a 10 percent increase in the index is associated with a 6 percent increase in assets in the LYO. Among the health variables, the indicator variable for psychological problems has a strong negative effect in two of the three pathways, and a stroke has a negative effect for persons who are single throughout our sample. Surprisingly, the onset of heart problems is estimated to have a positive effect on assets in the last year observed for two of the three pathways.

Education is very strongly related to assets in the LYO for both the 1→1 and the 2→1 groups. For example, for the 1→1 group an individual with a college degree is estimated to have a 67 percent increase in assets in the LYO relative to an individual with less than a high school degree. For the 2→1 group the comparable increase is 59 percent. For the 2→2 group the education effects are much smaller. Somewhat paradoxically, the coefficient on the indicator variable for having attained at least a college degree, 0.190, is smaller than the coefficient for some college, 0.252, although the hypothesis of equal effects could not be rejected at standard significance levels.

An indicator variable for psychological problems (emotional, nervous,

Table 4.7   Personal attributes associated with the change in assets between first and last year observed, persons age fifty-one to sixty-one in 1992 (dependent variable is log of assets in last year observed)

	Two person to two person				One person to one person				Two person to one person			
Variable	Coefficient	t-stat	Coefficient	t-stat	Coefficient	t-stat	Coefficient	t-stat	Coefficient	t-stat	Coefficient	t-stat
Log(assets in FYO)	0.849	40.44	0.804	35.92	0.970	23.98	0.872	20.22	1.060	11.59	0.965	10.20
Years since FYO			0.007	1.17			-0.001	-0.04			-0.002	-0.05
Age in FYO			-0.004	-0.47			0.073	2.68			0.074	1.84
Health in FYO			0.001	0.58			0.006	2.14			0.016	3.45
Cancer			0.027	0.47			-0.120	-0.54			-0.010	-0.03
Heart problems			-0.019	-0.31			-0.545	-2.62			0.320	0.97
Stroke			-0.188	-2.65			-0.506	-1.83			-0.507	-1.24
Lung disease			-0.318	-4.49			-0.105	-0.45			0.475	1.37
Psychological problems			-0.202	-2.74			-0.825	-3.30			-0.540	-1.70
Diabetes			-0.059	-0.94			0.143	0.60			0.884	2.40
High school degree			0.225	3.39			0.224	1.04			-0.229	-0.79
Some college			0.369	4.66			0.219	0.89			0.175	0.48
College or more			0.438	5.07			0.541	2.03			0.186	0.36
Constant	1.917	7.48	2.267	8.54	0.062	0.14	0.544	1.14	-1.212	-1.11	-1.262	-1.12
R^2	0.656		0.681		0.69		0.723		0.45		0.525	
N	858		858		261		260		166		166	

Notes: Sample excludes all persons who were alive when last observed. The variable "age in LYO" is the number of years over the age of fifty-three in the LYO.

Table 4.8   Personal attributes associated with the change in assets between first and last year observed, persons age seventy or older in 1993 (dependent variable is log of assets in last year observed)

Variable	2-person to 2-person				1-person to 1-person				2-person to 1-person			
	Coefficient	t-stat	Coefficient	t-stat	Coefficient	t-stat	Coefficient	t-stat	Coefficient	t-stat	Coefficient	t-stat
Log(assets in FYO)	0.894	57.25	0.868	50.11	0.841	42.94	0.820	40.41	0.910	22.71	0.870	20.00
Years since FYO			-0.014	-2.34			-0.044	-4.58			-0.045	-2.95
Age in FYO			-0.003	-0.77			-0.008	-1.25			-0.011	-0.88
Health in FYO			0.000	-0.39			0.003	1.83			0.006	2.32
Cancer			0.002	0.03			0.101	0.89			-0.009	-0.05
Heart problems			0.108	2.12			0.190	2.13			-0.081	-0.56
Stroke			0.051	0.96			-0.252	-2.67			-0.167	-1.11
Lung disease			-0.040	-0.61			-0.107	-0.83			0.243	1.20
Psychological problems			-0.148	-2.51			-0.421	-3.90			-0.260	-1.65
Diabetes			-0.069	-1.06			-0.110	-0.76			-0.253	-1.08
High school degree			0.083	1.64			0.281	3.36			0.160	1.13
Some college			0.252	3.95			0.279	2.73			0.297	1.76
College or more			0.190	2.80			0.674	5.29			0.586	3.12
Constant	1.299	6.77	1.657	8.04	1.520	6.80	1.899	7.75	0.606	1.25	1.273	2.47
R^2	0.71		0.709		0.544		0.567		0.44		0.465	
N	1,338		1,338		1,548		1,546		659		660	

Notes: Sample excludes all persons who were alive when last observed. The variable "age in LYO" is the number of years over the age of seventy in the LYO.

or psychiatric problems) has the most robust negative effect on assets in the LYO, looking across all persons age fifty-one to sixty-one in 1992 and seventy and older in 1993 and across the three family status pathways. In addition, health in the first year observed is associated with greater assets in the LYO for all groups except the 2→2 group.

We illustrate the relative magnitudes of the effects reported in table 4.6 by simulating asset balances for various covariate combinations using the specification without year effects. Table 4.9 presents simulated asset balances based on the estimates for ages fifty-one to sixty-one in 1992 and table 4.10 presents simulations for those over seventy in 1993. The first two rows of each table show the simulated assets in the LYO for a baseline person who has $100,000 of assets in the FYO, for each of the four levels of education, and the weighted average across all education groups. The first row reports assets in the LYO when all covariates except assets in the FYO and education are set to their sample means. The first entry in the first row of table 4.9 shows that assets fall by about $16,000 (from $100,000 to $84,139) for persons without a high school degree. The remaining entries in this row show terminal assets for persons with other levels of education. The differences by level of education are substantial, especially since we condition on assets in the FYO both in the estimation and in the simulation. The last entry in the row shows that average assets remain almost constant between the FYO and LYO. The second row shows the results of the same simulation, except

Table 4.9   Simulated assets in LYO for baseline person with $100,000 of assets in FYO, based on estimates for persons age fifty-one to sixty-one in 1992

| Baseline assets and attribute change | Level of education | | | | |
	Less than high school ($)	High school degree ($)	Some college ($)	College or more ($)	All ($)
Baseline assets in LYO					
Mean attributes	84,139	102,309	108,296	127,120	101,921
No health conditions	95,785	116,470	123,286	144,714	116,028
Change in attribute					
Health in FYO					
25th percentile	79,253	96,937	102,006	154,114	96,001
75th percentile	89,955	109,382	115,782	174,927	108,966
Family status					
2→1	69,198	84,142	89,065	104,546	83,821
2→2	93,220	113,351	119,984	181,274	112,920
Health conditions					
None	95,785	116,470	123,286	144,714	116,028
Stroke	72,126	87,702	92,834	108,970	87,369
Psychological problems	64,347	90,403	95,693	112,325	90,059

that all of the health condition variables are set to zero rather than to their means. The last entry in this row shows that, on average, persons who do not experience any health events increase asset balances between the FYO and the LYO.

The remaining rows of table 4.9 show the simulated level of assets in the LYO when selected attributes are set at specified values and the other covariates are set to their means. For example, averaging over all education groups (the last column), an increase in health in the FYO from the 25th percentile to the 75th percentile is associated with an increase in assets in the LYO from $96,001 to $108,966. Overall, the relationship between health in the FYO and assets in the LYO is modest, although statistically significant. However, both changes in family status and changes in health conditions have substantial effects on assets in the LYO. For example, using the coefficients in the "all" column, persons who are continuously married are predicted to have approximately $29,000 more in assets in the LYO, $83,821 versus $112,920, than persons who went from a two-person household to a one-person household. The two most important health conditions, stroke and psychological problems, are each associated, on average, with a $25,000 to $30,000 reduction in assets.

Table 4.10 presents comparable results for persons age seventy and older in 1993. The last entry of the first row of simulations suggests that, on average, the assets of this group declined modestly between the FYO and the LYO. The second row shows that assets would have been only marginally higher if the baseline person had experienced no health conditions. A comparison with the previous table suggests that the effect of health conditions is much greater for the younger than for the older cohort. This may be because an adverse health shock at a younger age reduces earnings and potential pension and Social Security accruals, in addition to creating expenditure needs. The effects of most of the other covariates are of similar orders of magnitude for the two age cohorts.

4.4 Summary

We have considered the determinants of assets as individuals approach the end of life, comparing asset balances when individuals in the Health and Retirement Study (HRS) were last observed prior to death with comparable data measures in the first year the individuals were included in the survey. We have data through 2012 for members of two HRS cohorts—respondents age fifty-one to sixty-one who were first observed in 1992, and respondents age seventy and older who were first observed in 1993. Thus we are able to study the evolution of assets for as many as nineteen years.

We first document levels of total assets, housing assets, and financial assets near the end of life for each of the HRS cohorts. Asset balances are quite persistent in the later stages of life. For the younger cohort, 70

Table 4.10   Simulated assets in LYO for baseline person with $100,000 of assets in FYO, based on estimates for persons age seventy or older in 1993

Baseline assets and attribute change	Less than high school ($)	High school degree ($)	Some college ($)	College or more ($)	All ($)
			Level of education		
Baseline assets in LYO					
Mean attributes	74,487	84,559	99,432	111,752	86,024
No health conditions	76,396	86,225	101,980	114,615	88,227
Change in attribute					
Health in FYO					
25th percentile	72,284	82,057	96,490	108,445	83,478
75th percentile	80,874	91,809	107,957	121,333	93,399
Family status					
2→1	62,062	70,453	82,845	93,109	71,673
2→2	92,008	104,448	122,820	138,037	106,257
Health conditions					
None	76,396	86,725	101,980	114,615	88,227
Stroke	71,336	80,981	95,225	107,023	82,384
Psychological problems	61,663	70,000	82,313	92,511	71,213

percent of those with less than $50,000 in total assets when last surveyed before death also had fewer than $50,000 in assets when first surveyed. For the older cohort, 52 percent of those with less than $50,000 in assets when last surveyed before death also had fewer than $50,000 in assets when first surveyed. Low levels of both housing and financial assets are also persistent. Those who had substantial assets at the end of life also had substantial asset balances when first observed. The persistence of wealth is confirmed in a series of figures showing median total assets in each survey wave between the wave first observed and the last wave observed before death. For the younger cohort the path of assets is essentially flat. For older cohorts there is some evidence of a modest decline. These findings suggest that the low level of retirement wealth of many households at the time of retirement documented in many studies, including Poterba (2014) and the US Government Accountability Office (2015), is a key contributor to low levels of wealth for individuals near the end of life.

We relate the change in assets between the first and last year observed to individual attributes and to changes in these attributes. We obtain estimates for each subgroup, those in the HRS who were fifty-one to sixty-one in 1992 and those in the AHEAD who were seventy or older in 1993, and for persons in each family status pathway. This includes those who were in two-person households in both the FYO and the LYO, those who were in one-person households in both the FYO and the LYO years, and those who were in a one-person household in the LYO but a two-person household in the FYO.

We pay particular attention to how the onset of chronic conditions, an individual's level of education, and changes in family composition, such as death of a spouse, are associated with changes in assets. Simulation results based on our regression estimates suggest that on average, assets remain roughly constant between the FYO and the LYO for the younger cohort and decline modestly for the older cohort. For those who do not experience a health event or family disruption, the asset profile slopes upward for the younger cohort and slightly downward for the older cohort. However, for individuals who experience adverse health events, such as a stroke or the onset of psychological problems, the decline in assets can be quite large. Similarly, individuals who experience a change in household composition, to one-person from two-person, on average also experience substantial declines in wealth.

Taken as a whole, these results suggest that the level of assets of individuals approaching the end of life is determined primarily by the assets these individuals held many years earlier. Most of those with limited assets at death also had limited assets earlier in life. They did not run out of assets in retirement; they never had many assets to begin with. However, there are also some individuals who entered retirement with modest or even large asset balances and experienced health shocks or family disruption that resulted in significant declines in assets. For the cohort age fifty-one to sixty-one in 1992, we find little evidence of asset decline among persons who did not experience health shocks or family disruption. For these individuals, there is no evidence that asset balances are being depleted by normal consumption expenditure in retirement. For older persons, it is also the case that assets at death are determined primarily by asset balances earlier in retirement. However, for those in our sample who were over the age of seventy in 1993, and who were therefore mostly over ninety by 2012, there is some evidence that assets decline modestly prior to death, even in the absence of health or family shocks. The onset of health conditions can have large negative consequences for asset balances of the older cohort as well, but on the whole the effects of health conditions are smaller than for the younger cohort.

A natural extension of this project would ask what individuals might have done earlier in life to avoid reaching late life with few resources. We will pursue this issue in future analysis. For those who are observed with lower assets in the LYO than in the FYO, purchasing an annuity earlier in life might have improved well-being in later years. To assess this possibility we plan to calculate the potential annuity income that each individual could have obtained by purchasing an annuity in the first year observed. We also plan to estimate the number of individuals who saved very little while working.

One explanation of low saving, which is difficult to evaluate, is that some households do not earn enough to both meet their spending requirements, and save, while working. Analyzing the dispersion of accumulated financial assets for those who are in the bottom quartile or half of the lifetime earning distribution could shed light on this hypothesis. Previous research, including Venti and Wise (1998, 1999), Hendricks (2007), Yang (2009), and Bozio, Emmerson, and Tetlow (2011), has shown that at each level of (lifetime) earnings, there are both high and low savers. This suggests that "low earnings" can only provide a partial explanation for low assets late in life, but this possibility warrants further investigation.

References

Banerjee, Sudipto. 2015. "A Look at the End of Life Financial Situation in America." *EBRI Notes* 36 (April):2–10.

Bozio, Antoine, Carl Emmerson, and Gemma Tetlow. 2011. "How Much Do Lifetime Earnings Explain Retirement Resources?" IFS Working Paper no.11/02, Institute for Fiscal Studies. http://www.ifs.org.uk/wps/wp1102.pdf.

DeNardi, Mariacristina, Eric French, and John B. Jones. 2015. "Saving after Retirement: A Survey." NBER Working Paper no. 21268, Cambridge, MA.

Coile, Courtney, and Kevin Milligan. 2009. "How Household Portfolios Evolve after Retirement: The Effect of Aging and Health Shocks." *Review of Income and Wealth* 55 (2): 226–48.

French, Eric, Mariacristina DeNardi, John Bailey Jones, Olesya Baker, and Phil Doctor. 2006. "Right before the End: Asset Decumulation at the End of Life." *Economic Perspectives* 2006 (Q3): 2–13.

Hendricks, Lutz. 2007. "Retirement Wealth and Lifetime Earnings." *International Economic Review* 48 (2): 421–56.

Johnson, Richard, Gordon Mermin, and Cori Uccello. 2006. "When the Nest Egg Cracks: Financial Consequences of Health Problems, Marital Status Changes, and Job Layoffs at Older Ages." Washington, DC, Urban Institute. January. http://www.urban.org/sites/default/files/alfresco/publication-pdfs/411265-When-the-Nest-Egg-Cracks.PDF.

Lee, Jinkook, and Hyungsoo Kim. 2007. "A Longitudinal Analysis of the Impact of Health Shocks on the Wealth of Elders." *Journal of Population Economics* 21:217–30.

Marshall, Samuel, Kathleen McGarry, and Jonathan Skinner. 2011. "The Risk of Out-of-Pocket Health Care Expenditure at End of life." In *Explorations in the Economics of Aging*, edited by David A. Wise. Chicago: University of Chicago Press.

Poterba, James. 2014. "Retirement Saving in an Aging Society." *American Economic Review* 104 (May): 1–33.

Poterba, James, Steven Venti, and David Wise. 2010. "The Asset Cost of Poor Health." NBER Working Paper no. 16389, Cambridge, MA.

———. 2012. "Were They Prepared for Retirement? Financial Status at Advanced Ages in the HRS and AHEAD Cohorts." In *Investigations in the Economics of Aging*, edited by David A. Wise. Chicago: University of Chicago Press.

————. 2013. "Health, Education, and the Post-Retirement Evolution of Household Assets." *Journal of Human Capital* 7 (4): 297–339.

Rohwedder, Susann, Steven J. Haider, and Michael Hurd. 2006. "Increases in Wealth among the Elderly in the Early 1990s: How Much is Due to Survey Design?" *Review of Income and Wealth* 52:509–24.

Sevak, Purvi, David Weir, and Robert Willis. 2003/2004. "The Economic Consequences of a Husband's Death: Evidence from the HRS and AHEAD." *Social Security Bulletin* 65 (3): 31–44.

Smith, James P. 1999. "Healthy Bodies and Thick Wallets: The Dual Relation between Health and Economic Status." *Journal of Economic Perspectives* 13 (2): 145–66.

————. 2004. "Unraveling the SES-Health Connection." *Population and Development Review Supplement: Aging, Health and Public Policy* 30:108–32.

————. 2005. "Consequences and Predictors of New Health Events." In *Analyses in the Economics of Aging*, edited by David A. Wise, 213–40. Chicago: University of Chicago Press.

US Government Accountability Office. 2015. *Retirement Security: Most Households Approaching Retirement Have Low Savings.* Washington, DC: GAO.

Venti, Steven, and David Wise. 1998. "The Cause of Wealth Dispersion at Retirement: Choice or Chance?" *American Economic Review Papers and Proceedings* 88 (2): 185–91.

————. 1999. "Lifetime Income, Saving Choices, and Wealth at Retirement." In *Wealth, Work, and Health: Innovations in Survey Measurement in the Social Sciences*, edited by J. Smith and R. Willis. Ann Arbor: University of Michigan Press.

Wu, Stephen. 2003. "The Effects of Health Status Events on the Economic Status of Married Couples." *Journal of Human Resources* 38 (1): 219–30.

Yang, Fang. 2009. "Accounting for the Heterogeneity in Retirement Wealth." CRR Working Paper no. 2009-6, Boston College, Center for Retirement Research. March.

Comment   Brigitte C. Madrian

In their chapter "What Determines End-of-Life Assets? A Retrospective View," Poterba, Venti, and Wise trace the evolution of assets with age using data through 2012 for HRS respondents age fifty-one to sixty-one in 1992 and for AHEAD respondents age seventy and older in 1993. Their analysis documents several interesting patterns. First, they find that asset balances are quite persistent. As one might expect, individuals with substantial assets when last observed also had substantial assets when first observed. What is more striking is their finding that most individuals who are last observed with a low level of assets (< $50k) also had a low level of assets when first

Brigitte C. Madrian is the Aetna Professor of Public Policy and Corporate Management at the Harvard Kennedy School and a research associate and co-director of the Household Finance Working Group at the National Bureau of Economic Research.

For acknowledgments, sources of research support, and disclosure of the author's material financial relationships, if any, please see http://www.nber.org/chapters/c13630.ack.

observed; for the most part, individuals who are poor in old age did not become poor in old age, they started poor. Second, Poterba, Venti, and Wise find that for the (younger) HRS cohort, median asset levels change very little with age (over the range of observed ages), whereas for the (older) AHEAD cohort, median asset levels do decline over time. If these wealth patterns with respect to age are not cohort specific, they suggest that on average, older individuals are able to live well into their seventies before drawing down their assets. Finally, because there is heterogeneity across households in the evolution of wealth, Poterba, Venti, and Wise delve beyond the averages to examine the factors that impact how wealth changes over time. They find that health shocks and family disruption (e.g., death of a spouse) result in a significant decline in assets between the first and last year that individuals are observed for both the HRS and the AHEAD cohorts. On the other hand, individuals with higher levels of educational attainment and no health problems actually see their assets increase over time, as do coupled individuals without a family disruption.

This set of findings is an important contribution to the literature on the financial well-being of older individuals. It highlights both the source and magnitude of the financial shocks that older individuals face. It also highlights the demographic factors that are correlated with how well individuals weather financial shocks in old age.

One of the striking findings in this chapter is the sizable negative impact that health shocks have on wealth. Indeed, as noted above, the authors find that for individuals in good health and with at least some college education, average wealth actually increases with age. Because HRS and AHEAD respondents are only surveyed every two years, one limitation of these findings is that they likely do not completely account for the impact on assets of medical spending during the last year of life. Riley and Lubitz (2010) find that the 5 percent of Medicare beneficiaries who die in any given year account for approximately one-quarter of total Medicare expenditures, while Barnato et al. (2004) calculate that annual per capita Medicare-covered hospital expenditures are six times higher for decedents than for survivors. If individuals who die face similarly large disparities in out-of-pocket expenditures in their last year of life relative to those who survive, the impact of health shocks on assets as calculated in this chapter is likely understated because the last observation on wealth of those who die may be up to two years before the date of death.

The authors could address this issue by exploiting variation in the timing between the date of death and the date of the last year observed (LYO) asset level. Among those who die, some will have died very shortly after the survey in which their assets were last observed, while others will have died up to two years later. If health shocks in the last year of life negatively impact assets, we should see a large decline in the level of assets between the final survey and the survey two years prior for those who die shortly after their last survey interview because for many of these decedents, the health shock that preceded death will have started having a financial impact between these last two surveys. In contrast, for those who die much closer to two years after the last survey, the difference in the level of assets between the final survey and the survey two years prior to the final survey should be much smaller as the financial shock that accompanies the health shock preceding death will more likely have occurred after the final observation on assets. Thus, we would expect to see a positive correlation between the length of time between the last interview and a decedent's date of death and the change in assets observed between the last and the penultimate surveys. This type of analysis would shed some light on the evolution of financial well-being, not just over the longer multiyear time horizon currently analyzed in the chapter, but over a relatively shorter horizon focused on the final months leading up to death.

A potentially important factor that could influence the evolution of assets in old age that is not examined in the chapter is mortality expectations: How long do individuals anticipate they (or their spouse) will live? As noted earlier, one of the findings in the chapter is that for the HRS cohort, the average level of assets does not decline with age; in contrast, the average level of assets does show a pattern of decline with age for those in the AHEAD cohort, particularly for the older members of the AHEAD cohort (those age seventy-six and older in 1993, see the last panel of figure 4.2). One difference between the older members of the AHEAD cohort and the (younger and older) members of the HRS cohort is that the AHEAD cohort is much closer in age to their life expectancy at the start of the survey than are members of the HRS cohort. If individuals self-manage their wealth in retirement rather than fully annuitizing it, age relative to life expectancy will be a key parameter in any model of wealth evolution, yet it is not included in the analysis in this chapter. Both the HRS and the AHEAD ask respondents to give subjective survival forecasts for the likelihood that they will live to particular ages. These questions have been shown in previous research to be correlated with behaviors linked to mortality such as smoking and exercise (Hurd and McGarry 1995; Manski 2004), although their relationship to actual mortality experiences is the subject of some debate (Hurd and McGarry 2002; Perozek 2008; Elder 2013).

It would be extremely interesting to incorporate some measure of mortality expectations into a future analysis of wealth evolution. Figure 4.2 in the chapter shows that in both the HRS and the AHEAD cohorts, those individuals who are still alive in the last survey year have a much higher level of assets in the first survey year than do individuals who died in the intervening years. Did these individuals who are still alive at the time of the last survey have a higher subjective survival forecast at the time of the initial survey that would lead them to acquire more assets before retirement? And once in retirement, do these individuals spend down their wealth more slowly? If individuals can predict their own mortality with some degree of accuracy, they may rationally save less while working if they expect to die young, and they may rationally spend down their assets in retirement more quickly, especially following a health shock, because they do not anticipate living much longer. Whether or not this is true in the data remains to be seen, but the analysis is a logical extension of what is in this chapter, and would help speak to policy issues around retirement income adequacy and the market for annuities.

References

Barnato, Amber E., Mark B. McClellan, Christopher R. Kagay, and Alan M. Garber. 2004. "Trends in Inpatient Treatment Intensity among Medicare Beneficiaries at End of Life." *Health Services Research* 39 (2): 363–76.
Elder, Todd E. 2013. "The Predictive Validity of Subjective Mortality Expectations: Evidence from the Health and Retirement Study." *Demography* 50 (2): 569–89.
Hurd, Michael, and Kathleen McGarry. 1995. "Evaluation of the Subjective Probabilities of Survival in the Health and Retirement Study." *Journal of Human Resources* 30 (S1): S268–92.
———. 2002. "The Predictive Validity of Subjective Probabilities of Survival." *Economic Journal* 112:966–98.
Manski, Charles. 2004. "Measuring Expectations." *Econometrica* 72 (5): 1329–76.
Perozek, M. 2008. "Using Subjective Expectations to Forecast Longevity: Do Survey Respondents Know Something We Don't Know?" *Demography* 45 (1): 95–113.
Riley, Gerald F., and James D. Lubitz. 2010. "Long-Term Trends in Medicare Payments in the Last Year of Life." *Health Services Research* 45 (2): 565–76.

5

Understanding the Improvement in Disability-Free Life Expectancy in the US Elderly Population

Michael Chernew, David M. Cutler, Kaushik Ghosh, and Mary Beth Landrum

Understanding how healthy lifespans are changing over time is central to public policy. For example, policies such as increasing the age of eligibility for Social Security or Medicare only make sense if healthy life expectancy is increasing for the vast bulk of the population. Accurate measurement of healthy life expectancy is thus essential in the welfare evaluation of such policies. Moreover, a good deal of medical spending is predicated on the idea that more intensive treatment improves quality-adjusted life expectancy. Measuring the relationship between medical advances and healthy life expectancy thus contributes to our understanding the value of medical advances and may provide insights into the causes of, and perhaps persistence of, improvements in healthy life expectancy.

Data on life expectancy are easy to obtain, but data on healthy life expectancy are more difficult. To a great extent, this is because there is no single measure of good or bad health commonly accepted in the literature. Our past work (Cutler, Ghosh, and Landrum 2014), along with much of the literature, focuses on disabled and nondisabled life expectancy. We define disability as an indicator for whether an individual has an impairment with

Michael Chernew is the Leonard D. Schaeffer Professor of Health Care Policy and the director of the HealthCare Markets and Regulation (HMR) Lab in the Department of Health Care Policy at Harvard Medical School and a research associate of the National Bureau of Economic Research. David M. Cutler is Harvard College Professor and the Otto Eckstein Professor of Applied Economics at Harvard University and a research associate of the National Bureau of Economic Research. Kaushik Ghosh is a research specialist at the National Bureau of Economic Research. Mary Beth Landrum is professor of health care policy, with a specialty in biostatistics, in the Department of Health Care Policy at Harvard Medical School.

This research was funded by the National Institute on Aging (P01AG005842) and Pfizer. We are grateful to Jonathan Skinner for helpful comments. For acknowledgments, sources of research support, and disclosure of the authors' material financial relationships, if any, please see http://www.nber.org/chapters/c13631.ack.

any Activity of Daily Living (ADL) or Instrumental Activity of Daily Living (IADL). We calculate the number of years a person turning sixty-five in different years can expect to live with and without a disability.

Our previous study shows that disability-free life expectancy has increased significantly at older ages in the United States. Between 1992 and 2005, for example, life expectancy increased by 0.7 years. Disability-free life expectancy increased by 1.6 years; disabled life expectancy fell by 0.9 years. Other results have reached similar conclusions about increases in disability-free life expectancy over time (Crimmins, Saito, and Ingegneri 1997, 2001, 2009; Manton, Gu, and Lowrimore 2008; Cai and Lubitz 2007). However, other work that defines healthy life expectancy based on presence of disease have come to an opposite conclusions finding that length of life with disease has increased (Crimmins and Beltrán-Sánchez 2010). This is consistent with findings from our previous work and others that while disease prevalence has increased, disability conditional on disease has declined (Cutler, Ghosh, and Landrum 2014; Freedman et al. 2007; Crimmins et al. 1993, Crimmins, Saito, and Reynolds 1997; Crimmins 2004; Manton, Corder, and Stallard 1993, 1997; Manton and Gu 2001; Manton, Gu, and Lamb 2006). However, little research has examined why disability-free life expectancy has increased so greatly, and in particular, what role medical advances may have played in this.

We address these issues in this chapter. Our analysis has three specific goals. First, we calculate disabled and disability-free life expectancy for a longer period of time than has been done previously. Our past research examined data from 1992 to 2005. In this chapter, we extend the analysis to 2008. This by itself does not change the conclusions materially, but the additional three years does encompass an era of relatively low growth in medical spending, so it is important to note that even with slow medical care cost increases, disability-free life expectancy kept increasing.

Second, we examine which medical conditions are associated with the greatest additions to disability-free life expectancy. We decompose both mortality and disability into fifteen medical conditions, ranging from acute but recoverable diseases such as heart disease and vision impairment, to chronic degenerative conditions such as Alzheimer's disease and Parkinson's disease, to chronic but nonfatal conditions such as arthritis and diabetes. Our central finding is that the vast bulk of the increase in disability-free life expectancy is accounted for by improvements in acute, recoverable conditions—two in particular: heart disease and vision problems. The prevalence of serious heart disease has declined over time, and for both conditions, people with the condition are in better health than they were formerly.

Our third goal is the most speculative: we seek to understand how much improvements in medical care have contributed to the health improvements associated with heart disease and vision problems. This analysis is the most speculative because we do not have great causal identification. We can observe trends in treatments and health, but we do not have an ideal way to turn these trends into causal statements. To make a stab at the causal question, we use two methodologies. In the case of cardiovascular disease, we combine trends in treatments over time with clinical trial evidence on the impact of different treatments on mortality and disability. The specific estimates are those used in the IMPACT mortality model, which we parameterize to the elderly population we study. Our results show that use of effective treatments has improved at a rate that the clinical literature suggests would have led to roughly half the health improvements that we observe. Most of the treatment improvements are pharmaceutical—cholesterol-lowering agents and antihypertensives are the major ones, but some are surgical as well.

In the case of vision, we focus primarily on increased use of cataract surgery. Fewer people have vision impairments late in the first decade of the twenty-first century than did in the early 1990s, and this seems proximately related to the increased use of cataract surgery over time. The clinical literature does not suggest a meaningful impact of cataract surgery on health-related quality of life. However, using data on individual transitions between more and less disabled states, we show significant benefits of cataract surgery on both vision and disability trends. People who receive cataract surgery are less likely to experience adverse disability trends than people who do not receive cataract surgery, controlling for the prior year's level of vision impairment. We thus conclude that it is likely that the growing use of cataract surgery explains some of the improvement in health over time.

The outline of the chapter is as follows. In the first section, we examine the overall trends in mortality and disability. Section 5.2 shows the changes in disability-free and disabled life expectancy. In section 5.3, we estimate the impact of medical conditions and demographic variables on disability. In section 5.4, we calculate the disability-free and disabled life expectancy by disease. Section 5.5 examines the pharmaceutical and surgical interventions that may have caused the declines in major cardiovascular events and mortality. Section 5.6 examines the factors responsible for improvements in vision problems. Finally, in section 5.7 we discuss our findings and conclude.

5.1 Health Trends among the Elderly

5.1.1 Life Expectancy

Life expectancy is a function of mortality rates. The mortality data are standard mortality rates from the National Center for Health Statistics. The data on disability comes from the Medicare Current Beneficiary Survey (MCBS), sponsored by the Center for Medicare and Medicaid Services (CMS). We discuss our specific measures of disability below.

Life expectancy in most developed countries increases regularly, and it has continued to do so in recent years. Figure 5.1 shows the change in life

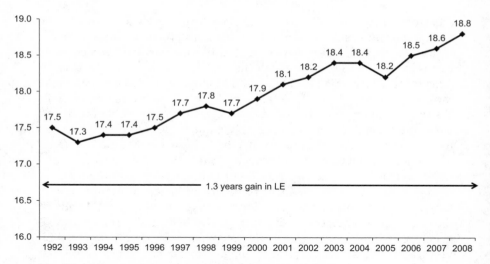

Fig. 5.1   Life expectancy at age sixty-five (total population)

Source: Data are from the Vital Statistics of the United States from the Centers for Disease Control and Prevention/National Center for Health Statistics.

expectancy at sixty-five years of age between 1992 and 2008. Over this time period, life expectancy increased by 1.3 years (17.5 to 18.8), or nearly one year per decade.

Relative to our earlier analysis, which ended in 2005, life expectancy increased by another 0.6 years between 2005 and 2008. Some of this increase is anomalous, given the unusual drop in life expectancy in 2005. Even taking out this year, however, life expectancy increases show no sign of slowing down, even in an era where medical spending increases were very low (Cutler and Sahni 2013).

For our analysis in this chapter, we care about mortality by cause in addition to overall mortality. Cause of death is reported on each death record. These causes are not believed to be wholly accurate. Death is declared when the heart stops, and thus a larger number of deaths are attributed to heart failure than is likely true. Nonetheless, it is not obvious that this will bias trends in mortality reporting over time. Without any alternative, we utilize these causes of death data.

Death codes change over time, and so the mortality rate by cause changes for that reason. Prior to year 1999, deaths were classified by the International Classification of Diseases, Ninth Revision (ICD–9), and from 1999 onward the causes of death are classified by the International Classification of Diseases, Tenth Revision (ICD–10). We use comparability ratio for the cause of death between ICD-9 and ICD-10 to compare causes of death in different periods. Comparability ratios for the broad aggregates of death that we examine are very close to 1.

We look at fifteen specific causes of death. The causes are defined to match the MCBS. We find the closest mortality cause for the questions that people are asked about directly in the MCBS (e.g., "Has a doctor [ever] told [you/(SP)] that [you/he/she] had a myocardial infarction or heart attack?"). Generally, these are causes that are commonly reported, but not always. For example, the MCBS asks about vision problems. The closest NCHS category is death from "diseases of the eye and adnexa," which is generally not reported separately. We group the fifteen causes into several categories, based on organ system: cardiovascular disease (ischemic heart disease and stroke); cancer (four specific sites and all others); central nervous system (Alzheimer's disease and Parkinson's disease); diseases of the respiratory system; musculoskeletal disease (broken hip, rheumatoid arthritis, and nonrheumatoid arthritis); diabetes; and diseases of the eye and adnexa.

Many chronic diseases have low mortality, but nonetheless contribute to deaths in other ways. For example, very few people have diabetes as the primary cause of death, but diabetes contributes to heart disease, kidney disease, and other conditions that kill many people. A richer model would account for this disease causality, relating chronic diseases to other diseases that ultimately kill them. We do not do that here.

Figure 5.2 shows the NCHS mortality rates per 100,000 (age-sex adjusted) by disease for two time periods: 1991–1994 and 2006–2009. Each data point

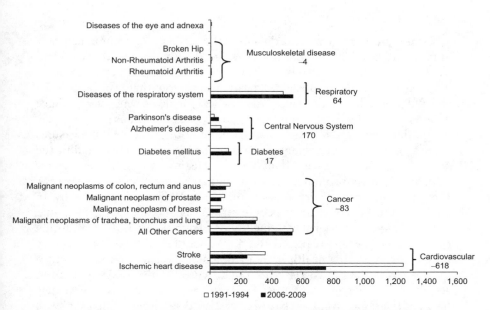

Fig. 5.2   NCHS causes of death for age sixty-five and older: Mortality rates per 100,000 (age-sex adjusted)
Source: Data are from the Centers for Disease Control and Prevention/National Center for Health Statistics on Causes of Death. The change in death rate is for two time periods, 1991– 1994 and 2006–2009.

is age and sex adjusted to the population in 2000. Within each interval, we take a simple average of death rates in each of the four years. The age-sex-adjusted death rates for cardiovascular diseases have the biggest decline (–618), followed by cancer (–83). Of the cancers we can attribute, the biggest reduction is in cancer of the trachea, bronchus, and lung—a cause strongly associated with tobacco use. However, mortality from other cancers is declining as well, and preventive efforts and medical treatments likely play a role in declining cancer mortality (Cutler 2008).

Deaths from diseases of the central nervous system increased the most by 170, with Alzheimer's disease being particularly important. Death from respiratory disease and diabetes increased as well.

In our work below, we translate these changes in mortality into changes in life expectancy, using standard cause-deletion techniques. To find the increase in life expectancy from one cause, we hold constant death rates from every other cause and change death rates for only the cause we are considering. This step involves an important assumption—that the change in death from one cause does not affect death from other causes. As an example of this, if medical treatment for smokers with cardiovascular disease improves, we might expect age- and sex-adjusted mortality rates for cancers caused by tobacco use to increase. Absent more detailed knowledge of interactions among causes of death, we make the independence assumption.

5.1.2 Disability

To measure disability, we use data from the Medicare Current Beneficiary Survey (MCBS). The MCBS, sponsored by the Centers for Medicare and Medicaid Services (CMS), is a nationally representative survey of aged, disabled, and institutionalized Medicare beneficiaries that oversamples the very old (age eighty-five or older) and disabled Medicare beneficiaries. Since we are interested in health among the elderly, we restrict our sample to the population age sixty-five and older. A number of surveys have measures of disability in the elderly population (Freedman et al. 2004), including the National Health Interview Study and the Health and Retirement Study. Still, the MCBS has a number of advantages relative to these other surveys. First, the sample size is large, about 10,000 to 18,000 people annually. In addition, the MCBS samples people regardless of whether they live in a household or a long-term care facility or switch between the two during the course of the survey period. Third, the set of health questions is very broad, encompassing health in many domains. Fourth, and importantly, individuals in the MCBS have been matched to Medicare death records. As a result, we can measure death for over 200,000 people, even after they have left the survey window. The MCBS started as a longitudinal survey in 1991. In 1992 and 1993, the only supplemental individuals added were to replace people lost to attrition and to account for newly enrolled beneficiaries. Beginning in 1994, the MCBS began a transition to a rotating panel design, with a four-year sample inclusion. About one-third of the sample was rotated out in 1994, and new members were included in the sample. The remainder of the original sample was rotated out in subsequent years. We use all interviews that are available for each person from the start of the survey in 1991 through 2009. The MCBS has two samples: a set of people who were enrolled for the entire year (the Access to Care sample) and a set of ever-enrolled beneficiaries (the Cost and Use sample). The latter differs from the former in including people who die during the year and new additions to the Medicare population. The primary data that we use are from the health status questionnaire administered in the fall survey, which defines the Access to Care sample. We thus use the Access to Care data. We date time until death from the exact date at which the Access to Care Survey was administered to the person.

To account for demographic changes in the Medicare population over this time frame, we adjust survey weights so that the MCBS population in each year matches the population in the year 2000 by age, gender, and race. All of our tabulations are weighted by these adjusted weights.

The MCBS is matched to death records available in the Medicare denominator files. As a result, we can measure death for all beneficiaries, even after they have left the survey. The death dates are available through 2012. For each individual interviewed between 1991 and 2009, we can determine if they died in the next twelve months or survived that period, died between twelve and twenty-four months or not, twenty-four and thirty-six months or not, or survived at least thirty-six months.

Trends in the distribution of time until death are shown in figure 5.3. The share of the population that is within one year of death declines from approximately 5.5 percent in 1991 to 4.5 percent in 2009, reflecting the overall reduction in mortality. The share of the population one to two years from death and two to three years from death declines as well. Correspondingly, the share of the population that is three or more years from death increased by about 0.18 percentage points annually, also shown in figure 5.3.

The MCBS asks a number of questions about a respondent's ability to function and independently perform basic tasks, shown in table 5.1. Six questions are asked about each of ADL and IADL limitations. The prevalence of each impairment is also shown in the table. The most common ADL impairment is difficulty walking, experienced by one-quarter of the population. The most common IADL impairment is doing heavy housework, which is experienced by one-third of the elderly population.

Figures 5.4A and 5.4B show the trends in ADL and IADL limitations from 1991 to 2009. We show the annual rate in the figure and (in the legend) report the annual percentage point changes between 1991–1994 and 2006–2009 in each impairment. People reporting ADL difficulties in bathing declined the most, by 0.35 percentage points annually. Other ADL difficulties also declined over the eighteen years: walking (0.34 percentage point

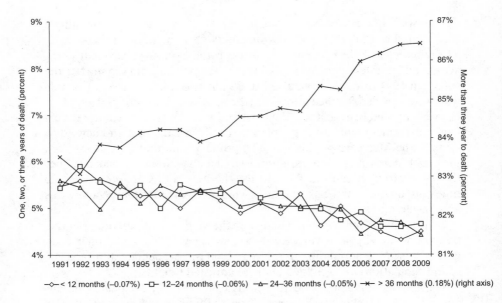

Fig. 5.3   Population distribution by time until death

Source: Data are from the Medicare Current Beneficiary Survey and Medicare denominator files linked to MCBS 1991–2009. Reported statistics is weighted to the population distribution in 2000 by age, sex, and race.

Table 5.1   Health status questions in the MCBS, 1991–2009

Num.	Question	Prevalence (%)
Activities of Daily Living says difficulty doing by himself/herself because of health or physical problem		
1	Bathing or showering	15
2	Going in or out of bed or chairs	15
3	Eating	5
4	Dressing	10
5	Walking	26
6	Using the toilet	8
Instrumental Activities of Daily Living: Difficulty doing the following activities by yourself because of health or physical problem		
7	Using the telephone	10
8	Doing light housework (like washing dishes, straightening up, or light cleaning)	16
9	Doing heavy housework (like scrubbing floors or washing windows)	34
10	Preparing own meals	14
11	Shopping for personal items	18
12	Managing money (like keeping track of expenses or paying bills)	11
Disability (any ADL/IADL difficulty)		45

Source: Tabulations are from the MCBS Access to Care sample for 1991–2009 and use sample weights adjusted to a constant year 2000 population by age, gender, and race.

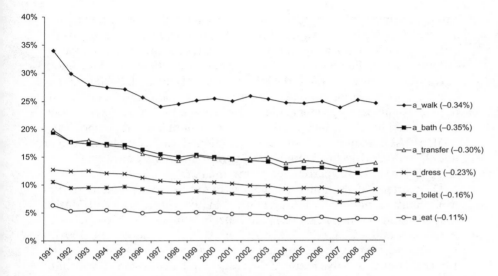

Fig. 5.4A   ADL limitations in elderly Medicare beneficiaries
Note: Data are from the Medicare Current Beneficiary Survey 1991–2009, and are weighted to the population distribution in 2000 by age, sex, and race.

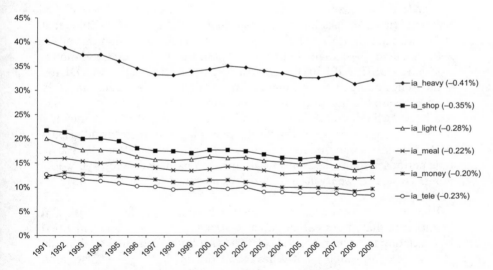

Fig. 5.4B   IADL limitations in elderly Medicare beneficiaries
Note: Data are from the Medicare Current Beneficiary Survey 1991–2009, and are weighted to the population distribution in 2000 by age, sex, and race.

annual decline); going in or out of bed or chairs (0.30 percentage point decline); dressing (0.23 percentage point decline); using the toilet (0.16 percentage point decline); and eating (0.11 percentage point decline annually).

Among IADL limitations, doing heavy housework (like scrubbing floors or washing windows) showed the biggest decline from 1991 to 2009 (7 percentage points overall and 0.41 percentage points annually). Again, this decline is significantly greater in the period between 1991and 1998 than later.

The disability metric we use is the share of the population that reports any ADL or IADL limitation. Using this definition, disability was 49.5 percent in 1991–1994 and declined roughly by 7 percentage points between 1991–94 and 2006–2009, or 0.5 percentage points annually.

This pattern of declining disability is found in most previous studies using multiple nationally representative surveys (Freedman and Martin 1998; Freedman, Martin, and Schoeni 2002; Freedman et al. 2004; Schoeni, Freedman, and Wallace 2001; Schoeni et al. 2005; Cutler 2001a, 2001b). For example, a working group analyzing trends in disability from the early 1980s to 2001 across five national data sets found a consistent 1 percent to 2.5 percent annual decline in ADL disability during the mid- to late 1990s (Freedman et al. 2004; Chen and Sloan 2015). A sharp decline in walking problems and heavy housework between 1992 and 1998 is also reported in some other studies (Crimmins 2004).

That said, the literature is not entirely uniform. Crimmins (2004) reported that trends in ADL disability is not consistent across studies (Crimmins et al. 2001; Crimmins, Saito, and Reynolds 1997; Liao et al. 2001; Manton and Gu 2001; Schoeni, Freedman, and Martin 2008). Further, an update from the working group (Freedman et al. 2013) found declines in IADL and ADL disability only among those ages eighty-five and older between 2000 and 2008.

To measure lifetime disability, we need to know disability by time until death. A decline in disability matters less for healthy life expectancy if it occurs at the very end of life than if it represents a sustained period prior to death. To understand the change in disability by time until death, we use the time periods in figure 5.3: < twelve months to death, twelve to twenty-four months to death, twenty-four to thirty-six months to death, and >thirty-six months to death.

Figure 5.5 shows the trend in disability by time until death. This figure is similar to that in our earlier paper (Cutler, Ghosh, and Landrum 2014), but updating the data through 2009. The vast bulk of the reduction in disability is among people a few years away from death. People who are more than thirty-six months away from death showed a decline of 0.5 percentage points between 1991–94 and 2006–2009. Disability is high and has remained so for people within one year of death; about 80 percent of this population is disabled, and that has not changed over time.

The reduction in disability farther away from death implies that there is a compression of morbidity into the period just before death (Cai and Lubitz

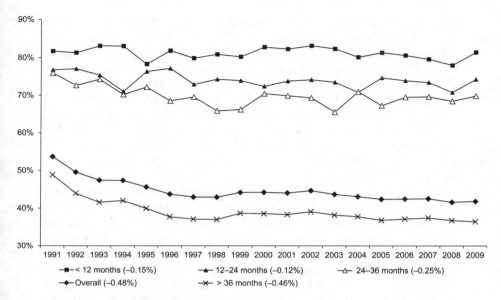

Fig. 5.5   ADL/IADL disability by time until death

Source: Data are from the Medicare Current Beneficiary Survey and Medicare denominator files linked to MCBS 1991–2009, and are weighted to the population distribution in 2000 by age, sex, and race.

2007; Cutler, Ghosh, and Landrum 2014). In the next section, we combine the NCHS period life tables and disability data to calculate disability-free and disabled life expectancy.

5.2   Disability-Free and Disabled Life Expectancy

In this section, we extend our previous research (Cutler, Ghosh, and Landrum 2014) and include more recent years of data to measure the changes in disability-free and disabled life expectancy.

The starting point for our analysis is the standard measure of life expectancy:

$$(1) \quad LE(a) = \sum_s \left\{ \Pr\left[\text{Survive } a+s \,\middle|\, \text{Alive } a\right] + .5 * \Pr\left[\text{Die at } a+s \,\middle|\, \text{Alive } a\right]\right\}.$$

Starting at age a, every (probabilistic) year that the average person survives adds one year to life expectancy. A person who dies in a year is assumed to live half the year, and thus adds half that amount to life expectancy.

To account for disability, we modify equation (1). For those in the last year of life, we weight the half year they expect to live by the share of the people in that half year who are not disabled. Similarly, we weight the years lived by those one year away from death, two years away from death, three years away from death, and more than three years away from death by the share of population in those intervals who are not disabled. Adding this up over all future ages yields disability-free life expectancy. Disabled life expectancy is the difference between total life expectancy and disability-free life expectancy. We can form disability-free life expectancy and disabled life expectancy for any year in which we have mortality and disability data. To match our results above, we estimate these values in two time periods: 1992 and 2008. The mortality data are from those exact years. The disability data are from 1991–1994 and 2006–2009. Although, disability data is available for individual years, we used the combined sample to provide more reliable estimates.

We present all of our calculations for a person age sixty-five in those years. Relative to our calculations in the previous section, we make one additional refinement. Where our aggregate trends were on an age-adjusted basis, here we need to disaggregate disability by age and time until death. Rather than calculating means across single-year age by time-until-death cells, which would involve many small cells, we instead use regression analysis to smooth disability rates by age and time until death. Specifically, we estimate a regression model relating disability to ten age-sex dummy variables (sixty-five to sixty-nine male, sixty-five to sixty-nine female, seventy to seventy-four male, seventy to seventy-four female, etc.), and time to death dummy variables. We estimate this regression separately for pooled 1991–1994 data and pooled 2006–2009 data. We use these regression results to predict disability rates for each person and then average predictions by single year of age. We match these to life tables in 1992 and 2008 and calculate disability-free and disabled life expectancy.

Figure 5.6 shows the trend in total life expectancy, disability-free life expectancy, and disabled life expectancy for the overall population at age sixty-five in 1991–1994 and 2006–2009. Life expectancy at age sixty-five was 17.5 years in 1992. Reflecting the fact that about half the elderly population is disabled, about half of those years were disabled. As noted earlier, life expectancy increased by 1.3 years between 1992 and 2008. The increase in disability-free life expectancy was greater than the total increase in life expectancy—1.8 years in total. The residual was a reduction in disabled life expectancy of 0.5 years. Thus, according to both metrics (the change in disabled life expectancy as well as the share of life that is spent disability free), morbidity is being compressed into the period just before death.

These results are consistent with our early findings (Cutler, Ghosh, and Landrum 2014). In our previous research, we found that for a typical person age sixty-five, life expectancy increased by 0.7 years between 1992 and 2005. Disability-free life expectancy increased by 1.6 years, while disabled life expectancy fell by 0.9 years. In the last three years, then, disability-free life expectancy increased by 0.2 years, although the disabled life expectancy increased by 0.4 years.

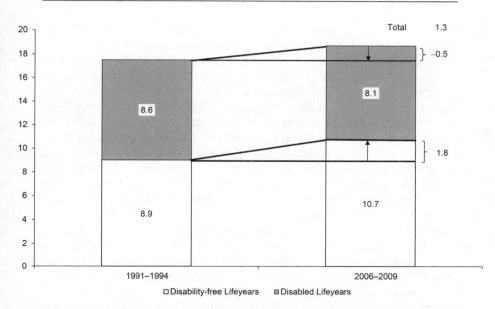

Fig. 5.6   Trend in disabled and disability-free life expectancy at age sixty-five
Note: The figure combines life expectancy data from the NCHS with imputed disability rates by age and time until death from MCBS data linked to Medicare.

In the next section, we examine the prevalence of self-reported diseases in the MCBS and how medical conditions affect disability.

5.3   Medical Conditions Affecting Disability

There is an extensive literature documenting the medical conditions that have the greatest impact on mortality and morbidity in older Americans. The Global Burden of Disease study (JAMA 2013) examined 291 diseases and injuries to identify the leading contributors to morbidity and mortality in the United States. This effort is the most exhaustive report. Ischemic heart disease, lung cancer, stroke, and chronic lung disease were the largest contributors to mortality, while musculoskeletal and mental illness were major contributors to disability. However, few results are reported by age group, and many of the top conditions are less relevant in elderly populations (for example, road injuries). Other studies looking at the burden of diseases include Wang et al. (2012), Salomon et al. (2012), and Murray et al. (2013).

Cutler, Landrum, and Stewart (2008) used data from the National Long-Term Care Survey and found that the probability of being disabled because of the cardiovascular disease fell from 9.4 percent in 1989 to 8.0 percent in 1999. Landrum, Stewart, and Cutler (2008) examined the onset of disability attributable to medical conditions as coded in the Medicare claims and compared these results to respondents' self-report of the cause of their disability. Because of their high prevalence and strong association with disability onset, they found that arthritis, dementia, and cardiovascular disease were the most important contributors to disability. Several studies have examined respondents' self-reported cause of their disability in national surveys (Landrum, Stewart, and Cutler 2008; Martin, Schoeni, and Andreski 2010). Arthritis, back pain, heart disease, diabetes, mental illness, and vision problems are the most common reported causes. Similar patterns are documented in all studies: cardiovascular disease, diabetes, lung disease, and Alzheimer's are a major contributor to death and disability, while musculoskeletal, mental illness, and vision problems are major contributors to morbidity. Cancer remains a major source of mortality, but is relatively minor in its contribution to disability.

The MCBS asks extensive medical condition questions, which we use to classify diseases. The questions are generally of the form, "Has a doctor (ever) told (you/[SP]) that (you/he/she) had a myocardial infarction or heart attack?" The first set of health questions is about medical events the person has experienced. These include cancers (lung cancer, breast cancer, prostate cancer, colorectal cancer, and other cancer); cardiovascular conditions (heart disease, stroke), diseases of the central nervous system (Alzheimer's disease, Parkinson's disease), musculoskeletal problems (rheumatoid arthritis, nonrheumatoid arthritis, broken hip), pulmonary disease, diabetes, and vision problems. The prevalence of these conditions is asked about, not the incidence rate.

Trends in age-sex-adjusted disease prevalence are reported in table 5.2. The prevalence of self-reported breast and prostate cancer is increasing, respectively, at 0.04 and 0.13 percentage points annually. Breast and prostate cancer screenings are increasingly common among the elderly and are mostly paid for by Medicare. Thus, the likelihood of early detection and treatment of these cancers may be becoming more common. Cardiovascular disease prevalence has declined markedly, including both ischemic heart disease (0.44 percentage point decline annually) and stroke (0.03 percentage point decline annually). Alzheimer's disease is increasing by 0.07 percentage points annually. There has been an increase in the prevalence of nonfatal disease over time, as more people report nonrheumatoid arthritis (0.18 percentage points annually) and, particularly, diabetes (0.51 percentage points point annually). People reporting vision problems have declined substantially (0.91 percentage points annually). The prevalence of pulmonary disease has also increased (0.17 percentage points annually).

To determine the impact of each disease on disability, we relate disability in the early time period of the sample (1991–1994) and the later time period (2006–2009) to demographic and medical factors using a linear probability model:

(2) $\text{Disability}_{it} = \beta_{D,t} \cdot \text{Demographics}_{it} + \beta_{C,t} \cdot \text{Medical Conditions}_{it} + \varepsilon_{it},$

Table 5.2   **Self-reported medical event questions in the MCBS**

Num.	Ever told have	Prevalence (%)	Annual % point change (1991–1994 to 2006–2009)
	Cancer		
1	Lung cancer	0.9	0.02
2	Breast cancer	4.4	0.04
3	Prostate cancer	3.4	0.13
4	Colorectal cancer	2.5	−0.04
5	Other cancer	7.0	−0.13
	Cardiovascular disease		
6	Ischemic heart disease	25.6	−0.44
7	Stroke	11.2	−0.03
	Central Nervous system		
8	Alzheimer's disease	5.2	0.07
9	Parkinson's disease	1.6	−0.01
	Musculoskeletal disease		
10	Rheumatoid arthritis	10.4	−0.11
11	Non-rheumatoid arthritis	46.0	0.18
12	Broken hip	4.1	−0.11
13	Pulmonary disease	14.0	0.17
14	Diabetes	18.7	0.51
15	Vision problems	31.4	−0.91

Source: Tabulations are from the MCBS Access to Care sample for 1991–2009 and use sample weights and use sample weights adjusted to a constant year 2000 population by age, gender, and race.

where *i* denotes individuals, and *t* denotes the period (1991–1994 or 2006–2009). Demographics include ten age-sex dummy variables and time-to-death dummy variables. Individuals may show up multiple times in the regression, depending on how frequently they are interviewed. For accurate standard errors, this should be accounted for. In the regression, we have clustered by individual id and reported the robust standard errors.

Table 5.3 shows the results of the regression. Columns (1) and (2) in show the average prevalence and regression coefficients obtained by regressing disability on demographic variables for the 1991–1994 period. Columns (3) and (4) show the same results for 2006–2009. Both the demographic and clinical covariates are strongly associated with disability. Older age is associated with higher disability, although this relationship decreased slightly over our study period. People are less disabled the further away they are from death. All of the clinical covariates are associated with higher disability rates, as we would expect. In most cases the coefficients are smaller in the 2006–2009 cohort, suggesting that these conditions are less disabling over time. Two exceptions are Alzheimer's disease and Parkinson's, which are more strongly associated with disability in the later time period.

We perform an Oaxaca decomposition to understand how much of the reduction in disability can be explained by changes in the prevalence of

Table 5.3   Regressions explaining disability

					Oaxaca decomposition		
	Prev. 91–94 (%)	Coeffs. (rob. se) 91–94	Prev. 06–09 (%)	Coeffs. (rob. se) 06–09	Effect of change in beta X * DBETA (%)	Effect of change in X BETA * DX (%)	Net effect (%)
Total					*-5.6*	*-1.8*	*-7.4*
Central nervous system					***0.3***	***0.2***	***0.5***
Alzheimer's	4.7	0.25 (0.01)	5.8	0.28 (0.01)	0.1	0.2	0.4
Parkinson's	1.8	0.18 (0.02)	1.6	0.24 (0.02)	0.1	0.0	0.1
Cardiovascular disease					*-1.7*	*-0.8*	*-2.5*
Ischemic heart disease	29.5	0.11 (0.01)	22.9	0.06 (0.01)	-1.5	-0.7	-2.2
Stroke	11.3	0.16 (0.01)	10.9	0.14 (0.01)	-0.2	-0.1	-0.3
Pulmonary disease	13.3	0.14 (0.01)	15.9	0.13 (0.01)	**-0.02**	**0.4**	**0.3**
Diabetes	16.2	0.11 (0.01)	23.8	0.12 (0.01)	***0.1***	***0.9***	***0.9***
Musculoskeletal disease					**-0.3**	**-0.2**	**-0.5**
Rheumatoid arthritis	12.3	0.22 (0.01)	10.7	0.20 (0.01)	-0.3	-0.4	-0.6
Nonrheumatoid arthritis	43.5	0.13 (0.01)	46.2	0.12 (0.01)	-0.2	0.4	0.2
Broken hip	5.2	0.13 (0.01)	3.5	0.16 (0.01)	0.2	-0.2	-0.1
Cancer					**-0.3**	**-0.03**	**-0.3**
Lung cancer	0.7	0.09 (0.03)	1.1	0.08 (0.02)	0.0	0.0	0.0
Brest cancer	4.2	0.04 (0.02)	4.8	0.00 (0.01)	-0.2	0.0	-0.1
Prostate cancer	2.2	0.02 (0.02)	4.1	-0.01 (0.01)	-0.1	0.0	0.0
Colorectal cancer	2.9	0.03 (0.02)	2.3	0.03 (0.02)	0.0	0.0	0.0
Other cancer	8.4	0.05 (0.01)	6.5	0.05 (0.01)	-0.1	-0.1	-0.2

Vision problem							
Vision problem	38.4	0.13 (0.01)	24.7	0.13 (0.01)	0.1	-1.7	-1.7
Time to death					-4.5	-0.4	-4.9
12–24 months	5.5	-0.04 (0.01)	4.8	-0.04 (0.01)	0.0	0.0	0.0
24–36 months	5.4	-0.04 (0.01)	4.6	-0.07 (0.01)	-0.1	0.0	0.0
> 36 months	83.6	-0.19 (0.01)	86.2	-0.24 (0.01)	-4.4	-0.5	-0.1
Other demographics					0.9	0.0	0.9
Male 70 to 74 years	11.9	0.01 (0.01)	11.9	0.00 (0.01)	-0.1	0.0	-0.1
Male 75 to 79 years	9.5	0.06 (0.01)	9.5	0.04 (0.01)	-0.2	0.0	-0.2
Male 80 to 84 years	5.6	0.14 (0.01)	5.6	0.13 (0.01)	-0.1	0.0	-0.1
Male 85 years +	3.8	0.28 (0.02)	3.8	0.22 (0.01)	-0.2	0.0	-0.2
Female 65 to 69	12.7	0.10 (0.01)	12.7	0.08 (0.01)	-0.3	0.0	-0.3
Female 70 to 74	14.5	0.12 (0.01)	14.5	0.09 (0.01)	-0.4	0.0	-0.4
Female 75 to 79	13.1	0.19 (0.01)	13.1	0.15 (0.01)	-0.5	0.0	-0.5
Female 80 to 84	9.2	0.28 (0.01)	9.2	0.22 (0.01)	-0.5	0.0	-0.5
Female 85 years +	9.1	0.37 (0.01)	9.1	0.35 (0.01)	-0.2	0.0	-0.2
Constant	100.0	0.27 (0.01)	100.0	0.30 (0.01)	3.3	0.0	3.3

Note: The table is a decomposition of changes in the measure of disability indicated in the columns. We estimate equations of the form: $D_{it} = X_{it}\beta_t + \varepsilon_{it}$, for two time periods: 1991–1994 and 2006–2009. The table shows Oaxaca decomposition, the predicted percentage point change in D_{it} resulting from changes in the X variables, decomposed into demographics and condition prevalence, and changes in the βs, decomposed into those for conditions, those for demographics, and the constant term. Robust standard errors are reported in parentheses.

the covariates versus changes in the impact of covariates on disability (the coefficients). The Oaxaca decomposition is reported in the last three columns of the table. The first column in the Oaxaca decomposition shows the change in disability due to change in the impact of covariates (coefficients), holding prevalence constant at its 1991–1994 level. The next column shows the change in disability due to change in prevalence, holding the impact of each coefficient constant at the 1991–1994 level. The final column shows the net change.

Between 1991–1994 and 2006–2009, disability decreased by 7.4 percentage points. Out of that, 5.6 percentage points is associated with a change in the impact of covariates on disability, and the remaining 1.8 percentage points is due to change in prevalence holding the impact constant. The biggest contributors to the total disability decline are cardiovascular disease (2.5 percentage points) and vision problems (1.7 percentage points). Both the prevalence of cardiovascular diseases decreased (explaining 0.8 percent of disability decline) as well as its impact on disability (explaining 1.7 percent). Vision problems remained equally disabling in the later period, but declined in prevalence. Cancers (0.3 percentage points) and musculoskeletal diseases (0.5 percentage points) both have declined marginally. In contrast, Alzheimer's disease (0.5 percentage points) and diabetes (0.9 percentage points) have increased disability points.

Even given these conditions, people are less disabled further away from death. Among the time-to-death dummies (12 to twenty-four months, twenty-four to thirty-six months, >thirty-six months), >thirty-six months have the biggest decline in disability (about 5 percentage points). The disability changes attributed to the time-to-death dummy variables are mostly factors that remained unexplained. This may include medical conditions not captured in the MCBS, environmental factors (ramps, disability accessible buildings), changes in living conditions (married, assisted living), other medical treatments, or unmeasured changes in the severity of conditions that are occurring over time. Understanding these other factors is an important issue for future research.

5.4   Disability-Free and Disabled Life Expectancy by Disease

The results in the previous section show us which diseases are affecting disability. In this section, we calculate disability-free and disabled life expectancy by disease.

To calculate the disability-free life expectancy by disease, we used a simulation method based on regression coefficients reported in table 5.3. For each disease, we simulate the impact of changes in the disease prevalence and impact on disability by changing the prevalence and coefficient for that particular disease in the 1991–1994 data to its 2006–2009 level. We then re-predict disability by age and time until death using the new coefficients and disease probabilities. In performing this simulation, we add one additional wrinkle, allowing the disease prevalence to vary by age group. We match the disease prevalence by ten age-sex groups (sixty-five to sixty-nine male, sixty-five to sixty-nine female, seventy to seventy-four male, seventy to seventy-four female, etc.).

On the demographic side, all age-sex dummy variables are adjusted to 2000 level. So, the only other variable for which we did the simulation are the time-to-death dummy variables. We simulated these variables all at once, that is, we changed the coefficients and prevalence rates of all time-to-death variables to their 2006–2009 level jointly, and then repredicted disability.

Once we have the change in disability due to each disease, we combine this with the change in life expectancy due to that disease, using the methodology described in the previous section. The result is a calculation of the change in disability-free and disabled life expectancy due to each disease.

Figure 5.7 shows the change in disability-free and disabled life expectancy resulting from changes in each medical condition. Adding across all conditions, disability-free life expectancy increased by 1.8 years and disabled life expectancy decreased by 0.5 years. These are the same as in figure 5.6, though these estimates are derived by adding across all conditions and thus could differ from the estimates in figure 5.6 because of covariance effects.

The biggest increase in disability-free life expectancy is from cardiovascular disease (0.85 years). Roughly 50 percent of the increase in disability-free

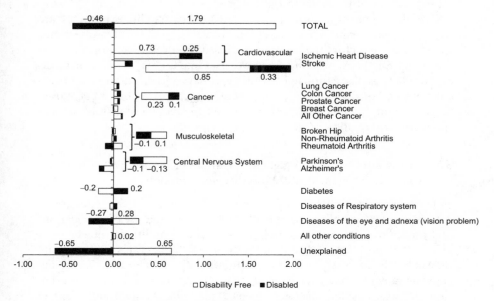

Fig. 5.7   Change in disabled and disability-free life expectancy at age sixty-five by disease (1991–1994 versus 2006–2009)

Note: The figure combines life expectancy data from the NCHS combined with causes of death data and imputed disability rates by age and time until death from MCBS data linked to Medicare.

life expectancy is from the cardiovascular disease, primarily heart disease. However, improvements in survival in those with cardiovascular disease also led to a modest increase in disabled life expectancy. Consistent with previous literature (Landrum, Stewart, and Cutler 2008) cancer remains a major source of mortality and contributes modestly to disability. Improvements in survival rates among those with cancer led to an increase in disability-free life expectancy of about 0.23 years. Vision problems show a significant impact on disability-free life expectancy (0.28 years). There is no increase in life expectancy from vision impairment, so all of this change comes from a reduction in disabled life expectancy.

Increased prevalence and impact of diseases of the central nervous system (Alzheimer's and Parkinson's) have reduced disability-free life expectancy by 0.13 years. The diseases of the central nervous system are very important as they have significant impacts on both morbidity and mortality. For diabetes, the disability-free life expectancy declined by 0.2 years.

The penultimate row of the table shows the impact of causes of death we have not separately delineated. These residual causes of death have a small aggregate effect on disability-free life expectancy. The final row shows the unexplained change in disability for those three or more years from death, which translates into 0.65 years of disability-free life expectancy and—since this is not associated with any mortality reduction—a reduction in disabled life expectancy of the same amount.

Overall, the most important gains in disability-free life expectancy are from cardiovascular disease and vision problems. In the next two sections, we explore the factors that may have caused the decline in mortality and morbidity for these two conditions. We examine the importance of medicines and revascularization in preventing primary and secondary cardiovascular events. We also explore the impact of surgical procedures like cataract surgery on improving vision problem and its impact on vision-related measurements and quality of life.

5.5   Pharmaceutical and Surgical Interventions in Reducing Cardiovascular Incidence, Mortality, and Morbidity

The question we address in this section is how much of the reduction in cardiovascular mortality can be explained by increased use of medications and procedures. Previous research has shown for conditions such as musculoskeletal problems and circulatory disorders, higher rates of surgery are plausibly related to reduced disability (Cutler 2005). There are also studies showing how pharmaceutical agents play an important role in the prevention of cardiovascular disease (Downs et al. 1998; Weisfeldt and Zieman 2007). And deaths from cardiovascular disease have greatly declined among the elderly in the United States over the past decades (Rosen et al. 2007). We examine how these trends are related.

We have two measures of cardiovascular disease: ischemic heart disease and stroke. Ischemic heart disease happens when there is reduced blood flow to the heart. Acute myocardial infarction or heart attack is the most serious form of ischemic heart disease, when the blood flow to the heart is abruptly interrupted, causing part of the heart muscle to die. A stroke happens when poor blood flow to the brain or a hemorrhage in the brain leads to death of part of the brain. Historically, heart attack and strokes are a major cause of death in the United States.

Figures 5.8 and 5.9 show more detail on death from these two causes. The mortality rate for ischemic heart disease has declined significantly over time (figure 5.8), from an age-adjusted rate of 1,250 per 100,000 in 1992–1994 to 749 per 100,000 in 2006–2009 ($p < 0.001$). The decline was significantly greater from 2001–2009 (35 percent) than prior to 2001 (17 percent). Figure 5.9 shows the trends in stroke mortality. Stroke mortality also declined significantly over time, from an age-adjusted rate of 357 per 100,000 in years

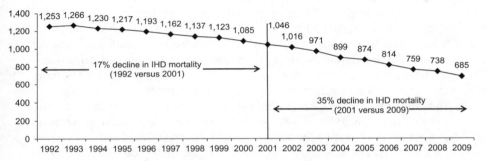

Fig. 5.8   IHD mortality rates per 100,000 (age-sex adjusted)
Source: Data are from the Centers for Disease Control and Prevention/National Center for Health Statistics on Causes of Death and microdata on mortality available at the National Bureau of Economic Research.

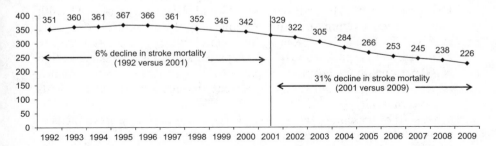

Fig. 5.9   Stroke mortality rates per 100,000 (age-sex adjusted)
Source: Data are from the Centers for Disease Control and Prevention/National Center for Health Statistics on Causes of Death and microdata on mortality available at the National Bureau of Economic Research.

1992–1994 to 240 per 100,000 in 2006–2009 ($p < 0.001$). Again, the reduction was greater after 2001 (31 percent) than before (6 percent).

Understanding how medical treatments or other changes influence these trends is challenging. The natural econometric technique is to relate receipt of the technology to reduced mortality. This is problematic, however, because receipt of different therapies is not random. For example, people who are more severely ill are more likely to receive more intensive technologies. Those same people are also more likely to die. Thus, receipt of intensive technologies is often associated with higher mortality in a cross section, even if the technology is actually effective.

A natural solution to the endogeneity problem is to instrument for technology receipt. In preliminary analysis, we spent some time evaluating potential instruments, including area-level treatment rates and their changes. However, there were no characteristics of areas or their changes that led to plausible instruments for technology receipt.

As a result, we follow a different path. We use the IMPACT model (Ford et al. 2007; Capewell, Morrison, and McMurray 1999; Capewell et al. 2010) to gauge the impact of treatment trends on mortality among US adults sixty-five years and older between 1992 and 2009. The IMPACT model is a multistate model explaining coronary heart disease mortality. The model divides the population into two groups: patients receiving medical and surgical treatments for heart disease and those who are not. It then estimates the contribution of treatment and risk factor changes (smoking, high systolic blood pressure, elevated total blood cholesterol, obesity, diabetes, and physical inactivity) to mortality. Within each disease state, clinical literature is used to parameterize the impact of different treatments and risk factors on mortality. The model was developed for the population as a whole (ages twenty-five to eighty-four); we parameterize the model to estimate the causes of mortality reduction in the elderly.

The rates of medical and surgical treatments and risk factors are calculated using various data sources, including NHDS (National Hospital Discharge Survey), Medicare data, MCBS, and NHANES (National Health and Nutrition Examination Survey), following the methodology of Ford et al. (2007). Similarly, we follow the assumptions of Ford et al. (2007) in assuming that the proportion of treated patients actually taking medication is 100 percent among hospitalized patients, 70 percent among symptomatic patients in the community, and 50 percent among asymptomatic patients in the community.

We start by presenting general trends in risk factors and the use of medications among the population overall, and for those with prior heart disease. We use data from NHANES, which measures cardiovascular risk factors such as total cholesterol, HDL cholesterol, blood pressure, body mass index, Hemoglobin A1c, body mass index, and smoking status. We use several years of data: 1988–1994 and biennial data from 1999 to 2000 through 2011 to 2012. Table 5.4 reports the trend in cardiovascular risk factors. As

Table 5.4 Prevalence of cardiovascular risk factors in NHANES subjects age ≥ sixty-five years during years and Medicare enrolled 1988–1994, 1999–2000, 2001–2004, 2005–2008, and 2009–2012

	Men					Women				
	1988–1994	1999–2000	2001–2004	2005–2008	2009–2012	1988–1994	1999–2000	2001–2004	2005–2008	2009–2012
Age	73	73	74	73	73	74	74	74	74	74
Diabetes (%)	12	14	18	20	22	12	14	17	19	20
HbA1c > 6.5%	11	13	12	13	15	10	10	10	12	13
Current smoker (%)	14	12	9	9	7	11	9	6	6	6
Systolic blood pressure	139	138	134	134	132	142	147	142	140	136
Total cholesterol	209	202	194	181	178	231	224	216	207	205
HDL cholesterol	46	47	48	49	50	56	57	61	60	60
Body mass index	26	28	28	29	28	27	28	28	28	29

Notes: The table combines NHANES 2001–2002 and 2003–2004; NHANES 2005–2006 and 2007–2008; and NHANES 2009–2010 and 2011–2012.

is well known, the elderly population has become more obese over time. Even still, total cholesterol levels have decreased in both men and women, and HDL cholesterol (good cholesterol) has increased. This is quite plausibly a result of greater statin use. Systolic blood pressure has also been decreasing marginally in both men and women. The prevalence of diabetes has increased in both men and women, and the prevalence of high HbA1c levels has increased.

Since smoking and obesity are the two most significant risk factors for cardiovascular disease, we focus on them in some detail. Figure 5.10 shows the trends in smoking and obesity in the elderly Medicare population. Obesity has increased markedly over time, while smoking has declined. Stewart, Cutler, and Rosen (2009) found that if past obesity trends continued unabated, the negative effects on the health of the US population will increasingly outweigh the positive effects gained from declining smoking rates.

The elderly population is now treated more aggressively to control cardiovascular risk. Statins are one well-known example. Statins help reduce the level of low-density lipoproteins (LDL) in the blood and also help with modulation of oxidative stress (Beltowski 2005) that may eventually lead to heart attack. Antihypertensive drugs include beta-blockers, angiotensin-

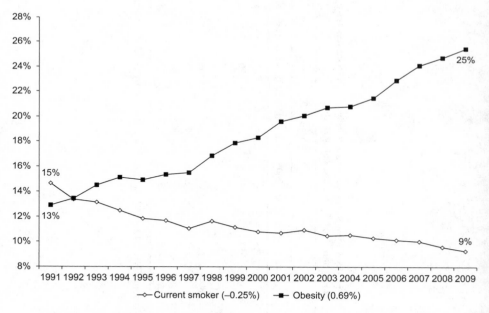

Fig. 5.10   Smoking and obesity prevalence in age sixty-five and older Medicare beneficiaries

Source: Data are from the Medicare Current Beneficiary Survey and Medicare denominator files linked to MCBS, 1991–2009, and are weighted to the population distribution in 2000 by age, sex, and race.

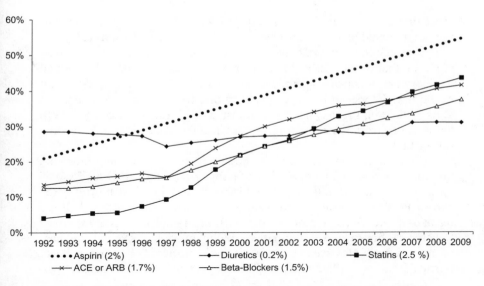

Fig. 5.11   Trends in cardiovascular medication usage in age sixty-five and older Medicare beneficiaries

Sources: Data on medication usage (statins, ACE or ARB, beta-blockers, and diuretics) is from Prescribed Medicine Events in the MCBS data. Rates are adjusted to 2000 population by age, sex, and race. The aspirin usage from the 1992 to 1994 period is from NHANES III, and the later period is from MEPS 2007. We did a linear interpolation for the intermediate years.

converting enzyme (ACE) inhibitors, angiotensin receptor blockers (ARBs), and diuretics. Aspirin use is also increasingly common. Literature suggests that low-dose aspirin helps reduce cardiovascular disease incidence and recurrence.

Figure 5.11 shows the trends in the use of these medications in the elderly community population, and figure 5.12 shows similar trends among patients with ischemic heart disease. The data on medication usage is from the Prescribed Medicine Events file in the MCBS that contains cost and utilization of prescribed medicines for the community population. Statin usage increased the most (2.5 percentage points annually in the population without IHD), though the use of beta-blockers (1.5 percentage points annually) and ACE inhibitors (1.7 percentage points annually) also increased markedly. The use of diuretics increased marginally (0.2 percentage point annually). Aspirin is available over the counter and thus is not in the prescribed medicine file. We obtain usage in the earlier time period (1992–1994) from NHANES III, with later data from the 2007 Medical Expenditure Panel Survey (MEPS). We used a linear interpolation to fill in the intermediate years. For this reason, we show the plots for aspirin use in dotted lines. Use among the population with IHD increased even more rapidly. In addition, procedure rates increased rapidly in the IHD population with a 2.0 percentage point annual increase in primary percutaneous interventions (PCI).

To estimate the impact of these changes on cardiovascular disease mortality, we first calculate the difference between the observed and expected number of deaths from ischemic heart disease in 2009. Compared to what would have happened had age-specific mortality rates remained constant at its 1992 level, the decline in age-adjusted death rate resulted in 228,910 fewer deaths from ischemic heart disease in 2009. This is shown in the first row of table 5.5.

The remaining rows of table 5.5 shows how this reduction in mortality distributes across treatments and risk factors. All told, the IMPACT model estimates that about half of reduced ischemic heart disease mortality (51 percent) is a result of improved treatment, about slightly less than half is a result of improved risk factors (44 percent), and a small share is unexplained (5 percent). Improvement in inpatient treatments only explained 8 percent of improvement. However, secondary prevention after MI had major effects, particularly, statins (9 percent), warfarin (1 percent), beta-blockers (11 per-

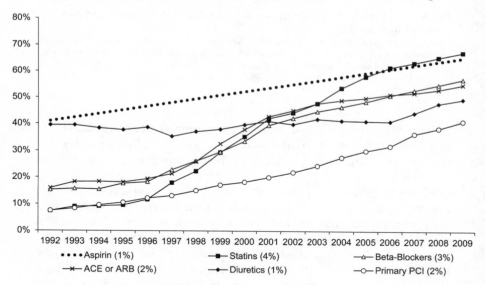

Fig. 5.12   Trends in medication usage in ischemic heart disease patients (sixty-five years and older)

Sources: Data on medication usage is from (statins, beta-blockers, ACE or ARB, diuretics) Prescribed Medicine Events in the MCBS data. Rates are adjusted to 2000 population by age, sex, and race. Aspirin usage for the earlier period is from NHANES III and the later year is from MEPS. The intermediate years are linear interpolations. Primary PCI usage is from 5 percent Medicare sample for people hospitalized for ischemic heart disease (410.X–414.X). Primary PCI is defined as having a PCI on the same day or the next day of an ischemic heart disease hospitalization.

Table 5.5   IMPACT mortality model estimated deaths prevented or postponed in the
                   elderly United States population in 2009

	Number of deaths	Percent of total change
Total change relative to expectations	−228,910	
Treatments	−117,521	51
Ischemic heart disease hospitalization (aspirin, beta-blockers, ACE inhibitors, primary PCI and CABG)	−18,158	8
Secondary prevention after MI		
Aspirin	−2,399	1
Beta-blocker	−25,476	11
ACE inhibitor	−12,752	6
Statins	−19,827	9
Warfarin	−2,195	1
Rehabilitation	−9,299	4
Secondary prevention after CABG or PTCA (aspirin, beta-blockers, ACE inhibitor, statins, rehabilitation)	−2,270	1
Chronic angina (CABG, angioplasty, aspirin, statins)	1,268	−1
Antihypertensive for hypertension treatment	−8,895	4
Statins for lipid reduction treatment	−17,538	8
Risk factors	**−100,511**	**44**
Smoking prevalence (%)	−19,299	8
Systolic blood pressure (mm hg)	−51,270	22
Total cholesterol (mmol/liter)	−68,787	30
Physical inactivity (%)	−3,924	2
Body mass index (BMI)	13,254	−6
Diabetes prevalence (%)	29,515	−13

Note: In the risk factor calculations for systolic blood pressure, the number of deaths excludes people receiving treatment for hypertension and for total cholesterol. The number of deaths excludes patients receiving statins. Risk factor estimates are from NHANES. The treatment data comes from several sources including NHDS, Medicare data, MCBS and some other studies.

cent), and ACE inhibitors (6 percent). Primary prevention was also a major contributor, including statins for lipid reduction (8 percent) and hypertension treatment (4 percent). The impact of other treatments was smaller.

Considering risk factor changes, the biggest changes were reduced total cholesterol (30 percent) and blood pressure (22 percent). These are each separate from treatment in that the estimated decline in blood pressure and cholesterol is among those who do not report taking medication. That said, the Ford et al. (2007) study does not adjust its estimate of population trends among the nontreated for the fact that increased numbers of people—likely with high levels of cholesterol and blood pressure—are being treated. Thus, it is possible that selection effects contribute to the magnitude of the risk factor estimates, making these estiamtes overstated. Smoking reduction contributed 8 percent, while increased BMI and diabetes led to 19 percent more deaths. Overall, these findings are close to Ford's 2007 study for the adult population ages twenty-five to eighty-four, which found a 47 percent reduction due to treatment and 44 percent due to risk factors.

Using the IMPACT model, we simulated the annual impact of treatment and risk factor changes for ischemic heart disease mortality rates between 1992 and 2009. Figure 5.13 shows the results. The line with squares shows the conterfactual mortality rate per 100,000 if the mortality rate by age remained constant at its 1992 level and only the population totals changed. The line with diamonds shows the actual mortality trend in ischemic heart disease between 1992 and 2009. The line with triangles shows the simulated effect of treatment and improvements in risk factors combined on mortality. The fact that the simulated mortality tracks the actual mortality shows that the model as a whole fits very well. The line with x-marks divides the total effect found by the model into a treatment component (the upper part) and a risk factor component (the lower part). Almost all of the changes in the 1990s are due to treatment; those after 2000 are a mix of treatment and risk factor changes. Figures 5.14 and 5.15 show the effect of individual medications and risk factors on mortality. Between 1992 and 2009, increased use of statins for primary and secondary prevention saved roughly 48,000 lives. Increased use of ACE inhibitors and beta-blockers in IHD patients saved another 43,000 lives. Other studies have found similar impact of greater satin use. For example, Grabowski et al. (2012) found that statin therapy reduced low-density lipoprotein levels by 18.8 percent, which translated into roughly 40,000 fewer deaths.

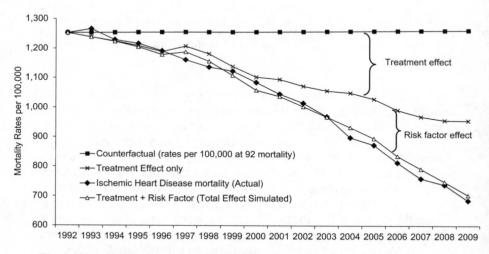

Fig. 5.13   Ischemic heart disease mortality rates per 100,000: Actual versus simulated

Source: Data are from the Centers for Disease Control and Prevention/National Center for Health Statistics on Causes of Death and the US Census of population.

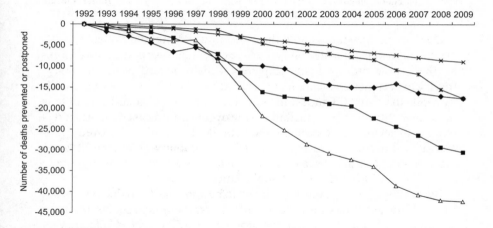

→×— Anti-hypertensive treatments (non-Ihd cohort)

→*— Statins + Warfarin (primary prevention in non-Ihd cohort)

→♦— Ihd hospitalization (410.XX- 414.XX) (Aspirin, Beta-blockers, ACE inhibitors Resuscitation, Primary PCI and CABG)

→■— Statins + Warfarin (Ihd patients)

→△— ACE inhibitors & Beta-Blockers (ihd-patients)

Fig. 5.14   Estimated deaths prevented or postponed in the elderly United States population: Treatment effect

Source: The treatment effects are calculated using data from NHDS, MCBS, Medicare and other sources cited in Ford et al. (2007).

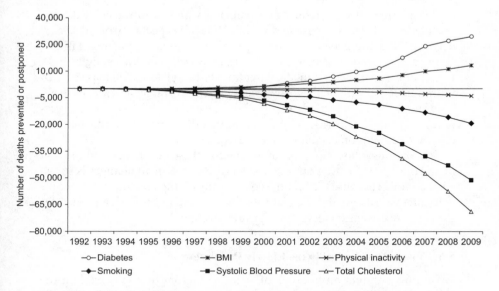

Fig. 5.15   Estimated deaths prevented or postponed in the elderly United States population: Risk factors

Source: The risk factors are calculated using data from NHANES and MCBS.

One central question is how these mortality changes are related to the overall improvement in disability-free life expectancy we noted above. Linking these two estimates is not completely straightforward, as the disability-free life expectancy estimates include changes in both disability and mortality, while the IMPACT model includes mortality only. To understand how these mortality changes contribute to the overall improvement in disability-free life expectancy, we need to understand whether the improvement in mortality is accompanied by a reduction in disability or whether it keeps more people alive in a disabled state. The former would add much more to disability-free life expectancy than the latter.

By and large, the interventions shown to be important in reducing mortality are those that reduce the incidence of adverse events and enable improved functioning after an event, not just prolong survival for those who are very disabled. This is shown directly in the 12 percent of reduced deaths accounted for by primary prevention—generally associated with fewer acute events—and indirectly in the secondary prevention after an MI. For example, statins and antihypertensive agents decrease cardiovascular symptoms in addition to reducing heart attacks and strokes. Still, to be conservative, we assume that medical treatments reduce mortality and the prevalence of acute cardiovascular events, but leave unaffected disability for those who have had a cardiovascular event. We model this empirically as treatment affecting mortality and the prevalence of disease, but not disability conditional on having ischemic heart disease.

Considering only the reduction in mortality and cardiovascular disease prevalence yields an increase in disability-free life expectancy of 0.53 years between 1992 and 2008 (compared to 0.73 years including changes in disability conditional on ischemic heart disease as well, as shown in figure 5.7). If half of this is a result of medical treatments, this yields an increase of 0.26 years associated with medical advance. This is a very large increase; by itself, it accounts for 15 percent of the total increase in disability-free life expectancy over this time period. Figure 5.16 shows the impact of cardiovascular disease treatment on disability-free life expectancy.

The obvious follow-up question is whether these benefits exceed the cost of the therapies. Costing out the impact of the treatment changes is somewhat complex because the lifetime costs of any therapy include what people will suffer who do not die of cardiovascular disease. For this reason, we defer the cost-effectiveness calculation for future research.

5.6   Vision Impairment in the Elderly Population

We now conduct an analysis of possible factors that may explain the change in disability-adjusted life expectancy associated with vision impairment. The trend in having a current vision problem is shown in figure 5.17. Current vision problems have declined from about 40 percent of the elderly

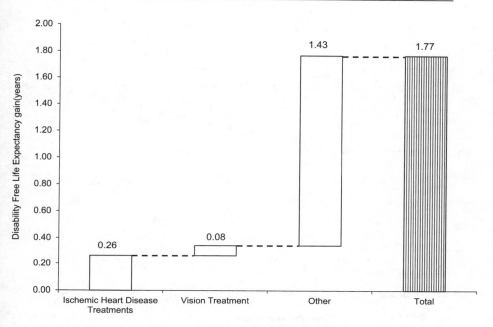

Fig. 5.16   Impact of treatments on changes in disability-free life expectancy at age sixty-five

Note: The figure combines life expectancy data from the NCHS with imputed disability rates by age and time until death from MCBS data linked to Medicare.

population to about 25 percent. This decline has been noted in other studies (Freedman and Martin 1998; Cutler 2001a, 2001b; Freedman et al. 2007; Cutler, Ghosh, and Landrum 2014).

There are several reasons why people may have vision problems, and thus several treatments for them. The most prevalent source of vision problems in the elderly is cataracts, a condition in which the lens of the eye becomes progressively opaque. Most cataracts are a natural process of aging. Other possible causes of vision impairment include glaucoma, diabetic retinopathy, and macular degeneration (Kasper 1989).

Cataract surgery is the most common treatment for cataracts in the United States. Figure 5.17 also shows the percentage of people who have had cataract surgery in the elderly Medicare population. This is from a self-reported question the first year that an individual is in the survey. Self-reported cataract surgery increased from 20 percent to 33 percent. The decline in current vision problems looks like a mirror image of increase in cataract surgery, both in number (16 percent decline versus a 13 percent increase) and in timing. It is thus plausible that people are reporting fewer vision problems as a result of greater use of cataract surgery.

For comparison, the bottom line of the figure shows treatment for macu-

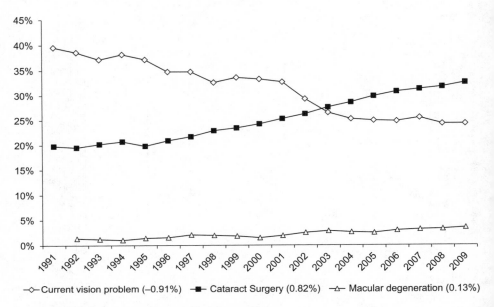

--◇--Current vision problem (–0.91%)   ---■--- Cataract Surgery (0.82%)   --△-- Macular degeneration (0.13%)

Fig. 5.17   Cataract surgery and vision problems
Source: Data are from the Medicare Current Beneficiary Survey and Medicare denominator files linked to MCBS 1991–2009, and are weighted to the population distribution in 2000 by age, sex, and race.

lar degeneration, measured by claims for macular degeneration drugs. This is also increasing over time, though the rates are much lower.

The question is whether the increased use of cataract surgery can explain the reduction in vision impairment, and thus reduced disability. We started in the same way for cardiovascular disease, in particular by examining the literature on the impact of cataract surgery on disability. Table 5.6 contains a brief literature review of studies documenting vision changes and broader changes in health-related quality of life after cataract surgery. The first part of the table shows clear evidence that cataract surgery results in fewer vision problems. Studies show improvements in Snellen visual acuity, improvements in self-reported trouble with vision, and also improvements in VF-14 scores and NEI-VFQ25 scores in a period four to six months after cataract surgery.

Despite these improvements in vision, however, studies of health-related quality of life, shown in the lower panel of the table, indicate no significant change in periods after cataract surgery. This is true for measures such as the Euroqual-5D (EQ-5D), the SF-12, and the SF-36. This result is confusing, since the evidence presented earlier shows that vision problems are a significant cause of disability. That said, none of these survey instruments are a perfect match for our measure of ADL and IADL disability.

To better understand the impacts of cataract surgery on vision problems

Table 5.6   **Effectiveness and use of cataract surgery on vision problems and disability**

Findings	Study
Vision problems	
Improvement in Snellen visual acuity	Steinberg et al. (1994)
	Mangione et al. (1994)
	Javitt et al. (1993)
Improvement in self-reported trouble with vision	Steinberg et al. (1994)
Improvements in VF-14 score	Steinberg et al. (1994)
	Owsley et al. (2007)
Improvements in NEI-VFQ25 score	Groessl et al. (2013)
Health-related quality of life (HRQOL)	
EQ-5D shows insignificant change	Foss et al. (2006)
SF-12 shows insignificant change	Castells et al. (2006)
No significant impact on SF-36 physical functioning	Mangione et al. (1994)
	Owsley et al. (2007)

Note: **Snellen visual acuity** test is decimal acuity with 1.0 representing 20/20 vision. **VF-14** is a method for assessing the quality of the visual function of those with cataracts in daily living from the patient's viewpoint, developed in 1994 by Steinberg et al. **VFQ-25** is the product of an item-reduction analysis of the longer field test version of the survey called the fifty-one-item National Eye Institute Vision Function Questionnaire (NEI-VFQ). **EQ-5D** is a standardized instrument for use as a measure of health outcomes. **SF-12** is a short-form 12 health survey that was developed for the Medical Outcomes Study (MOS). **SF-36** is a thirty-six-item, patient-reported survey of patient health commonly used to determine the cost effectiveness of medical treatments.

and disability, we look at trends in vision-problem reporting and disability within individuals who have and have not received cataract surgery. The idea is that if cataract surgery changes the trend in vision degradation over time, this might be apparent by following individual health trends. Of course, such an effect is not guaranteed to be found. For example, if people who have cataract surgery are at the poor end of the vision distribution, their vision might deteriorate even if cataract surgery prevents a more rapid deterioration. Conversely, if the nonvision health of people who receive cataract surgery is better, their health transitions may have been relatively better even without the cataract surgery. This is the endogeneity issue noted above. In the case of vision, we do not have a disease model we can use for validation.

Our regressions for vision impairment are of the form:

$$(3)\ VI_{it} = \beta_C * \text{Cataract Surgery}_{it} + \beta_D * \text{Demogs}_{it} + \beta_M * \text{Medical Conditions}_{it}$$
$$+ \beta_S * \text{Social Factors}_{it} + \beta_V * VI_{it-1} + \varepsilon_{it},$$

where VI is the degree of vision impairment (ordered, as described below) and VI_{it-1} is a set of dummy variables representing the answers in the prior year of the survey. Cataract Surgery$_{it}$ is a dummy variable indicating a claim for cataract surgery between the previous interview date and the current interview date (interviews are generally in the fall). Demographics include age-sex dummy variables and a time trend. We also control for four groups of medical conditions: chronic disabling (Alzheimer's, Parkinson's, and pulmonary), recoverable acute events (ischemic heart disease, stroke, and broken hip), nonfatal chronic conditions (diabetes and arthritis), and cancer. Social factors may influence disability as well. We address this with dummy variables for whether the person is married and whether they live alone. The latter variable is partly endogenous—people who are less healthy may not be able to live alone; the former is plausibly more exogenous. Since 2002, the MCBS has asked about three levels of vision impairment: no vision problem, a little vision problem, and a lot of vision problem. We order them in that fashion (healthiest is 0 and a lot of vision problems is 2) and estimate an ordered probit model. Prior to 2002, the MCBS also included a category for whether the individual was blind. The share of people reporting blindness is small, so we include this with the group reporting a lot of vision problems. Because the relationship between past vision impairment and current vision impairment may change in the year that the survey questionnaire changes, however, we omit data from 2002 from the regression.

We estimate a separate but similar model for disability. In this case, we form an ordered variable for no disability, IADL disability only, 1–2 ADLs, and 3+ ADLs (in this case, from 0 to 3, where higher numbers indicate worse health). We also include dummies for lagged disability status and lagged vision impairment as independent variables.

To measure cataract surgery during the course of our sample, we use MCBS fee-for-service cost and use data (recall that self-reports of cataract surgery receipt are asked only in the first year of the survey). Eligible CPT codes include simple cataract surgery (66984), complex cataract surgery (66982), removal of lens material (66840, 66850, 66852, 66920, 66930, 66940), and intracapsular cataract surgery (66983).

The results of the two regressions are reported in table 5.7. The model for vision impairment is in the left panel, and the model for disability is in the right panel. Each model estimates the coefficients on the indicated variables and a series of cut points for the different variables; we report the coefficient estimates, but not the cut point estimates. The fit of the vision impairment model is reasonable, with a pseudo-R^2 of 19 percent. All the variables have expected signs and most are statistically significant. The cataract surgery dummy variable is negative and significant ($p < 0.001$) indicating an improvement in reporting of vision problems in people having cataract surgery. To interpret the magnitude of the coefficient, we repredicted the probability of having no vision problem, a little vision problem, and a lot of vision problems for those who received cataract surgery under the counterfactual that they had not received surgery. The predicted impact of cataract surgery for no vision problem rises from 59.4 percent to 62.0 percent, a little vision problem falls from 29.3 percent to 27.9 percent, and the probability of having a lot of vision problems falls from 11.3 percent to 10.1 percent.

Table 5.7   **Vision problem acuity and disability states: Ordered probit model**

	Vision problem		Disability	
	Coef.	Robust std. err.	Coef.	Robust std. err.
Cataract surgery receipt (t –1 to t)	−0.092	0.024	−0.126	0.021
Year trend	−0.026	0.001	−0.004	0.001
Age 70–74 male	0.009	0.023	0.042	0.023
Age 75–79 male	0.139	0.023	0.175	0.024
Age 80–84 male	0.171	0.023	0.359	0.024
Age 85+ male	0.213	0.025	0.593	0.024
Age 65–69 female	0.103	0.026	0.163	0.027
Age 70–74 female	0.091	0.022	0.172	0.022
Age 75–79 female	0.147	0.022	0.298	0.022
Age 80–84 female	0.208	0.022	0.434	0.022
Age 85+ female	0.217	0.022	0.675	0.022
Nonwhite	−0.017	0.014	0.035	0.012
Married	0.019	0.013	−0.214	0.011
Living alone	0.042	0.013	−0.190	0.011
Ischemic heart disease	0.117	0.010	0.102	0.009
Stroke	0.127	0.013	0.307	0.012
Alzheimer's disease	−0.250	0.020	0.671	0.018
Parkinson's disease	0.129	0.031	0.416	0.031
Broken hip	0.044	0.019	0.268	0.019
Pulmonary disease	0.117	0.012	0.205	0.011
Diabetes	0.135	0.011	0.213	0.010
Arthritis	0.208	0.010	0.168	0.009
Cancer	0.052	0.011	0.056	0.010
A little vision problem (previous year)	1.086	0.010	0.057	0.010
A lot of vision problem (previous year)	1.954	0.021	0.143	0.016
IADL limitation only (previous year)	—	—	0.891	0.012
1–2 ADL limitations (previous year)	—	—	1.437	0.013
3+ ADL limitations (previous year)	—	—	2.746	0.022
N	109,728		109,728	
Pseudo-R^2	0.188		0.303	

Source: Data are from the MCBS cost and use sample for 1992–2009 and use sample weights adjusted to a constant year 2000 population by age, gender, and race. The ordinal dependent variable for vision problem is: no vision problem, a little vision problem, and a lot vision of problem. The ordinal dependent variable for disability is no IADL/ADL limitations, IADL limitations only, 1–2 ADL limitations, and 3+ ADL limitations.

As expected, difficulty with vision increases with age and diseases—the nonfatal chronic conditions (arthritis, diabetes) have the biggest impact on vision acuity. Also interestingly, there is no trend in vision impaiment for married people, but vision worsens for people who are living alone.

The right columns of the table examine the impact of cataract surgery on disability. The model fit is again reasonable, with a pseudo-R^2 of 30 percent. A good share of this is a result of the fact that disability does not change greatly over time, and we include prior year's disability in the model. The cataract surgery dummy is also negative and significant ($p < 0.001$), implying a reduction in the extent of disability after cataract surgery. Again, to better interpret the coefficient, we repredicted the probability of the various levels of disability for those who received cataract surgery if they had not received surgery. The predicted probability of having no limitations falls from 55.5 percent to 52.0 percent, the predicted probability of an IADL limitation only increases from 14.3 percent to 14.9 percent, the predicted probability of having 1–2 ADL limitations increases from 18.8 percent to 20.2 percent, and the predicted probability of having 3+ ADL limitations increases from 11.4 percent to 12.9 percent.

One way to gauge the magnitude of these coefficients is to compare them with other variables. We focus on two other malleable variables: marital status and living alone. Married people have better trends in health than unmarried people. Roughly speaking, the impact of being married is twice the impact of having cataract surgery. Also interestingly, those living alone have improved health over time. We suspect this is a result of selection; those with materially worse health will move in with relatives or move to an institution. The correlation between cataract surgery and each of these variables is small; the coefficient on cataract surgery is essentially unchanged controlling for marital status and living arrangements. This lends some support to the idea that the coefficient on cataract surgery is picking up the true effect of medical care changes, not just other attributes of the individual.

A second way to gauge the magnitude of this coefficient is to consider its implication for the time series. As figure 5.17 shows, the share of people receiving cataract surgery increased by 13 percentage points over our time series. If each cataract surgery operation reduces the probability of being disabled by 3.5 percentage points, the implied reduction in disability is 0.5 percentage points. Table 5.3 shows that disability fell by 1.7 percentage points due to fewer vision impairments. Thus, the increase in cataract surgery explains 27 percent of the improved health related to vision impairment over time. This translates into 0.08 years gain in disability-free life expectancy due to increase in cataract surgery, or roughly 5 percent of the total increase in disability-free life expectancy.

Even this estimate, while large, is likely to be an underestimate, as cataract surgery may explain the trend in vision and thus disability in years beyond its receipt. Thus, we conclude that cataract surgery has an important impact on disability trends over time.

5.7   Conclusion

Our analysis of disability-free life expectancy yields three important conclusions. First, we show that over the 1991–2009 period, disability-free life expectancy rose and disabled life expectancy declined. These results mirror our earlier findings, but extend the years for which we have this information.

Second, we identify the diseases that contribute most to the improvement in disability-free life expectancy. Quantitatively, the largest contributions come from cardiovascular disease and vision problems. Cardiovascular disease contributes to both mortality and morbidity improvements; the impact of vision impairment is entirely through morbidity. Our results attribute 63 percent of the improvement in disability-free life expectancy to these two conditions.

Third, and more speculatively, we consider the factors that lead to improvements in these conditions. For neither condition can we do the type of rigorous empirical research that would identify a population effect with a very high degree of reliability. Nonetheless, our methodologies have strengths. In the case of cardiovascular disease, we use a well-validated model to identify the role of medical treatments versus social factors in improved health. These results show that a bit under half of the mortality reduction from cardiovascular disease is a result of improved medical treatments, translating into about 0.26 years of disability-free life, or roughly 15 percent of the overall increase in disability-free life expectancy.

Our results on vision problems are less certain, since no validated models for vision impairment exist that are comparable to those for cardiovascular disease. The major medical treatment change for people with vision impairment over this time period is the increased use of cataract surgery. Cataracts are the primary source of vision impairment in the elderly population, and cataract surgery has diffused widely. Our results on within-person changes in vision impairment and disability show that receipt of cataract surgery is associated with improved vision and disability trends. We estimate that one-quarter of the reduction in disability due to poor vision results from greater use of cataract surgery. This translates into about 5 percent of the overall increase in disability-free life expectancy. The result on improved vision after cataract surgery mirrors the clinical literature. The finding of reduced disability is novel; studies have not shown a very large improvement in disability after cataract surgery. It is unclear if the difference in results is due to our larger sample sizes, to having measures more focused on disability, or to a tendency to perform cataract surgery in the healthiest members of the population. To the extent that these findings are not driven by selection, however, they indicate real and large benefits of diffusion of cataract surgery.

The important question raised by our results is to identify the other contributors to improved population health over time. There are some conditions that our data do not ask about—mental illness and musculoskeletal issues (back pain, for example)—that have been shown to be major contributors to disability in other studies (JAMA 2013). Other data that have information on these conditions would be a valuable addition to what we present here.

In addition, recent work has documented a slowdown or even reversal of improvements in morbidity and mortality in more recent periods, particularly in the near elderly (Martin, Schoeni, and Andreski 2010; Chen and

Sloan 2015; Case and Deaton 2015). Moreover, improvements in health have been concentrated in high socioeconomic populations (Chetty et al. 2016). The combination of medical, social, and environment factors that have led to better health is a major topic for future research.

References

Beltowski, J. 2005. "Statins and Modulation of Oxidative Stress." *Toxicol Mech Methods* 15 (2): 61–92.

Cai, L., and J. Lubitz. 2007. "Was There Compression of Disability for Older Americans from 1992 to 2003?" *Demography* 44 (3): 479–95.

Capewell, S., E. Ford, J. Croft, J. Critchley, K. Greenlund, and D. Labarthec. 2010. "Cardiovascular Risk Factor Trends and Potential for Reducing Coronary Heart Disease Mortality in the United States of America." *Bulletin of the World Health Organization* 88:120–30.

Capewell, S., C. Morrison, and J. McMurray. 1999. "Contribution of Modern Cardiovascular Treatment and Risk Factor Changes to the Decline in Coronary Heart Disease Mortality in Scotland between 1975 and 1994." *Heart* 81 (4): 380–86.

Case, A., and A. Deaton. 2015. "Rising Morbidity and Mortality in Midlife among White Non-Hispanic Americans in the 21st Century." *Proceedings of the National Academy of Sciences* 112 (49): 15078–83.

Castells, X., M. Comas, J. Alonso, M. Espallargues, V. Martinez, J. Garcia-Arumi, and M. Castilla. 2006. "In a Randomized Controlled Trial, Cataract Surgery in Both Eyes Increased Benefits Compared to Surgery in One Eye Only." *Journal of Clinical Epidemiology* 59:201–07.

Chen, Y., and F. A. Sloan. 2015. "Explaining Disability Trends in the US Elderly and Near-Elderly Population." *Health Services Research* 50 (5): 1528–49.

Chetty, Raj, Michael Stepner, Sarah Abraham, Shelby Lin, Benjamin Scuderi, Nicholas Turner, Augustin Bergeron, and David Cutler. 2016. "The Association between Income and Life Expectancy in the United States, 2001–2014." *Journal of the American Medical Association*. Published online April 10, 2016. doi:10.1001/jama.2016.4226.

Crimmins, E. 2004. "Trends in the Health of the Elderly." *Annual Review of Public Health* 25:79–98.

Crimmins, E., and H. Beltrán-Sánchez. 2010. "Mortality and Morbidity Trends: Is There Compression of Morbidity?" *Journal of Gerontology: Social Sciences* 66B (1): 75–86.

Crimmins, E., M. Hayward, A. Hagedorn, Y. Saito, and N. Brouard. 2009. "Change in Disability-Free Life Expectancy for Americans 70 Years Old and Older." *Demography* 46 (3): 627–46.

Crimmins, E., and D. Ingegneri. 1993. "Trends in Health among the American Population." In *Demography and Retirement: The Twenty-First Century*, edited by A. M. Rappaport and S.J. Schieber, 225–42. Westport, CT: Praeger.

Crimmins, E., and Y. Saito. 2001. "Trends in Healthy Life Expectancy in the United States, 1970–1990: Gender, Racial, and Educational Differences." *Social Science and Medicine* 52 (11): 1629–41.

Crimmins, E., Y. Saito, and D. Ingegneri. 1989. "Changes in Life Expectancy and Disability-Free Life Expectancy in the United States." *Population and Development Review* 15 (2): 235–67.

————. 1997. "Trends in Disability-Free Life Expectancy in the United States, 1970–1990." *Population and Development Review* 23:555–72.

Crimmins, E., Y. Saito, and S. Reynolds. 1997. "Further Evidence on Recent Trends in Two Sources: The LSOA and the NHIS." *Journal of Gerontology: Social Sciences* 52B (2): S59–71.

Cutler, D. M. 2001a. "The Reduction in Disability among the Elderly." *Proceedings of the National Academy of Science* 98 (12): 6546–47.

————. 2001b. "Declining Disability among the Elderly." *Health Affairs* 20 (6): 11–27.

————. 2005. "Intensive Medical Technology and the Reduction in Disability." In *Analyses in the Economics of Aging*, edited by David A. Wise. Chicago: University of Chicago Press.

————. 2008. "Are We Finally Winning the War on Cancer?" *Journal of Economic Perspectives* 22 (4): 3–26.

Cutler, D. M., K. Ghosh, and M. Landrum. 2014. "Evidence for Significant Compression of Morbidity in the Elderly US Population." In *Discoveries in the Economics of Aging*, edited by David A. Wise, 21–50. Chicago: University of Chicago Press.

Cutler, D. M., M. Landrum, and K. Stewart. 2008. "Intensive Medical Care and Cardiovascular Disease Disability Reductions." In *Health in Older Ages: The Causes and Consequences of Declining Disability among the Elderly*, edited by D. M. Cutler and D. A. Wise. Chicago: University of Chicago.

Cutler, D. M., and N. Sahni. 2013. "If Slow Rate of Health Care Spending Growth Persists, Projections May Be Off by $770 Billion." *Health Affairs* 32 (5): 841–50.

Downs, J. R., M. Clearfield, S. Weis, E. Whitney, D. R. Shapiro, P. A. Beere, A. Langendorfer, E. Stein, W. Kruyer, and A. M. Gotto. 1998. "Primary Prevention of Acute Coronary Events with Lovastatin in Men and Women with Average Cholesterol Levels: Results of AFCAPS/TexCAPS." *Journal of the American Medical Association* 279 (20): 1615–22.

Ford, E. S., U. A. Ajani, J. B. Croft, J. A. Critchley, D. R. Labarthe, T. E. Kottke, W. H. Giles, and S. Capewell. 2007. "Explaining the Decrease in US Deaths from Coronary Disease, 1980–2000." *New England Journal of Medicine* 356:2388–98.

Foss, A. J., R. H. Harwood, F. Osborn, R. M. Gregson, A. Zaman, and T. Masud. 2006. "Falls and Health Status in Elderly Women Following Second Eye Cataract Surgery: A Randomised Controlled Trial." *Age Ageing* 35:66–71.

Freedman, V. A., E. Crimmins, R. F. Schoeni, B. C. Spillman, H. Aykan, E. Kramarow, K. Land, J. Lubitz, K. Manton, L. G. Martin, D. Shinberg, and T. Waidmann. 2004. "Resolving Inconsistencies in Trends in Old-Age Disability: Report from a Technical Working Group." *Demography* 41 (3): 417–41.

Freedman, V. A., and L. G. Martin. 1998. "Understanding Trends in Functional Limitations among Older Americans." *American Journal of Public Health* 88 (10): 1457–62.

Freedman, V. A., L. G. Martin, and R. F. Schoeni. 2002. "Recent Trends in Disability and Functioning among Older Adults in the United States: A Systematic Review." *Journal of the American Medical Association* 288 (24): 3137–46.

Freedman, V. A., R. F. Schoeni, L. G. Martin, and J. C. Cornman. 2007. "Chronic Conditions and the Decline in Late-Life Disability." *Demography* 44 (3): 459–77.

Freedman, V. A., B. C. Spillman, P. M. Andreski, J. C. Cornman, E. M. Crimmins, E. Kramarow, J. Lubitz, et al. 2013. "Trends in Late-Life Activity Limitations in the United States: An Update from Five National Surveys." *Demography* 50 (2): 661–71.

Grabowski, D. C., D. N. Lakdawalla, D. P. Goldman, M. Eber, L. Z. Liu, T. Abdelgawad, A. Kuznik, M. E. Chernew, and T. Philipson. 2012. "The Large Social

Value Resulting from Use of Statins Warrants Steps to Improve Adherence and Broaden Treatment." *Health Affairs* 31 (10): 2276–85.

Groess, E. J., L. Liu, M. Sklar, S. R. Tally, R. M. Kaplan, and T. G. Ganiats. 2013. "Measuring the Impact of Cataract Surgery on Generic and Vision-Specific Quality of Life." *Quality of Life Research* 22 (6): 1405–14.

Javitt, J. C., M. H. Brenner, B. Curbow, M. W. Legro, and D. A. Street. 1993. "Outcomes of Cataract Surgery: Improvement in Visual Acuity and Subjective Visual Function after Surgery in the First, Second, and Both Eyes." *Archives of Ophthalmology* 111 (5): 686–91.

Journal of the American Medical Association (JAMA). 2013. "The State of US Health 1990–2010. Burden of Diseases, Injuries, and Risk Factors." US Burden of Disease Collaborators. *Journal of the American Medical Association* 310 (6): 591–606.

Kasper, R. L. 1989. "Eye Problems of the Aged." In *Clinical Aspects of Aging*, 3rd ed., edited by W. Reichel, 445–53. Baltimore: Williams & Wilkins.

Landrum, M., K. Stewart, and D. M. Cutler. 2008. "Clinical Pathways to Disability." In *Health at Older Ages: The Causes and Consequences of Declining Disability among the Elderly*, edited by David Cutler and David Wise. Chicago: University of Chicago Press.

Liao, Y., D. L. McGee, G. Cao, and R. S. Cooper. 2001. "Recent Changes in the Health Status of the Older US Population: Findings from the 1984 and 1994 Supplement on Aging." *Journal of the American Geriatrics Society* 49: 443–49.

Mangione, C. M., R. S. Phillips, M. G. Lawrence, J. M. Seddon, E. J. Orav, and L. Goldman. 1994. "Improved Visual Function and Attenuation of Declines in Health-Related Quality of Life after Cataract Extraction." *Archives of Ophthalmology* 112 (11): 1419–25.

Manton, K. G., L. S. Corder, and E. Stallard. 1993. "Estimates of Change in Chronic Disability and Institutional Incidence and Prevalence Rates in the US Elderly Population from the 1982, 1984, and 1989 National Long-Term Care Survey." *Journal of Gerontology: Social Sciences* 48:S153–66.

———. 1997. "Chronic Disability Trends in Elderly United States Populations: 1982–1994." *Proceedings of the National Academy of Science* 94:2593–98.

Manton, K. G., and X. Gu. 2001. "Changes in the Prevalence of Chronic Disability in the United States Black and Nonblack Population above Age 65 from 1982 to 1999." *Proceedings of the National Academy of Science* 98:6354–59.

Manton, K. G., X. Gu, and V. L. Lamb. 2006. "Change in Chronic Disability from 1982 to 2004/2005 as Measured by Long-Term Changes in Function and Health in the US Elderly Population." *Proceedings of the National Academy of Science* 103 (48): 18374–79.

Manton, L. G., X. Gu, and G. R. Lowrimore. 2008. "Cohort Changes in Active Life Expectancy in the US Elderly Population: Experience from the 1982–2004 National Long-Term Care Survey." *Journals of Gerontology Series B: Psychological Sciences and Social Sciences* 63 (5): S269–81.

Martin, L. G., V. A. Freedman, R. F. Schoeni, and P. M. Andreski. 2010. "Trends in Disability and Related Chronic Conditions among People Ages Fifty to Sixty-Four." *Health Affairs* 29:725–31.

Martin, L. G., R. F. Schoeni, and P. M. Andreski. 2010. "Trends in Health of Older Adults in the United States: Past, Present and Future." *Demography* 47:S17–40.

Murray, C., T. Vos, R. Lozano, M. Naghavi, A. Flaxman, C. Michaud, M. Ezzati, et al. 2013. "Disability-Adjusted Life Years (DALYs) for 291 Diseases and Injuries in 21 Regions, 1990–2010: A Systematic Analysis for the Global Burden of Disease Study 2010." *Lancet* 380 (9859): 2197–223.

Owsley, C., G. McGwin, K. Scilley, G. C. Meek, D. Seker, and A. Dyer. 2007. "Impact of Cataract Surgery on Health-Related Quality of Life in Nursing Home Residents." *British Journal of Ophthalmology* 91 (10): 1359–63.

Rosen, A. B., D. M. Cutler, D. Norton, H. M. Hu, and S. Vijan. 2007. "The Value of Coronary Heart Disease Care for the Elderly: 1987–2002." *Health Affairs* 26 (1): 111–23.

Salomon, J., H. Wang, M. Freeman, T. Vos, A. Flaxman, A. Lopez, and C. J. L. Murray. 2012. "Healthy Life Expectancy for 187 Countries, 1990–2010: A Systematic Analysis for the Global Burden Disease Study 2010." *Lancet* 380 (9859): 2144–62.

Schoeni, R. F., V. A. Freedman, and L. G. Martin. 2008. "Why is Late-Life Disability Declining?" *Milbank Quarterly* 86 (1): 47–87.

Schoeni, R. F., V. A. Freedman, and R. B. Wallace. 2001. "Persistent, Consistent, Widespread, and Robust? Another Look at Recent Trends in Old-Age Disability." *Journal of Gerontology: Social Sciences* 56B:S206–18.

Schoeni, R., L. Martin, P. Andreski, and V. Freedman. 2005. "Persistent and Growing Socioeconomic Disparities in Disability among the Elderly: 1982–2002." *American Journal of Public Health* 95 (11): 2065–70.

Steinberg, E. P., J. M. Tielsch, O. D. Schein, J. C. Javitt, P. Sharkey, S. D. Cassard, M. W. Legro, et al. 1994. "National Study of Cataract Surgery Outcomes: Variation in 4-Month Postoperative Outcomes as Reflected in Multiple Outcome Measures." *Ophthalmology* 101 (6): 1131–40.

Stewart, S. T., D. M. Cutler, and A. B. Rosen. 2009. "Forecasting the Effects of Obesity and Smoking on US Life Expectancy." *New England Journal of Medicine* 361:2252–60.

Wang, H., L. Dwyer-Lindgren, K. Lofgren, J. K. Rajaratnam, A. Rector, C. Levitz, A. Lopez, and C. Murray. 2012. "Age-Specific and Sex-Specific Mortality in 187 Countries, 1970–2010: A Systematic Analysis for the Global Burden of Disease Study 2010." *Lancet* 380 (9859): 2071–94.

Weisfeldt, M. L., and J. Z. Zieman. 2007. "Advances in the Prevention and Treatment of Cardiovascular Disease." *Health Affairs* 26 (1): 25–37.

Comment   Jonathan Skinner

The chapter by Chernew, Cutler, Ghosh, and Landrum is an ambitious one that covers considerable ground, ranging from updated measures of disability compression in the United States to the key question of how much the diffusion of health care technology has contributed to improving health outcomes. First, the authors have revisited the questions posed in Cutler, Ghosh, and Landrum (2014) to test whether the decline in disability (and increase in disability-free days) has continued through 2008; the reassuring answer is yes. But they go beyond this question to dig in more as to the

Jonathan Skinner is the James O. Freedman Presidential Professor of Economics at Dartmouth College, professor of community and family medicine at the Dartmouth Institute for Health Policy and Clinical Practice, and a research associate of the National Bureau of Economic Research.

For acknowledgments, sources of research support, and disclosure of the author's material financial relationships, if any, please see http://www.nber.org/chapters/c13632.ack.

causes of this continued decline: Which medical conditions have made the greatest contribution to the rise in disability-free survival, and more importantly, how much of the disease-specific declines in morbidity and mortality can be attributed to the diffusion of medical innovations such as statins or aspirin? These are great questions, and the authors have done an excellent job of addressing them using a variety of data from the demography and clinical literatures.

In my comments, I have no quarrel with the central conclusion of the chapter, but instead focus on three separate issues raised at different points in the chapter. The first is an intriguing pattern that the authors uncover regarding trends in disability prior to death. While the trend for ADL/IADL measures in the two to three years prior to death exhibited a steady decline, the fraction of people with a disability has remained stubbornly fixed at roughly four-fifths between 1991 and 2009 for those in the last year of life (their table 5.5). This might appear to be puzzling; generally, we might expect disability rates to be declining across the life cycle. But perhaps this is not so puzzling after all: people still have to die of something, and it would be surprising to find a rise in (e.g.) the fraction of sudden cardiac arrest or accidental deaths—more common causes of death among the nondisabled. Still, the empirical patterns uncovered by Chernew et al. suggest a slightly more nuanced view of disability.

For example, suppose disability arises from two general causes. The first is associated with medical factors that are not immediately life threatening, such as diabetes, depression, stable angina, or arthritis, where lifestyle changes and medical innovations might be most effective in reducing both prevalence of the disease, and ensuring that the disease is less likely to result in disability. It is these kinds of disability that we observe most often among those in the second or third year prior to death. The second type of disability arises from serious medical conditions associated with an elevated likelihood of mortality. For example, Class IV congestive heart failure (CHF) has as much as a 50 percent risk of one-year mortality (Ahmed, Aronow, and Fleg 2006), as well as a poor quality of life associated with it, and so we might be expected to find more of these CHF patients in the (unfortunate) group within one year of death. Thus moving from the second or third year prior to death into those just prior to death may represent a fundamental shift in the type of disability, with the second type far less likely to exhibit secular improvement.

Second, the authors show a substantial improvement in vision during this period, one that seems difficult to explain solely through the increase in cataract surgery. The authors have certainly done their best to solve this puzzle, with a careful read of the clinical literature and clever regression analysis. I do not have much to add to their inquiries, except to suggest that the improvement in vision may be associated with other non-cataract-related improvements in health. For example, high blood pressure is a risk factor for vision impairment, so improved cardiovascular health will reduce vision impairment as well (van Leeuwen et al. 2003). Even among diabetics, whose population is on the rise, there has been a growth in monitoring and control, with eye examinations for diabetic patients the standard of care during the past decade. Thus the remarkable decline in vision impairment may be a dividend arising from other sources of health improvement.

Third, the authors have provided further understanding of the fundamental causes for the increase in disability-free life years. Rather than estimate treatment effects from their data, they correctly turned to the comprehensive IMPACT study (Ford et al. 2007) that uses evidence from randomized trials on drugs or cardiovascular treatments to impute how the diffusion of medical treatments (and pharmaceutical use) might have affected patient health. The authors perform this accounting exercise for cardiovascular disease, and find that roughly half of the improvement in disability-free years arises from medical treatments.

They are most likely right, but I would still argue that one must be careful in translating estimates of effectiveness from randomized trials to actual outcomes in the larger community. This was shown first in an earlier study by Wennberg et al. (1998) who compared the mortality rate for carotid endarterectomy reported in the randomized clinical trial (RCT) (e.g., 0.6 percent) with actual mortality in community-based hospitals, which was as much as 2.5 percent depending on the volume of surgical procedures. The differences in outcomes arise because the institutions in the RCT were so selective in choosing appropriate patients for the trials, and because the overall quality of the institutions that performed RCTs—typically academic medical centers—were higher than average community-based hospitals (Wennberg et al. 1998).

While Chernew et al. do not use estimates of carotid endarterectomies in their own analysis, they do use estimates of benefits arising from the increase in (e.g.) statin and estimated aspirin use, so similar issues could arise for their estimates. For example, one recent study from Finland showed substantially lower marginal health effects of statin use once one accounted for the poor adherence with the drug regimen observed in the community (Aarnio et al. 2015). Another study effects of aspirin use found evidence of its impact on lowering the incidence of cancer, but suggested that the "use of aspirin in the general population does not have a major impact on cardiovascular mortality." (Cuzik et al. 2015). This does not detract from the view that advances in treatment had an impact on health outcomes, but it does suggest some caution in interpreting estimates from randomized trials as applying to treatments performed in the general population.

With this concern set aside, one can only hope that this team of researchers will return to the question of why disability rates continue to fall among those not receiving new medical or pharmaceutical treatments in an environment of stagnating health care spending. It is an important question, and surely one of the few reassuring trends that we see in US health care.

References

Aarnio, Emma, Maarit J. Korhonenemail, Risto Huupponenemail, and Janne Martikainenemail. 2015. "Cost-Effectiveness of Statin Treatment for Primary Prevention in Conditions of Real-World Adherence—Estimates from the Finnish Prescription Register." *Atherosclerosis* 239 (1): 240–47.
Ahmed Ali, Wilbert S. Aronow, and Jerome L Fleg. 2006. "Higher New York Heart Association Classes and Increased Mortality and Hospitalization in Heart Failure Patients with Preserved Left Ventricular Function." *American Heart Journal* 151 (2): 444–50.
Cutler, D. M., K. Ghosh, and M. Landrum. 2014. "Evidence for Significant Compression of Morbidity in the Elderly US Population." In *Discoveries in the Economics of Aging*, edited by David A. Wise, 21–50. Chicago: University of Chicago Press.
Cutler, D. M., M. Landrum, and K. Stewart. 2008. "Intensive Medical Care and Cardiovascular Disease Disability Reductions." In *Health at Older Ages: The Causes and Consequences of Declining Disability among the Elderly*, edited by David M. Cutler and David A. Wise. Chicago: University of Chicago.
Cuzick, J., M. A. Thorat, C. Bosetti, P. H. Brown, J. Burn, N. R. Cook, L. G. Ford, et al. 2015. "Estimates of Benefits and Harms of Prophylactic Use of Aspirin in the General Population." *Annals of Oncology* 26:47–57.
Ford, E. S., U. A. Ajani, J. B. Croft, J. A. Critchley, D. R. Labarthe, T. E. Kottke, W. H. Giles, and S. Capewell. 2007. "Explaining the Decrease in US Deaths from Coronary Disease, 1980–2000." *New England Journal of Medicine* 356:2388–98.
van Leeuwen, Redmer, M. Kamran Ikram, Hans Vingerling, Jacqueline C. M. Witteman, Paulus de Jong, and Albert Hofman. 2003. "Blood Pressure, Atherosclerosis, and the Incidence of Age-Related Maculopathy: The Rotterdam Study." *Investigative Ophthalmology & Visual Science* 44:3771–77.
Wennberg, David E., F. Lee Lucas, John D. Birkmeyer, Carl E. Bredenberg, and Elliott S. Fisher. 1998. "Variation in Carotid Endarterectomy Mortality in the Medicare Population: Trial Hospitals, Volume, and Patient Characteristics." *Journal of the American Medical Association* 279:1278–81.

6

Are Black-White Mortality Rates Converging?
Acute Myocardial Infarction in the United States, 1993–2010

Amitabh Chandra, Tyler Hoppenfeld, and Jonathan Skinner

6.1 Introduction

There is a vast literature documenting the presence of pervasive racial disparities in US health care (IOM 2002). More recently, researchers have studied changes over time in the extent of racial and socioeconomic disparities, to test whether the public focus on disparities in health care has led to fundamental changes in practice styles, improved sensitivity by health care providers to different cultural norms, and less biased treatment and outcome decisions. In many cases, there has been a notable reduction in the magnitude of disparities in treatment and the use of "effective" care (Trivedi et al. 2005; Trivedi et al. 2011; Jha et al. 2005). There is less progress, however, with respect to racial disparities in overall health outcomes (e.g., Meara, Richards, and Cutler 2008).

How can this puzzle be explained? Many efforts to address disparities have focused on how physicians treat patients of different races and ethnicities. For example, the public knowledge that stenting rates for black patients are so much lower than those for white patients could lead to cardiologists at the margin to question their decisions not to provide stents to their black patients. An increasing share of minority health professionals could also

Amitabh Chandra is the Malcolm Wiener Professor of Social Policy and Director of Health Policy Research at the Harvard Kennedy School of Government and a research associate of the National Bureau of Economic Research. Tyler Hoppenfeld is a research fellow in the Evidence for Policy Design program at Harvard University. Jonathan Skinner is the James O. Freedman Presidential Professor of Economics at Dartmouth College, professor of community and family medicine at the Dartmouth Institute for Health Policy and Clinical Practice, and a research associate of the National Bureau of Economic Research.

For acknowledgments, sources of research support, and disclosure of the authors' material financial relationships, if any, please see http://www.nber.org/chapters/c13643.ack.

lead to a decline in the extent of disparities in treatments of diverse patient populations. Over a sufficiently lengthy period of time, we might expect to see a convergence in treatment patterns as a result of efforts to reduce both implicit and explicit biases in health care within the hospital.

A much different source of health disparities arises from the fact that black and white patients go to different providers. One study, for example, documented that nearly half of all black acute myocardial infarction (AMI) patients were admitted to 571 hospitals serving just 7 percent of white AMI patients (Skinner et al. 2005). The authors estimated that most of the gap between black and white ninety-day mortality was the consequence of the quality of the hospital to which the patient was admitted, and not because of how black and white patients were treated within the hospital.

Should we expect a convergence in this quality differential across hospitals? Unfortunately, even if all physicians and health professionals were entirely bias-free with regard to race and ethnicity, we would still observe disparities in outcomes if black or Hispanic patients were admitted to hospitals with lower average quality. The question of convergence here is related to two quite different factors: whether patient demand leads to migration toward high-quality hospitals (Chandra et al. 2013), and whether there is a convergence in the quality of hospitals as poor-performing hospitals catch up over time (Skinner and Staiger 2015).

To test these hypotheses, this chapter uses a two-decade time-series approach to test for convergence in hospital quality between black and white patients admitted to hospital for acute myocardial infarction, or AMI. Using a sample of more than four million patients, we do not find evidence of convergence of black and white ninety-day mortality rates. From 1993 to 1998, black AMI patients experienced risk-adjusted mortality rates 0.4 percentage points greater than white AMI patients. After increasing to a gap of 1.6 percentage points from 1999 to 2005, by 2006–2010 the gap had been attenuated to 1.0 percentage points, still more than double the initial disparity in 1993–1998.

With regard to the sources of this widening in outcomes, we use an Oaxaca-Blinder decomposition to consider separately the "within-hospital" sources of racial disparities in outcomes and the "between-hospital" measure capturing black AMI patients going to hospitals with higher (white) mortality rates. Of the overall racial disparity in risk-adjusted outcomes, most was the consequence of between-hospital differences in quality; black patients were admitted to lower-quality hospitals (where quality was measured by risk-adjusted outcomes for white patients), and these between-hospital disparities have shown little evidence of convergence.

At the same time, the within-hospital disparities have been growing. One potential explanation for such differences is the use of percutaneous coronary interventions (PCI), which includes angioplasty and stenting, during the index admission—a marker for "primary" and highly effective surgical treatment for AMI. We find indeed that while rates of PCI trended upward for both black and white patients, the trend was more pronounced for white patients within hospitals—in other words, the rapid diffusion of this treatment is likely to have exacerbated disparities in health outcomes within hospitals.

In sum, we do not find evidence that black patients have sorted or migrated to higher-quality hospitals. These results are therefore supportive of models in which there is little convergence in mortality across hospitals between black and white AMI patients (Skinner and Staiger 2015). To the extent that more productive hospitals with better outcomes expand by increasing volume (as in Chandra et al. 2013), they may do so by drawing from people with similar race or ethnicities, and less through a reduction in segregation of hospital admissions.

6.2   Literature and Theory

The standard model of racial disparities in health care focuses on the clinical encounter, and embodies the idea that a provider treats two identical patients, one white and the other black, differently. Treatment differences in the clinical encounter may occur because there is explicit discrimination where a provider consciously withholds valuable care from minority patients. But disparities may also arise from implicit discrimination, where a harried provider operating in a time-sensitive environment makes unconscious mental decisions that are detrimental to minorities. Stereotyping is one manifestation of this indiscretion and it occurs when a provider uses a patient's race to deduce information about the benefit of treatment (Balsa and McGuire 2003). If African American patients are perceived as less likely to be compliant, then a physician may assume that her African American patient is less compliant. Such biases are compounded by poor communication between providers and their patients, which may create enormous psychological barriers to minority patients seeking care (van Ryn and Burke 2000). Similarly, minority patients may be treated by different physicians within a hospital, for example, by residents rather than attending physicians. If the quality of care differs between black and white patients, we would term this "within-hospital" disparities.[1]

Our earlier work focused on a different source of racial disparities capturing the idea that racial disparities in care are partially the consequence of differences in where minorities and whites receive care. Using five years of Medicare data from 1997 to 2001, Skinner et al. (2005) found that racial

---

1. Strumpf (2011) found that variations in quality of primary care by physicians varied more with respect to the specific physician providing the care than it did with regard to the match, or "concordance," of patient race or ethnicity and the physician's race or ethnicity. To the extent that physician quality varies across hospitals, this would again argue for between-hospital disparities rather than within-hospital disparities.

disparities could primarily be attributed to the treatment of black patients at hospitals with poor risk-adjusted outcomes rather than by worse outcomes for black patients within hospitals. This finding was consistent with studies indicating that black patients are more likely to be treated at hospitals with lower rates of evidence-based treatments and protocols and higher surgical mortality (Barnato et al. 2005; Bradley et al. 2004; Konety, Vaughan Sarrazin, and Rosenthal 2005; Rothenberg et al. 2004).

Differences in where minorities are treated have to do with factors such as insurance and lower socioeconomic status, as well as historical patterns of discrimination and neighborhood segregation. Yet geographical treatment patterns, even for AMI patients being rushed to the hospital, are not set in stone. As Doyle et al. (2015) have found, hospital treatment patterns for AMI patients are strongly affected by which ambulance firm picks up the patient, so the potential is great for regionalization policies to encourage ambulances (and patients) to seek care at high-volume cardiac centers rather than low-volume or low-quality hospitals.

The empirical question is whether there should be convergence in quality across hospitals. If the reason why hospitals exhibit lower quality is because they are less likely to adopt new and effective technologies, or because they are more likely to adopt low-quality technologies, as in Skinner and Staiger (2015), then we might not expect convergence. As the lagging hospitals finally adopt the innovations that rapid-adopting hospitals have been using for years, the rapid-adoption hospitals have already moved on to a new technology, leading to a lack of convergence. Indeed, Skinner and Staiger (2015) found no evidence of convergence, in the sense that the lagging hospitals with low diffusion rates caught up to the rapid-adoption hospitals with high diffusion rates.

Conversely, more productive hospitals, in the sense of providing better health outcomes for AMI patients, have been shown to experience more rapid growth in patient populations (Chandra et al. 2013). In their model, demand-side factors would lead to convergence in hospital quality over time. A variant of this hypothesis would be that more productive hospitals would draw patients of similar race and ethnicity, but not draw new patients from across race and ethnicity; in this case we could observe a convergence in hospital quality within white and black patient populations, but no convergence between racial or ethnic groups.

Our analytic framework is a simple Oaxaca-Blinder decomposition exercise. At a point in time, the black-white difference in the probability of person i, of race j and in year t, dying post-AMI, m_{jti}, is given by

(1) $$m_{jti} = x_{jti}\beta_j + \delta_{kt} + \epsilon_{jti}.$$

In this linear probability model, mortality is a function of an individual's risk characteristics x_{jti}, times the race-specific coefficient β_j, plus the hospital- and time-specific quality measure δ_{kt}, $k = 1, \ldots K$. The hospital-specific effect captures a variety of different treatment approaches (and expertise), as well as differences in treatment of patients within hospitals by race. For example, if white AMI patients are more likely to receive primary reperfusion than black patients in hospital k, then δ_{kw} will be more likely to be much less than δ_{kb} (that is, a lower mortality rate for white patients in that hospital than for black patients in the same hospital).

The average mortality between black and white AMI patients, again at a point in time is

(2) $$M_{bt} - M_{wt} = \left(X_{bt} - X_{wt}\right)\beta + \sum_{k=1}^{K}[\delta_k\left(\mu_{bk} - \mu_{wk}\right)] + \omega,$$

where M_{kt} is the average mortality, X the average value for the vector of comorbidities and risk adjusters, Z the average value of the treatments within hospitals, μ_{jk} is the mean fraction of people of race or ethnicity j who are admitted to hospital j, and ω_t captures the additional terms in general Oaxaca-Blinder decompositions reflecting differences in black and white coefficients (since we now assume a common β for black and white patients), and thus reflects a residual term. A simplified version of the hospital-specific effect of racial representation creates 10 deciles of hospitals where hospitals are allocated into deciles depending on the fraction of black patients admitted for AMI.

6.3 Data and Methods

The data set used was a 100 percent sample of Medicare Provider Analysis and Review (MEDPAR) data on Medicare fee-for-service billing information for all patients hospitalized for AMI between January 1993 and December 2010, with follow-up data extending to December 2011. The sample was further restricted to only patients seen at hospitals that treated at least ten Medicare patients for AMIs. The criterion for determining the presence of AMI from the claims was a hospital admission with a primary diagnosis of AMI, without evidence of an AMI in the prior year.

Using information from the Medicare Denominator File, patients were categorized as black and white,[2] while other race/ethnicity groups were excluded because of small sample sizes. The initial sample comprised 4,250,422 qualifying AMI events. Of these, 149,380 (3.5 percent) patients were excluded because they were neither black nor white, and an additional 3,556 (0.08 percent) patients were excluded because they were seen at hospitals that treated fewer than ten patients for AMI in the study period. This left 4,097,486 (96 percent of original sample) patients who were assigned to the first hospital recording an AMI primary diagnosis code, regardless of future treatment location.

---

2. There is a very strong correlation between black racial measures in the Medicare claims data and self-reported racial identity (Arday et al. 2000).

This sample was used to calculate the percentage of all AMI patients in a hospital who were black. We then created approximate deciles of this measure to provide a summary measure of the extent to which a hospital serves the black community. Patient counts in each of these deciles were not exactly 10 percent of the sample because patients in a given hospital were retained in the same decile category. We report summary statistics for each decile in table 6.1.

The primary measure of outcomes was risk-adjusted mortality at ninety days from initial admission (sensitivity analysis is described below). Ninety-day mortality is likely to capture the total outcome of decisions that affect both short- and medium-term mortality (such as coronary artery bypass graft surgery, which can reduce medium-term mortality, but carries short-term perioperative risk), while still capturing differences in hospital care, rather than differences in postacute care. Previous uses of these outcome data have been described elsewhere (McClellan, McNeil, and Newhouse 1994; McClellan and Noguchi 1998; Kessler and McClellan 2000; Skinner et al. 2003). As noted by previous studies, measures of hospital performance that use patient outcome data can be biased if hospitals serve patients with different average severity levels, however, measures of risk-adjusted AMI

Table 6.1   Distribution of patients and hospitals across years within study sample

Year	Number of black patients	Total patients	Number of hospitals
1993	14,148	239,345	4,864
1994	14,833	242,804	4,861
1995	14,911	244,791	4,837
1996	15,139	244,264	4,788
1997	15,162	238,913	4,722
1998	15,350	239,590	4,705
1999	16,335	243,939	4,669
2000	16,990	249,819	4,662
2001	17,609	250,342	4,643
2002	18,268	255,005	4,553
2003	18,516	252,374	4,471
2004	17,542	239,676	4,497
2005	16,157	223,321	4,414
2006	15,124	204,796	4,253
2007	13,772	192,606	4,185
2008	13,657	188,034	4,154
2009	13,103	175,142	4,077
2010	12,962	172,636	4,037
Total	279,578	4,097,397	6,250

Notes: The sample used is a census of the Medicare fee-for-service population hospitalized for AMI between January 1993 and December 2010. The sample was further restricted to only patients seen at hospitals that treated at least ten Medicare patients for AMIs. The criterion for determining the presence of AMI from the claims was a hospital admission with a primary diagnosis of AMI, without evidence of an AMI within the prior year.

mortality have been shown to be valid indicators of hospital quality and have been incorporated into hospital profiling efforts (Davies et al. 2001).

This method of risk adjustment is not intended to be a comprehensive measure of a patient's well-being, as it leaves out a wide variety of relevant information, ranging from tobacco smoking status to clinical impressions and lab values. This set of controls is not sufficiently comprehensive to eliminate omitted variable bias, but it gives insight into the direction of that bias. As long as the unobserved health status of a patient is correlated with their observed health status, we can identify the direction of the bias, but not the magnitude.

To adjust for risk, we control for age nonparametrically in five-year increments, and allow each age category to interact with sex. We control for pre-existing conditions using indicator variables for vascular disease, pulmonary disease, dementia, diabetes, renal failure, and cancer. Also included were year categorical variables and categorical variables that indicate the severity of the AMI, whether anterior, inferior, subendocardial, or a reference "other" category.

There are a range of potential health outcomes that are of interest following an AMI, including diminished cardiac output, reduced cognitive function and loss of independence, but we use mortality because it is unambiguous and reported with high reliability. While it would be of interest to study the incidence of congestive heart failure (CHF) following an AMI, the reporting and diagnosis of CHF depends on both the judgment of treating physicians, as well as the patient's access to follow-up care.

We estimated logistic regression models for both mortality and PCI use by first calculating year-specific rates by race, or aggregating the data to create early (1993–1998), middle (1999–2005), and late (2006–2010) rates of mortality, again by race. For ninety-day mortality, this is the basic racial disparity we seek to explain (that is, the left-hand side of equation 1). We then add comorbidities (thus capturing the effect of average differences in patient characteristics X) and hospital effects (capturing the average differences in hospital quality).

A simple way to demonstrate the "across-hospital" effect is to calculate the mortality rate for white patients if they had been admitted to hospitals in the same proportion as for black patients. In other words, if 1.4 percent of all black AMI patients were admitted to Hospital H, and the white mortality rate there was 19.2 percent, then the weighted average of this "white patients admitted to black hospitals" measure would reflect the 19.2 percent white mortality rate but weighted by the percentage of black patients, 1.4 percent (see Skinner et al. 2005).

All statistical analysis was performed in STATA 13.1.

6.4   Results

Table 6.1 presents the distribution of patients and hospitals across years within study sample. There is a rise in the number of AMI patients initially, reflecting a growth in the Medicare population, but the total number then declines, particularly near the end of the period, for two reasons. First, there was a rise in patients moving into Medicare Advantage managed care, and thus out of fee-for-service care, leading to a smaller denominator of fee-for-service patients over time. And second, there has been a general decline in the incidences of AMI (Likosky et al. 2013).

Table 6.2 presents summary statistics for fee-for-service Medicare beneficiaries who were treated for AMI between 1993 and 2010. The table illustrates the construction of the deciles used in the analysis, as well as the wide variation in the racial composition of patients at different hospitals. Focusing on the statistics at the bottom of the left column, the average Medicare AMI patient was treated in a hospital where 6.82 percent of AMI patients were black. The typical black patient, however, was treated at a hospital where 23.57 percent of all patients were black, while the typical white patient was treated at a hospital where just 5.60 percent of patients were black. Patients treated at hospitals with the highest proportion of black patients were disproportionately from the South, and living in poorer ZIP codes (not reported).

In figure 6.1, panels A, B, and C, we show the fraction of black and white AMI patients by decile for each of the three periods: 1993–1998, 1999–2005, and 2006–2010. It is clear that black and white AMI patients tend to be admitted to different hospitals (as in Skinner et al. 2005). However, there does not appear to be a trend in the extent to which black and white patients are admitted to largely different hospitals. Thus, as a first test, there is no evidence of convergence in the degree of segregation of hospital AMI admissions.

One concern is that white patients in disproportionately black hospitals are in worse health to begin with; thus, it would be no surprise to show that such patients experience worse health outcomes owing to unmeasured co-morbidities. Figure 6.2 presents an index of AMI severity across each of the ten hospital deciles; this measures predicted mortality based on recorded comorbidities and AMI presentation, but controls for age, race, sex, and the racial composition of the patients treated at the same hospital. There do not appear to be differences in the underlying risk of mortality across hospital type, making it less likely that unobservable confounding variables could explain the differences we find (Altonji et al. 2010).

Figure 6.3 shows regression estimates from a model that risk adjusts and allows for different mortality rates by race and by hospital decile. While the confidence intervals are fairly wide, they still demonstrate that for the time

Table 6.2   Summary statistics of patients and hospitals by decile of the share of black AMI patients admitted

Deciles of percentage of black patients	Percent of all patients at hospital who are black	Min. percent	Max. percent	Percent in urban area	Average stay (days)	Number of patients	Average hospital size (pts. in sample)	Number of hospitals
Lowest decile	0.05	0.0	0.2	31.15	4.8	410,070	1,048	2,222
2nd	0.36	0.2	0.6	61.91	5.7	409,583	2,076	397
3rd	0.81	0.6	1.1	72.38	5.9	410,591	2,126	379
4th	1.43	1.1	1.9	73.15	6.3	409,516	2,360	404
5th	2.43	1.9	3.0	70.40	6.5	410,254	2,664	399
6th	3.62	3.0	4.3	75.90	6.5	408,457	2,606	362
7th	5.40	4.3	6.8	80.23	6.6	409,950	2,499	427
8th	8.24	6.8	10.3	80.44	7.0	410,904	2,688	410
9th	13.77	10.3	17.6	70.92	6.8	408,749	2,262	471
Highest decile	32.18	17.6	100.0	70.86	6.9	409,323	1,761	811
White patients	5.60	0.0	98.9	68.07	6.2	3,817,819		
Black patients	23.57	0.0	100.0	77.82	7.2	279,578		
Total	6.82	0.0	100.0	68.74	6.3	4,097,397	2,209	6,283

Notes: The sample used is a census of the Medicare fee-for-service population hospitalized for AMI between January 1993 and December 2010. The sample was further restricted to only patients seen at hospitals that treated at least ten Medicare patients for AMIs. The criterion for determining the presence of AMI from the claims was a hospital admission with a primary diagnosis of AMI, without evidence of an AMI within the prior year.

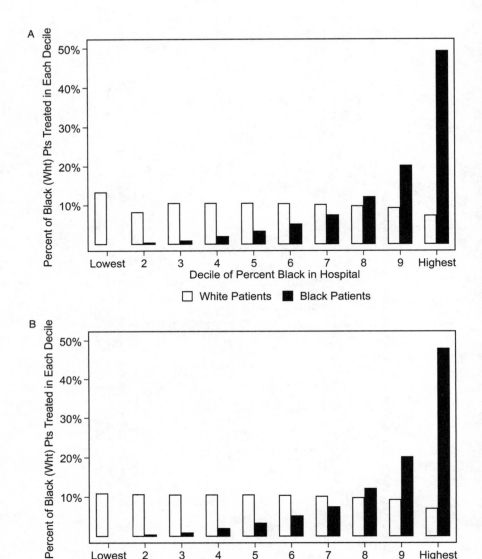

Fig. 6.1 Distribution of black and white patients by percent black admitted to hospital

Notes: Panel A: Distribution of patients by race (1993–1998); panel B: Distribution of patients by race (1999–2005). After discarding hospitals with fewer than ten patients over the study period, hospitals are ranked by the degree to which they serve the black population over the entire study period. The bars titled "Black Patients" indicate the percent of the black population that is treated in each grouping of hospitals.

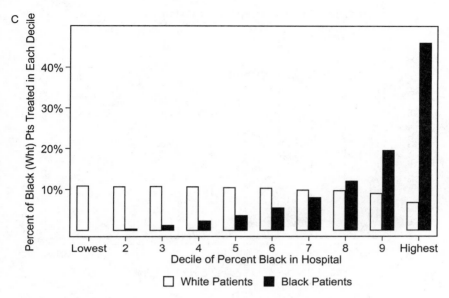

Fig. 6.1   (cont.)l

Note: Panel C: Distribution of patients by race (2006–2010).

period we consider, most of the variation in mortality arose from the hospital to which patients were admitted, rather than differences that occurred within the hospital. (Figure 6.4 shows the same results, but with Hospital Referral Region [HRR] fixed effects).

Figure 6.5 shows time trends in the risk-adjusted ninety-day mortality risk. For both black and white patients there was a marked decline in mortality during this period, but there is no evidence of less overall disparity in hospital mortality. As detailed in table 6.3, during the later period (2006–2010) there was a gap of 1 percentage point between black ninety-day mortality (18.8 percent) and white ninety-day mortality (17.8 percent). Had the white patients been admitted to hospitals using the same frequency as black patients, then the average white mortality rate would have been 18.5 percent. The within-hospital racial disparity is therefore 0.3 percent (18.8 percent–18.5 percent) and the across-hospital disparity is the remaining 0.7 percent, a slight reduction from the 0.9 percent gap in the early period and the 1.0 percent difference in the middle period.

The introduction of HRR fixed effects does not substantially change the pattern of results that we find, suggesting that the broad patterns of between-hospital disparity we find are not driven by regional differences. In other words, the evidence is weak that patient migration (or shutting down of hospitals) has led to a reduction in disparities across hospitals.

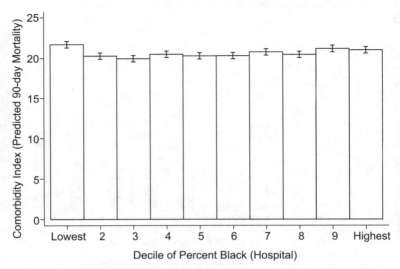

Fig. 6.2   Index of comorbidity and AMI severity by percent of admitted patients who are black

Note: Figure reports predicted ninety-day mortality for white patients across deciles of percent black. Predicted mortality is calculated using all the risk adjusters in the data, including age and sex. Risk adjustment includes controls for vascular disease, pulmonary disease, dementia, diabetes, renal failure, cancer, and the location of the heart attack within the heart: anterior, inferior, subendocardial, or a reference "other" category.

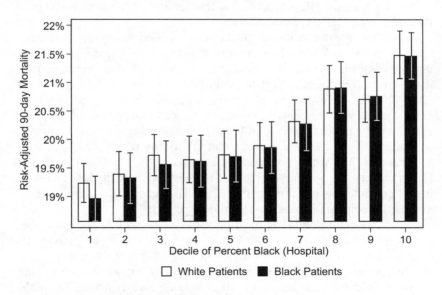

Fig. 6.3   Risk-adjusted mortality by hospital decile and race

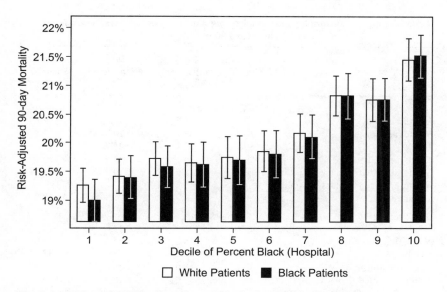

Fig. 6.4   Risk- and HRR-adjusted mortality by hospital decile and race

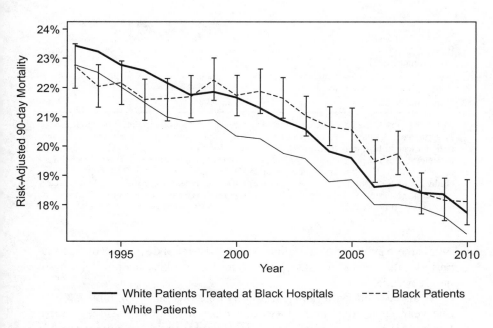

Fig. 6.5   Risk-adjusted ninety-day AMI mortality

Note: Risk adjustment includes controls for age, sex, vascular disease, pulmonary disease, dementia, diabetes, renal failure, cancer, and the location of the heart attack within the heart: anterior, inferior, subendocardial, or a reference "other" category.

Table 6.3   Mortality rates at thirty-day, ninety-day, and one-year horizons by race and hospital admission patterns

	Overall (%)	Early (1993–1998) (%)	Middle (1999–2005) (%)	Late (2006–2010) (%)
Ninety days				
White	19.7	21.7	19.8	17.8
White (unadjusted)	19.7	23.1	20.3	17.8
Black	20.7	22.1	21.4	18.8
Black (unadjusted)	20.8	24.1	23.0	20.1
White, admitted to black hospitals	20.6	22.6	20.8	18.5
White, admitted to black hospitals (unadjusted)	20.7	24.2	21.3	18.5
Thirty days				
White	14.6	16.4	14.6	13.1
White (unadjusted)	14.6	18.3	15.2	12.8
Black	14.6	15.7	15.0	13.1
Black (unadjusted)	14.6	18.0	16.2	13.3
White, admitted to black hospitals	15.3	17.0	15.3	13.6
White, admitted to black hospitals (unadjusted)	15.3	19.2	15.9	13.3
One year				
White	28.6	31.2	28.8	25.9
White (unadjusted)	28.6	31.4	29.4	26.9
Black	32.0	33.5	32.8	29.6
Black (unadjusted)	32.0	35.5	35.7	33.2
White, admitted to black hospitals	29.7	32.4	30.0	26.6
White, admitted to black hospitals (unadjusted)	29.7	32.8	30.8	27.9

Note: The sample used is a census of the Medicare fee-for-service population hospitalized for AMI between January 1993 and December 2010. The sample was further restricted to only patients seen at hospitals that treated at least ten Medicare patients for AMIs. The criterion for determining the presence of AMI from the claims was a hospital admission with a primary diagnosis of AMI, without evidence of an AMI within the prior year. Risk adjustment includes controls for vascular disease, pulmonary disease, dementia, diabetes, renal failure, cancer, and the location of the heart attack within the heart: anterior, inferior, subendocardial, or a reference "other" category.

Nor is there evidence of a decline in within-hospital disparities during this period—the "black" versus "white admitted to black hospital" lines are nearly parallel.

We also consider alternative mortality horizons, shown in table 6.3 with one-year, thirty-day, and ninety-day mortality rates for three groups: black AMI patients, white AMI patients, and white AMI patient mortality weighted by hospital admission patterns for black AMI patients, across the three periods of analysis. There is a clear gradient showing worse outcomes for black AMI patients at longer horizons. While the gap in between-hospital mortality variation is larger at 365 days (1.2 percent in the early period, and 1.3 percent in the middle period), there is a modest decline as for the later period (0.8 percent).

Why are health outcomes so much worse for black patients at longer horizons? One reason might be that we have not adequately adjusted for other comorbidities that affect longer-term longevity. In a separate analysis (not reported here), we considered this puzzle using more detailed risk adjustment based on HCC scores (hierarchical condition category) for more recent data. While HCC scores are known to be sensitive to overadjustment (e.g., Einav et al. 2015; Song et al. 2010), our results suggested that much of the gap at both thirty days and 365 days could be explained by differential adjustment. Thus, we are more confident about changes over time in black and white rates than about comparing black and white rates at a point in time.

Why might there be so little gain in within-hospital mortality disparity? In the early period, the within-hospital gap was −0.5 percent (that is, white mortality rates, with hospital weights determined by black hospital admissions, were higher than for black mortality rates with the same hospital

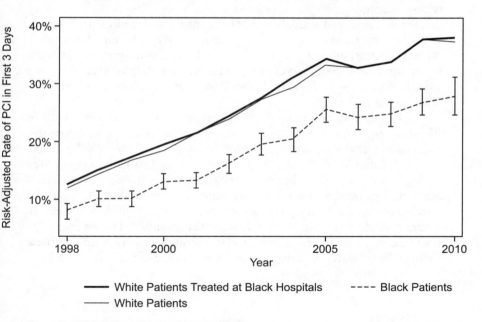

Fig. 6.6 Risk-adjusted rate of prompt PCI
Note: Rates of PCI in the first three days after hospital admission have climbed dramatically, with black patients receiving PCI at rates significantly below whites. This gap persists through the study period, and does not close in the later years.

weights). In the later period, nearly two decades later, the within-hospital gap had flipped to 0.7 percent. One reason is shown in figure 6.6; rates of percutaneous coronary interventions (PCI), which have been steadily rising for all patients over this period, but where the absolute gap in PCI rates has been increasing even more rapidly. While the proportional difference may have shrunk during this period, what matters for the gap in mortality is the incremental value of the procedure times the fraction of AMI patients who receive the treatment. And this has been rising, from a few percentage points in the mid-1990s, to roughly 10 percentage points in 2010.

6.5   Conclusion

During the 1993–2010 period, there was a tremendous increase in the scientific literature on racial disparities in health care. Based on these findings, one would have expected proactive efforts by providers to narrow health disparities, particularly for disparities occurring within hospitals. For acute myocardial infarction in the elderly population, we observe a remarkable decline in mortality over the past several decades. However, the decline in mortality was not associated with a reduction in mortality differentials within hospitals, nor did we observe a significant reduction in mortality disparities associated with black AMI patients being admitted to hospitals with disproportionately high risk-adjusted mortality rates for whites. While there was some hint of an improvement in the across-hospital gap between the middle (1999–2005) and late (2006–10) periods, additional years of data would be necessary to discern whether it was statistical noise or a long-term improvement.

The fact that black and white AMI patients go to different hospitals is, in many respects, the consequence of racial segregation in where people live, and not a systematic effort to discriminate against black AMI patients. That is, we should not be surprised to find that AMI patients living in Mississippi are more likely to be admitted to hospitals with disproportionately black patient populations than AMI patients living in North Dakota. Of greater interest for policy purposes is segmentation of markets not driven by distance alone, that is, black patients who are admitted to lower-quality hospitals when there are higher-quality hospitals nearby. Studying these more granular travel patterns is a topic for future research.

References

Altonji, Joseph G., Timothy Conley, Todd E. Elder, and Christopher R. Taber. 2010. "Methods for Using Selection on Observed Variables to Address Selection on Unobserved Variables." Unpublished Manuscript.

Arday, S. L., D. R. Arday, Stephanie Monroe, and J. Zhang. 2000. "HCFA's Racial and Ethnic Data: Current Accuracy and Recent Improvements." *Health Care Financing Review* 21 (4): 107–16.

Balsa, Ana I., and Thomas G. McGuire. 2003. "Prejudice, Clinical Uncertainty and Sterotyping as Sources of Health Disparities." *Journal of Health Economics* 22 (1): 89–116.

Barnato, Amber E., F. Lee Lucas, Douglas Staiger, David E. Wennberg, and Amitabh Chandra. 2005. "Hospital-Level Racial Disparities in Acute Myocardial Infarction Treatment and Outcomes." *Medical Care* 43 (4): 308–19.

Bradley, Elizabeth H., Jeph Herrin, Yongfei Wang, Robert L. McNamara, Tashonna R. Webster, David J. Magid, Martha Blaney, et al. 2004. "Racial and Ethnic Differences in Time to Acute Reperfusion Therapy for Patients Hospitalized with Myocardial Infarction." *Journal of the American Medical Association* 292 (13): 1563–72.

Chandra, Amitabh, Amy Finkelstein, Adam Sacarny, and Chad Syverson. 2013. "Healthcare Exceptionalism? Productivity and Allocation in the US Healthcare Sector." NBER Working Paper no. 19200, Cambridge, MA.

Davies, Sheryl M., Jeffrey Geppert, Mark McClellan, Kathryn M. McDonald, Patrick S. Romano, and Kaveh G. Shojania. 2001. "Refinement of the HCUP Quality Indicators." Agency for Healthcare Research and Quality (US). http://archive.ahrq.gov/clinic/tp/hcupqitp.htm.

Doyle, Joseph, John Graves, Jonathan Gruber, and Samuel Kleiner. 2015. Measuring Returns to Hospital Care: Evidence from Ambulance Referral Patterns." *Journal of Political Economy* 123 (1): 170.

Einav, Liran, Amy Finkelstein, Raymond Kluender, and Paul Schrimpf. 2015. "Beyond Statistics: The Economic Content of Risk Scores." NBER Working Paper no. 21304, Cambridge, MA.

Institute of Medicine (IOM). 2002. *Unequal Treatment: Confronting Racial and Ethnic Disparities in Health Care.* Washington, DC: National Academy Press.

Jha, A., E. S. Fisher, Z. Li, E. J. Orav, and A. M. Epstein. 2005. "Racial Trends in the Use of Major Procedures among the Elderly." *New England Journal of Medicine* 353 (7): 683–91.

Kessler, Daniel P., and Mark B. McClellan. 2000. "Is Hospital Competition Socially Wasteful?" *Quarterly Journal of Economics* 115 (2): 577–615.

Konety, Suma H., Mary S. Vaughan Sarrazin, and Gary E. Rosenthal. 2005. "Patient and Hospital Differences Underlying Racial Variation in Outcomes after Coronary Artery Bypass Graft Surgery." *Circulation* 111:1210–16.

Likosky, Donald S., Weiping Zhou, David J. Malenka, William B. Borden, David J. Malenka, William B. Borden, Brahmajee K. Nallamothu, and Jonathan Skinner. 2013. "Growth in Medicare Expenditures for Patients with Acute Myocardial Infarction: A Comparison of 1998 through 1999 and 2008." *JAMA Internal Medicine* 173 (22): 2055–61.

McClellan, M., B. J. McNeil, and J. P. Newhouse. 1994. "Does More Intensive Treatment of Acute Myocardial Infarction in the Elderly Reduce Mortality? Analysis Using Instrumental Variables." *Journal of the American Medical Association* 272 (11): 859–66.

McClellan, M., and Haruko Noguchi. 1998. "Technological Change in Heart-Disease Treatment. Does High Tech Mean Low Value?" *American Economic Review (Proceedings)* 88 (2): 90–96.

Meara, Ellen R., Seth Richards, and David M. Cutler. 2008. "The Gap Gets Bigger: Changes in Mortality and Life Expectancy, by Education, 1981–2000." *Health Affairs* 27 (2): 350–60.

Rothenberg, Barbara M., Thomas Pearson, Jack Zwanziger, and Dana Mukamel. 2004. "Explaining Disparities in Access to High-Quality Cardiac Surgeons." *Annals of Thoracic Surgery* 78:18–24. doi:10.1016/j.athoracsur.2004.01.021.

Skinner, Jonathan, Amitabh Chandra, Douglas Staiger, Julie Lee, and Mark McClellan. 2005. "Mortality after Acute Myocardial Infarction in Hospitals That Disproportionately Treat Black Patients." *Circulation* 112 (17): 2634–41.

Skinner, Jonathan, and Douglas Staiger. 2015. "Technology Diffusion and Productivity Growth in Health Care." *Review of Economics and Statistics* 97 (5): 951–64.

Skinner, Jonathan, James N. Weinstein, Scott M. Sporer, and John E. Wennberg. 2003. "Racial, Ethnic, and Geographic Disparities in Rates of Knee Arthroplasty among Medicare Patients." *New England Journal of Medicine* 349 (14): 1350–59.

Song, Yunjie, Jonathan Skinner, Julie Bynum, Jason Sutherland, John E. Wennberg, and Elliott S. Fisher. "Regional Variations in Diagnostic Practices." *New England Journal of Medicine* 363 (1): 45–53.

Strumpf, Erin C. 2011. "Racial/Ethnic Disparities in Primary Care: The Role of Physician-Patient Concordance." *Medical Care* 49 (5): 496–503.

Trivedi, Amal N., Regina C. Grebla, Steven M. Wright, and Donna L. Washington. 2011. "Despite Improved Quality of Care in the Veterans Affairs Health System, Racial Disparity Persists for Important Clinical Outcomes." *Health Affairs* 30 (4): 707–15.

Trivedi, Amal N., A. M. Zaslavsky, E. C. Schneider, and J. Z. Ayanian. 2005. "Trends in the Quality of Care and Racial Disparities in Medicare Managed Care." *New England Journal of Medicine* 353 (7): 692–700.

van Ryn, Michelle, and Jane Burke. 2000. "The Effect of Patient Race and Socio-Economic Status on Physician's Perceptions of Patients." *Social Science and Medicine* 50 (6): 813–28.

Comment   David R. Weir

This chapter is a good example of the strengths of this research program in the economics of aging. It deals with a problem of first-order importance for the health and well-being of the older population. It utilizes data that are both appropriate and all-but-definitive for the question. The methods are careful but not overwrought, letting the data speak for themselves. The conclusion is well supported by the evidence, and points clearly to the next steps to be taken in the research agenda.

Racial disparities in health and aging are substantial. According to the National Center for Health Statistics (NCHS) life tables for 2010, life expectancy at age fifty is 3.3 years longer for white men than African Americans (12 percent longer), and 2.2 years longer for white women than for black

David R. Weir is a research affiliate of the Population Studies Center and a research professor at the Survey Research Center, both at the University of Michigan, and director of the Health and Retirement Study (HRS).

For acknowledgments, sources of research support, and disclosure of the author's material financial relationships, if any, please see http://www.nber.org/chapters/c13644.ack.

women (7 percent longer). When we factor in morbidity, as in a measure of healthy life expectancy, the differences are even greater. Combining morbidity data from HRS 2010 with the NCHS life tables, healthy life expectancy at age fifty is 4.1 years longer for white men than African Americans (24 percent) and 5.1 years longer for white women than for black women (31 percent).

Racial disparities in health have been a major public policy concern for many years. "Healthy People" expresses US policy goals by decade. The goal for the 1990s was to reduce health disparities by 2000. The goal in the first decade of the twenty-first century was to eliminate health disparities by 2010. Having largely failed to meet either goal, the goals for this decade are to achieve health equity, eliminate disparities, and improve the health of all groups. Understanding why such oft-stated policy goals are so resistant to progress is an important topic for scientific research.

This chapter focuses on outcomes of acute myocardial infarction (AMI), that is, heart attacks. This is clearly an important category of health event both for its frequency in the population and its impact on health and mortality. They begin with a good theoretical framework delineating the possible sources of race differences in AMI outcomes into three categories: (a) different risk (individual characteristics that relate to outcomes), (b) discrimination within hospitals (differential results by race within hospitals, conditional on individual characteristics), and (c) segregated access (correlation between racial composition of patient pool and outcomes).

They use the universe of Medicare hospital records for 1993–2010, limited to patients who were on a fee-for-service basis (necessary to have good data records in the Medicare claims), and to hospitals who treated at least ten such cases in a year (it is not clear what fraction of all AMI cases are excluded by this). With over four million observations, this is clearly an impressive data source for the problem, and largely free of sample selection issues.

Risk adjustment for individual risk is a pretty familiar concept in health economics as in the medical care business. It is often not very intellectually satisfying, and the authors do not provide much detail on their modeling choice, which relies mainly on detail of the location and severity of the heart damage from the infarct. As they note, there are other characteristics (e.g., smoking) that would be relevant but cannot be included. Overall, observable risk did not vary much across hospitals arrayed from low to high percentage of black patients. It seems then that the adjustments are adequate to the task, which is to demonstrate that (a) individual differences in ex ante risk are small relative to differences in outcomes, and (b) they can be adequately removed.

The chapter thus focuses mainly on the question of whether worse outcomes for blacks occur mainly within hospitals or between hospitals. The evidence is very clear that most of the racial gap arises between hospitals.

Whites and blacks have very similar outcomes within hospitals. The overall gap is due to the fact that blacks go to hospitals that have, on average, worse outcomes for patients of all races.

One minor concern with the use of Medicare records for racial disparities is the quality of the race information on the Medicare files. Race is imported into the Centers for Medicare and Medicaid Services (CMS) records from Social Security records, which capture race as a self-report at the time of application or at other encounter events such as claiming benefits. The authors are aware of the issue, and refer to work based on the Medicare Current Beneficiary Survey (MCBS) that suggests it is good enough. Using HRS linked to Medicare, it is possible to examine not only the concordance of self-report but also concordance with genetic data. Black race is highly accurate in the Medicare claims—very few HRS self-reported or genetically identifiable blacks are recorded as anything other than black in Medicare data, and vice versa. The problem is with identifying whites as distinct from other races, and in particular, Hispanic ethnicity. Roughly 6 to 8 percent of Medicare "whites" are either Hispanic or some other race. The possible concern for this chapter is that whites in majority-black hospitals may be disproportionately other minorities and so their outcomes may understate the effect of discrimination within hospitals.

The time-series aspect of the data is also used effectively to understand the problem. First, treatment quality and survival from AMI has been improving everywhere. Against this backdrop of improvement, the gap between good hospitals and bad hospitals has stayed about the same over time. Significantly, the size of the gap between good and bad hospitals, and the overall black/white gap in ninety-day survival, is equivalent to about five years of progress. Thus, the bad hospitals of 2010 are substantially better at survival from AMI than were the good hospitals of 1993.

What do the chapter's findings suggest for the future of research on this topic? The authors seem most interested in medical performance—understanding what makes good hospitals good and bad ones bad. In a dynamic world of rapid improvement everywhere, this is a question mainly about the diffusion of technological change and not a question of static differences. What seems more persistent is the association of racial composition with position in the quality hierarchy of hospitals. That is a question more economic and less medical in nature. Why do blacks persist in going to bad hospitals? Acute myocardial infarction is largely an emergency condition and most patients will either be delivered by ambulance or go to a nearby facility. The extra time it would take to search for a better hospital and get there would outweigh any benefit of better treatment. Thus, geographic location is the primary reason for where people get AMI care and the most likely cause of the persistent association of racial composition and quality is the economic process allocating lower-quality inputs to hospitals located in minority-serving areas.

Finally, it should be noted that differences in medical care are not the primary source of racial disparities in health, just as differences in medical care are not the reason why the United States lags behind other countries in health. The racial gap in life expectancy at age fifty is equivalent to about twenty years of progress, compared with the AMI survival gap studied here that represents about five years of progress. Differences in health at the population level arise mainly from differences in incidence of things like hypertension and diabetes that elevate risk for more severe conditions. Research and policy aimed at reducing racial disparities should focus more on primary prevention.

Measuring Disease Prevalence in Surveys
A Comparison of Diabetes Self-Reports, Biomarkers, and Linked Insurance Claims

Florian Heiss, Daniel McFadden, Joachim Winter,
Amelie Wuppermann, and Yaoyao Zhu

7.1 Introduction

Reliable measures of disease prevalence are crucial for answering many empirical research questions in health economics, including the causal structures underlying the correlation between health and wealth. Much of the existing literature on the health-wealth nexus relies on survey data (for example, those from the US Health and Retirement Study [HRS]). Such survey data typically contain self-reported measures of disease prevalence, which are known to suffer from reporting error. Two more recent developments—the collection of biomarkers and the linkage with data from administrative sources such as insurance claims—promise more reliable measures of disease prevalence. In this chapter, we systematically compare these three measures of disease prevalence.

Florian Heiss is the Chair of Statistics and Econometrics at the University of Dusseldorf. Daniel McFadden is the Presidential Professor of Health Economics at the University of Southern California. He has joint appointments at the USC Sol Price School of Public Policy and the Department of Economics at USC Dornsife College. He is also a research associate of the National Bureau of Economic Research. Joachim Winter is the Chair of Empirical Economic Research at the University of Munich. Amelie Wuppermann is assistant professor of economics at the University of Munich. Yaoyao Zhu is a PhD candidate in economics at the University of Southern California.

This research was funded by the Behavioral and Social Research program of the National Institute on Aging (grants P01AG05842-18, P01AG033559, R56AG026622-01A1, and RC4AG039036), with additional support from the E. Morris Cox Fund at the University of California, Berkeley. We gratefully acknowledge comments by James P. Smith and other participants of the NBER Economics of Aging Conference, Carefree, AZ, May 2015. We thank Patricia St. Clair for invaluable help with the data and Ingrid Hagele and Katrin Poschen for excellent research assistance. For acknowledgments, sources of research support, and disclosure of the author's or authors' material financial relationships, if any, please see http://www.nber.org/chapters/c13637.ack.

This work extends an existing literature that compares survey self-reports and biomarker-based measures of disease prevalence. These papers focus on diabetes (Goldman et al. 2003; Baker, Stabile, and Deri 2004; Smith 2007; Barcellos, Goldman, and Smith 2012; Chatterji, Joo, and Lahiri 2012) and/or hypertension (Goldman et al. 2003; Johnston, Propper, and Shields 2009; Barcellos, Goldman, and Smith 2012; Chatterji, Joo, and Lahiri 2012). These are all diseases for which biomarkers can be obtained relatively easily in community surveys such as the HRS.[1] Data linkage provides another opportunity to verify survey self-reports. Two recent studies, Wolinsky et al. (2014) and Yasaitis, Berkman, and Chandra (2015), compare survey self-reports of different conditions with diagnoses documented in Medicare claims data that have been linked to the HRS data. Sakshaug, Weir, and Nicholas (2014) are the first to compare measures from all three data sources: self-reports, biomarkers, and claims data. They document large differences in diabetes prevalence between HRS self-reports and linked Medicare claims and show that self-reported diabetes aligns more closely with the biomarker data. Taking the biomarker data as a "gold standard" they conclude that diabetes prevalence in the Medicare claims data is too high. The present chapter takes a closer look at the three different measures of diabetes in the HRS, biomarker, and linked Medicare claims data. In particular, our analysis takes the perspective that all three measures may suffer from measurement error.

Substantively, the results from prior literature show that survey respondents tend to underreport the prevalence of diabetes and hypertension compared to "objective" measures from biomarkers. There are socioeconomic status (SES) gradients both in prevalence itself and in the measurement error contained in self-reports, but they are not necessarily the same.

Goldman et al. (2003) find in data from Taiwan that survey self-reports vastly underestimate the prevalence of hypertension, but yield a reasonable accurate estimate of diabetes prevalence. The accuracy of self-reports is predicted by age, education, time of the most recent health exam, and cognitive function.

For the United States, Smith (2007) documents predictors of diabetes prevalence and undiagnosed diabetes using data from three National Health and Nutrition Examination Survey (NHANES) waves. He finds that diabetes prevalence is predicted primarily by excessive weight and obesity. Inheritance of diabetes through parents is also important. These forces were only partially offset by improvements in the education of the population over time. Further, Smith shows that about one in five male diabetics were

1. Other surveys used in related studies include the National Health and Nutrition Examination Survey (NHANES) in Smith (2007) and Barcellos, Goldman, and Smith (2012); the Health Survey for England (HSE) in Johnston, Propper, and Shields (2009); and the Canadian National Population Health Survey (NPHS) in Baker, Stabile, and Deri (2004). A related study that uses the HRS is Chatterji, Joo, and Lahiri (2012).

undiagnosed in the 1999–2002 NHANES waves. While race and ethnic differentials in undiagnosed diabetes were eliminated over the last twenty-five years, the disparities became larger across other measures of disadvantage such as education. Undiagnosed diabetes is a particularly severe problem among the obese, a group at much higher risk of diabetes onset. Also for the United States and with NHANES data, Barcellos, Goldman, and Smith (2012) study undiagnosed diabetes among Mexican immigrants. The striking finding is that these immigrants might be much less healthy than previously thought because diseases remain undiagnosed at a much higher rate than among other groups of the US population. With respect to diabetes, Barcellos et al. document that about half of recent immigrants with the disease remain undiagnosed.

An important issue is whether the measurement error contained in survey self-reports is related to socioeconomic status (SES). The findings in Smith (2007) and Barcellos, Goldman, and Smith (2012) suggest that this is indeed the case for diabetes in the United States. Similar SES gradients in undiagnosed hypertension have been documented by Johnston, Propper, and Shields (2009) for England.

Curiously, when comparing self-reports and insurance claims data, Wolinsky et al. (2014), and Yasaitis, Berkman, and Chandra (2015) document that the measurement error in survey self-reports may also go the other way: Wolinsky et al. (2014) document over- as well as underreporting of different health conditions and health care use in survey data as compared to claims. The authors find an SES gradient with respect to wealth in the accuracy of the self-reports. Yasaitis, Berkman, and Chandra (2015) focus on acute myocardial infarctions (AMI) and find that less than half of those who reported a heart attack in their HRS sample had evidence of acute cardiovascular hospitalizations in the Medicare claims data. Further, they did not find associations between demographic characteristics and the frequency with which self-reported AMI was verified by Medicare claims.

Not only survey self-reports, but also measures of disease prevalence constructed from claims data may be subject to measurement error. Sakshaug, Weir, and Nicholas (2014) find that roughly 8 percent of HRS respondents in 2006 do not report having been diagnosed with diabetes but are identified as diabetics based on the linked Medicare claims. Among these cases, almost 64 percent do not have diabetes according to the available biomarker information, suggesting that the procedure of identifying diabetes cases in the claims data may lead to false positives.

The literature thus suggests that neither self-reports nor claims data may deliver reliable measures of health conditions and that both measures may be subject to Type I and Type II errors. The possibility of measurement error in the biomarker data, however, has received less attention. The present chapter further explores this issue. Furthermore, the question of whether the different errors are predicted by SES is still open and the present chapter presents some additional evidence. A potentially important consideration, which we will not address in this chapter, is to what extent selectivity in linked samples—due to incomplete consent of survey respondents to either biomarker measurement or to claims data linkage—contributes to observed SES gradients in the various measures of disease prevalence and the associated measurement errors.

The remainder of the chapter is structured as follows: We discuss the data used in section 7.2. Section 7.3 contains the results, and section 7.4 concludes with a summary of our findings and a discussion of avenues for future research.

7.2 Data

In the analysis presented in the chapter, we use three linked data sets: biomarker data on diabetes prevalence are taken from the HRS (2006 and 2008), self-reports of diabetes are taken from the RAND HRS data set (where SES covariates are readily defined), and claims-based information on diabetes prevalence is taken from Medicare claims that are linked to HRS respondents. The latter data are provided by the Medicare Research Information Center (MedRic). Column (1) of table 7.1 displays the number of observations in each of these data sets. Column (2) shows the number of observations with nonmissing diabetes indicators. Comparing these two columns shows that the rates of missing items (due to nonresponse or other reasons) are low.

Columns (3), (4), and (5) contain diabetes prevalence in each of the data sets. In the biomarker data, we use glycated hemoglobin (HbA1c) levels with 6.5 percent as a threshold (the NHANES equivalent value);[2] in the RAND HRS data, we use the self-reported diagnosed diabetes; in the claims data, we use an "ever had" diabetes claims indicator as provided by MedRIC. The latter is based on the procedure used to identify diabetes in other commonly used Medicare claims data by the Chronic Conditions Data Ware-

---

2. The HbA1c level captures chronic hyperglycemia and has traditionally been used to monitor diabetes treatment (e.g., Bonora and Tuomilehto 2011). In this respect, the American Diabetes Association recommends that HbA1c levels are regularly checked for diabetes patients and patients should try to reach specific HbA1c target levels (usually < 7 percent, but for some patients lower targets, such as <6.5 percent, may be appropriate) as lower HbA1c levels are associated with lower risk of diabetes-related complications. The use of HbA1c screenings as a diagnostic tool for diabetes has only started recently, after extensive research had demonstrated its value for identifying undiagnosed diabetes (e.g., Rohlfing et al.2000; Bennett, Guo, and Dharmage 2007) although other authors conclude that it is not a reliable measure to detect diabetes (Reynolds, Smellie, and Twomey 2006). In the United States, the American Diabetes Association started to recommend HbA1c screening as a test for diabetes in 2010 (American Diabetes Association 2010). HbA1c levels below 5.7 percent are considered normal, levels 5.7–6.5 percent are considered as prediabetes, and levels above 6.5 percent indicate diabetes (American Diabetes Association 2015).

Table 7.1   **Prevalence of diabetes—Comparisons across measures**

	(1)	(2)	(3)	(4)	(5)
			Diabetes indicators		
	N	N	HbA1c> = 6.5%	Self-reported (%)	Claims (%)
2006					
Biomarkers	6,735	6,517	12.38	n/a	n/a
HRS	18,469	18,435	NA	19.60	n/a
MedRIC (HRS-claims)	11,323	11,323	n/a	n/a	25.34
2008					
Biomarkers (total)	6,329	6,256	15.04	n/a	n/a
Biomarkers (biosafe lab)		4,347	14.49	n/a	n/a
Biomarkers (flex lab)		1,909	16.29	n/a	n/a
HRS	17,217	17,185	n/a	21.57	n/a
MedRIC (HRS-claims)	10,597	10,597	n/a	n/a	29.86
Linked sample					
All individuals					
2006	4,118	3,956	16.66	22.27	24.32
2008	3,904	3,853	18.82	24.27	28.13
Excluding individuals in HMOs					
2006		2,517	16.01	21.97	26.36
2008		2,370	18.99	22.70	30.51

Notes: Column (1) displays overall numbers of observations in each data set. Column (2) limits to those observations with information on diabetes. Diabetes indicators in the claims data are based on the Chronic Conditions Data Warehouse (CCW) definitions; those based on HbA1c biomarkers use NHANES equivalent definitions.

house (CCW).[3] In the 2006 biomarker data, for instance, 12.38 percent of respondents have diabetes according to their HbA1c level, while 19.6 percent of the respondents from 2006 HRS report ever having been diagnosed with diabetes in the HRS. In the linked MedRIC claims data, 25.34 percent of individuals are identified as diabetics. As these samples contain different individuals that vary in age, for example, the rates are, however, not directly comparable across data sources.

As biomarker data are collected in the HRS only every second wave, the biomarker samples are substantially smaller than the full HRS. In addition, not all respondents consent to biomarker measurement and/or claims data

---

3. However, in the MedRIC claims data, the diabetes flag is coded as either 0 or 1 with no missing values, while in the other CMS Medicare data, it is coded in 4 levels: (a) incomplete claims coverage for the reference period and diagnosis not found; (b) incomplete claims coverage for the reference period and diagnosis found; (c) complete claims coverage for the reference period and diagnosis not found; and (d) complete claims coverage for the reference period and diagnosis found. In the MedRIC claims data, we do not know how the cases with incomplete claims were coded.

linkage, which results in a further loss of survey cases. However, consent rates in the HRS are generally high.[4] After merging the three data sets, we have 4,118 observations for year 2006 and 3,904 observations for year 2008. Excluding cases with missing information on diabetes-related variables, the linked data contain 3,956 individuals in 2006 and 3,853 individuals in 2008. This includes individuals with different types of Medicare coverage, in particular, individuals who are in traditional Medicare (in a fee-for-service [FFS] plan) and individuals who are in a Health Maintenance Organization (HMO) through Medicare Advantage. For individuals in HMOs we do not observe all relevant claims and we thus conduct most analyses excluding this group of individuals.[5] Excluding HMO individuals and focusing on nonmissing diabetes-related variables, we have 2,517 observations for 2006 and 2,370 observations for 2008.

Columns (3), (4), and (5) of the bottom panel of table 7.1 display diabetes prevalence rates for the linked samples. Even in the linked sample diabetes prevalence is lowest according to the biomarker data and highest in the claims data. This pattern is similar in both years and aligns with the findings of Sakshaug, Weir, and Nicholas (2014), who only analyzed the 2006 HRS data.[6] We explore these patterns in more detail in the next section.

7.3   Results

We first consider diabetes prevalence by gender and by educational levels (table 7.2). For education, we use the five education categories in the RAND HRS data: less than high school; GED; high school graduates; some college; college and above. Results in the lower panels of table 7.2 show educational gradients in diabetes based on all three diabetes indicators. For both genders and in all education groups in both years, diabetes prevalence is lowest according to the HbA1c and highest in the claims data.

Table 7.3 shows two-way within-respondent comparisons of the different measures for the years 2006 and 2008. For all measures and in both years, the concordance across different measures is quite high. The first panel,

4. According to the HRS biomarker documentation, in 2006 the consent rate for obtaining dried blood spots from which the HbA1c measure is extracted was 83 percent and the completion rate, conditional on consent, was 97 percent. The overall completion rate was 81 percent. In 2008, the overall completion rate was 87 percent. According to the MedRIC documentation, over 80 percent of all HRS respondents who are eligible for Medicare provided their identification numbers so that claims data could be linked.

5. In the analyses that do not include information in the claims data, this restriction is not necessary. The results are almost identical when individuals in HMOs are included and thus not discussed further. They are available upon request.

6. Sakshaug et al. also exclude individuals in HMOs. In addition, they restrict their analysis to individuals older than sixty-five who are not veterans. Although we do not implement these additional restrictions, our results are almost identical. While Sakshaug et al. report that 27.3 percent in their linked sample have diabetes according to the claims data in 2006, in our sample definition 26.4 percent are identified as diabetics in the claims.

Table 7.2   **Diabetes by gender and education**

	N	(%)	HbA1c> = 6.5%	Self-reported (%)	Claims (%)
			Diabetes indicators		
			Gender		
2006					
Male	1,079	42.89	14.92	23.63	27.53
Female	1,437	57.11	12.38	20.72	25.45
	Chi-square test		3.4204	3.0445	1.3660
	P-value		0.0640	0.0810	0.2430
2008					
Male	997	42.41	18.65	27.08	33.73
Female	1,354	57.59	14.39	19.46	28.12
	Chi-square test		7.7434	19.2020	8.5989
	P-value		0.0050	0.0000	0.0030
			Education		
2006					
Less than high school	515	20.47	18.06	29.13	35.53
GED	124	4.93	19.35	23.39	28.23
High school graduate	840	33.39	12.59	20.78	26.48
Some college	516	20.51	9.90	18.83	22.33
College and above	521	20.70	12.48	19.58	20.54
	Chi-square test		19.612	20.912	35.982
	P-value		0.001	0.000	0.000
2008					
Less than high school	520	22.12	23.53	32.26	41.18
GED	108	4.59	17.59	30.56	41.67
High school graduate	777	33.05	14.32	21.74	29.67
Some college	455	19.35	16.96	18.26	25.43
College and above	491	20.89	10.37	16.46	22.56
	Chi-square test		35.552	47.704	55.167
	P-value		0.000	0.000	0.000

Notes: Excluding individuals who have Medicare coverage through an HMO.

for example, compares diabetes according to the biomarker data and self-reports in 2006 and 2008. In 2006, roughly 10 percent of individuals report having been diagnosed with diabetes and have an HbA1c level higher than 6.5 percent. Another 75 percent of individuals report not having been diagnosed with diabetes and have an HbA1c level lower than 6.5 percent. For 85 percent of cases, self-reports and biomarker data thus align. The respective results for 2008 are almost identical. In both years, 15 percent of respondents have inconsistent results according to the two diabetes indicators. In 2006, 3.26 percent (4.05 percent in 2008) of respondents have HbA1c levels higher than 6.5 percent but do not report diabetes (which may reflect cases of undiagnosed diabetes) while 11.76 percent (10.55 percent in 2008) of the individuals have HbA1c levels lower than 6.5 percent but report having

Table 7.3   **Comparison of measures of diabetes**

	(%)	(%)
HRS self-reported diabetes and biomarker		
2006 (N = 2,517)	HRS self-reported diabetes	
Biomarker	Yes	No
HbA1c level (%) > = 6.5	10.21	3.26
HbA1c level (%) < 6.5	11.76	74.77
2008 (N = 2,370)		
HbA1c level (%) > = 6.5	12.15	4.05
HbA1c level (%) < 6.5	10.55	73.25
Diabetes according to claims and biomarker		
2006 (N = 2,517)	Diabetes according to claims	
Biomarker	Yes	No
HbA1c level (%) > = 6.5	9.57	3.89
HbA1c level (%) < 6.5	16.77%	69.77
2008 (N = 2,370)		
HbA1c level (%) > = 6.5	12.45	3.76
HbA1c level (%) < 6.5	18.06	65.74
HRS self-reported diabetes and according to claims		
2006 (N = 2,517)	Diabetes according to claims	
Self-reports	Yes	No
HRS self-reported diabetes: Yes	18.87	3.10
HRS self-reported diabetes: No	7.47	70.56
2008 (N = 2,370)		
HRS self-reported diabetes: Yes	20.93	1.77
HRS self-reported diabetes: No	9.58	67.72

Notes: Excluding individuals who have Medicare coverage through an HMO.

been diagnosed with diabetes. The latter cases may reflect overdiagnoses or diabetes cases that are successfully treated. We explore the possibility of under- and overdiagnosis in the self-reports in more detail below (in tables 7.4 and 7.5).

In the middle panel of table 7.3, we compare diabetes according to bio-markers and claims data. In this comparison, roughly 21 percent of respondents have inconsistent results; 3.89 percent of the sample in 2006 and 3.76 percent in 2008 have no diabetes claims, yet have HbA1c levels that exceed 6.5 percent; and 16.77 percent in 2006 and 18.06 percent in 2008 have diabetes claims, but their HbA1c level is below 6.5 percent.

The bottom panel of table 7.3 compares HRS self-reported diabetes with diabetes according to the claims data. The discrepancies are even smaller than when comparing the other measures: 3.1 percent of the sample in 2006 and 1.77 percent in 2008 report ever having been diagnosed with diabetes but have no diabetes claims, while 7.47 percent of the respondents in 2006 and 9.58 percent in 2008 report not having been diagnosed with diabetes but are identified as diabetic in the claims data. The latter findings are again very similar to Sakshaug, Weir, and Nicholas (2014) who report that in 2006 7.7 percent of individuals have diabetes according to the claims data but do not report having been diagnosed with diabetes.

In tables 7.4 and 7.5, we try to reconcile the discrepancies that arise when comparing the self-reports and the biomarker data. Table 7.4 focuses on the possibly "overdiagnosed" cases, while table 7.5 focuses on the possibly "undiagnosed" cases. Table 7.4 displays self-reported medical treatment for individuals who report that they have been diagnosed with diabetes but do not have diabetes according to the biomarker data. In both years, a large fraction among these individuals report taking swallowed medication (almost 74 percent in 2006 and 69 percent in 2008). Furthermore, between 13 and 14 percent report being treated with insulin. Combining the two treatments, 81 percent in 2006 and 77 percent in 2008 report being treated for diabetes. A majority of the differences between self-reports and biomarker data in diabetes may thus stem from successfully treated diabetes cases rather than overreporting in the self-reported data. This is also plausible, as the American Diabetes Association (2015), for example, suggests that providers may recommend patients to target HbA1c levels below 6.5 percent, as this lowers the risk of diabetes-related complications.

Table 7.5 focuses on individuals with high HbA1c levels who do not report having diabetes. There are two main explanations for why individuals do not report diabetes while their HbA1c levels are above 6.5 percent. First, they may have been diagnosed with diabetes but they simply forget to—or do not want to—mention it during the HRS interview. Second, they may not know that they have diabetes. While for individuals who report not having been diagnosed with diabetes there is no information on treatment in the HRS survey, we can look at the claims data to investigate whether these individuals receive treatment for diabetes and have taken diabetes screenings. Table

Table 7.4   **Reconciliation HRS self-reports and biomarker information–Medical treatment among seemingly false positive self-reports**

	Swallowed medication			Insulin			Either of the two treatments		
	Yes (%)	No (%)	Missing (%)	Yes (%)	No (%)	Missing (%)	Yes (%)	No (%)	Missing (%)
2006 (N = 296)	73.65	25.68	0.68	14.53	84.80	0.68	81.42	17.91	0.68
2008 (N = 250)	68.80	30.80	0.40	13.20	86.40	0.40	76.80	22.80	0.40

Notes: Excluding individuals who have Medicare coverage through an HMO.

Table 7.5   **Reconciliation HRS self-reports and biomarker information—Claims and diabetes screening among seemingly false negative self-reports**

2006	N = 82 (%)		N = 22 (%)	N = 21 (enrolled in Medicare for at least 2 years before earliest diabetes diagnosis) (%)
Diabetes claims: Yes	26.83	Percent ever had glucose test before earliest indication of diabetes	45.45	47.62
		Percent ever had HbA1c test before earliest indication of diabetes	68.18	61.90
		Percent ever had screening test before earliest indication of diabetes	81.82	76.19
Diabetes claims: No	73.17	Percent ever had glucose test	23.33	Percent had glucose test in recent two yrs. 11.67
		Percent ever had HbA1c test	15.00	Percent had HbA1c test in recent two yrs. 8.33
		Percent ever had screening test before the HRS 2006 interview	31.67	Percent ever had screening test in recent two yrs. 18.33

2008	N = 96		N = 23	N = 22 (enrolled in Medicare for at least two years before earliest diabetes diagnosis)
Diabetes claims: Yes	23.96	Percent ever had glucose test before earliest indication of diabetes	43.48	40.91
		Percent ever had HbA1c test before earliest indication of diabetes	78.26	68.18
		Percent ever had screening test before earliest indication of diabetes	82.61	72.73%
Diabetes claims: No	76.04	Percent ever had glucose test	31.51	Percent had glucose test in recent two yrs. 6.85
		Percent ever had HbA1c test	23.29	Percent had HbA1c test in recent two yrs. 6.85
		Percent ever had screening test before the HRS 2008 interview	43.84	Percent ever had screening test in recent two yrs. 12.33

Notes: Excluding individuals who have Medicare coverage through an HMO.

7.5 shows that 26.8 percent of "undiagnosed" cases in 2006 and almost 24 percent in 2008 are identified as diabetics in the claims data. As this suggests that individuals receive treatment for diabetes, the fraction of truly undiagnosed cases reduces from 3.26 percent to 2.4 percent in 2006 and from 4.05 percent to 3.1 percent in 2008. Diabetes screenings are identified in the claims based on CPT-4 and ICD-9 diagnosis codes. As the list shown below indicates, we identify two types of tests: a glucose test and a glycated hemoglobin (HbA1c) test. Furthermore, there is a general code for diabetes screening: 82947 Assay Body Fluid Glucose; 82950 Glucose Test; 82951 Glucose Tolerance Test (GTT); 83036 Glycated Hemoglobin (HbA1c) Test; and V77.1 Screen for diabetes mellitus.

Based on this information, we construct three indicators: (a) whether an individual has taken a glucose test, (b) whether an individual has taken an HbA1c test, and (c) whether an individual has taken a glucose or HbA1c test. For individuals who have high HbA1c levels but do not report having been diagnosed with diabetes and are not identified as diabetic in the claims data, we investigate whether they have taken a screening test before the HRS survey date. We further check whether this group of people has taken a screening test in the two years before their HRS interview. For individuals who have high HbA1c levels and diabetes claims but do not report diabetes, we show the fraction of individuals who took the different screening tests before the onset of diabetes in their claims records.

The results in table 7.5 indicate that 32 percent of individuals with high HbA1c levels but no self-reported diabetes and no claims in 2006 and 44 percent among these individuals in 2008 have taken at least one diabetes screening test before their HRS interview. When restricting it to a two-year time horizon before the HRS interview, only 18 percent in 2006 and 12 percent in 2008 have taken a test. This compares to 82–83 percent among individuals with diabetes claims. This suggests that a large fraction of individuals with high biomarker data but no diabetes according to self-reports or claims data truly have undiagnosed diabetes.

Next, we study how having undiagnosed diabetes varies by gender. Table 7.6 displays within comparisons of the biomarker and self-reported diabetes measures by gender and year. Furthermore, it investigates for potential cases of undiagnosed diabetes (high HbA1c but no diabetes according to self-reports) whether individuals are identified as diabetics based on their Medicare claims. The results are very similar across gender and years. Self-reported diabetes and diabetes in the biomarker data align for roughly 85 percent of individuals. The fraction of potentially false positives (or overdiagnoses) in the self-reported data is between 10 and 11 percent; the fraction of potentially false negatives (or undiagnosed cases) is 3–4 percent. The fraction who have high HbA1c levels, no self-reports, and also do not have diabetes according to their Medicare claims varies across genders and years. However, these differences are not statistically significantly different

Table 7.6   Comparison of self-reports, biomarker data, and claims by gender

	HRS self-reported diabetes: Male			HRS self-reported diabetes: Female		
	Yes (%)		No (%)		Yes (%)	No (%)
2006	$N = 1,097$				$N = 1,438$	
HbA1c level (%) >= 6.5	11.49		3.19		9.11	3.27
HbA1c level (%) < 6.5	11.76		71.92		11.61	76.01
	3.19 (obs. = 35)		3.27 (obs. = 47)			
	Diabetes according to claims: Yes		34.29		Diabetes according to claims: Yes	21.28
	Diabetes according to claims: No		65.71		Diabetes according to claims: No	78.72
2008	$N = 1,008$				$N = 1,362$	
HbA1c level (%) >= 6.5	15.28		3.37		9.84	4.55
HbA1c level (%) < 6.5	11.81		69.51		9.62	75.99
	3.37 (obs. = 34)		4.55 (obs. = 62)			
	Diabetes according to claims: Yes		20.59		Diabetes according to claims: Yes	25.81
	Diabetes according to claims: No		79.41		Diabetes according to claims: No	74.19

Notes: Excluding individuals who have Medicare coverage through an HMO.

from zero.[7] Overall, we do not find evidence of gender differences in undiagnosed diabetes.

An important issue in the literature on diabetes prevalence is its gradient in SES. We study whether SES is a predictor of diabetes prevalence as well as prevalence of undiagnosed diabetes among all diabetics. We define the latter two measures based on different combinations of the three available measures. Tables 7.7 and 7.8 present summary statistics of different demographic and socioeconomic variables as measured in the HRS data for 2006 and 2008, respectively.

The means of the variables are presented for the entire linked samples (excluding individuals in HMOs) and separately for individuals with and without diabetes according to the three different measures. The last three columns of tables 7.7 and 7.8 display means for the groups of individuals who potentially have undiagnosed diabetes according to three different definitions that we discuss further below.

For both years and across all three measures of diabetes, tables 7.7 and 7.8 suggest that race, ethnicity, education, earnings, wealth, and self-assessed health status are associated with diabetes prevalence. Among individuals with diabetes, a lower share is white and a higher share is Hispanic. In addition, diabetics have on average lower education, lower income, and lower wealth than nondiabetics and more of them rate their health as fair or poor. Furthermore, as one would expect, individuals with diabetes have a higher body mass index (BMI) on average and fewer among them report doing vigorous exercise.

While tables 7.7 and 7.8 analyze each diabetes measure separately, one could also combine the three available measures in different ways. The following analysis is a first attempt in that direction. We start with counting everyone as diabetic who either reports having been diagnosed with diabetes, or has an HbA1c that exceeds 6.5 percent, or has diabetes in the claims data. However, we also rely on self-reports and biomarker data alone to facilitate comparison of our results to the earlier literature that had no matched claims data. Table 7.9 provides means of the demographic, socioeconomic, and health- and health insurance-related variables for these two different definitions of diabetes and both years of data. To simplify comparisons, table 7.9 also displays means for individuals that are only identified as diabetics in the claims data. The results suggest that the latter group is slightly older, more likely to be white and female, has higher wealth, better self-rated health, and slightly lower BMI compared to individuals who either report having been diagnosed with diabetes or have high HbA1c levels. In addition, they naturally have a lower HbA1c level on average compared to the other groups of diabetics. While this group may indeed include certain individuals who are falsely classified as diabetics as Sakshaug, Weir, and Nicholas

---

7. Results available upon request.

Table 7.7   Summary statistics 2006

Variable	Whole linked sample	HbA1c >= 6.5%	HbA1c < 6.5%	SR diabetes: Yes	SR diabetes: No	Diabetes claims: Yes	Diabetes claims: No	Undiagnosed diabetes 1: High HbA1c no self-reports	Undiagnosed diabetes 2: High HbA1c, no self-reports, no claims	Undiagnosed diabetes:3: High HbA1c, no self-reports, no claims, no screening in past two years
Age	72.80	71.98	72.92	71.93	73.04	73.82	72.43	73.21	72.67	72.08
Age > = 65	0.88	0.86	0.89	0.86	0.89	0.93	0.87	0.91	0.90	0.90
Race (white)	0.88	0.79	0.89	0.82	0.89	0.83	0.90	0.74	0.80	0.78
Hispanic	0.05	0.10	0.04	0.09	0.04	0.09	0.04	0.05	0.05	0.06
Female	0.57	0.53	0.58	0.54	0.58	0.55	0.58	0.57	0.62	0.61
Married	0.63	0.60	0.64	0.62	0.64	0.60	0.65	0.59	0.57	0.57
Education: High school and above	0.80	0.73	0.81	0.73	0.81	0.72	0.82	0.76	0.78	0.78
Indiv. earnings	5,449.77	4,301.37	5,628.52	3,436.00	6,016.79	2,706.23	6,430.88	5,067.02	6,658.27	7,882.57
HH income	57,303.95	44,182.31	59,346.30	45,022.89	60,761.90	42,544.32	62,582.07	41,909.11	42,702.33	45,441.74
HH income (median)	36,380.00	31,988.00	37,381.00	31,060.00	38,400.00	31,164.00	38,376.00	29,533.27	27,404.00	30,651.00
HH wealth	577,488.4	413,044.5	603,083.7	429,214.0	619,237.8	428,920.2	630,617.2	319,767.9	317,605.80	337,720.0
HH wealth (median)	264,400.0	155,000.0	284,152.0	177,000.0	299,530.0	177,000.0	300,000.0	173,763.0	195,040.0	195,080.0
Covered by EGHP	0.46	0.41	0.47	0.43	0.47	0.43	0.47	0.39	0.37	0.41
Poor/fair general health status	0.29	0.41	0.27	0.45	0.25	0.42	0.24	0.26	0.23	0.22
BMI	27.71	30.18	27.32	30.44	26.93	29.36	27.11	28.92	29.06	29.58
Total cognition	22.03	21.26	22.15	21.31	22.23	21.05	22.41	20.96	21.69	21.66
Ever smoker	0.58	0.58	0.58	0.59	0.57	0.59	0.57	0.50	0.53	0.53
Current smoker	0.11	0.10	0.11	0.10	0.12	0.10	0.12	0.09	0.07	0.08
Vigorous exercise	0.34	0.24	0.35	0.26	0.36	0.27	0.36	0.30	0.32	0.31
Part A enrollment	0.92	0.94	0.92	0.93	0.91	0.99	0.89	0.98	0.97	0.96
Part B enrollment	0.86	0.89	0.86	0.89	0.85	0.96	0.83	0.91	0.91	0.90
Drug coverage (part D or other sources)	0.79	0.79	0.79	0.81	0.78	0.85	0.76	0.80	0.85	0.82
Medicaid	0.07	0.12	0.06	0.11	0.06	0.11	0.06	0.10	0.10	0.06
Observations	2,517	339	2,178	553	1,964	663	1,854	82	60	49

Notes: Excluding individuals who have Medicare coverage through an HMO. Means of respective variables, unless indicated otherwise. EGHP indicates employer-sponsored health insurance.

Table 7.8 Summary statistics 2008

Variable	Whole linked sample	HbA1c >= 6.5%	HbA1c < 6.5%	SR diabetes: Yes	SR diabetes: No	Diabetes claims: Yes	Diabetes claims: No	Undiagnosed diabetes 1: High HbA1c no self-reports	Undiagnosed diabetes 2: High HbA1c, no self-reports, no claims	Undiagnosed diabetes:3: High HbA1c, no self-reports, no claims, no screening in past two years
Age	73.88	72.95	74.06	72.48	74.29	74.16	73.76	74.31	73.41	73.33
Age > = 65	0.95	0.93	0.95	0.91	0.96	0.93	0.96	0.97	0.96	0.95
Race (white)	0.87	0.77	0.89	0.80	0.89	0.82	0.89	0.78	0.77	0.78
Hispanic	0.07	0.11	0.06	0.11	0.05	0.11	0.05	0.07	0.04	0.05
Female	0.57	0.51	0.59	0.49	0.60	0.53	0.59	0.65	0.63	0.63
Married	0.56	0.53	0.57	0.53	0.57	0.51	0.58	0.54	0.59	0.58
Education: High school and above	0.78	0.68	0.80	0.68	0.81	0.70	0.81	0.77	0.78	0.75
Indiv. earnings	4,370.63	4,172.96	4,408.85	3,652.10	4,581.64	2,356.04	5,255.00	6,931.84	8,850.69	8,884.38
HH income	53,895.97	43,758.34	55,856.11	43,815.66	56,856.23	41,008.84	59,553.16	51,761.80	58,736.68	57,430.32
HH income (median)	35,009.00	30,300.00	36,000.00	28,804.00	37,936.00	28,804.00	37,936.00	32,052.00	41,235.00	41,197.50
HH wealth	577,099.4	401,678.5	611,017.6	356,055.1	642,013.1	393,180.8	657,835.9	395,058.30	439,706.5	428,768.7
HH wealth (median)	232,750.0	123,750.0	262,500.0	139,000.0	288,500.0	139,000.0	288,500.0	169,000.0	232,000.0	234,000.0
Covered by EGHP	0.43	0.39	0.43	0.42	0.43	0.41	0.44	0.42	0.48	0.45
Poor/fair general health status	0.32	0.49	0.28	0.48	0.27	0.46	0.25	0.33	0.32	0.28
BMI	27.87	30.64	27.34	30.60	27.07	29.84	27.01	29.03	29.53	29.56
Cognition	21.80	20.84	21.98	20.96	22.04	20.74	22.26	21.52	22.33	22.13
Ever smoker	0.58	0.61	0.58	0.64	0.57	0.62	0.57	0.51	0.47	0.44
Current smoker	0.11	0.11	0.11	0.11	0.11	0.10	0.12	0.10	0.11	0.09
Vigorous exercise	0.33	0.23	0.35	0.27	0.35	0.26	0.36	0.24	0.27	0.28
Part A enrollment	0.99	0.98	0.99	0.98	0.99	0.99	0.99	0.99	1.00	1.00
Part B enrollment	0.93	0.93	0.93	0.92	0.93	0.96	0.92	0.92	0.92	0.92
Drug coverage (part D or other sources)	0.88	0.90	0.88	0.91	0.88	0.91	0.87	0.90	0.93	0.92
Medicaid	0.10	0.17	0.08	0.18	0.07	0.17	0.06	0.09	0.06	0.06
Observations	2,370	384	1,986	538	1,832	723	1,647	97	73	64

Notes: Excluding individuals who have Medicare coverage through an HMO. Means of respective variables unless indicated otherwise.

Table 7.9   **Summary statistics—Cases with diabetes according to different measures**

| | 2006 | | | 2008 | | |
Variable	Self-reports or biomarker	Self-reports or biomarker or claims	Claims only	Self-reports or biomarker	Self-reports or biomarker or claims	Claims only
Age	72.09	73.02	76.55	72.76	73.80	77.09
Age > = 65	0.87	0.89	0.98	0.92	0.93	0.96
Race (white)	0.81	0.82	0.84	0.80	0.81	0.87
Hispanic	0.09	0.08	0.07	0.11	0.10	0.08
Female	0.54	0.56	0.61	0.52	0.54	0.61
Married	0.62	0.61	0.57	0.53	0.53	0.51
Education: High school and above	0.73	0.74	0.75	0.70	0.71	0.76
HH wealth	415,080.8	420,042.10	439,020.44	362,013.10	399,387.3	513,974.5
HH wealth (median)	162,000.0	175,000.0	234,550.0	125,000.0	155,000.0	228,408.7
Covered by EGHP	0.43	0.43	0.46	0.42	0.42	0.42
Poor/fair general health status	0.42	0.40	0.33	0.46	0.44	0.39
BMI	30.25	29.72	27.69	30.36	29.79	28.01
Cognition	21.26	21.17	20.86	21.05	20.99	20.82
Ever smoker	0.58	0.59	0.60	0.62	0.60	0.56
Current smoker	0.10	0.10	0.10	0.11	0.10	0.10
Vigorous exercise	0.27	0.27	0.29	0.26	0.26	0.27
Part A enrollment	0.93	0.95	0.99	0.98	0.99	1.00
Part B enrollment	0.89	0.91	0.96	0.92	0.94	0.98
Drug coverage (part D or other sources)	0.81	0.82	0.85	0.91	0.91	0.91
Medicaid	0.11	0.11	0.08	0.16	0.15	0.12
Observations	635	801	166	635	839	204

Notes: Excluding individuals who have Medicare coverage through an HMO. Means of respective variables unless indicated otherwise.

(2014) suggest, it may also include individuals whose diabetes is under control through treatment and who thus do not report having diabetes.

The results presented in tables 7.10 and 7.11 explore predictors of diabetes in multivariate regressions. In table 7.10, all individuals who have diabetes according to either of the three measures are classified as diabetics. In table 7.11, diabetes is defined according to self-reports only, using biomarker data as a predictor for self-reported diabetes. Both tables include average marginal effects after probit estimation for the years 2006 (columns [1]–[3]) and 2008 (columns [4]–[6]). For each year, the first column displays results for demographic and socioeconomic variables only, the second column adds health indicators and health behavior as explanatory variables, and the third column adds information on an individual's insurance status.

The results in table 7.10 confirm many of the findings from the descriptive analyses in tables 7.7 and 7.8 and are in line with the earlier literature studying predictors of diabetes. Individuals who are white are less likely to have diabetes, and those who are Hispanic are more likely to have diabetes. In addition there are gradients in education and wealth, although the former is no longer significantly different from zero when health indicators and behaviors are included. Individuals who rate their health as fair or poor have a 10 to 13 percentage points higher probability of having diabetes compared to individuals who rate their health as better. In addition, diabetes risk is positively related to BMI and negatively to doing vigorous exercise. These associations do not change when insurance status is included. The results in table 7.11 indicate that the HbA1c level is a very significant predictor of self-reported diabetes, even when controlling for all the other demographic, socioeconomic, health- and health insurance-related variables. Many of the latter variables do not significantly predict self-reported diabetes when HbA1c is included (e.g., race, ethnicity), mainly self-reported general health and BMI remain robust and strong predictors above and beyond the HbA1c level.[8]

The descriptive analysis above already suggested that measures of undiagnosed diabetes depend on the data sources and how they are combined. In the final set of analyses we therefore study alternative definitions of undiagnosed diabetes that combine information from all three sources of prevalence data in different ways:

1. Undiagnosed1: HbA1c level > = 6.5 percent, but no self-reported diabetes.
2. Undiagnosed2: HbA1c level > = 6.5 percent, but no self-reported diabetes and no diabetes in claims data.

8. For the results presented in tables 7.10 and 7.11, we additionally explored changes when using categories of BMI instead of the linear value, when restricting the sample to individuals age sixty-five and older, and when replacing household wealth with household income. The results were remarkably similar and are thus not shown here. They are, however, available upon request.

Table 7.10   **Probability of diabetes (according to any of the three measures)—Marginal effects after probit estimation**

	2006			2008		
	SES	+health indicators	+insurance status	SES	+health indicators	+insurance status
Age	0.002*	0.003**	0.003*	0.000	0.003**	0.003*
	[0.0012]	[0.0015]	[0.0016]	[0.0013]	[0.0016]	[0.0016]
White	−0.148***	−0.081**	−0.089***	−0.140***	−0.094***	−0.101***
	[0.0306]	[0.0327]	[0.0335]	[0.0314]	[0.0324]	[0.0330]
Hispanic	0.162***	0.128***	0.130**	0.136***	0.077*	0.050
	[0.0458]	[0.0490]	[0.0506]	[0.0429]	[0.0433]	[0.0451]
Female	−0.035*	−0.027	−0.033	−0.071***	−0.056***	−0.058***
	[0.0195]	[0.0215]	[0.0217]	[0.0205]	[0.0210]	[0.0212]
Married	−0.001	0.004	0.002	−0.037*	−0.019	−0.018
	[0.0208]	[0.0219]	[0.0224]	[0.0213]	[0.0214]	[0.0218]
Education: High school	−0.053**	0.007	0.006	−0.067***	−0.011	−0.003
and above	[0.0244]	[0.0255]	[0.0264]	[0.0256]	[0.0264]	[0.0270]
HH wealth/1,000,000	−0.413***	−0.269**	−0.281***	−0.331***	−0.208**	−0.183*
	[0.1068]	[0.1067]	[0.1070]	[0.0987]	[0.0967]	[0.0951]
Poor/fair general health		0.105***	0.103***		0.136***	0.132***
status		[0.0240]	[0.0243]		[0.0238]	[0.0243]
BMI		0.019***	0.020***		0.019***	0.018***
		[0.0018]	[0.0018]		[0.0017]	[0.0017]
Cognition		−0.005**	−0.006**		−0.004*	−0.004*
		[0.0023]	[0.0024]		[0.0023]	[0.0024]
Ever smoker		0.021	0.025		0.010	0.007
		[0.0208]	[0.0209]		[0.0207]	[0.0209]
Current smoker		−0.066**	−0.067**		−0.035	−0.046
		[0.0322]	[0.0326]		[0.0336]	[0.0337]
Vigorous exercise		−0.051**	−0.052**		−0.036*	−0.035
		[0.0211]	[0.0212]		[0.0218]	[0.0219]
Enrolled in part B			0.074**			0.055
			[0.0351]			[0.0375]
Drug coverage (part D			0.041			0.086***
or other sources)			[0.0270]			[0.0300]
Medicaid			0.012			0.097**
			[0.0443]			[0.0424]
Covered by EGHP			0.007			0.031
			[0.0202]			[0.0205]
Observations	2,517	2,172	2,127	2,369	2,221	2,177

Notes: Excluding individuals who have Medicare coverage through an HMO. Average marginal effects after probit estimation. Dependent variable = 1 if individual diabetic according to any of the three measures (self-reports, biomarker, or claims).

***Significant at the 1 percent level.

**Significant at the 5 percent level.

*Significant at the 10 percent level.

Table 7.11 **Probability of self-reported diabetes—Marginal effects after probit estimation**

	2006			2008		
	SES	+health indicators	+insurance status	SES	+health indicators	+insurance status
HbA1c Level	0.211***	0.187***	0.187***	0.185***	0.167***	0.165***
	[0.0082]	[0.0087]	[0.0087]	[0.0074]	[0.0077]	[0.0077]
Age	−0.002**	−0.001	−0.002	−0.003***	−0.002	−0.002
	[0.0009]	[0.0012]	[0.0012]	[0.0009]	[0.0012]	[0.0012]
White	−0.008	0.012	0.009	−0.007	0.018	0.014
	[0.0214]	[0.0221]	[0.0228]	[0.0208]	[0.0205]	[0.0212]
Hispanic	0.010	−0.006	−0.009	0.040	0.002	−0.010
	[0.0319]	[0.0331]	[0.0341]	[0.0303]	[0.0291]	[0.0294]
Female	−0.018	−0.016	−0.019	−0.062***	−0.054***	−0.056***
	[0.0151]	[0.0168]	[0.0170]	[0.0151]	[0.0156]	[0.0158]
Married	−0.002	−0.005	−0.005	−0.021	−0.016	−0.016
	[0.0160]	[0.0171]	[0.0175]	[0.0154]	[0.0157]	[0.0161]
Education: High school and above	−0.029	0.009	0.007	−0.057***	−0.027	−0.031
	[0.0188]	[0.0193]	[0.0200]	[0.0191]	[0.0196]	[0.0204]
HH wealth/1,000,000	−0.083	−0.009	−0.018	−0.192**	−0.120	−0.110
	[0.0755]	[0.0764]	[0.0775]	[0.0807]	[0.0781]	[0.0773]
Poor/fair general health status		0.088***	0.090***		0.064***	0.063***
		[0.0194]	[0.0197]		[0.0178]	[0.0181]
BMI		0.010***	0.011***		0.007***	0.007***
		[0.0014]	[0.0014]		[0.0012]	[0.0012]
Cognition		−0.003	−0.003*		−0.003**	−0.003*
		[0.0018]	[0.0018]		[0.0017]	[0.0018]
Ever smoker		0.013	0.014		0.012	0.011
		[0.0161]	[0.0163]		[0.0151]	[0.0153]
Current smoker		−0.043*	−0.044*		−0.039*	−0.037
		[0.0246]	[0.0250]		[0.0226]	[0.0230]
Vigorous exercise		−0.028*	−0.026		0.010	0.011
		[0.0811]	[0.0167]		[0.0165]	[0.0166]
Enrolled in part B			0.037			−0.003
			[0.0274]			[0.0280]
Drug coverage (part D or other sources)			0.034*			0.054***
			[0.0207]			[0.0211]
Medicaid			0.030			0.045
			[0.0361]			[0.0314]
Covered by EGHP			0.017			0.023
			[0.0159]			[0.0152]
Observations	2,517	2,172	2,127	2,325	2,178	2,135

Notes: Excluding individuals who have Medicare coverage through an HMO. Average marginal effects after probit estimation. Dependent variable = 1 if individual has self-reported diabetes.

***Significant at the 1 percent level.

**Significant at the 5 percent level.

*Significant at the 10 percent level.

3. Undiagnosed3: HbA1c level > = 6.5 percent, but no self-reported diabetes, no diabetes in claims data, and no glucose/HbA1c screening test two
years before the interview.

The first measure uses only information from self-reports and biomarker
data. Individuals are coded as having undiagnosed diabetes if their HbA1c
level is above 6.5 percent, but they do not report having been diagnosed
with diabetes, that is, this definition ignores information from claims. In the
second definition we incorporate the information from the claims data: only
individuals who have an elevated HbA1c level but neither report diabetes in
the HRS nor have diabetes related claims are coded as having undiagnosed
diabetes. In the third definition we further require that individuals have not
taken a screening test in the two years before the HRS interview.

The last three columns of tables 7.7 and 7.8 show means of the different
demographic, socioeconomic, and health-related variables for the three different definitions of undiagnosed diabetes. Compared to individuals with
diabetes, fewer among the undiagnosed are Hispanic, a larger share has at
least a high school degree, they have higher average income, higher median
wealth (although the mean is lower in 2006), and fewer rate their health as
fair or poor. These findings are somewhat surprising—as they suggest that,
if at all, individuals with higher SES have a higher risk of undiagnosed diabetes. In order to shed additional light on this, the final set of regressions
studies these relationships in multivariate analyses.

In the multivariate analyses of predictors of undiagnosed diabetes, the
undiagnosed cases are compared to those who have diagnosed diabetes. In
the first definition, a diagnosis of diabetes can come from self-reports or
biomarkers, in the second and third definitions, individuals who only have
diabetes according to the claims data are also coded as diabetic. Results for
the first definition are presented in table 7.12, for the second in table 7.13,
and for the third in table 7.14. Interestingly, fair or poor self-rated health
is the only predictor of undiagnosed diabetes that is robust and significant
across all definitions and in almost all specifications. It is conceivable that
a diabetes diagnosis leads individuals to rate their health as fair or poor,
so the question of causality has to be left open. In addition, in some of
the specifications some of the socioeconomic or health-related variables
significantly predict undiagnosed diabetes. However, the patterns are not
consistent across years. Overall, there is thus no systematic relationship of
any of our measures of undiagnosed diabetes with demographic or socioeconomic characteristics. Neither is there an impact of cognition, known
risk factors, such as BMI or exercise, or health insurance status. Given the
richness of our data and findings in the earlier literature we reviewed above,
this is perhaps a bit surprising.

Table 7.12   Probability of undiagnosed diabetes (undiagnosed1)

	2006			2008		
	SES	+health indicators	+insurance status	SES	+health indicators	+insurance status
Age	0.003	0.001	0.001	0.005**	0.002	0.002
	[0.0017]	[0.0024]	[0.0024]	[0.0019]	[0.0026]	[0.0026]
White	−0.063	−0.063	−0.071	−0.038	−0.052	−0.056
	[0.0397]	[0.0468]	[0.0485]	[0.0399]	[0.0451]	[0.0466]
Hispanic	−0.052	−0.063	−0.053	−0.020	0.015	0.030
	[0.0414]	[0.0461]	[0.0491]	[0.0498]	[0.0609]	[0.0665]
Female	0.006	−0.004	0.001	0.091***	0.075**	0.078**
	[0.0286]	[0.0336]	[0.0334]	[0.0293]	[0.0321]	[0.0326]
Married	−0.002	0.003	−0.001	0.038	0.028	0.029
	[0.0297]	[0.0333]	[0.0336]	[0.0307]	[0.0328]	[0.0335]
Education: High school and above	0.023	0.004	−0.002	0.047	0.030	0.022
	[0.0300]	[0.0375]	[0.0389]	[0.0319]	[0.0378]	[0.0393]
HH wealth/1,000,000	−0.228	−0.326	−0.295	0.013	−0.037	−0.023
	[0.2262]	[0.2656]	[0.2559]	[0.1711]	[0.1907]	[0.1831]
Poor/fair general health status		−0.088***	−0.092***		−0.075**	−0.075**
		[0.0305]	[0.0307]		[0.0324]	[0.0329]
BMI		−0.001	−0.001		−0.004	−0.005*
		[0.0028]	[0.0028]		[0.0027]	[0.0027]
Cognition		−0.001	0.001		0.002	0.002
		[0.0035]	[0.0036]		[0.0038]	[0.0039]
Ever smoker		−0.043	−0.040		−0.045	−0.041
		[0.0332]	[0.0330]		[0.0332]	[0.0334]
Current smoker		0.065	0.066		0.043	0.041
		[0.0710]	[0.0716]		[0.0637]	[0.0638]
Vigorous exercise		0.013	0.006		−0.030	−0.031
		[0.0351]	[0.0343]		[0.0347]	[0.0350]
Enrolled in part B			−0.011			−0.011
			[0.0634]			[0.0608]
Drug coverage (part D or other sources)			−0.054			−0.005
			[0.0505]			[0.0572]
Medicaid			−0.052			−0.056
			[0.0485]			[0.0464]
Covered by EGHP			−0.025			−0.043
			[0.0304]			[0.0320]
Observations	635	542	532	635	584	575

Notes: Excluding individuals who have Medicare coverage through an HMO. Average marginal effects after probit estimation. Sample includes individuals identified as diabetics in self-reports or biomarker data. Dependent variable = 1 if diabetes in biomarker data, but not according to self-reports.

***Significant at the 1 percent level.

**Significant at the 5 percent level.

*Significant at the 10 percent level.

Table 7.13   Probability of undiagnosed diabetes (undiagnosed2)

	2006			2008		
	SES	+health indicators	+insurance status	SES	+health indicators	+insurance status
Age	−0.000	−0.001	−0.001	−0.000	−0.001	−0.001
	[0.0012]	[0.0017]	[0.0017]	[0.0013]	[0.0017]	[0.0017]
White	−0.003	−0.001	−0.002	−0.036	−0.053	−0.064*
	[0.0248]	[0.0289]	[0.0298]	[0.0299]	[0.0344]	[0.0368]
Hispanic	−0.033	−0.043	−0.035	−0.051*	−0.042	−0.030
	[0.0281]	[0.0290]	[0.0328]	[0.0262]	[0.0315]	[0.0379]
Female	0.012	0.011	0.013	0.041**	0.025	0.026
	[0.0198]	[0.0225]	[0.0225]	[0.0202]	[0.0221]	[0.0225]
Married	−0.007	−0.006	−0.010	0.036*	0.026	0.022
	[0.0210]	[0.0231]	[0.0235]	[0.0213]	[0.0227]	[0.0233]
Education: High school	0.018	0.002	−0.002	0.017	−0.006	−0.017
and above	[0.0211]	[0.0267]	[0.0279]	[0.0227]	[0.0281]	[0.0302]
HH wealth/1,000,000	−0.180	−0.256	−0.204	0.018	−0.002	0.000
	[0.1851]	[0.2146]	[0.1947]	[0.1000]	[0.1172]	[0.1209]
Poor/fair general health		−0.048**	−0.043**		−0.034	−0.033
status		[0.0204]	[0.0207]		[0.0219]	[0.0225]
BMI		−0.000	−0.000		−0.001	−0.001
		[0.0019]	[0.0020]		[0.0018]	[0.0018]
Cognition		0.001	0.002		0.004	0.003
		[0.0025]	[0.0025]		[0.0026]	[0.0027]
Ever smoker		−0.003	−0.004		−0.046**	−0.046*
		[0.0219]	[0.0220]		[0.0233]	[0.0236]
Current smoker		−0.022	−0.016		0.029	0.033
		[0.0345]	[0.0367]		[0.0459]	[0.0478]
Vigorous exercise		0.009	0.004		−0.004	−0.008
		[0.0239]	[0.0235]		[0.0241]	[0.0244]
Enrolled in part B			−0.008			−0.005
			[0.0471]			[0.0447]
Drug coverage (part D or			0.019			0.017
other sources)			[0.0282]			[0.0356]
Medicaid			−0.043			−0.055**
			[0.0288]			[0.0271]
Covered by EGHP			−0.024			−0.014
			[0.0206]			[0.0219]
Observations	801	698	683	837	776	761

Notes: Excluding individuals who have Medicare coverage through an HMO. Average marginal effects after probit estimation. Sample includes individuals identified as diabetics in self-reports, biomarker, or claims data. Dependent variable = 1 if diabetes in biomarker data, but not according to self-reports and claims.

***Significant at the 10 percent level.

**Significant at the 5 percent level.

*Significant at the 1 percent level.

Table 7.14 Probability of undiagnosed diabetes (undiagnosed3)

	2006			2008		
	SES	+health indicators	+insurance status	SES	+health indicators	+insurance status
Age	−0.001	−0.002	−0.002	−0.000	−0.001	−0.001
	[0.0011]	[0.0016]	[0.0016]	[0.0012]	[0.0016]	[0.0016]
White	−0.012	−0.008	0.000	−0.019	−0.028	−0.037
	[0.0237]	[0.0269]	[0.0262]	[0.0269]	[0.0303]	[0.0325]
Hispanic	−0.018	−0.028	−0.028	−0.044*	−0.036	−0.028
	[0.0276]	[0.0283]	[0.0283]	[0.0241]	[0.0288]	[0.0339]
Female	0.009	0.008	0.007	0.034*	0.018	0.018
	[0.0180]	[0.0203]	[0.0204]	[0.0191]	[0.0210]	[0.0214]
Married	−0.007	−0.012	−0.010	0.028	0.017	0.015
	[0.0190]	[0.0212]	[0.0213]	[0.0202]	[0.0214]	[0.0220]
Education: High school and above	0.013	0.000	0.005	0.001	−0.024	−0.032
	[0.0193]	[0.0247]	[0.0245]	[0.0224]	[0.0282]	[0.0300]
HH wealth/1,000,000	−0.086	−0.122	−0.121	0.014	−0.005	−0.005
	[0.1435]	[0.1599]	[0.1566]	[0.0961]	[0.1120]	[0.1118]
Poor/fair general health status		−0.047***	−0.044**		−0.045**	−0.045**
		[0.0183]	[0.0186]		[0.0201]	[0.0206]
BMI		0.000	−0.000		−0.000	−0.001
		[0.0017]	[0.0018]		[0.0017]	[0.0017]
Cognition		0.001	0.001		0.002	0.002
		[0.0023]	[0.0023]		[0.0024]	[0.0025]
Ever smoker		−0.001	0.001		−0.047**	−0.047**
		[0.0198]	[0.0199]		[0.0219]	[0.0222]
Current smoker		−0.008	−0.009		0.004	0.006
		[0.0335]	[0.0334]		[0.0402]	[0.0418]
Vigorous exercise		−0.003	−0.002		−0.002	−0.005
		[0.0209]	[0.0210]		[0.0227]	[0.0230]
Enrolled in part B			−0.014			0.003
			[0.0427]			[0.0404]
Drug coverage (part D or other sources)			0.004			0.003
			[0.0277]			[0.0357]
Medicaid						−0.045*
						[0.0259]
Covered by EGHP			−0.008			−0.020
			[0.0188]			[0.0205]
Observations	801	698	686	837	776	761

Notes: Excluding individuals who have Medicare coverage through an HMO. Average marginal effects after probit estimation. Sample includes individuals identified as diabetics in self-reports, biomarker, or claims data. Dependent variable = 1 if diabetes in biomarker data, but not according to self-reports and claims, and has not taken a diabetes screening two years before the HRS interview.

***Significant at the 1 percent level.
**Significant at the 5 percent level.
*Significant at the 10 percent level.

7.4   Summary and Outlook

In this chapter we compare three measures of diabetes using HRS data: the commonly used survey measure on diabetes, diabetes according to HbA1c levels collected in the HRS biomarker data, and diabetes in the Medicare insurance claims linked to the HRS data. Self-reported diabetes and diabetes information from biomarker data align for a large part of our sample (85 percent). Using information on self-reported medication from the HRS as well as information from claims data help to shed light on the differences between the self-reports and the biomarker data. Most of the differences can likely be explained by the fact that treatment lowers HbA1c levels in some cases even below the 6.5 percent threshold. When considering the three data sources, roughly 2–3 percent of individuals have diabetes according to HbA1c but do not report diabetes, and do not receive diabetes treatment according to their claims records. Even in the Medicare population there is thus a fraction of individuals who likely have undiagnosed diabetes. Somewhat surprisingly, however, we do not find that the probability of being undiagnosed is related to socioeconomic status.

Importantly, comparing the three measures of diabetes as well as taking into account information on treatment suggests that none of the three measures should be taken as a gold standard. In particular, our results stress that both the presumably more objective biomarker as well as the claims data suffer from error just as the self-reports. While the biomarker data can be influenced by treatment and thus may not identify cases as diabetic because their diabetes is well managed, the claims data may potentially falsely classify individuals as diabetics (e.g., Sakshaug, Weir, and Nicholas 2014). In addition, individuals who have diabetes but are not treated for it will also be misclassified based on the claims data.

We envision that future research will move beyond the descriptive analysis of the data we presented in this chapter. A statistical model could start from a framework (e.g., Wansbeek and Meijer 2000) in which true disease prevalence is unobserved, with survey self-reports, biomarkers, and administrative claims data being three indicators that all potentially suffer from measurement error. Such a model could be used to construct a more reliable measure of prevalence, which in turn could be employed as a predictor in substantive analysis, for example, mortality prediction or studies of health care use.

Another issue that future research might address is that typically not all respondents of a survey provide consent to biomarker measurement or administrative record linkage. Also, while biomarker data and administrative linkages potentially improve measurement of disease prevalence in community surveys, they involve costs as well. Both these issues could be addressed jointly in a statistical decision framework motivated by a total survey error cost perspective (Groves 1989). Specifically, this approach could address the questions of whether collecting biomarkers or administrative linkage are worth their costs, which of them is the more cost effective, and whether including both of them is the best option.[9] The required cost and benefit calculations are, however, more straightforward for a biomarker such as HbA1c as its only purpose is the measurement of diabetes prevalence, while linked insurance claims data can serve many purposes so that their benefits are harder to quantify. To end on a positive note, one of our results was that adding claims information to combined self-reports and biomarkers reduces undiagnosed diabetes cases from 3.26 percent to 2.4 percent in 2006 and from 4.05 percent to 3.1 percent in 2008, that is, by between one-quarter and one-third. Thus, including all three measures in a major study such as the HRS improves measurement of disease prevalence substantially.

References

American Diabetes Association. 2010. "Standards of Medical Care in Diabetes—2010." *Journal of Clinical and Applied Research in Education* 33 (Supp. 1): 11–61.

———. 2015. "Standards of Medical Care in Diabetes—2015." *The Journal of Clinical and Applied Research in Education* 38 (Supp. 1): 1–94.

Baker, Michael, Mark Stabile, and Catherine Deri. 2004. "What Do Self-Reported, Objective, Measures of Health Measure?" *Journal of Human Resources* 39:1067–93.

Barcellos, Silvia, Dana Goldman, and James P. Smith. 2012. "Undiagnosed Disease, Especially Diabetes, Casts Doubt on Some of Reported Health 'Advantage' of Recent Mexican Immigrants." *Health Affairs* 31:2727–37.

Bennett, C. M., M. Guo, and S. C. Dharmage. 2007. "HbA1c as a Screening Tool for Detection of Type 2 Diabetes: A Systematic Review." *Diabetic Medicine* 24:333–43.

Bonora, Enzo, and Jaako Tuomilehto. 2011. "The Pros and Cons of Diagnosing Diabetes with A1c." *Diabetes Care* 34 (Supp. 2): 184–90.

Chatterji, Pinka, Heesoo Joo, and Kajal Lahiri. 2012. "Beware of Being Unaware: Racial/Ethnic Disparities in Chronic Illness in the USA." *Health Economics* 21:1040–60.

Goldman, Noreen, I-Fen Lin, Maxine Weinstein, and Yu-Hsuan Lin. 2003. "Evaluating the Quality of Self-Reports of Hypertension and Diabetes." *Journal of Clinical Epidemiology* 56:148–54.

Groves, Robert M. 1989. *Survey Errors and Survey Costs*. New York: Wiley.

Johnston, David, Carol Propper, and Michael Shields. 2009. "Comparing Subjective and Objective Measures of Health: Evidence from Hypertension for the Income/Health Gradient." *Journal of Health Economics* 28:540–52.

Manski, Charles F., and Francesca Molinari. 2008. "Skip Sequencing: A Decision Problem in Questionnaire Design." *Annals of Applied Statistics* 2:264–85.

---

9. We are aware of only one paper that formally studies costs and benefits of decisions in survey design, although in a different context (Manski and Molinari 2008).

Reynolds, Timothy, Stuart Smellie, and Patrick Twomey. 2006. "Glycated Haemo-globin (HbA1c) Monitoring." *British Medical Journal* 333 (7568): 586–88.

Rohlfing, C. L., R. R. Little, H. H. Wiedmeyer, J. D. England, R. Madsen, M. I. Harris, K. M. Flegal, M. S. Eberhardt, and D. E. Goldstein. 2000. "Use of GhB (HbA1c) in Screening for Undiagnosed Diabetes in the US Population." *Diabetes Care* 23:187–91.

Sakshaug, Joseph W., David R. Weir, and Lauren H. Nicholas. 2014. "Identifying Diabetics in Medicare Claims and Survey Data: Implications for Health Services Research." *BMC Health Services Research* 14 (150): 1–6.

Smith, James P. 2007. "Nature and Causes of Trends in Male Diabetes Prevalence, Undiagnosed Diabetes, and the Socioeconomic Status Health Gradient." *Proceedings of the National Academy of Sciences of the United States of America* 204:13225–31.

Wansbeek, Tom, and Erik Meijer. 2000. *Measurement Error and Latent Variables in Econometrics*. Amsterdam: Elsevier.

Wolinsky, Frederik D., Michael P. Jones, Fred Ullrich, Yiyue Lou, and George L. Wehby. 2014. "The Concordance of Survey Reports and Medicare Claims in a Nationally Representative Longitudinal Cohort of Older Adults." *Medical Care* 52 (5): 462–68.

Yasaitis, Laura, Lisa Berkman, and Amitabh Chandra. 2015. "Comparison of Self-Reported and Medicare Claims-Identified Acute Myocardial Infarction." *Circulation* 131:1477–85.

Comment   James P. Smith

In a thought-provoking chapter, Heiss et al. raise several important questions about the appropriate way to measure diabetes prevalence in household surveys. While diabetes is the disease at issue in the chapter, the same questions would arise with many other disease outcomes. Three common measures of diabetes prevalence are used and compared in their analysis—self-reports of ever being diagnosed by a doctor, the common HbA1c diabetes biomarker being above the standard American threshold of 6.5 percent, and a diabetes diagnosis mentioned in Medicare claims data. The question the authors ask is whether the three measures are "consistent" and which one is "correct."

Figure 7C.1, derived from the chapter, illustrates the central finding of the chapter by showing diabetes prevalence rates for a sample of HRS respondents who had their diabetes measured in all three ways in 2006 and in 2008. Rates of diabetes prevalence are clearly quite different using the three

James P. Smith holds the Distinguished Chair in Labor Market and Demographic Studies at the RAND Corporation.

These comments were written with the support of grants from the National Institute of Aging and were delivered at a NBER conference on the Economics of Aging, Carefree, Arizona, May 2015. For acknowledgments, sources of research support, and disclosure of the author's material financial relationships, if any, please see http://www.nber.org/chapters/c13638.ack.

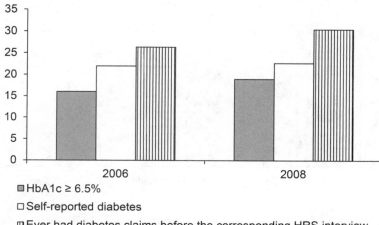

■ HbA1c ≥ 6.5%

□ Self-reported diabetes

⊞ Ever had diabetes claims before the corresponding HRS interview

Fig. 7C.1   Diabetes indicators

measures—19.0 percent for the biomarker measure, 22.7 percent for the self-report of ever diagnosed, and 26.4 percent using Medicare claims data.

The discrepancy between the biomarker index and the ever self-report is easy to explain since they are actually measuring very different things. The self-report is obtained from a question to respondents about whether they had *ever* been diagnosed by a doctor while the biomarker is an indicator of whether the respondent *currently* exceeds the diabetes threshold of 6.5 percent. There is no real inconsistency between these two measures since they are in fact measuring very different things (Smith 2007). Biomarker values above the diagnosis threshold for those who claimed they were never diagnosed are a possible indication of undiagnosed disease, an important phenomenon in itself. Similarly, biomarker values below the diagnosis threshold for those who claimed they were diagnosed in the past may indicate that the respondent is managing the disease well. Thus, there is no fundamental inconsistency between the ever self-report of diagnosis and the current biomarker indicator. They should be used together as they are in the chapter to provide insights into diagnosis, undiagnosis, and good disease management.

The real puzzle centers on the claim data measure, which is much higher than either of the other two. If it was the "correct" measure, it would imply that we are seriously underestimating diabetes prevalence in the age fifty and older population in the United States.

Figure 7C.2 uses the same data as in figure 7C.1, but rearranges it to highlight changes over time between the 2006 and 2008 waves. Once again, the depiction of trends varies significantly depending on which measure is used. While self-reports of ever diagnosed show very little change between the two HRS waves (less than 1 percentage point), the change is almost 3

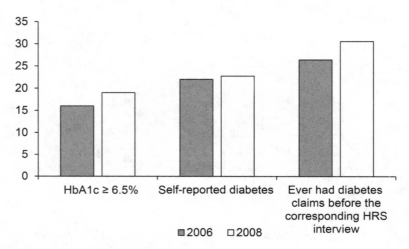

Fig. 7C.2   Diabetes indicators

percentage points using the biomarker and 4 percentage points using claims data. It would be useful as well for research to focus also on the reasons for the discrepancies in the three measures in measuring changes in diabetes prevalence over time. Secular trends in diabetes prevalence are equally as important as comparisons at a moment in time, the primary focus of this chapter.

My main suggestion at the conference to the authors is that they extend their analysis from simply doing cross-sectional comparisons between the three prevalence measures by using the panel nature of HRS data, which contain repeat measures of all three prevalence concepts. Not only would this address another central question of the nature of secular changes in diabetes prevalence, but multiple measures in the HRS panel for all three diabetes prevalence measures can go a long way to cleaning each measure of any reporting errors that may be present.

Table 7C.1 illustrates the potential contribution of the panel component of HRS to measurement of the ever self-report of disease for three diseases—cancer, diabetes (the relevant disease for this chapter), and hypertension (HBP). These data are derived from the first eight waves of the original HRS sample. In this table, a "no" answer to the diabetes question is translated into a zero while a "yes" answer is translated into a 1. The first two columns list the fraction of respondents who always answered "no" or always "yes" to the ever self-report question. For diabetes, for eight waves in a row, 74.6 percent of HRS respondents said "no"; 6.4 percent said "yes" to the ever-diagnosed diabetes question, so we should be very confident in this 81 percent subsample who is a diabetic and who is not.

The interesting case is when there is not complete consistency in responses

Table 7C.1   HRS disease measurement on ever self-report (prevalence)

Diseases	All 0s (%)	All ones (%)	Mixed (%)	All 1s after all 0s (%)	0s after 1s (%)	0s after 1s "corrected" (%)
Cancer	82.0	3.9	14.1	11.9	2.2	1.0
Diabetes	74.6	6.4	19.0	15.1	3.9	0.7
HBP	33.6	29.0	37.5	27.0	9.5	3.7

over the eight waves so that we translate respondents' answers into mixed values of 0s and 1s. For diabetes, this represents 19 percent of the cases. However, values of zeros (not a diabetic) followed by a series of 1s are fully consistent since that simply means that there was an onset of diabetes during the first eight HRS waves that was not contradicted in a future wave. That situation represents 15.1 percent of the cases, leaving only 3.9 percent of cases with an obvious inconsistency (a 0 that follows a 1). One in twenty-five is not so bad.

The situation is even not near that dire, since many of these inconsistences are easy to repair. For example, a zero followed by two 1s and then followed by five 0s should, in this author's opinion, be changed to all 0s since five times in a row in the more recent waves of HRS the respondent said he/she was not told he/she was a diabetic. Thus, the use of the panel data in HRS results in a big decrease in measurement error and a big increase in signal/noise for self-reports of prevalence, and especially, and even more importantly, for the incidence of diabetes.

As table 7C.1 shows, the situation is very similar for "self-reports of ever-diagnosed cancer," but there remain a larger fraction of uncertain diagnosis for hypertension, a far less serious disease. But for all the diseases in HRS the use of the full panel waves of responses helps a great deal in determining with good confidence whether a respondent was ever diagnosed with a particular disease.

Next consider the use of the biomarker index HbA1c, a measure of the percent of hemoglobin molecules bound to glucose (Goldman et al. 2003). Biomarker data are a very useful addition to population-based aging surveys, but they should not be treated as an uncontested gold standard. Biomarkers suffer from their own forms of measurement error and there is often inconsistency between alternative biomarkers meant to measure the same thing. For diabetes, HbA1c and fasting glucose would be an excellent example. Fasting glucose is typically the clinical measure used to diagnose in the doctor's office, while HbA1c is the standard survey population measure since it does not require respondents to fast. Incomplete fasting and momentary stress affect the accuracy of both measures.

As mentioned above the most important point is that self-reports of diabetes and an HbA1c threshold are measuring ever diagnosed, and now there is no real inconsistency in their values. Instead of diagnosis, biomarkers are most useful in combination with self-reports of ever diagnosed as an indicator of undiagnosed disease or well-managed disease. It is also an excellent indicator of disease severity by using the continuous measure of the biomarker outcome. For example respondents scoring above 8 in their HbA1c test not only are much more likely to be diabetics, they also are much more likely to suffer from a more serious level of the disease.

Since biomarkers are now measured in every other wave of HRS, I would make the same comment about biomarkers that I made about "ever" self-report above. They are most useful when the full set of panel data available across all waves is employed. Having a respondent above the diagnosis threshold in multiple waves of the survey should be a reliable indication that she is, in fact, a diabetic.

I finish with the third measure—the report of diabetes in Medicare claims data. The real puzzle of the chapter is why the prevalence report of diabetes is so much higher in claims data compared to the self-report of ever diabetes. This difference is not unique to anything about the HRS since similar levels of self-reports of ever diabetes have been found in NHANES for the same age group as HRS (Sakshaug, Weir, and Nicholas 2014). Similar to this chapter, Sakshaug et al. also report much higher rates of diabetes prevalence in claims data compared to ever self-reports.

There is a natural temptation to treat claims data as the real gold standard, but in my view that would be a mistake. It might not even rank as a bronze standard. There are several reasons for this. First, diabetes is often put on claims data to justify taking blood—the "rule out" hypothesis—or to give a warning sign and to have a talk with the patient. Sakshaug, Weir, and Nicholas (2014) also report that the higher rates of diabetes prevalence in claims data are due to false positives and may indicate intensive monitoring of prediabetes patients, especially those with other cardiovascular risk factors. Once again, researchers may be on safer ground if they use multiple waves of the claims data as well. It might even be better to use two or more visits to the doctor to confirm the diabetes diagnosis.

Conclusions

In this intriguing and stimulating chapter, Heiss et al. demonstrate that using three common alternative measures of disease prevalence—self-reports of past prevalence, a common biomarker (HBa1c), and being listed in Medicare claims data—over the same sample of respondents produces very different measures of diabetes prevalence. From highest to lowest prevalence, claims data are ranked the highest and the biomarker the lowest.

In my view, comparing the three measures and looking for a winner in which is the best measure of diabetes prevalence is not really the thing to do. Rather the issue is how to use them together, especially using the panel aspect of the data to obtain better health measurement and not just for knowing diabetes prevalence.

References

Goldman, N., I. Lin, M. Weinstein, and Y. Lin. 2003. "Evaluating the Quality of Self-Reports of Hypertension and Diabetes." *Journal of Clinical Epidemiology* 56:148–54.

Sakshaug, J. W., D. R. Weir, and L. H. Nicholas. 2014. "Identifying Diabetics in Medicare Claims and Survey Data: Implications for Health Services Research." *BMC Health Services Research* 14:150.

Smith, J. P. 2007. "Nature and Causes of Male Diabetes Trends, Undiagnosed Diabetes, and the SES Health Gradient." *Proceedings of National Academy of Sciences* 104 (33): 13225–31.

Challenges in Controlling Medicare Spending
Treating Highly Complex Patients

Thomas MaCurdy and Jay Bhattacharya

8.1 Introduction

Medicare expenditures are rising at a persistent rate, with the government unable to maintain current levels of per capita services in the next several decades without either substantial increases in taxes or large reductions in other domestic spending. Over the long term, Medicare faces significant financial challenges because of rising overall health-care costs, increasing enrollment as the population ages, and a decreasing ratio of workers to enrollees. Total Medicare spending is projected to increase from 15 percent of all federal outlays in 2010 to nearly 18 percent of outlays by 2020, reaching 4 percent of the gross domestic product (GDP). By 2035, Medicare expenditures are expected to consume almost 6 percent of GDP.

Any policy offering hope of success in mitigating the unsustainable rise in Medicare expenses must focus its impacts on the highest-cost users of Medicare. For example, a May 2005 Congressional Budget Office analysis found that Medicare users who were ranked in the top 5 percent of health

Thomas MaCurdy is professor of economics and senior fellow of The Hoover Institution, Stanford University, a senior research associate of Acumen LLC, and a research associate of the National Bureau of Economic Research. Jay Bhattacharya is professor of medicine at Stanford University, a senior research associate at Acumen LLC, and a research associate of the National Bureau of Economic Research.

This research was supported by contract RTOP CMS-08–026 from the Office of the Actuary (OACT) of the Centers for Medicare and Medicaid Services (CMS). Bhattacharya's work was partly supported by National Institute on Aging grant #P01AG005842. Any opinions expressed in this document do not necessarily represent the official position or policy of either OACT or CMS. The authors thank Mallory Bounds and Dan Rogers for expert research assistance and Todd Caldis and John Poisal for many useful comments. For acknowledgments, sources of research support, and disclosure of the authors' material financial relationships, if any, please see http://www.nber.org/chapters/c13645.ack.

expenditures accounted for 43 percent of all expenditures, those ranked in the top 10 percent accounted for 61 percent of expenditures, while those ranked in the top 25 percent accounted for 81 percent of all expenditures (CBO 2005). Clearly, Medicare is unlikely to control spending growth unless it also controls spending growth of costs for high-cost users because that is where the bulk of expenditures can be found.

Determining the characteristics of the high-intensity users is not as easy a task as one might first surmise, for this alone provides few insights unless one can also develop profiles linking attributes of these groups to their intense utilization. Uncovering such attributes reveals what behaviors policies must alter to be successful in curtailing program costs. For example, studies indicating that the majority of high-cost users are in their last year of life suggest that a large fraction of expenditures go to postponing inevitable mortality, implying that society must value short extensions in life at high values to justify the expenditures. Further, it suggests that capping expenses per person over a year will have only a minor impact on mortality, for such a policy primarily brings about an inevitable death earlier. Alternatively, programs proposed in Medicare to manage diseases or chronic conditions maintain that these afflictions identify high-cost users and that improved treatment will lower overall expenditures by preventing worsening circumstances leading to utilization of expensive services.

This study reveals that beneficiaries with multiple illnesses cost considerably more than would be predicted by adding up the costs of treatments for each disease/illness condition in isolation; increasing the number of comorbidities induces a multiplicative rather than an additive cost structure. While it is well known that patients with multiple comorbidities (i.e., patients with more than one disease) account for a disproportionate amount of expenditures and mortality (see Sorace et al. 2011), the critical link between medical complexity and costs is not well understood. Moreover, the findings presented here highlight further complications since the patterns of disease/illness combinations are quite diverse with individual combinations populated by small numbers of patients. These empirical findings demonstrate that most Medicare expenditures are associated with small sets of medically complex patients.

The depictions of high-cost users uncovered in this study provide important policy insights into the designs of both Medicare reimbursements and approaches for incentivizing medical practices likely to be effective in lowering the growth of Medicare spending. In the area of reimbursement policy, the findings suggest that the risk-adjustment models currently used by Medicare inadequately compensate for complex patients due to their cost structure that principally assumes linearity in health-condition indicators. In the area of policies aimed at encouraging medical practices to focus on lowering the expenses of treating high-cost patients, quality-improvement

programs such as disease management and care coordination must be formulated to individualize treatments necessary for patients suffering from
a wide array of illnesses. Although these forms of medical practice can
offer flexibility in dealing with comorbidities, the level of variability in comorbidities documented in this chapter indicates that care-coordination
models will be continually challenged with novel clinical situations. The
relatively common occurrence of rare disease/illness combinations explains
why popular care-management paradigms have not produced anticipated
cost savings and have frequently led to higher overall expenditures.

What follows in this chapter is organized into four remaining sections.
Section 8.2 describes our approach for measuring the illness complexity of
Medicare patients and presents the incidence and composition of illnesses
among the patient population. Section 8.3 documents the extent to which
medically complex patients have higher costs than patients with less complexity. Section 8.4 briefly discusses several implications regarding Medicare
reimbursement policies. Finally, section 8.5 presents a summary of results.

8.2   Illness Complexity of Medicare Patients

This section describes the approach implemented in this analysis to assess
the illness complexity of Medicare patients. To characterize the relationship
between medical expenses and the complexity of patients' health status,
the analysis first adopts a systematic method for classifying patient comorbidities, and then investigates how expenditures increase with increasing patient complexity. Section 8.2.1 explains the approach for classifying
patients based on their illnesses and number of comorbidities, and section
8.2.2 presents the incidence and composition of illnesses among the patient
population.

8.2.1   Classification of Illnesses and Comorbidities

Since one of our essential goals in this research is to characterize patient
complexity, we must first choose a disease classification system. In this
choice, we are guided by several principles. First, we focus on a disease classification system based upon a system that is in active use by the Centers
for Medicare and Medicaid Services (CMS) for the purposes of provider
payment, risk adjustment, or other important activities. This principle guar-
antees that our results will have direct operational implications for Medicare.

Second, we analyze disease classification systems that range from simpler
to more detailed for the purposes of sensitivity analysis. Our choice of disease classification system has direct implications for our calculation of the
number of patients with a distinct combination of diseases. A simple classification system, which aggregates many similar diseases, will necessarily
elide clinical differences between patients. For instance, such a system might

group together patients with early and late-stage cancer. A too-simple classification system will thus produce an underestimate of the range of patients with differing combinations of conditions.

Conversely, an overly detailed classification system makes clinical distinctions that, while important to medical personnel caring for patients, are not particularly important in predicting health care expenditures. Such a system will produce an overestimate of the range of patients with differing combinations of conditions. By analyzing multiple disease classification systems ranging from simpler to more detailed, our estimates will bracket the true complexity of Medicare patients.

Patients' diseases and comorbidities are key inputs into many of Medicare's payment systems. Perhaps the most well-known disease classification system used by CMS is the Hierarchical Condition Category (HCC) system. Medicare Advantage uses the HCC methodology, for instance, to amend a beneficiary's premiums based on the beneficiary's risk factors. This system is based on an underlying disease classification system, called condition categories (CCs), which though not as detailed as the full ICD-9 or ICD-10 disease classification system, still contains considerable detail distinguishing between various disease conditions. In this chapter, we adopt and analyze the CC disease classification system since it meets both of our selection principles—the system is in use by Medicare, and it makes useful distinctions between diseases in classifying patient disease.

Our second selection principle requires us to consider a simpler classification system in addition to the detailed CC system. To this end, this analysis develops an illness condition (IC) classification system to identify the health conditions a patient has in a given month. This IC classification system is based on a simplification of the CC system. The following discussion describes the IC classification system and the process used to measure illness complexity.

Medicare uses a total of seventy-one different CCs to compute cost differentials, where each CC identifies whether a beneficiary experiences a particular illness.[1] A CC is assigned based on the diagnosis codes (ICD-9-CM) recorded on the individual's Parts A and B fee-for-service (FFS) claims, including those from inpatient (IP), skilled nursing (SNF), home health (HH), hospice (HS), outpatient (OP), physician (PB), and durable medical equipment (DME) claim files. Some groups of CCs identify the same illness, with individual CCs measuring different levels of severity within the illness; other CCs identify unique illnesses. Assigning a hierarchy to the CCs linked to a common illness produces the HCC representing this group.

The IC classification system developed here represents an alternative aggregation of the CC system, with the goal of aggregating CCs to ICs by

---

1. The standard seventy CCs used to calculate risk scores are incremented by renal failure, which is used as a separate risk-adjustment factor.

unique illnesses. In particular, the analysis groups each CC in a set designating the same illness at different severity levels and into a single IC. Table 8.1 presents the complete mapping of CCs to the IC system. The left column designates a unique number for each of the forty-four ICs for identification purposes, the center column describes the illness defined by the IC, and the last column lists the set of CCs aggregated into the IC. Among the forty-four ICs, sixteen of them are aggregations of multiple CCs while the remaining twenty-eight each belong to a distinct CC illness category. For example, IC 8, myocardial infarction, consists of three CCs used in the HCC methodology to compute cost differentials: 81, 82, and 83. Conversely, IC 17, HIV/AIDS, only includes one CC.

Our IC classification system is more appropriate for our purposes than the HCC classification system. The latter system assigns patients a diagnosis code at the top of a hierarchy on the basis of the relative expenditures required for caring for patients with the conditions that make up that hierarchy. This procedure suppresses the complexity of caring for patients with conditions that are both high and low in the hierarchy. Instead, our IC system lumps together patients in the CC hierarchy, and thus reduces the *observed* clinical heterogeneity of patients. Our IC results are meant to be compared against our CC results, which (unlike the HCC or IC systems) reflect all of the complexity in the CC system.

8.2.2   Incidence and Composition of Illnesses

Our analysis characterizes the illness complexity of a patient by counting the number of distinct combinations of ICs and CCs afflicting the patient during each month making up a calendar year. The assignment of a CC and an IC in a month is determined by checking diagnoses on eligible FFS claims in the five-month window surrounding the selected month, with the window comprised of the current month, the two months prior, and the two months after.[2] For the depiction of the health experiences presented here, the following empirical analysis calculates measures using the universe of FFS Medicare beneficiaries who had continuous Part A and B enrollment in 2009 while alive, preceded by two months of A and B enrollment in 2008 and followed by two months of A and B enrollment in 2010. The population consists of 32.9 million beneficiaries, 1.46 million of whom died during 2009.

Table 8.2 summarizes the incidence of each IC, as well as the number of distinct IC combinations and the total and average costs associated with

2. The assignment applies the same algorithm used in the CMS risk-adjustment model. Considering inpatient, outpatient, and physician claims eligible for CMS risk adjustment, the algorithm excludes denied claims and claims that are not from an approved provider type. It further excludes physician and outpatient claims where the procedure codes indicate the claim was primarily used for laboratory tests, equipment, supplies, orthopedic, ambulance, or radiology services. The results presented in this chapter registers occurrence of a health condition when relevant diagnoses show up on at least one claim in the five-month window. The findings reported here change only marginally if a two-claim threshold replaces the one claim criteria.

Table 8.1   **List of illness categories**

IC number	Illness category	CCs included
1	Cancer	7–10
2	Diabetes	15–19, 119
3	Liver	25–27
4	Substance abuse	51–52
5	Schizophrenia/depression (psychiatric)	54–55
6	Shock	2, 79
7	Respiratory arrest	77–78
8	Myocardial infarction	81–83
9	Stroke	95–96
10	Renal failure	129–31
11	Skin ulcers	148–49
12	Head injury	154–55
13	Opportunistic infections	5, 111–12
14	Paralysis	67–68, 100
15	Vertebral/spinal disorders	69, 157
16	Peripheral vascular disorders	104–5
17	HIV/AIDS	1
18	Protein-calorie malnutrition	21
19	Intestinal obstruction/perforation	31
20	Pancreatic disease	32
21	Inflammatory bowel disease	33
22	Bone/joint/muscle infect/necrosis	37
23	Rheum. arthritis/inflam. conn. tissue	38
24	Severe hematological disorders	44
25	Disorders of immunity	45
26	Muscular dystrophy	70
27	Polyneuropathy	71
28	Multiple sclerosis	72
29	Parkinson's and Huntington's disease	73
30	Seizure disorders and convulsions	74
31	Coma, brain compression/anoxic damage	75
32	Congestive heart failure	80
33	Specified heart arrhythmias	92
34	Cerebral palsy, other paralytic syndromes	101
35	Cystic fibrosis	107
36	Chron. obstructive pulmonary disease	108
37	Nephritis	132
38	Extensive third-degree burns	150
39	Hip fracture/dislocation	158
40	Traumatic amputation	161
41	Major comp. of medical care/trauma	164
42	Major organ transplant status	174
43	Artificial opens for feeding/elimination	176
44	Amputee status/lower limb/amput. compl.	177

Table 8.2   Incidence, composition, and costs of illness categories

Illness category (IC)	No. beneficiaries	No. bene. months	No. distinct IC combinations	No. distinct CC combinations	Total Medicare part A/B cost (millions $)	Average cost per bene. month ($)
Respiratory arrest	189,289	764,396	229,443	361,823	12,580	16,458
Third-degree burns	1,941	7,545	2,565	2,905	116	15,427
Cerebral palsy	162,329	595,668	162,188	235,816	6,762	11,353
Malnutrition	803,879	3,251,735	637,787	1,121,418	33,504	10,303
Opportunistic infections	860,009	3,457,486	561,525	1,101,990	30,513	8,825
Traumatic amputation	54,785	262,230	60,160	104,924	2,194	8,368
Artificial openings for feeding/elimination	367,252	1,836,347	365,456	569,180	15,260	8,310
Shock	2,623,864	11,470,864	1,120,007	2,551,410	82,772	7,216
Intestinal obstruction/perforation	834,837	3,400,597	441,813	774,567	23,766	6,989
Amputation	151,113	828,813	137,673	279,793	5,694	6,870
Trauma	1,426,494	6,378,361	615,012	1,239,189	42,745	6,702
Bone/joint/muscle infection	398,169	1,929,716	269,033	497,871	11,927	6,180
Hip fracture/dislocation	601,626	2,889,510	244,021	421,016	15,908	5,505
Severe hematological disorder	406,786	2,345,658	261,575	482,959	12,163	5,185
Disorders of immunity	345,965	1,776,422	176,886	328,699	9,165	5,159
Paralysis	720,901	3,881,990	431,552	796,082	19,943	5,137
Head injury	308,769	1,318,585	171,933	270,757	6,532	4,954
Major organ transplant	77,623	562,163	69,222	119,296	2,735	4,865
Nephritis	314,648	1,569,702	156,675	337,230	7,146	4,552
Skin ulcers	1,663,903	8,970,141	672,330	1,575,324	38,646	4,308
Renal failure	3,864,397	24,942,694	1,062,844	2,769,880	96,517	3,870
Pancreatic disease	544,758	2,627,137	242,323	420,950	10,050	3,825
Stroke	1,879,021	9,679,151	642,118	1,287,280	36,974	3,820
Vertebral/spine	881,076	4,161,272	320,248	595,480	14,813	3,560

(continued)

Table 8.2 continued

Illness category (IC)	No. beneficiaries	No. bene. months	No. distinct IC combinations	No. distinct CC combinations	Total Medicare part A/B cost (millions $)	Average cost per bene. month ($)
Cystic fibrosis	8,692	49,527	7,549	9,651	170	3,442
Myocardial infarction	3,305,127	16,554,603	608,504	1,706,839	56,106	3,389
Substance abuse	608,278	3,098,318	256,207	467,987	10,472	3,380
Coma	5,045,466	31,684,378	1,082,904	2,770,567	106,357	3,357
Liver	454,089	2,691,715	234,741	481,393	8,975	3,334
Heart arrhythmias	179,279	971,264	103,150	150,316	2,943	3,030
Seizure disorders and convulsions	1,177,065	7,592,712	462,119	814,415	20,736	2,731
Peripheral vascular disease	6,344,000	39,468,824	1,086,509	2,816,761	101,168	2,563
Polyneuropathy	2,116,592	11,783,943	503,750	1,143,192	29,163	2,475
Inflammatory bowel disease	312,395	1,856,224	128,624	196,399	4,569	2,461
Congestive heart failure	4,814,660	35,550,728	844,886	2,052,953	87,305	2,456
COPD	5,493,492	36,042,267	920,743	2,224,269	86,409	2,397
Muscular dystrophy	22,961	140,401	16,262	20,883	325	2,316
Parkinson's/Huntington's	570,521	4,317,794	196,521	345,475	9,326	2,160
Cancer	4,396,160	31,904,703	619,102	1,708,936	62,600	1,962
HIV/AIDS	116,835	1,089,221	55,540	86,946	1,967	1,806
Multiple sclerosis	182,011	1,422,276	76,445	113,731	2,513	1,767
Psychiatric	2,514,992	19,416,247	499,391	1,042,345	33,113	1,705
Rheumatoid arthritis	1,741,038	12,050,335	303,015	578,686	18,256	1,515
Diabetes	8,657,223	76,192,689	1,088,021	3,278,663	114,998	1,509

beneficiaries with each IC. The second column reports the number of unique beneficiaries afflicted by the IC at least one month during 2009, and the third lists the total number of beneficiary months with an assignment to the IC. The next two columns present the total number of *unique* IC combinations among beneficiary months classified into each IC and the number of *unique* CC combinations among beneficiary months classified into each IC, respectively. The calculation of Medicare payment includes all FFS claims for a beneficiary with service dates in that month, and the totals sum across months assigned to the designated IC.

Table 8.2 shows that there are many complex patients within each IC, and there is extreme variability among these patients regarding the combinations of comorbid conditions. Taking diabetes as an example, among the more than eight million patients in the diabetes IC category in 2009, there were over a million unique types of patients on the basis of IC combinations and over 3.2 million unique types of patients when characterized on the basis of the less aggregated CC system. This example demonstrates incredible clinical heterogeneity among diabetic Medicare patients, regardless of whether a more or less detailed clinical classification system is used to characterize comorbid conditions. Thus, the particular set of comorbid conditions experienced by a given diabetes patient may be rare among other diabetes patients, and the same holds true for patients classified into the other ICs reported above. Since IC and CC combinations in table 8.2 are defined at the month level, an individual beneficiary whose set of comorbidities changes across the year may account for multiple IC or CC combinations.

To provide a sense of the dynamics of individuals across states of illness complexity, table 8.3 broadly examines patients' transitions across complexity spells. A spell here represents the span of time that a patient is classified in a given range of complexity levels. The spell ends when either the patient's complexity level changes, the patient dies, or calendar year 2009 ends. This table demonstrates that "very complex" spells (consisting of seven or more ICs), while comparatively rare, are substantially more costly than less complex spells. Across the study period, about 5 percent of the total spells fell into the "very complex" category. The average monthly cost for these spells is $11,276, nearly three times the cost of "complex" spells (consisting of

Table 8.3   **Transitions across spells of different illness complexities**

Classification of spell complexity	No. spells	Avg. length of spell (months)	Avg. monthly cost ($)	Share of spells ending in less complex (%)	Share of spells ending in more complex (%)	Share of spells ending in death (%)	Share of spells ending in the end of period (%)
Sick (1–3 ICs)	27,563,337	6.1	705	31	15	2	52
Complex (4–6 ICs)	7,055,328	3.5	3,478	51	14	6	29
Very complex (7 + ICs)	1,785,517	3.5	11,276	54	—	18	29

four to six ICs) and nearly sixteen times the cost of "sick" spells (consisting of one to three ICs). Moreover, the high costs of "very complex" spells are not exclusively driven by expensive services associated with end-of-life care. About 18 percent of spells within this category ended in death, but over half ended with the patient moving to a lower level of complexity. Thus, complex patients do not tend to die at the end of a disease spell, but very often survive and transition into a healthier state.

8.3   Medical Expense of Comorbidities

To explore the extent to which medically complex patients—those with more ICs in a given month—have higher costs than patients with less complexity, this section elaborates the relationship between costs and illness complexity in the Medicare population. Section 8.3.1 describes the distribution of Medicare expenditures across incidence of illness complexity, and section 8.3.2 details how costs are compounded by any increase in illness complexity.

8.3.1   Relating Costs to Illness Complexity

Table 8.4 characterizes medical condition complexity by evaluating the number of combinations of ICs and CCs present in a patient during a month, and then measures the incidences of each status along with showing heterogeneity of illnesses within the status and costs associated with the level of complexity. The first group of columns shows the incidence of various illness complexities in the Medicare population in 2009. About 65 percent (21.4 of 32.9 million) of beneficiaries experienced at least one month with no ICs, and 45 percent of beneficiary months in 2009 have no IC occurrence. The second group displays the number of distinct combinations of ICs and CCs making up each illness complexity level. The last group of columns present total Medicare expenditures in the months associated with each level of illness complexity, along with the average payment per beneficiary month, the average payment per IC per month, and the marginal change in the average cost per IC per month attributable to increasing medical complexity by an incremental IC.

Table 8.5 presents an alternative depiction of the information in table 8.4 showing the cost of caring for beneficiaries categorized by their highest degree of illness complexity experienced during 2009. This table shows that 31 percent of beneficiaries experienced no ICs throughout the year, and that these beneficiaries jointly had nearly 113 million months of enrollment in 2009. For 6 percent of beneficiaries, their most complex month of illness complexity involved having four simultaneous ICs, and these beneficiaries jointly accounted for about 37 million months of enrollment in 2009. The remaining columns in table 8.5 present numbers analogous to those in table 8.4 with calculations done for the months listed in the third column.

Table 8.4 Expansion of costs associated with illness complexity

No. illness categories	No. beneficiaries with illness complexity for at least one month	No. bene. months with illness complexity	Share of illness complexity months (%)	No. distinct IC combinations associated with illness complexity	No. distinct CC combinations associated with illness complexity	Total Medicare payments ($millions)	Share of Medicare payments (%)	Avg. payment per bene. month ($)	Avg. payment per IC per month ($)	Marginal change in payment per IC per month ($)
0	21,447,305	166,847,086	45.48	0	0	$24,921	8.3	149	—	—
1	17,168,325	96,090,578	26.19	44	168	$40,788	13.6	424	424	—
2	11,216,501	48,797,948	13.30	932	8,446	$41,238	13.8	845	423	−2
3	6,862,826	24,476,762	6.67	10,784	109,686	$37,343	12.5	1,526	509	86
4	4,223,018	12,926,046	3.52	60,332	452,557	$32,864	11.0	2,542	636	127
5	2,654,623	7,235,988	1.97	175,975	868,816	$28,282	9.4	3,909	782	146
6	1,699,076	4,229,539	1.15	305,757	1,043,544	$23,692	7.9	5,602	934	152
7	1,092,717	2,531,285	0.69	368,524	962,929	$19,164	6.4	7,571	1,082	148
8	698,512	1,527,395	0.42	354,040	762,048	$15,049	5.0	9,853	1,232	150
9	440,125	915,266	0.25	294,004	540,338	$11,371	3.8	12,424	1,380	149
10	273,395	545,512	0.15	223,347	353,639	$8,337	2.8	15,282	1,528	148
11	166,927	320,362	0.09	156,254	219,663	$5,988	2.0	18,693	1,699	171
12	99,502	185,079	0.05	101,968	131,150	4,102	1.4	22,164	1,847	148
13	58,070	105,008	0.03	63,159	76,583	2,718	0.9	25,883	1,991	144
14	32,373	56,797	0.02	36,248	42,379	1,671	0.6	29,428	2,102	111
15	17,184	29,507	0.01	19,558	22,516	985	0.3	33,389	2,226	124
>15	10,900	25,702	0.01	18,064	20,403	997	0.3	38,791	2,320	94

Table 8.5   Costs of treating beneficiaries classified by their highest degree of illness complexity

No. illness categories	No. beneficiaries with illness complexity in most complex month	No. bene. months	Share of beneficiaries (%)	No. distinct IC combinations associated with illness complexity	No. distinct CC combinations associated with illness complexity	Total Medicare payments ($millions)	Share of Medicare payments (%)	Avg. payment per bene. month ($)	Avg. payment per IC per month ($)	Marginal change in payment per IC per month ($)
0	10,234,740	112,667,232	31.12	0	0	13,918	4.6	124	—	—
1	8,185,024	92,820,030	24.89	45	168	28,329	9.5	305	494	—
2	5,351,918	61,080,948	16.28	970	7,645	34,460	11.5	564	448	-46
3	3,283,812	37,321,325	9.99	10,819	88,339	35,132	11.7	941	494	46
4	2,052,791	23,028,297	6.24	58,718	362,531	33,496	11.2	1,455	573	79
5	1,320,342	14,507,768	4.02	175,436	771,449	30,728	10.3	2,118	670	97
6	870,727	9,337,048	2.65	330,990	1,084,757	27,328	9.1	2,927	773	103
7	575,924	6,021,968	1.75	453,591	1,192,854	23,388	7.8	3,884	879	107
8	378,487	3,863,796	1.15	503,611	1,117,835	19,341	6.5	5,006	988	109
9	244,062	2,443,357	0.74	486,185	932,916	15,317	5.1	6,269	1,096	108
10	154,311	1,521,062	0.47	422,644	709,197	11,730	3.9	7,712	1,207	111
11	96,052	935,066	0.29	337,620	502,903	8,754	2.9	9,362	1,326	118
12	58,529	563,452	0.18	249,240	336,485	6,308	2.1	11,195	1,443	117
13	34,907	333,435	0.11	171,989	215,993	4,396	1.5	13,185	1,552	109
14	20,134	191,839	0.06	110,886	131,701	2,914	1.0	15,188	1,652	100
15	11,142	105,815	0.03	67,013	76,649	1,827	0.6	17,265	1,740	87
>15	10,900	103,422	0.03	70,938	79,290	2,142	0.7	20,715	1,845	105

Table 8.4 further reveals that beneficiaries with multiple complex illnesses account for most Medicare spending. Only about 1 percent of beneficiary months have six ICs, and yet these months alone account for 8 percent of Medicare spending. Less than 1 percent of beneficiary months have eight assigned ICs, and yet these months account for 5 percent of Medicare spending. By contrast, the months with no IC nearly make up about *half* the months during the year, and yet only 8 percent of spending occurs in these months. The average monthly cost of caring for such beneficiaries is about $149. The average monthly cost of care per beneficiary rises steeply as the number of ICs rises, with the average monthly cost of caring for patients with five ICs nearly ten times the cost of caring for beneficiaries with one IC, and only a third of the cost of caring for patients with nine ICs.

Comparing the results in tables 8.4 and 8.5 suggest that illness complexity tends to be a transitional state for individuals. Whereas table 8.5 indicates that about 7 percent of beneficiaries concurrently experience six or more ICs sometime during the year, table 8.4 shows that these experiences account for only about 3 percent of total months of services during the year. This implies that Medicare patients who suffer from many comorbid conditions either develop additional conditions or recover from some their conditions later in the year. Beneficiaries who simultaneously experience six or more ICs sometime during the year receive 41 percent of Medicare services, but the months when care is given for six or more ICs account for only 31 percent of Medicare expenditures. This indicates that beneficiaries suffering from six or more ICs typically do not spend all of the year with this severity of illness complexity.

Figures 8.1 and 8.2 summarize the results in table 8.4. Figure 8.1 depicts the distribution of the number of months with different levels of illness complexity and the average cost associated with these months. As the figure illustrates, the average monthly cost sharply increases with illness complexity, even as the number of beneficiary months decreases. Figure 8.2 shows the relationship between the share of Medicare beneficiaries and share of expenditures by number of patient ICs. According to this figure, patients with five or more coexisting ICs represent only about 11 percent of the Medicare population but account for 41 percent of Medicare expenditures. Beneficiaries with six or more ICs account for only 3 percent of months, but 31 percent of payments.

These findings support the conclusion that the majority of medical expenditures are for complex (high comorbidity) medical patients. As increased patient complexity (high comorbidity) is strongly associated with higher Medicare expenses, ignoring the complexity of patient health circumstances leads to overestimating of Medicare expenditures for less complex patients and underestimating of Medicare expenditures for more complex patients. For example, ignoring this synergistic effect will lead to an overestimation

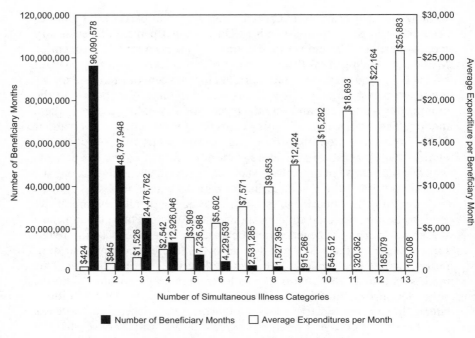

Fig. 8.1   Number beneficiary months and per-month spending by illness complexities

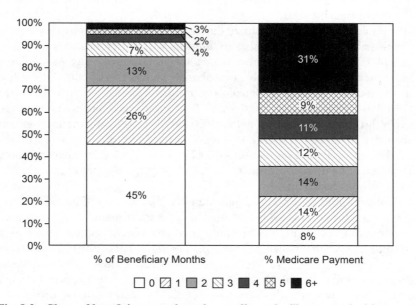

Fig. 8.2   Share of beneficiary months and expenditures by illness complexities

of Medicare expenditures of about $2,500 for a patient with no ICs, and an underestimation of about $1,300 for a patient with five ICs.

Tables 8.4 and 8.5 also highlight that patient heterogeneity increases dramatically with the number of coexisting conditions. According to table 8.4, 11.2 million of total service months with two concurrent ICs are associated with only about 900 distinct combinations of ICs and over 8,000 combinations of CCs; by way of contrast, the 1.7 million service months with six ICs involve over 305,000 combinations of ICs and over one million combinations of CCs.

The average number of beneficiary months per distinct IC combination also falls as the number of simultaneously experienced illness categories increases. For Medicare beneficiaries in the IC = 6 classification of service months, the numbers in table 8.4 imply on average about fourteen patient months per distinct IC combination and a little more than four patient months per distinct CC combination.

Table 8.5 also shows that for the nearly one million beneficiaries who experience more than seven ICs sometime during the year, these patients must be concurrently treated for over 2.4 million unique combinations of ICs and more than four million unique combinations of CCs, which translates into four distinct CC combinations per Medicare highly complex patient.

Regardless of the perspective used here to assess medical complexity, patients become increasingly distinct and increasingly unique as the number of comorbidities grows.

8.3.2   Comorbidities Entail Compounding Medical Costs

Because medical conditions interact to increase the cost of care, beneficiaries with multiple illnesses have greater expenditures than would be predicted by treating each condition in isolation. Figure 8.3 depicts this trend by graphing the relationship conveyed by the last column of table 8.4. The figure shows that the monthly cost per IC increases by $100–$150 for each additional IC beyond three. Consequently, the average cost of treating each illness category compounds as illness complexity increases. For example, the cost of treating a beneficiary's diabetes, CHF, and COPD is more expensive for a patient with another IC than for a beneficiary with no other ICs.

The implications of figure 8.3 on Medicare spending are best summarized by inferring how monthly expenditures per beneficiary change with added illness complexity. Our purpose is to make clear in a stylized way how each additional diagnosis adds to the average cost of caring for a patient by imposing marginal costs above and beyond the costs of caring for a patient with fewer diagnoses. Let $\$AE_n$ denote average monthly Medicare expenditure per beneficiary with n illness conditions. Figure 8.1 implies the following approximate difference equation for $n = 1$ IC conditions:

$$(1) \qquad \$AE_{n+1} = \$AE_n + \$425$$

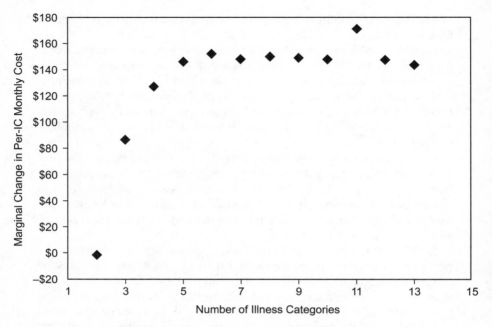

Fig. 8.3   Increment to per-IC monthly cost of increasing illness complexity

or, after rearranging difference equation (1):

(2) $$\$AE_{n+1} = (n+1) \cdot \frac{\$AE_n}{n} \text{ with } \$AE_n = \$425.$$

From figure 8.3, it is clear that each additional IC condition diagnosed adds an additional amount to the average costs of caring for a patient. To simplify matters, we assume that each additional IC condition above the first one adds \$140 to average costs. Thus, for $n \geq 2$ IC conditions

(3) $$\$AE_{n+1} = (n+1) \cdot \left(\frac{\$AE_n}{n} + \$140 \right).$$

Equations (1) and (3) provide an approximate depiction of the results shown in the last column of table 8.5. These equations clearly depict the compounding effect on cost of increasing illness complexity. Not only does the average monthly costs of treating ICs rise due to the cost of treating the additional IC, the costs of treating each of the preexisting ICs also rises. So, for instance, as a given beneficiary shifts to having five ICs from four, on average *each* of this person's five conditions cost about \$140 more to treat than if this individual had just four ICs.

Figure 8.4 plots the relationship between predicted monthly expenditures and the numbers of concurrent illness categories implied by formulas (1)–

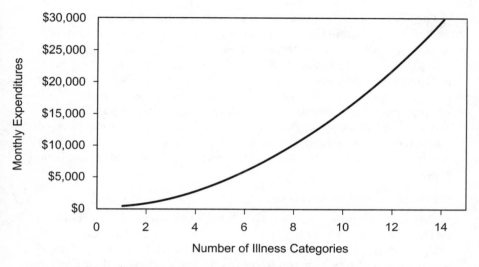

Fig. 8.4   **Predicted average monthly expenditures with increasing illness complexity**

(3). It is the counterpart of monthly expenditure bars depicted in figure 8.1; the close tracking of predicted monthly expenditures in figure 8.4 to the observed monthly expenditures in figure 8.1 verifies the accuracy of the above formulas in characterizing the dependence of average monthly Medicare spending on the number of IC conditions. The key point to note in figure 8.4 is that, after the first two health conditions, further increases in the number of illness categories leads to rapidly increasing growth in predicted average monthly expenditures by Medicare.

8.4   Policy Implications of Findings

Better managing the care of high-cost patients is a central tenet of many health reform proposals such as Accountable Care Organizations (ACOs), disease management, and pay-for-performance. These reimbursement policies focus on establishing incentives for providers to implement innovative and evidence-based treatment guidelines to care efficiently for patients, especially those with multiple chronic diseases that are known to consume a disproportionate share of Medicare resources. One prominent component of these polices involves the application of risk-adjustment modifiers to amend provider payments by accounting for patients' preexisting conditions. A second component includes the promotion of integrated care management of patients with multiple chronic conditions to lower expenses for treating patients with projected high costs. The portrait of high-cost users presented above offers a useful setting for considering the designs of both these policy components.

The following discussion explores the implications of the above empirical findings in adapting the risk-adjustment and coordination-of-care programs currently found in Medicare to enhance their chances of attaining savings in medical costs. Section 8.4.1 explores some of the reasons why complex patients might have costs that increase nonlinearly with their number of health conditions. Section 8.4.2 examines the implications of our results for appropriate risk adjustment of Medicare payments to providers who care for complex patients. Section 8.4.3 briefly assesses the consequences of our results for disease management programs. Finally, section 8.4.4 broadly considers data analytic methods to cope with patient heterogeneity and complexity.

8.4.1   Likely Drivers of Increased Costs

The above empirical findings establish a clear correlation between an increased number of health conditions and increased cost associated with each condition. They also show that the effect becomes more pronounced as patient complexity increases. To assess the implications of these findings further, the following discussion contemplates what might be the source of these increased costs.

One possible source is that synergistic relationships between conditions limit physicians' ability to provide cost-effective treatment. For example, the best medication for one condition may be contraindicated by another condition, as when an angiotensin-converting enzyme (ACE) inhibitor normally prescribed for congestive heart failure becomes contraindicated when the patient is also taking nonsteroidal anti-inflammatory drugs (NSAIDs) or diuretics for a different condition. This requires the physician to choose alternative therapies that are likely to be more expensive or less effective (if they are neither of these things, they would likely be the preferred therapy). The more conditions a patient has, the more likely that he or she will have one or more synergistic interactions that mandate a change in treatment. Thus, limited treatment options available to complex patients may contribute to the higher costs associated with treating such patients.

A second driver of high health care costs among complex patients may be the paucity of reliable data on unique condition combinations and treatment interactions. With every additional condition a patient has, the number of potential combinations of those conditions increases dramatically. A patient with two ICs will have one of a possible 946 different IC combinations. A patient with three ICs has over 13,000 IC combinations. This complexity is borne out by the actual patient data. Of the roughly three million Medicare patients that have three ICs, there are over 9,000 unique patient types (when categorized by ICs), each of which may present different contraindications and complications. When facing a dearth of well-established treatment protocols for highly complex patients, physicians may need to resort to trial and error that can directly increase costs as a result of the need for additional services, and indirectly increase costs by introducing possible treatment complications, which will also require attention.

Compounding this problem is the reality that highly complex patients are more likely to require the services of multiple specialists, who may be either unaccustomed or unequipped to work together. In situations where the right combination of specialists are unable to share data and coordinate a plan of care, one would expect to see an escalation in costs, owing to certain inefficiencies (e.g., redundant tests) and the need for trial and error in treatment as described in the previous paragraph. These shortcomings may be less pronounced in the context of managed care, which theoretically would draw some advantages from its integrated delivery methods. As information from Medicare-managed care plans was not included in this study, future research may be required to see if the synergistic effects of comorbidities are less pronounced in a managed care setting; however, the common use of capitation payments may complicate efforts to determine the exact cost per patient.

8.4.2   Implications for Risk Adjustment

To compensate physicians for providing care to Medicare patients with medical complications, CMS uses risk-adjustment methods to award higher payments for serving these beneficiaries. These adjustments are necessary to reimburse providers adequately for the increased time and resources involved in the care of complex patients. Risk adjustment is used, for example, to reimburse managed care plans, calculating bundled payments for end-stage renal disease (ESRD) patients and payment for inpatient hospitalizations (Newhouse et al. 2011). Furthermore, risk-adjustment methods are a critical element in the viability and success of the state-level health insurance exchanges called for in the Affordable Care Act (ACA), matching compensation to differences in enrollees' health status across different health plans (Weiner et al. 2012).

Without appropriate risk adjustment, providers may be overpaid for some types of patients and underpaid for others. If payments do not match the level of resources used to care for different groups of patients, providers will have an incentive to avoid care of certain populations (the undercompensated) versus an incentive to provide care to others (the overcompensated). For example, Part D Medicare payments have been shown not to reimburse insurers sufficiently for the relatively high medication use of low-income populations, creating perverse incentives for plans to avoid this part of the Part D market (Hsu et al. 2010). In addition, incorrect risk adjustment creates incentives for providers to counsel the use of services that are more lucrative, whether or not these services are medically appropriate. Adequate risk adjustment of provider payments will increase in importance as Medicare continues to move away from a FFS payment model toward episode-based or capitated payment policies.

The CMS currently risk adjusts payments according to the presence of medical conditions identified for Medicare patients based on diagnostic claims coding, and categorizes these according to specific HCCs. The CCs, which are also used in the present analysis, represent more than 200 illnesses/diseases organized into organ systems upon which a hierarchy based on the severity of the disease is then applied to obtain seventy HCCs (Pope et al. 2004). Payments are adjusted according to a formula based upon multivariate regression of total Medicare payments on these individual conditions and six interactions of HCCs, with weights for each of the health conditions determined by the regression coefficients. The current CMS risk-adjustment model takes into account four two-way and two three-way interactions among six common and high-cost chronic diseases (Frogner et al. 2011). The presence of combinations of these specific conditions increases reimbursements above the individual payments for any individual condition alone.

Our results strongly suggest that the accounting for a small set of interactions between chronic conditions in risk-adjustment methods is insufficient to capture the costs associated with the complexity of caring for patients with more than two or three conditions. Each extra condition adds considerable complexity to patient management, as the optimal care for one of the conditions may impinge on or even prevent the treatment of other conditions. Further, the medical expenditures required to care for such complicated patients grows strongly and non-linearly with the number of conditions. Any appropriate risk-adjustment methodology must account for this sort of complexity.

Addressing this problem in CMS's risk-adjustment methodology will be a challenging task given a further dispiriting implication of our results. The above findings reveal that a very large number of combinations of conditions (whether measured by CCs or ICs) exist within the group of patients with any given number of conditions. This implies that among complex Medicare patients there are very few patients with *any particular* combination of conditions despite the fact that our analysis considers the universe of Medicare beneficiaries. Consequently, a risk-adjustment methodology that takes into account the full complexity of disease interactions will thus face the problem of very small sample sizes in many of the disease combination cells, hampering the ability of an analyst to produce reliable estimates of risk-adjustment modifiers.

8.4.3   Implications for Disease Management

Patient complexity also raises important concerns about disease management and care coordination programs. Because there are an overwhelming number of potential combinations of ICs, it is not feasible to study every such combination. This has two profound implications for disease management. First, as already noted it is likely that providers will discover that certain preferred treatments are unavailable to them because of their interactions with other treatments or conditions, particularly those prescribed by other specialists. Second, even setting such contraindications to the side, it is likely that many health care providers will have limited experience with the precise combination of conditions presented in a given patient, and will face uncertainties in determining the optimal treatment. Taken together, these two factors greatly complicate the delivery of care for complex patients.

As noted previously, it is likely that highly complex patients will require treatment by a large number of specialists, who may not be used to working together, and who may disagree on how best to treat the patient. It would be expected for each type of specialist to be focused on treating their particular areas of specialty, and to be less aware of or concerned about the effects that their prescribed treatments may have on a patient's other coexisting conditions. This problem is likely to be especially pronounced among highly complex patients because the sheer number of specialists involved would make collaboration and complete access to all relevant medical records impractical. Absent a complete medical history and understanding of all coexisting patient conditions, patient care and treatment outcomes could suffer.

Thus, patient complexity of the sort characterized above poses a difficult challenge for disease management and care coordination programs. At the same time, traditional approaches to caring for complicated patients, which involve minimal communication among multiple autonomous providers, could produce even worse results than active disease management programs. At the very least, disease management programs might be better positioned to avoid duplication of tests, provide patient education, and perhaps prioritization of care when the best treatment for a condition affecting one organ system is contraindicated by the presence of another condition. Despite the challenges of multiple comorbid conditions, good disease management programs may be the only way to cope with patient complexity. It remains to be seen whether disease management programs can control the costs of care with complex patients, while maintaining high-quality outcomes.

8.4.4   Minimizing the Consequences of Patient Complexity

There are a number of potential courses of action that may help mitigate the consequences of high patient complexity. One question outside the scope of this research is whether integrated delivery models, such as those used by managed care plans, achieve a superior level of care for highly complex patients given their systems for sharing patient histories. As this has often been touted as a selling point by the managed care plans, it would be interesting to see whether either health care costs or health outcomes for highly complex patients in managed care settings differ meaningfully from their FFS counterparts. If so, issues of adverse selection aside, difficulties in sharing patient data across providers may be a material determinant of health care costs and patient health outcomes among complex patients.

A second option would be to improve access to patient records through continued shifts toward electronic recordkeeping. This would allow physicians treating highly complex patients to access the other conditions and treatments in their patients' medical histories more easily. In addition, if a Health Insurance Portability and Accountability Act-compliant patient database could be created, and made sufficiently accessible and searchable, physicians could draw upon the experiences of the select few others who have already treated similar combinations of conditions in the past, and avoid reinventing the wheel with trial and error each time a patient presents with an uncommon combination of conditions.

A related third option would be for CMS or the National Institute of Health to promote more research on effective disease management models for complicated patients. Given the small number of patients with a given mix of diagnoses and the large number of possible combinations, a complete catalog of best practices is not practical. However, a well-developed research program might uncover best practices among providers with the best results caring for complicated patients. A carefully developed set of principles for patient care developed from a comprehensive analysis of available data, rather than a cookbook of medicine, would likely prove useful to all providers.

8.5   Summary of Findings

The empirical results of this study tell a simple story: a substantial segment of the highest-cost users of Medicare consist of beneficiaries with highly complex and diverse arrays of medical conditions. About 52 percent of Medicare spending goes to treat 8 percent of the total service months when beneficiaries are afflicted by four or more major health conditions (e.g., cancer, diabetes, renal failure, chronic heart failure, etc.). During these periods of treatment, beneficiaries suffer from nearly 5.5 million combinations of major health conditions. Around 31 percent of spending goes to treat less than 3 percent of the time when Medicare beneficiaries suffer from six or more major health conditions; and, during these periods, beneficiaries suffer from nearly 4.2 million combinations of major conditions.

Translated into an annual context for beneficiaries, 18 percent of Medicare beneficiaries are afflicted by four or more major health conditions sometime during the year, and they account for 63 percent of total Medicare spending. These beneficiaries suffer from nearly 7.5 million combinations of major health conditions during the year. About 7 percent of Medicare beneficiaries are afflicted by six or more major health conditions and account for 41 percent of Medicare spending. These beneficiaries alone suffer from more than 6.4 million combinations of major illnesses, with an average of three distinct combinations per Medicare beneficiary with six or more health conditions. Regardless of the perspective used to assess medical complexity, patients are strikingly more expensive to treat and more distinct as the number of comorbidities grows.

References

Congressional Budget Office (CBO). 2005. "High Cost Medicare Beneficiaries." May. www.cbo.gov/sites/default/files/cbofiles/ftpdocs/63xx/doc6332/05-03-medi spending.pdf.

Frogner, B. K., G. F. Anderson, R. A. Cohen, and C. Abrams. 2011. "Incorporating New Research into Medicare Risk Adjustment." *Medical Care* 49 (3): 295–300.

Hsu, J., V. Fung, J. Huang, M. Price, R. Brand, R. Hui, B. Fireman, W. H. Dow, J. Bertko, and J. Newhouse. 2010. "Fixing Flaws in Medicare Drug Coverage that Prompt Insurers to Avoid Low-Income Patients." *Health Affairs* 29 (12): 2335–43.

Newhouse, J. P., J. Huang, R. J. Brand, V. Fung, and J. T. Hsu. 2011. "The Structure of Risk Adjustment for Private Plans in Medicare." *American Journal of Managed Care* 17 (6 spec. no.): e231–40.

Pope, G. C., J. Kautter, R. P. Ellis, A. S. Ash, J. Z. Ayanian, L. I. Lezzoni, M. J. Ingber, J. M. Levy, and J. Robst. 2004. "Risk Adjustment of Medicare Capitation Payments Using the CMS-HCC Model." *Health Care Financing Review* 25 (4): 119–41.

Sorace, J., H. H. Wong, C. Worrall, J. Kelman, S. Saneinejad, and T. MaCurdy. 2011. "The Complexity of Disease Combinations in the Medicare Population." *Population Health Management* 14 (4): 161–66.

Weiner, J. P., E. Trish, C. Abrams, and K. Lemke. 2012. "Adjusting for Risk Selection in State Health Insurance Exchanges Will Be Critically Important and Feasible, But Not Easy." *Health Affairs* 31 (2): 306–15.

Comment   Hidehiko Ichimura

A Summary

Main Findings

The chapter documents the authors' extremely interesting finding that a small fraction of "complex" patients constitute a major share of Medicare expenses. The authors use the universe of the 2009 Medicare claims to show that patients with six or more comorbid conditions (using forty-four illness categories they define for this study) constitute about 3 percent of the service months and 31 percent of Medicare spending, and patients with four or more comorbid conditions constitute about 8 percent of the service months and 52 percent of spending.

Patients with six or more comorbid conditions suffer from almost 4.2 million combinations of major conditions, and patients with four or more

Hidehiko Ichimura is professor of economics at the Graduate School of Economics at the University of Tokyo.

For acknowledgments, sources of research support, and disclosure of the author's material financial relationships, if any, please see http://www.nber.org/chapters/c13646.ack.

comorbid conditions suffer from almost 5.5 million combinations of major conditions over a five-month period.

In annual context for beneficiaries, 18 percent of Medicare beneficiaries experienced four or more major health conditions during 2009, and they accounted for 63 percent of total Medicare spending, suffering from almost 7.5 million combinations of major health conditions, and about 7 percent of Medicare beneficiaries experienced six or more major health conditions and they accounted for 41 percent of spending, suffering from more than 6.4 million combinations of major health conditions.

Implications

The authors argue that "risk-adjustment models currently used by Medicare inadequately compensate for complex patients" because they inadequately take into account the exponential nature of the costs with respect to the number of comorbidities. They also argue that "it is likely that many health care providers will have limited experience with the precise combination of conditions presented in a given patient, and will face uncertainties in determining the optimal treatment."

Authors' Suggestions

The authors suggest investigating the effectiveness of integrated delivery models (e.g., those used by managed care plans). They also suggest improving the sharing of information across different specialists "through continued shifts toward electronic recordkeeping" and suggest CMS or the NIH promote more research on effective disease management models for complicated patients.

Comments

Suggestions for Further Clarifications of the Situation

One of the main difficulties they point out about their findings is the difficulty health care providers will have given that they have limited experience with the precise combination of conditions presented in a given patient. To see if this is really the case, it will be useful to find out whether the top X highest frequency cells (say, $X = 10,000$ cells) among patients with four or more comorbid conditions amounts to a large fraction of total spending. This may give us cases to focus on to medically examine each of the X cases.

Finding out whether cells with more than N patients (say, $N = 1,000$ patients) amount to a large fraction of total spending may be useful. This may isolate cells so we have some hope of learning something from data.

To understand the source of the high cost, it may be useful to break up the per-month spending into different items such as hospital care, physician and clinical services, drugs, and so forth.

In order to address the coordination issue across specialists/departments, it may be useful to examine comorbidity issues using illness category classification based on relevant departments/specialists. One may redo the two exercises above using the classification.

Is the "Complexity" Issue Distinct from the "End-of-Life" Issue?

It may be useful to try to see to what extent the "high comorbidity-high cost" issue is distinct from the "high cost in the last year of life" issue. A simple measure may be to compute the number of patients who acquired new illness categories within X months prior to their death and have four or more major health conditions at death in a given year over the number of patients who die in the given year. One can do the same with spending, instead of numbers.

On a related issue, it will be useful to understand how the complexity develops. To understand this, it may be useful to distinguish patients who come into Medicare with multiple health problems from those who do not have any health problems (for, say, one year into the program). Among the latter group, it may be interesting to examine how the number of comorbid conditions progress over time to explore how different combinations of illness categories give rise to additional categories using a hazard function.

On the Interpretation of Table 8.4

Looking at table 8.4: 932 out of potential $_{44}C_2$ = 946 combinations are realized. Because of a very large number of observations, this implies a very accurate estimate of a low probability for fourteen combinations. Analogously, 10,784 out of potential $_{44}C_3$ = 13,244 combinations are realized. If the only low probability combinations are those fourteen cases, then the number of cells with low probability is below 14 × 44 and we have 2,460 cells with very low probability; there seems to be new information from this beyond what is implied by the earlier observation. Analogous observations can be made for other cells, too.

Accounting for the Benefit Side

It may be interesting to take into account the benefit side by defining "recovery" by "no illness in the same category within X years." One simple measure may be the average cost per recovery. A better measure may require using data that link health data and earnings data, for example. This type of measure may convey even a bleaker picture than that reported in this chapter.

Movies, Margins, and Marketing
Encouraging the Adoption of Iron-Fortified Salt

Abhijit Banerjee, Sharon Barnhardt, and Esther Duflo

9.1 Introduction

Anemia is estimated to affect 1.6 billion people worldwide (de Benoist et al. 2008). Iron deficiency is one of the leading causes of anemia, along with other nutritional deficiencies, illness and disease (diarrhea and malaria), and infections (parasites) (Viteri 1998). Anemia is associated with slower physical and cognitive development (Lozoff 2007), with potentially long-lasting effects (Lozoff et al. 2006). For working-age adults, productivity may be lowered by anemia, as feeling weak is the most common symptom of the disorder (Haas and Brownlie 2001). Severe anemia during pregnancy can lead to low birth weight and child mortality (Stoltzfus 2001). High rates

Abhijit Banerjee is the Ford Foundation International Professor of Economics and codirector of the Abdul Latif Jameel Poverty Action Lab (J-PAL) at the Massachusetts Institute of Technology and a research associate of the National Bureau of Economic Research. Sharon Barnhardt is the primary investigator of CESS Nuffield–Flame University and is affiliated with the Abdul Latif Jameel Poverty Action Lab (J-PAL). Esther Duflo is the Abdul Latif Jameel Professor of Poverty Alleviation and Development Economics, a cofounder and codirector of the Abdul Latif Jameel Poverty Action Lab (J-PAL) at the Massachusetts Institute of Technology, and a research associate of the National Bureau of Economic Research.

For financial support, we thank the International Initiative for Impact Evaluation, the UK Department for International Development, the US National Institutes of Health (P01AG005842), and the International Food Policy Research Institute. Dr. Vandana Shiva provided medical expertise and Tata Chemicals distributed DFS to stores through their stockists. For dedicated research support we are grateful to the team at J-PAL, including Urmi Bhattacharya, Shruti Bhimsaria, Anna George, Dwijo Goswami, Radhika Jain, Seema Kacker, Sweta Kumari, Bastien Michel, Prianthi Roy, Krutika Ravishankar, Achill Rudolph, Laura Stilwell, Niloufer Taber, Micah Villareal, and dozens of survey specialists. We thank Amitabh Chandra and participants at the Health and Aging conference at the Boulders, 2015, for comments. All errors are our own. For acknowledgments, sources of research support, and disclosure of the authors' material financial relationships, if any, please see http://www.nber.org/chapters/c13649.ack.

of anemia are observed broadly among older adults, among whom lower hemoglobin levels are associated with cognitive decline (Peters et al. 2008) and lower physical performance (Penninx et al. 2004).

Fortified foods are a potential solution for widespread iron-deficiency anemia (IDA).[1] Model-based estimates suggest that, compared to iron supplementation, iron fortification is less expensive and would be more cost effective at a large scale for reducing maternal and neonatal mortality (Baltussen, Knai, and Sharan 2004). For iron fortification to be effective, the fortified food must be something households routinely consume. Grains like wheat were seen as promising in north India, but only for the relatively richer households who buy flour. For poorer households who consume their own grains, fortification at small mills requires behavioral changes by households, which are unsustainable (Banerjee, Duflo, and Glennerster 2011).

Salt seems to be an ideal product to fortify: it is ubiquitous, cheap, and generally purchased from stores. Consumers have brand loyalty and prefer white, branded salt over the grayish traditional rock salt. Adding iron to branded salts thus seems to be a promising way to increase iron intake and reduce IDA if marketing campaigns can convince consumers to make the switch. Despite its promise, double-fortified salt (DFS) was not commercially available until recently, due to technical difficulties in ensuring the stability of both the iron and the iodine. In the middle of the first decade of the twenty-first century, India's National Institute of Nutrition (NIN, Hyderabad) developed DFS fortified with iron and iodine. Double-fortified salt is estimated to provide about 30 percent of the recommended daily allowance (RDA) of iron (National Institute of Nutrition [India] 2005) when consuming 10g salt per day regularly (fortified at 1mg iron/g salt) (Ranganathan and Sesikeran 2008). The NIN scientists first demonstrated the long-term safety of DFS in animal studies (Nair, Sesikeran, et al. 1998). They also established the stability and bioavailability of iron in DFS and the acceptability and effectiveness of DFS in school children and small-scale trials with tribal populations (Nair, Brahmam, et al. 1998; Brahmam et al. 2000; Sivakumar et al. 2001).

In the last five years, NIN and the Indian government have sought to encourage wider adoption of DFS. Since 2011, the NIN formulation of DFS can be manufactured by private companies through a license agreement requiring a certain percentage of production to be donated to charities such as school meal programs. In 2012, India's Department of Women and Child Welfare directed states to use DFS in the national midday meal

1. Bhutta, Salam, and Das (2013, 10) describe the full list of nutritional interventions aimed at women and children as "education, dietary modification, food provision, agricultural interventions, supplementation and fortification . . . alone and in combination, provision of financial incentives . . . home gardening and community-based nutrition education and mobilization programs."

scheme (school lunches) and the Integrated Child Development Scheme (Mudur 2013). Several manufacturers produce and market DFS, including Tata Chemicals Limited. Tata is one of the leading manufacturers of salt in India, and we used their DFS, branded as "Tata Salt Plus" for our study. The maximum retail price of Tata Salt Plus is twenty rupees (₹20) per kg, making it a relatively low-cost iron source, but around twice the price of regular iodized salt.[2]

Surprisingly, the nationwide scale-up of DFS in school meals and the approval for retail sales happened despite the lack of large-scale efficacy trials of DFS: we only have a few efficacy studies, all among women and children in carefully monitored environments (Mudur 2013).

This chapter is part of a larger project to fill this gap and assess the potential impact of a nationwide subsidy on double-fortified salt. There are three overarching questions to answer: (a) what would be the demand for DFS, even if it were subsidized, and at what price would demand be sustained over time? (b) could that demand be increased through marketing approaches? and (c) what is the population-wide impact of DFS?

We examined the first question in a previous paper (Banerjee, Barnhardt, and Duflo 2014) with a small-scale, individual-level, randomized pricing experiment to determine the demand curve for DFS. We found that demand falls sharply at a price of ₹10 per kilogram, the price of the cheapest alternative branded salt. Just under a third of the households seem willing to try it just below that price. To answer question (c) we set up two experiments. First, a free distribution experiment that will help us determine the causal impact of DFS consumption and, more broadly, whether demand multiplied by impact would be sufficient to make a difference in population health, cognitive and physical capacities, and productivity. Second, we designed a large-scale impact evaluation where all shopkeepers in 200 villages (randomly chosen out of 400) were given the opportunity to stock Tata Salt Plus at a special research MRP of ₹9, and we measured health and productivity outcomes at baseline and approximately three years after the introduction of the product.

This chapter focuses on question (b). We analyze a set of experiments conducted in the 200 villages where Tata Salt Plus was made available in order to understand whether different forms of social marketing can boost demand for double-fortified salt. Within these villages, we conducted the following experiments: First, we commissioned a high-production value twenty-six-minute edutainment movie and screened it during an intermission midway through a free showing of a very popular film. Modeled on a sitcom and starring prominent actors from local language cinema, the movie was widely seen and was entertaining as well as informative. This is in keeping with the effort of companies like MTV to convey health messages

2. Tata Salt, which is the highest-quality iodized salt available, normally sells for ₹15 per kg.

through entertaining TV shows, but contrasts with the more dour style of the traditional public health documentary. Second, we sought to incentivize shopkeepers by randomly providing either one or all of them in a given village with higher margins to sell the product (Ashraf, Bandiera, and Jack 2012). In a lighter touch experiment, we also hand delivered flyers in some villages to sample households: the idea was to make sure that households in the sample knew of the existence of the product. Finally, we distributed DFS to some households at no charge in order to measure the impact on actual consumption and downstream biological and economic impacts of having the salt at home for free. In this chapter, we use the results of free distribution on take-up as a benchmark for the effect of the other interventions.

9.2   Context and Data

9.2.1   Anemia in Bihar

Bihar is a large and poor state in north India, with nearly one-third of its 103 million residents living under the poverty line as of 2012 (Planning Commission 2013). According to the National Family Health Survey, 67 percent of adult women, 34 percent of adult men, and 78 percent of children under the age of three years suffered from some form of anemia in 2005–2006 (International Institute for Population Sciences [IIPS] and Macro International 2008). Wendt et al. (2015) found that only 37 percent of pregnant women in Bihar received the recommended iron supplement in 2007–2008 and only 24 percent of them consumed the supplement for ninety days. We worked across all fourteen administrative blocks of Bhojpur District (which has a population of 2.7 million). In the State Health Society's December 2015 ranking of districts in terms of medical service provision, Bhojpur came in at number twenty-six out of thirty-eight (State Health Society Bihar 2015). For the study, we randomly selected twenty-eight or twenty-nine villages in each block to get a total of 400 villages. Our "main" experiment is the marketing of double-fortified salt to shopkeepers in randomly assigned treatment villages compared to the remaining main control villages where DFS is not offered. We randomly assigned 50 percent of the villages in each block to the sales treatment and 50 percent to be control, ending up with 200 of each for the main experiment.

Our data come from detailed household surveys at baseline and endline. The timing of endline data collection was approximately two years after DFS was introduced.[3] Purchase data come from a household salt-purchase module, answered by the household head (male or female) who had the most knowledge about household purchases and assets. The baseline also includes modules on household composition, consumption and expenditure, use of

---

3. See appendix for a time line of all activities.

health services, time use, cognition, and physical health. Baseline data is described in some detail in Banerjee, Barnhardt, and Duflo (2014).

9.2.2 Baseline Data and Attrition

Table 9.1 shows some baseline descriptive statistics of the sample[4] and balance checks across treatment conditions. The households in the sample are poor but not exceptionally so by Indian standards. In the control group, 14.8 percent of individuals were anemic at baseline. The average household size is eight persons. Eighteen percent of the households have elderly members, an important target group for this study. Overall, the randomization seems to have produced very balanced experimental groups. The households that receive the free DFS intervention are somewhat less likely to have older members and an educated head.

Table 9.2 shows that 8 percent of households were lost to attrition in the 200 treatment villages, and there are no differences across samples. This chapter will focus on household-level variable "purchase," and here the attrition level is fairly low; therefore, we opted not to correct for attrition with bounds or other methods. At the individual level attrition is higher—in total, 20 percent of individuals surveyed at baseline were lost to follow-up. Table 9.3 shows that attritors were more likely to be men, less likely to be children, and less likely to be anemic. Most characteristics of the attritors are balanced across groups, with one exception: attritors tend to be poorer in the "basic" experiment villages (those receiving the 50 percent discount alone) and in the store-incentives villages but not in the movie or flyer experiment villages (column [7]).

9.3 Experiments and Assignments

In each main treatment village, a team of vendors approached every shop in the village, including both private *kirana* (grocery) stores and public distribution system (PDS or "fair price") shops. The team pitched the product, took orders, delivered salt to the shops, and accepted payment from the shopkeepers. Shops were then instructed to sell DFS at the special research price of ₹9 per kg, discounted from the retail price of ₹20 per kg. The price was prominently displayed on the packet.[5] The first time the village was visited for stocking, a marketing team from Tata Chemicals launched the product. To highlight the importance of a diet sufficiently rich in iron, team members played games that required endurance with children in the village, gave away T-shirts and hats to the winners, and explained the key benefits of consuming DFS. After approaching all shops in all 200 villages this way, a

---

4. Banerjee, Barnhardt, and Duflo (2014) has a much more detailed description of the baseline sample.

5. At this price level, Banerjee, Barnhardt, and Duflo (2014) established an initial take-up of approximately 30 percent in Behea Block of Bhojpur District.

Table 9.1   Balance checks, baseline characteristics

	Female (1)	Age (2)	Elderly (3)	Anemic (4)	Severely anemic (5)	HB concentration (6)	Consump. per capita in the past thirty days (in thous. of INR) (7)	HH head completed class 5 or above (8)	Number of HH Members (9)	HH includes only immediate family members (10)
Movie experiment	0.005	−0.425	−0.004	0.006	−0.001	−0.102**	0.021	0.048**	−0.186	0.010
	[0.006]	[0.335]	[0.006]	[0.007]	[0.002]	[0.050]	[0.077]	[0.023]	[0.298]	[0.016]
Flyer promotion experiment	−0.003	−0.595	−0.010	0.000	−0.001	0.068	−0.040	−0.033	0.377	−0.013
	[0.007]	[0.422]	[0.007]	[0.008]	[0.002]	[0.057]	[0.088]	[0.026]	[0.310]	[0.019]
Store incentive: All kiranas	0.004	0.328	0.004	−0.020**	−0.001	0.050	−0.066	−0.027	−0.229	0.011
	[0.008]	[0.418]	[0.007]	[0.009]	[0.002]	[0.063]	[0.099]	[0.028]	[0.363]	[0.019]
Store incentive: 1 kirana	0.003	0.093	0.004	0.001	0.002	−0.038	−0.090	0.017	−0.174	0.036*
	[0.008]	[0.423]	[0.008]	[0.009]	[0.002]	[0.063]	[0.097]	[0.029]	[0.408]	[0.020]
Free DFS households	−0.011	−1.439***	−0.024**	0.007	0.004*	−0.107	0.145	−0.078**	−0.120	0.017
	[0.009]	[0.542]	[0.010]	[0.011]	[0.002]	[0.065]	[0.131]	[0.040]	[0.558]	[0.026]
Basic treatment mean within treatment group	0.513	26.205	0.166	0.128	0.009	12.302	2.236	0.563	8.726	0.224
Main control group mean	0.515	26.522	0.182	0.148	0.008	12.196	2.074	0.574	8.429	0.231
Observations	19,998	19,998	19,998	17,342	17,342	17,342	19,852	18,677	19,997	19,976

Note: The sample excludes the control group for the main treatment. Regression includes block-level fixed effects. Regressors not reported include a dummy for free DFS villages and a dummy for non-store-incentive households within the main treatment villages. Standard errors are clustered at the village level for individual characteristics and at the household level for household characteristics. Intermediate family members include household head, wife/husband of household, and children of household head. The variable for consumption is measured in rupees. Standard errors in brackets.

***Significant at the 1 percent level.

**Significant at the 5 percent level.

*Significant at the 10 percent level.

Table 9.2   **Individual-level and household-level attrition by experiment type**

	Respondent lost to attrition since BL (1)	HH lost to attrition since BL (2)
Movie experiment	−0.009	0.004
	[0.012]	[0.010]
Flyer promotion experiment	0.013	−0.007
	[0.013]	[0.012]
Store incentive: All kiranas	0.020	0.013
	[0.013]	[0.013]
Store incentive: 1 kirana	0.023	0.005
	[0.015]	[0.014]
Free DFS households	−0.032**	−0.015
	[0.016]	[0.011]
Basic treatment mean within treatment group	0.206	0.081
Main control group mean	0.193	0.064
Observations	20,315	3,002

Note: The sample excludes the control group for the main treatment. Regression includes block-level fixed effects. Regressors not reported include a dummy for free DFS villages and a dummy for non-store-incentive households within the main treatment villages. Standard errors are clustered at the village level for individual characteristics and at the household level for household characteristics. Standard errors in brackets.

***Significant at the 1 percent level.
**Significant at the 5 percent level.
*Significant at the 10 percent level.

new round of stocking began. In all, we completed twelve rounds of stocking between August 2012 and May 2015. Tata stocked 446,732 kilograms of DFS, 160,958 in the PDS shops and 285,774 in private *kiranas*.

Within each village, we randomly selected fifteen households from the District Rural Development Authority household listing to form the measurement sample. All of the experiments reported in this chapter took place within the 200 main experiment villages and measured the impact on the nearly 3,000 measurement households living in them.[6]

Our earlier work in the district (Banerjee, Barnhardt, and Duflo 2014) suggested shopkeepers may have an important influence on which salt consumers choose. Our field team observed several shoppers ask for a package of salt and shopkeepers give a package without asking which brand or type the consumer wanted. This is confirmed in the reasons given to buy salt in the data we collected for this study: in the main experiment group with

6. In sixty-two randomly selected main treatment villages, we randomly assigned seven households to receive free DFS from May 2013 until the end-line survey back checking was completed. This was to measure the impact on health (not take-up, which is the focus of this chapter). We therefore control for both free DFS village and free DFS household in all of our regressions.

Table 9.3   Characteristics of those lost to attrition since baseline

	Female (1)	Age (2)	Elderly (3)	Anemic (4)	Severely anemic (5)	HB concentration (6)	Consump. per capita in the past thirty days (in thous. of INR) (7)	HH head completed class 5 or above (8)	Number of HH members (9)	HH includes only immediate family members (10)
Resp. lost to attrition since BL	-0.037*** [0.009]	0.928** [0.456]	-0.005 [0.008]	-0.037*** [0.008]	0.005** [0.002]	0.022 [0.050]	-0.054 [0.052]	-0.007 [0.016]	-0.330 [0.211]	-0.010 [0.012]
				Characteristics of those lost to attrition by experiment type						
Movie experiment * respondent lost to attrition since BL	0.035* [0.020]	2.457** [0.949]	0.033** [0.016]	-0.043*** [0.016]	0.010* [0.005]	-0.071 [0.102]	0.234** [0.116]	0.042 [0.034]	-0.735* [0.439]	0.027 [0.027]
Flyer promotion experiment * respondent lost to attrition since BL	-0.014 [0.022]	-2.172* [1.115]	-0.044** [0.018]	0.021 [0.016]	0.003 [0.006]	0.057 [0.109]	0.317*** [0.106]	0.034 [0.039]	0.550 [0.436]	-0.032 [0.031]
Store incentive: All Kiranas * respondent lost to attrition since BL	0.060*** [0.021]	-0.608 [1.133]	-0.006 [0.020]	-0.028 [0.020]	0.007 [0.006]	-0.091 [0.118]	-0.090 [0.135]	-0.004 [0.040]	0.346 [0.510]	0.001 [0.030]
Store incentive: 1 Kirana * respondent lost to attrition since BL	-0.008 [0.023]	0.301 [1.131]	-0.002 [0.019]	-0.040* [0.022]	0.011** [0.006]	0.002 [0.127]	-0.003 [0.134]	-0.024 [0.041]	0.694 [0.523]	-0.024 [0.030]
Free DFS households * respondent lost to attrition since BL	-0.027 [0.032]	1.813 [1.659]	0.022 [0.030]	-0.001 [0.030]	-0.002 [0.007]	-0.130 [0.177]	-0.072 [0.169]	-0.013 [0.054]	-0.855* [0.505]	0.020 [0.040]
Resp. lost to attrition since BL	-0.039 [0.024]	1.509 [1.225]	0.020 [0.020]	-0.012 [0.021]	-0.006 [0.005]	0.017 [0.135]	-0.267** [0.127]	-0.054 [0.048]	-0.783 [0.588]	0.015 [0.037]
Basic treatment mean within treatment group	0.513	26.205	0.166	0.128	0.009	12.302	2.236	0.563	8.726	0.224
Main control group mean	0.515	26.522	0.182	0.148	0.008	12.196	2.074	0.574	8.429	0.231
Observations	19,993	19,993	19,993	17,338	17,338	17,338	19,847	18,674	19,992	19,971

Note: The sample excludes the control group for the main treatment. Regression includes block-level fixed effects. Regressors not reported include dummies for all the treatment groups (without the interactions), as well as a dummy for free DFS villages and a dummy for non-store-incentive households within the main treatment villages. Also not reported is the interaction between currently or previously use DFS and non-store-incentive HHs, as well as the interaction between currently or previously use DFS and free DFS villages. Standard errors are clustered at the village level for individual characteristics and at the household level for household characteristics. The variable for consumption is measured in rupees. Standard errors in brackets.

***Significant at the 1 percent level.

**Significant at the 5 percent level.

*Significant at the 10 percent level.

no other intervention, 41 percent of households who bought DFS did so because it was what the shopkeeper gave them, and 8 percent because it was what he recommended. The shopkeeper's incentive to choose DFS over other brands or to exert more effort marketing DFS may be important in the adoption of DFS. On the other hand, previous research (Ashraf, Bandiera, and Jack 2012) raises the possibility that for a low-demand product that represents only a small part of the retail business, financial incentives may have no impact. In that study, financial incentives for selling female condoms were given to hairdressers. The setting here is different, however, because the product is less exotic and may be easier to convince households to try. In particular, households do regularly buy salt and the shopkeeper just needs to get them to buy this particular type. In contrast, in Ashraf, Bandiera, and Jack (2012), the average control group hairdressers only sold seven packs of two condoms over the course of a year.

Since the impact of retailer incentives is an empirical question, we conducted an experiment to determine the impact of increasing the private shopkeeper's margin on household adoption. This experiment happened during the fifth round of stocking (August–December 2013) in the 189 main treatment villages that had at least two *kiranas*. Shopkeepers selected for the treatment group got an additional discount of ₹3 per kg on the wholesale price of DFS, without any requirement to decrease the price charged to the final consumer. It was then the shopkeeper's choice to reduce the price, increase marketing, or do something else. We randomized these villages into three equal groups, those in which one shop gets the discount, all shops get the discount, and no shop gets the discount (control). This design was chosen to enable the study of how shopkeeper behavior (including price charged to customer and other marketing habits) depends on competition. Kumar, Rajiv, and Jeuland (2001) suggest that the pass-through may be limited when consumers lack information, and only a few retailers are offered the promotion. In the sixty-three villages where only one shop was given the discount, we randomly selected it from all shops in the village.

Notwithstanding the influence of shopkeepers, households are the eventual decision makers. An important challenge for the launch of a new product is making sure households know about it. Tata's launch in the villages addressed this need systematically across all sales villages. However, many of the villagers probably missed the launch event, and others may not have been persuaded by it: as discussed in Banerjee, Barnhardt, and Duflo (2014), our pilot experiment showed that various versions of the "standard" marketing package performed by Tata did not seem to increase the adoption rate. To address this issue, we commissioned the production of a twenty-six-minute movie about the health benefits of adequate iron consumption and the availability of iron in DFS. The film was meant to be entertaining, modeled on sitcoms and starring Bhojpuri actors (Bhojpuri is the local dialect of Hindi and has its own cinema industry). It tells the story of Bhim and his pregnant wife. Bhim is physically small and not very strong and wants to ensure that his son (he assumes he will have a son) will grow to be a strong man. A village nurse convinces his wife of the importance of taking iron for anemia as a way of making sure that the child is healthy and strong, and after initial misgivings Bhim is convinced as well.

Earlier research has shown that edutainment movies can be effective, but there are few randomized trials on the subject. Using a difference-in-difference strategy based on the gradual introduction of cable television, Jensen and Oster (2009) and La Ferrara, Chong, and Duryea (2012) show sizable effects of television on behavior. In India, the introduction of cable television is associated with improvements in women's status, including increases in reported autonomy and female school enrollment, and decreases in the acceptability of beating. In the case of Brazil, exposure to *Rede Globo* soaps featuring very small families was found to decrease fertility by an amount equivalent to the mother having two extra years of education.

Some studies focus, like us, on soap operas explicitly produced with education in mind. Rogers et al. (1999) and Rogers and Vaughan (2000) found that the radio soap opera *Twende Na Wakati* in Tanzania had strong behavioral effects on family planning. Exposure was nonrandom, however, and the survey just compared exposed to unexposed households. Using mixed methods and before-after designs, Usdin et al. (2005) and Solórzano et al. (2008) find encouraging effects on risky sexual behavior and gender-based violence indicators of two popular campaigns, *Soul City* in South Africa and *Puntos de Encuentro* in Nicaragua. Paluck and Green (2009) and Gunhild and Zia (2013), both randomized evaluations of soap operas, find positive impacts on conflict resolution and intergroup tolerance in Rwanda and on financial literacy outcomes in South Africa, respectively. Finally, Kearney and Levine (2014) estimate that the MTV reality series *16 and Pregnant* led to a 5.7 percent reduction in teen births across the United States, which is about one-third of the overall decline in the period they studied.

To maximize viewership, we showed the movie as an intermission between two halves of the classic film *Nadiya Ke Par*. We showed the film and our movie twice in each movie treatment village between October and December 2013. One screening was outdoors in the evening and intended for the entire village. The second showing was intended for women and kids, and we scheduled it the next day inside a school, day care, medical office, or somewhere else women would feel comfortable. To estimate movie viewership, we sent observers to twenty-five randomly selected villages to count the number of men and women present. We estimate that a total of slightly over 50,000 people saw the movie in total (about three-quarters of those in the general screening sessions, and one-quarter in the sessions for women and children), which we estimate was about 15 percent of everyone in the village (including children). We conservatively estimate (based on some auxiliary assumptions) that this means at least one adult male saw the movie in

20 percent of households and at least one adult female saw it in 9.3 percent of households.

We conducted the movie experiment in both main treatment and main control villages so that we could separately study the impact of the film's DFS promotion on adoption of the product where it was available in stores and the impact of the anemia-prevention information in villages where DFS was *not* sold. The movie experiment was stratified by block, village status in the main experiment, as well as by the free DFS experiment we simultaneously conducted. In total, we randomly assigned sixty-four out of the 200 main treatment villages to receive the movie screenings. This chapter focuses on the take-up of the fortified salt, so we focus on the part of the movie experiment that happened in the main treatment villages (since the salt was not available in the control villages).

To serve as a benchmark for those interventions, we also conducted a much lighter touch information experiment. We designed a flyer that simply informed a household about DFS and where it could be bought locally. We then delivered the flyer directly to our sample households in October and November 2013. The advantage of direct marketing is that the flyer has a greater chance of reaching those women who do not go outside the home very much, but who may have different preferences for investing in health or over brands of salt. Another reason for distributing the flyer was that, in the original marketing experiment, the reduction in prices was announced through vouchers distributed at home. The flyers would allow us to say something about the part of the impact of the vouchers that came from raised product awareness, rather than the price cut. The flyer experiment was stratified by the retail incentive, movie, and free DFS experimental status. In all, we assigned 150 villages (in the main treatment group) to receive flyers. All fifteen measured (sample) households were supposed to get the flyers.

Finally, in sixty-two villages, seven of the fifteen study households were provided with free double-fortified salt. The prime objective was to serve as a large-scale trial of the impact of double-fortified salt on health outcomes in a field setting, but this also provides a useful benchmark for the impact of the marketing experiment. The willingness to use the salt when received for free should be an upper bound for any potential impact of a marketing intervention.

9.4   Results

We estimate the impact of the marketing treatments using the main treatment sample of 200 villages. Given the multiple randomizations occurring across the same set of villages, we estimate all results in a single specification as follows:

(1) $$USE_{hv} = \alpha + \beta_1 * Movie_v + \beta_2 * Flyer_v + \beta_3 * AllStores_v$$
$$+ \beta_4 * OneStore_v + \beta_5 Free_h + X\gamma + e_{hv}$$

where X represents the controls: village randomized into free DFS treatment group, village not in retail incentive experiment (has < 2 *kiranas*), and fixed effects at the block level. Thus, each treatment coefficient can be interpreted as the impact of this particular modification compared to a situation where this modification is not present. We work with several versions of the USE variable: currently use, ever used, current and past use, number of times purchased (or received) DFS in the last year.

Results are presented in table 9.4. Without any additional intervention, just under 10 percent of households are currently using DFS (about two to three years after introduction of the product in their villages), and 20 percent have ever tried it. When DFS is distributed for free 54.6 percent of households do use it (9.8 percent + 44.8 percent), which probably represents an upper bound of what any kind of marketing could achieve. The difference between DFS and other preventive health products such as bed nets (see Dupas 2009) is that, even at zero price, not everybody is willing to use the product. While essentially all households accepted delivery of the salt, about half of them did something else with it. Anecdotal evidence suggests that they either gave it away, resold it, or fed it to cows.

Against this backdrop, the movie experiment has a large impact: it increases current take-up at end line, which took place between seven and sixteen months after the movie was shown, by 5.5 percentage points (57 percent) and "ever used" by 11.5 percentage points (22 percent). This is a much longer-term impact of a single exposure than what is typically evaluated. In most studies, the impact is measured while the movie is still being shown. We calculate that someone has seen the movie in 20 percent of households on average, so the impact per viewer is large. Of course, it could be that viewers share the information with others, so there is no implied instrumental variable estimate here. But it suggests that the movie was effective in convincing people to adopt double-fortified salt, and to stick with it over several rounds of purchases. The effect appears to be similar for households who receive free DFS and those who do not (the interaction of DFS and Movie is noisy, positive for current use, and negative for past use), and for those who are in the shopkeeper experiment and those who are not. It suggests that the movie shifted up the demand for DFS, regardless of the price point: it basically changed the "willingness to accept" the product rather than the willingness to pay.

In contrast with the results of Ashraf, Bandiera, and Jack (2012), increasing the retailer margin also leads to an increase in sustained adoption of double-fortified salt: the point estimate for "currently using DFS" is 5.5 percentage points, almost exactly identical to the impact of the movie. Interestingly, this is only true when all the retailers were offered the incentives. The point estimate impact of the one-shop treatment is either zero or negative.

Contrary to the movie—which led both to an increase in one-time purchases (trying out the product) and persistence—the store incentive has a

Table 9.4   Take-up results

	Currently using DFS (1)	Currently or previously used DFS (2)	Currently and previously used DFS (3)	Times in past year HH purchased DFS (4)	Currently using DFS (5)	Currently or previously used DFS (6)	Currently using DFS (7)	Currently or previously used DFS (8)
Movie experiment	0.056**	0.115***	0.085***	1.026*	0.052**	0.121***	0.042	0.127***
	[0.023]	[0.030]	[0.025]	[0.544]	[0.025]	[0.035]	[0.027]	[0.041]
Flyer promotion experiment	-0.002	-0.018	0.021	-0.284	-0.002	-0.019	-0.002	-0.018
	[0.023]	[0.034]	[0.026]	[0.546]	[0.024]	[0.034]	[0.024]	[0.034]
Store incentive: All kiranas	0.055*	0.023	0.035	0.235	0.055*	0.022	0.043	0.028
	[0.029]	[0.036]	[0.029]	[0.606]	[0.029]	[0.036]	[0.032]	[0.040]
Store incentive: 1 kirana	0.000	-0.044	-0.028	-0.954	0.000	-0.044	-0.002	-0.043
	[0.028]	[0.036]	[0.032]	[0.631]	[0.027]	[0.036]	[0.028]	[0.037]
Free DFS household	0.448***	0.517***	0.347***	2.862***	0.441***	0.529***	0.442***	0.528***
	[0.038]	[0.044]	[0.038]	[0.515]	[0.048]	[0.051]	[0.048]	[0.051]
Movie experiment * free DFS HH					0.020	-0.033	0.018	-0.032
					[0.066]	[0.066]	[0.066]	[0.066]
Movie experiment * store incentive: All kiranas							0.035	-0.016
							[0.052]	[0.065]
Basic treatment mean within treatment group	0.098	0.207	0.061	3.195	0.098	0.207	0.098	0.207
Observations	3,193	2,088	2,088	2,236	3,193	2,088	3,193	2,088

Note: The sample excludes the control group for the main treatment. Regression includes block-level fixed effects. Regressors not reported include a dummy for free DFS villages and a dummy for non-store-incentive households within the main treatment villages. Standard errors are clustered at the village level. Standard errors in brackets.

***Significant at the 1 percent level.

**Significant at the 5 percent level.

*Significant at the 10 percent level.

larger marginal impact on the fraction of households who persist with using the salt: the point estimate is smaller and insignificant for "ever purchased."

These results contrast with those for the flyer distribution, which only notified households at home of where in their villages fortified salt was being sold. That treatment had absolutely no impact on purchases. This suggests that the movie treatment affected purchase because it truly changed the way households thought about the salt, as opposed to merely reminding them of its availability.

Our next set of results on who currently uses DFS is presented in table 9.5. In that table, we run the following specification:

$$CHAR_{hv} = \alpha + \beta_1 * Movie_v * USE_{hv} + \beta_2 * Flyer_v * USE_{hv}$$
$$+ \beta_3 * AllStores_v * USE_{hv} + \beta_4 * OneStore_v * USE_{hv}$$
$$+ \beta_5 Free_h * USE_{hv} + \beta_6 USE_{hv} + X\gamma + e_{hv},$$

where $CHAR_{hv}$ is a particular household characteristic, measured at baseline (e.g., number of household members), and the vector of control variable including main effects for each treatment group. Few characteristics of households who take up DFS are systematically different, compared to nonusers. The only differences are that they have slightly more female members and the head is more likely to be educated. It does not seem to be the case that households with greater incidence of anemia are more likely to switch to DFS. The different treatments do not alter the composition of buyers in any important way either, with one exception: the "all store incentives" experiment seems to lead poorer households to purchase DFS than in the conditions without treatment. We need to take this finding with some caution, given the number of characteristics in the table, but it seems to be the one robust result. Based on the social marketing literature, one hypothesis we had was that the film could have been particularly effective on the type of families depicted in the movie, in this case a small nuclear family expecting their first child. We find no evidence for that.

The next two tables shed light on the mechanisms behind the effects, and suggest that although the movie and the store incentives had comparable impacts on purchase, the underlying reasons were very different. The movie informed households and led them to demand more double-fortified salt; the store incentives led shopkeepers to try to force households to buy it.

In table 9.6 we provide more evidence from a survey that we conducted with our study households in each village on average forty-five days after the store incentive experiments started—which was many months before the end-line survey showing the results above. This earlier survey focused on salt adoption and purchase and was conducted in all the villages that were part of the store incentive experiments. In table 9.7, we show data that comes from a survey conducted with shopkeepers.

Column (1) of table 9.6 mostly confirms the findings of table 9.4, with one exception: it seems to suggest that even the flyer led to some adoption

Table 9.5   Household characteristics of current DFS users

	Total number of females in HH (1)	Average age of HH members (2)	Total number of elderly HH members (3)	Total number of anemic HH members (4)	Average HB conc. of HH members (5)	Consump. per capita in the past thirty days (in thous. of INR) (6)	HH head completed class 5 or above (7)	Female HH head completed class 5 or above (8)	Total number of HH members (9)	HH includes only immediate family members (10)
Movie experiment * currently use DFS	0.371 [0.347]	-0.787 [1.006]	0.072 [0.104]	-0.050 [0.157]	0.115 [0.096]	-0.315 [0.199]	-0.005 [0.052]	0.077 [0.047]	0.624 [0.598]	-0.035 [0.042]
Flyer promotion experiment * currently use DFS	-0.578 [0.372]	0.954 [0.967]	-0.039 [0.103]	-0.047 [0.137]	0.079 [0.104]	-0.010 [0.205]	0.013 [0.052]	-0.006 [0.047]	-0.953 [0.630]	0.010 [0.046]
Store incentive: All kiranas * currently use DFS	-0.532 [0.453]	-0.439 [1.108]	-0.154 [0.114]	-0.207 [0.209]	0.103 [0.112]	-0.206 [0.270]	-0.076 [0.064]	-0.050 [0.057]	-0.696 [0.797]	0.045 [0.051]
Store incentive: 1 kirana * currently use DFS	-0.856* [0.437]	1.071 [1.272]	-0.147 [0.136]	-0.227 [0.223]	0.111 [0.123]	-0.244 [0.278]	-0.045 [0.065]	-0.044 [0.058]	-1.052 [0.770]	0.030 [0.061]
Free DFS household * currently use DFS	-0.232 [0.487]	0.869 [1.678]	0.008 [0.153]	0.365 [0.227]	-0.149 [0.168]	0.445 [0.318]	0.010 [0.076]	0.030 [0.073]	-0.187 [0.891]	0.001 [0.077]
Currently using DFS	0.821* [0.465]	-0.050 [1.378]	0.116 [0.144]	0.128 [0.222]	-0.041 [0.139]	0.253 [0.280]	0.134* [0.075]	0.070 [0.062]	0.973 [0.832]	-0.037 [0.063]
Basic treatment mean within treatment group	3.662	28.142	1.221	0.794	12.277	2.491	0.555	0.133	7.176	0.324
Main control group mean	3.667	28.673	1.263	0.923	12.228	2.266	0.545	0.216	7.104	0.314
Observations	3,193	3,193	3,193	3,152	3,152	3,174	2,990	2,841	3,193	3,192

Note: The sample excludes the control group for the main treatment. Regression includes block-level fixed effects. Regressors not reported include dummies for all the treatment groups (without the interactions), as well as a dummy for free DFS villages and a dummy for non-store incentive households within the main treatment villages. Also not reported is the interaction between currently or previously use DFS and non-store-incentive HHs, as well as the interaction between currently or previously use DFS and free DFS village. The variable female head of household is defined as either the wife of the head of the household or the head of the household. If there were multiple female heads for the household, then the highest education level out of all the female household heads was used. Standard errors are clustered at the village level. Standard errors in brackets. The variable for consumption is measured in rupees.

***Significant at the 1 percent level.

**Significant at the 5 percent level.

*Significant at the 10 percent level.

Table 9.6   HH take-up results from store incentive experiment

	Currently use DFS (1)	Selected DFS because contains iron or because it reduces anemia (2)	Selected DFS because contains iodine (3)	Selected DFS because of taste (4)	Selected DFS because of clean, white appearance (5)	Selected DFS because always buy the same thing (6)	Selected DFS because no other salt available (7)	Store owner gave or recommend DFS to respondent (8)	Amount paid for 1 packet of DFS (9)
Movie experiment	0.049**	0.086**	0.011	0.019	0.001	-0.074***	0.042	-0.093	-0.398**
	[0.024]	[0.039]	[0.033]	[0.043]	[0.036]	[0.028]	[0.057]	[0.061]	[0.182]
Flyer promotion experiment	0.039*	-0.045	-0.012	-0.003	-0.081	0.055*	0.068	-0.113	0.478***
	[0.023]	[0.044]	[0.046]	[0.055]	[0.051]	[0.032]	[0.069]	[0.070]	[0.182]
Store incentive: All kiranas	0.078***	-0.000	-0.085**	-0.013	0.040	-0.038	0.137**	-0.087	0.163
	[0.030]	[0.039]	[0.040]	[0.045]	[0.045]	[0.033]	[0.057]	[0.070]	[0.199]
Store incentive: 1 kirana	-0.031	0.057	0.023	0.022	-0.028	-0.011	0.117	-0.147*	0.078
	[0.022]	[0.055]	[0.055]	[0.060]	[0.060]	[0.043]	[0.072]	[0.076]	[0.160]
Basic treatment mean within treatment group	0.099	0.000	0.033	0.083	0.116	0.033	0.157	0.463	8.135
Observations	4,862	636	636	636	636	636	636	636	608

Note: The sample excludes the control group for the main treatment, free DFS households, and all households within the main treatment that were not part of the store incentive experiment. Columns (2)–(10) include only houses that were currently using DFS. Regression includes block-level fixed effects. A dummy for free DFS village was included in the regressions, but the coefficient is not reported. The amount paid for one packet of DFS is measured in rupees. Standard errors in brackets.

***Significant at the 1 percent level.

**Significant at the 5 percent level.

*Significant at the 10 percent level.

of DFS (3.9 percentage points). This is perhaps because the survey was conducted shortly after the flyer distribution (fifty days on average, between one and eighty days depending on the village), and households were persuaded to buy DFS once, but then stopped.

The next few columns look at stated reasons for buying DFS. Interestingly, *no one* in the control group reports buying DFS because it prevents anemia. In contrast, in the movie group, 8.6 percent of the DFS buyers say that they buy it because it reduces anemia and the fraction of buyers who buy DFS because this is what they have always done, goes down. Thus, the movie succeeded in conveying its message.

Another sign that the movie changed households' information is that they report paying less for the DFS in the movie villages. There was a scene in the film where the price of ₹9 for the double-fortified salt was clearly shown. Looking at the distribution of reported prices (results not shown) we find that they are more likely to report paying ₹9 (the official price) and less likely to report ₹10. This is not confirmed by what the shopkeepers report in table 9.7, but it is plausible that generally people do not know exactly how much they pay for salt. Those who saw the movie know the price better.

On the other hand, in the incentive for "all *kiranas*" treatment, households who bought DFS are much more likely to report that this was the only salt available. This suggests that, rather than lowering the price (which does not change, see column [6] in table 9.6) or selling the virtues of DFS (households are no more likely to buy it because it reduces anemia, but they are less likely to buy it because it contains iodine), the primary marketing strategy of the shopkeeper was to push it on people by claiming he did not have anything else, even if he did. Note that this was not done by simply treating DFS as the default: the fraction of purchasers who buy DFS because it was what the shopkeeper handed them or what he recommended actually goes down in the store incentive treatments. Instead, the main margin of influence seems to be not giving customers a choice.

In table 9.7 (columns [8] and [9]) we see that although shopkeepers who received the incentives were more likely to carry and display DFS, and carried more of it, most of them also carry other iodized salt, as well as in some cases unbranded rock salt, and that these proportions are not affected by receiving the incentives.

The behavior of the other shopkeepers in villages where only one shopkeeper got the incentive is interesting. While the incentivized shop behaves exactly like the shops in villages where all shops got the incentive, shops that are not getting the incentive are more likely to carry other types of branded salt relative to the control group (where no one got incentives). This may be to attract consumers with variety. Recall that about half of the households that are given DFS for free still do not want to use it. If the incentivized shopkeeper is more likely to claim that DFS is all he has, some consumers who are really averse to it probably decide to go to another shop to buy a substitute. Shops that carry the alternative will thus increase their sales.

Table 9.7   Store take-up results from store incentive experiment

	Ever sold DFS (1)	DFS currently in stock (2)	Number of 1 kg DFS packets in stock (3)	Amount at which store sells 1 kg of DFS (4)	Amount paid for 1 kg of DFS (5)	Profit from 1 kg of DFS (6)	DFS displayed in store (7)	Sell other iodized salt (not including DFS) (8)	Sell unbranded rock salt (9)
Movie experiment	-0.009 [0.031]	-0.060* [0.033]	1.456 [3.207]	0.039 [0.050]	0.175* [0.099]	-0.141 [0.107]	-0.035 [0.031]	-0.024 [0.022]	0.011 [0.034]
Flyer promotion experiment	-0.031 [0.033]	-0.003 [0.039]	3.192 [2.984]	0.002 [0.041]	0.125 [0.117]	-0.119 [0.119]	-0.006 [0.039]	0.019 [0.024]	0.008 [0.034]
Store incentive: All kiranas	0.074** [0.033]	0.190*** [0.040]	10.452*** [3.259]	-0.106** [0.051]	-1.228*** [0.123]	1.129*** [0.126]	0.143*** [0.041]	0.001 [0.028]	-0.011 [0.044]
Store incentive: 1 kirana	-0.022 [0.032]	-0.011 [0.037]	-0.662 [2.524]	-0.048 [0.043]	0.071 [0.069]	-0.101 [0.081]	-0.018 [0.042]	0.043* [0.024]	-0.065* [0.039]
Store incentive: 1 kirana * store chosen for incentive	0.050 [0.070]	0.143** [0.073]	4.296 [3.639]	-0.099 [0.080]	-1.219*** [0.341]	1.176*** [0.357]	0.217** [0.096]	-0.047 [0.053]	0.093 [0.078]
Basic treatment mean within treatment group	0.710	0.314	5.896	9.197	7.641	1.548	0.211	0.860	0.186
Observations	1,532	1,316	1,447	1,074	593	590	1,084	1,316	1,316

Note: The sample excludes the control group for the main treatment, free DFS households, and all households within the main treatment that were not part of the store incentive experiment. Regression includes block-level fixed effects. A dummy for free DFS villages was included in the regressions, but the coefficient is not reported. The amounts for columns (4)–(6) are measured in rupees. Standard errors in brackets.

***Significant at the 1 percent level.

**Significant at the 5 percent level.

*Significant at the 10 percent level.

There may then be two reasons why the overall take-up of the salt does not change relative to the control group. First, the shopkeeper with incentives may stop trying to impose double-fortified salt, as a result of this kind of competitive pressure. Second, there may be a composition effect, with purchases of DFS going up in the store that gets the incentive and down in the stores that do not (over and above the sorting of the clients). The former explanation is not consistent with the data, since the probability of DFS purchasers saying that they got it because it was the only one available goes up even when only one store receives the incentive. Therefore, the latter explanation is likely: shopkeepers that did not receive the incentive may have helped spread rumors that the salt was not good for people's health in order to depress demand. Anecdotal reports suggest that this was indeed the case.

9.5   Conclusion

The promise of double-fortified salt to reduce anemia and increase productivity rests on two premises: that households will be willing to buy it and use it, even at a reduced price—or potentially for free—and that it is effective enough, at the levels of fortification that are stable and safe, to make a real difference.[7]

This chapter addresses the first question. Double-fortified salt is a new product, with some characteristics that would positively influence adoption (it is clean and white, sold in a fancy packet with a trusted brand name) and some handicaps (people are generally reluctant to try new foods, there were some instances of food blackening early on). Moreover, many people did not understand the links between salt and anemia or between anemia and well-being. Clearly, the basic marketing campaign conducted by the manufacturer at launch was completely ineffective at conveying why this salt should be purchased: two years after the introduction of the product, absent any additional information campaign, *no one* who buys DFS knows that it helps reduce anemia, or reports buying it because it is good for the health of household members.

Even when the salt is provided for free, only about half of households actually use it for cooking. When they have to buy it just below half price, with no other intervention, about 20 percent of households give it a try, but only 10 percent still use it after about three years.

Against this backdrop, this chapter shows the power of a strong communication campaign, in the form of an entertaining movie that was seen by about 20 percent of the households in the village, in changing households' perception about the product. Consumption of doubled-fortified salt increased by 5.5 percentage points, an increase of 50 percent over the mean

---

7. In settings like schools where children have no choice about what they eat, only the second question is pertinent.

for households who have to buy the salt, and more than 10 percent over the mean usage among those who get it for free. Eight percent of households who buy DFS at endline do report that they bought this salt because it helps fight anemia (although that leaves 92 percent who do so for other reasons), and they pay a lower price on average (as advertised in the movie).

The chapter also highlights how powerful shopkeepers are in influencing what households do. A small increase in (all) retailer margins resulted in an increase in take-up at least as large as that caused by the movie screening. There is some ambiguity on how this was achieved. The retailers claim that they dropped the final price of the salt (very little). Village households do not report such a decline and instead claim that they bought the salt because it was the only one available. More generally, over half of the buyers of DFS report that they just bought what the shopkeeper gave them. On the other hand, when only one shopkeeper was given an incentive, the others seem to have reacted by being more likely to sell other types of salt. There was no increase in the overall take-up of DFS. Future research should investigate the impact of providing discounts to consumers versus providing them to shopkeepers, and, more generally, examine their potential as agents of change.

Appendix

9A.1   **Time line of activities**

Start	End	Activity
May 2011	March 2012	Baseline survey
October 2011	November 2011	Pricing experiment
August 2012	May 2015	Main experiment: DFS sales
February 2013	October 2013	Monitoring survey
May 2013	May 2015	Free DFS experiment
August 2013	December 2013	Retailer incentive experiment
October 2013	February 2014	Store & household take-up surveys
October 2013	December 2013	Movie experiment
October 2013	November 2013	Flyer experiment
July 2014	February 2015	End line survey

Note: The pricing experiment was conducted in Behea block with separate villages.

References

Ashraf, N., O. Bandiera, and K. Jack. 2012. "No Margin, No Mission? A Field Experiment on Incentives for Pro-Social Tasks." CEPR Discussion Paper no. 8834, Center for Economic and Policy Research.
Baltussen, R., C. Knai, and M. Sharan. 2004. "Iron Fortification and Iron Supple-

mentation are Cost-Effective Interventions to Reduce Iron Deficiency in Four Subregions of the World." *Journal of Nutrition* 134 (10): 2678–84.

Banerjee, A., S. Barnhardt, and E. Duflo. 2014. "Nutrition, Iron Deficiency Anemia, and the Demand for Iron-Fortified Salt: Evidence from an Experiment in Rural Bihar." In *Discoveries in the Economics of Aging*, edited by David A. Wise, 343–84. Chicago: University of Chicago Press.

Banerjee, A., E. Duflo, and R. Glennerster. 2011. "Is Decentralized Iron Fortification a Feasible Option to Fight Anemia among the Poorest?" In *Explorations in the Economics of Aging*, edited by David A. Wise, 317–44. Chicago: University of Chicago Press.

Bhutta, Z. A., R. A. Salam, and J. K. Das. 2013. "Meeting the Challenges of Micronutrient Malnutrition in the Developing World." *British Medical Bulletin* 106 (1): 7–17.

Brahmam, G., K. Nair, A. Laxmaiah, C. Gal Reddy, S. Ranganathan, M. Vishnuvardhana Rao, A. Naidu, et al. 2000. "Community Trials with Iron and Iodine Fortified Salt (Double Fortified Salt)." In *Proceedings of the 8th World Salt Symposium*, vol. 2, edited by Rob M. Geertman, 955–60. Amsterdam: Elsevier.

de Benoist, B., E. McLean, I. Egli, and M. Cogswell. 2008. "Worldwide Prevalence of Anaemia 1993–2005: WHO Global Database of Anaemia." Technical Report, Geneva, World Health Organization.

Dupas, P. 2009. "What Matters (and What Does Not) in Households' Decision to Invest in Malaria Prevention?" *American Economic Review* 99 (2): 224–30.

Gunhild, B., and B. Zia. 2013. "Harnessing Emotional Connections to Improve Financial Decisions: Evaluating the Impact of Financial Education in Mainstream Media." World Bank Policy Research Working Paper no. 6407. http://elibrary.worldbank.org/doi/abs/10.1596/1813-9450-6407.

Haas, J. D., and T. Brownlie. 2001. "Iron Deficiency and Reduced Work Capacity: A Critical Review of the Research to Determine a Causal Relationship." *Journal of Nutrition* 131 (2): 676S–90S.

International Institute for Population Sciences (IIPS) and Macro International. 2008. *National Family Health Survey (NFHS-3), India, 2005–06: Bihar*. Mumbai: IIPS.

Jensen, R., and E. Oster. 2009. "The Power of TV: Cable Television and Women's Status in India." *Quarterly Journal of Economics* 124 (3): 1057–94.

Kearney, M., and P. Levine. 2014. "Media Influences and Social Outcomes: The Effect of MTV's *16 and Pregnant* on Teen Childbearing." NBER Working Paper no. 19795, Cambridge.

Kumar, N., S. Rajiv, and A. Jeuland. 2001. "Effectiveness of Trade Promotions: Analyzing the Determinants of Retail Pass Through." *Marketing Science* 20 (4): 382–404.

La Ferrara, E., A. Chong, and S. Duryea. 2012. "Soap Operas and Fertility: Evidence from Brazil." *American Economic Journal: Applied Economics* 4 (4): 1–31.

Lozoff, B. 2007. "Iron Deficiency and Child Development." *Food & Nutrition Bulletin* 28 (suppl. 4): 560S–71S.

Lozoff, B., J. Beard, J. Connor, B. Felt, M. Georgieff, and T. Schallert. 2006. "Long-Lasting Neural and Behavioral Effects of Iron Deficiency in Infancy." *Nutrition Reviews* 64 (s2): S34–43.

Mudur, G. 2013. "Doubts on Fortified Midday-Meal Salt—Safe But No Clear Proof It Increases Haemoglobin: Scientists." *The Telegraph*, June 9.

Nair, K., G. Brahmam, S. Ranganathan, K. Vijayaraghavan, B. Sivakumar, and K. Krishnaswamy. 1998. "Impact Evaluation of Iron and Iodine Fortified Salt." *Indian Journal of Medical Research* 108:203.

Nair, K. M., B. Sesikeran, S. Ranganathan, and B. Sivakumar. 1998. "Bioeffect and

Safety of Long-Term Feeding of Common Salt Fortified with Iron and Iodine (Double Fortified Salt) in Rats." *Nutrition Research* 18 (1): 121–29.

National Institute of Nutrition (India). 2005. *Double Fortified Common Salt (DFS) as a Tool to Control Iodine Deficiency Disorders and Iron Deficiency Anaemia: A Report*. Hyderabad, National Institute of Nutrition.

Paluck, E. L., and D. P. Green. 2009. "Deference, Dissent, and Dispute Resolution: An Experimental Intervention Using Mass Media to Change Norms and Behavior in Rwanda." *American Political Science Review* 103 (4): 622–44.

Penninx, B. W., M. Pahor, M. Cesari, A. M. Corsi, R. C. Woodman, S. Bandinelli, J. M. Guralnik, and L. Ferrucci. 2004. "Anemia is Associated with Disability and Decreased Physical Performance and Muscle Strength in the Elderly." *Journal of the American Geriatrics Society* 52 (5): 719–24.

Peters, R., L. Burch, J. Warner, N. Beckett, R. Poulter, and C. Bulpitt. 2008. "Haemoglobin, Anaemia, Dementia and Cognitive Decline in the Elderly, A Systematic Review." *BMC Geriatrics* 8 (1): 18.

Planning Commission. 2013. "Press Note on Poverty Estimates, 2011–12." Technical Report, Government of India. http://planningcommission.nic.in/news/pre_pov2307.pdf.

Ranganathan, S., and B. Sesikeran. 2008. "Development of the Double-Fortified Salt from the National Institute of Nutrition." *Comprehensive Reviews in Food Science and Food Safety* 7 (4): 390. http://onlinelibrary.wiley.com/doi/10.1111/j.1541-4337.2008.00049.x/pdf.

Rogers, E. M., and P. W. Vaughan. 2000. "A Staged Model of Communication Effects: Evidence from an Entertainment-Education Radio Soap Opera in Tanzania." *Journal of Health Communication* 5:203–27.

Rogers, E. M., P. W. Vaughan, R. Swalehe, N. Rao, P. Svenkerud, and S. Sood. 1999. "Effects of an Entertainment-Education Radio Soap Opera on Family Planning Behaviour in Tanzania." *Studies in Family Planning* 30 (3): 193–211.

Sivakumar, B., G. N. V. Brahmam, K. M. Nair, S. Ranganathan, M. V. Rao, K. Vijayaraghavan, and K. Krishnaswamy. 2001. "Prospects of Fortification of Salt with Iron and Iodine." *British Journal of Nutrition* 85:S167–73.

Solórzano, I., A. Bank, R. Peña, H. Espinoza, M. Ellsberg, and J. Pulerwitz. 2008. "Catalyzing jPersonal and Social Change around Gender, Sexuality, and HIV: Impact Evaluation of *Puntos de Encuentro*'s Communication Strategy in Nicaragua." Unpublished Manuscript.

State Health Society Bihar. 2015. "District Ranking with Penalty." December. http://164.100.130.11:8091/ranking.html.

Stoltzfus, R. J. 2001. "Defining Iron-Deficiency Anemia in Public Health Terms: A Time for Reflection." *Journal of Nutrition* 131 (2): 565S–67S.

Usdin, S., E. Scheepers, S. Goldstein, and G. Japhet. 2005. "Achieving Social Change on Gender-Based Violence: A Report on the Impact Evaluation of Soul City's Fourth Series." *Social Science and Medicine* 61 (11): 2434–45.

Viteri, F. E. 1998. "Prevention of Iron Deficiency." In *Prevention of Micronutrients Deficiencies. Tools for Policymakers and Public Health Workers*, C. P. Howson, E. T. Kennedy, and A. Horwitz, 45–102. Washington, DC: National Academy Press.

Wendt, A., R. Stephenson, M. Young, A. Webb-Girard, C. Hogue, U. Ramakrishnan, and R. Martorell. 2015. "Individual and Facility-Level Determinants of Iron and Folic Acid Receipt and Adequate Consumption among Pregnant Women in Rural Bihar, India." *PLOS ONE* 10 (3): e0120404.

Suicide, Age, and Well-Being
An Empirical Investigation

Anne Case and Angus Deaton

10.1 Introduction

This chapter juxtaposes well-being measures and suicide rates. We use data from the United States and from other countries to examine patterns of suicide and well-being by age and across space.

Information on self-reported well-being (SWB) is now widely used in economics. Self-reported well-being measures correlate with traditional real income measures in the expected way, but are also sensitive to a wide range of other welfare-related circumstances and outcomes, holding out the possibility that they may provide a broader window into human well-being than does real income. Yet, at least since Lionel Robbins (1932) argued that psychological measures were unnecessary for economic analysis, economists have been wary of measures that are not backed up by observable behavior, and have given greater weight to preference revealed through choice than to

Anne Case is the Alexander Stewart 1886 Professor of Economics and Public Affairs and professor of economics and public affairs at the Woodrow Wilson School of Public and International Affairs and the economics department at Princeton University and a research associate of the National Bureau of Economic Research. Angus Deaton is the Dwight D. Eisenhower Professor of Economics and International Affairs at the Woodrow Wilson School of Public and International Affairs and the economics department at Princeton University and a research associate of the National Bureau of Economic Research.

Prepared for NBER Aging Conference, Carefree, Arizona, April 30 to May 2, 2015. Deaton acknowledges funding support from the Gallup Organization, with whom he is a consulting senior scientist, and from the National Institute on Aging through the NBER, grant numbers 5R01AG040629–02 and P01 AG05842–14, and through Princeton's Roybal Center for Translational Research on Aging, grant P30 AG024928. Case acknowledges support from the National Institute on Aging under grant P30 AG024361. We thank David Cutler and Julie Phillips for perceptive and helpful comments. For acknowledgments, sources of research support, and disclosure of the authors' material financial relationships, if any, please see http://www.nber.org/chapters/c13639.ack.

preferences that are self-reported. As noted by Daly, Wilson, and Johnson (2013), suicide should reveal unhappiness, at least in its most extreme form. Suicides are rare, 12.6 per 100,000 in the United States today, and while it is possible for those contemplating suicide to be extremely unhappy when other people are not, it is also true that shifts of the whole distribution will show up in the tails, dramatically so for many distributions. In consequence, if suicide rates were positively correlated or uncorrelated with well-being measures, we would have something of a paradox (Helliwell 2007). Such a paradox, if real, would cast some doubt on the validity of self-reported well-being. Alternatively, if we maintain the validity of well-being measures, the paradox would cast doubt on the usefulness of suicide as an overall indicator of population mental health. Studying the patterns of suicide and well-being can thus potentially contribute to an understanding of both. Such is our aim here. Our purpose is *not* to explain suicide by happiness—indeed it seems likely that each is affected by other, more fundamental causes—but to look for the negative correlation that these theories predict.

Hamermesh and Soss (1974) propose an "economic theory of suicide" that links suicide to intertemporal utility as used in theories of intertemporal choice of consumption and labor supply. Hamermesh and Soss postulate that people will kill themselves when the utility of being dead is higher than the utility of staying alive, a theory whose implications have been explored by them, and extended and corrected by Cutler, Glaeser, and Norberg (2001) and by Becker and Posner (2004). Goudie et al. (2014) use the same theory to link life satisfaction and risk taking and Chen et al. (2010) survey the field. Whether or not the utility of intertemporal choice in economics matches self-reported well-being, and if so how—for example, whether SWB is the integral over life, or the forward-looking integral, or instantaneous utility (felicity) for the period—remain open questions, but the links between suicide and SWB provide a fertile ground for testing the theory as well as for exploring the meaning of SWB itself.

There is a small previous literature that looks at SWB and suicide together. It includes the papers by Helliwell (2007), Daly and Wilson (2009), Daly, Wilson, and Johnson (2013), as well as the book by Layard (2005, 71), all of whom argue that the same factors that explain suicide also explain unhappiness or, more precisely, that the coefficients of the linear projections of suicide rates and SWB on selected covariates such as age, education, sex, race, time, and geography, have similar patterns in both sign and magnitude. We will follow this methodology; indeed, there is little alternative in the absence of baseline well-being data in large follow-up studies.

A few studies have found marked differences between suicide and SWB patterns in some contexts, including Daly et al. (2011) and Bray and Gunnell (2006), who examine suicide and life satisfaction over US states and European countries, respectively. Daly et al. find that suicide and life satisfaction are *positively* correlated across US states, while Bray and Gunnell find a negative correlation across European countries that is entirely driven by the comparison of Eastern with Western European countries; exclusion of the East results in a perverse positive correlation. We shall return to these results below.

We are aware of only one prospective study that gathers life satisfaction at baseline and follows individuals over time; Koivumaa-Honkanen et al. (2001) follow a sample of 29,173 Finnish adults from 1976 to 1995 and find that life satisfaction was protective against suicide. However, their measure of life satisfaction—the sum of Likert scores on four items, interest in life, happiness, ease of living, and loneliness—is quite different from what is usually called life satisfaction. The Finnish measure, as noted by the authors, is conceptually and empirically close to a measure of clinical depression, a well-established risk factor for suicide. That depression predisposes to suicide is consistent with a protective role for SWB, but is essentially a different finding.

One contribution of this chapter is to use Gallup data from the Gallup-Healthways Well-Being Index (GHWBI) for the United States, collected daily on a range of well-being measures—with nearly two million observations from 2008 through 2013—as well as the Gallup World Poll—which covers nearly all of the countries in Europe, the Organisation for Economic Co-operation and Development (OECD), and Latin America for which suicide data can be obtained from the World Health Organization's mortality database (WHO 2014) in conjunction with United Nations population data (UN 2014). Because the Gallup data contain several well-being measures, including life evaluation, happiness, worry, stress, and anger, we can explore the possibility that suicide links differently to these different evaluative and hedonic measures.

The Gallup surveys also collect data on physical pain, in the same format as the hedonics, asking whether the respondent experienced physical pain during a lot of the day prior to the interview. We do not think of physical pain as a well-being measure, but pain is a risk factor for suicide (Goldsmith et al. 2002), which makes it a useful variable in its own right. Pain is also associated with lower well-being, and so provides a potential link between suicide and SWB. Beyond that, obtaining the expected link between suicide and the pain measure from the Gallup data provides a baseline comparison for the hedonic measures. If pain as measured in the Gallup data is not correlated with suicide, it would not be surprising if the hedonics also are not; if pain is correlated with suicide, and the hedonics are not, we will have a stronger case against the link between SWB and suicide. We therefore examine pain along with the hedonics in most of the calculations below.

We begin (section 10.2) with summary data for the United States, tabulating suicide and SWB by age, sex, race, and education. Section 10.3 focuses on suicide and SWB over the days of the week; we argue that these patterns help discriminate between economic and other theories of suicide, rather in favor of the latter. Section 10.4 focuses on age and examines whether the famous U-shape of life evaluation over life, with older Americans doing better than those in middle age, has any counterpart in the suicide data. Section 10.5 turns to spatial patterns, across the states of the United States, as well as across countries of the OECD, Eastern Europe, and Latin America, with some attention to the age patterns within countries.

The suicide data come from the Compressed or Detailed Mortality Data from the Centers for Disease Control, available through the CDC Wonder website. At the end of section 10.2 we use the individual death records merged with population data from the American Community Survey (ACS), but we otherwise rely on tables generated by CDC Wonder. Suicides comprise deaths from intentional self-harm (ICD10 codes X60–84), as well as sequelae of intentional self-harm (ICD10 code Y87.0); we add the corresponding data from ICD9 in section 10.4. Some suicides are certainly misclassified, particularly into the category of deaths from events of undetermined intent, but here we adopt the narrow definition. All data on SWB and pain come from the GHWBI poll and, in section 10.5, from the Gallup World Poll.

10.2   Suicide and Well-Being in the United States Today

Table 10.1 presents some of the basic facts on suicide and well-being by three broad age groups of adults age twenty-five and older, by sex, and by education level. All data in the table are for 2013.

The relationship between suicide and well-being is like the curate's egg, good only in parts. Life evaluation (here the Cantril ladder, which ranges from 0 for the worst possible life to 10 for the best) is higher for women than for men—a standard finding in the literature—while women have more negative affect (especially stress and worry) than men and about the same amount of positive affect. Positive and negative affect measure short-run feelings ("Did you feel X during a lot of the day yesterday?" yes or no) with positive affect defined as the average of happiness, smiling, enjoyment, and not sad, while negative affect is the average of worry, anger, and stress. If (or when) suicide is an impulsive act, hedonic emotions are likely to be a better indicator than long-term life evaluation. Men are almost four times more likely to kill themselves than are women. While this is consistent in direction with women's higher life evaluation, it is not consistent with the patterns of affect. Adding physical pain only deepens the puzzle; in the Gallup data on pain, as well as across a range of morbidities (Case and Paxson 2005), women fare less well than men in all age groups.

Turning to age, we have the well-known U-shaped pattern of life evaluation for both men and women; for both sexes, life evaluation is at its lowest in middle age. If suicide rates are to match this, they should peak in middle age. This is true for women, but not for men. The suicide rate for men in

Table 10.1   Life evaluation, positive and negative affect, and suicide by age, sex, and
                    education (2013)

Outcome:	Education category:	Ages 25–34		Ages 35–54		Ages 55+	
		Men	Women	Men	Women	Men	Women
Suicide	Less than high school	26.43	6.51	25.95	7.20	26.53	3.79
	High school	29.34	7.74	32.06	10.26	32.47	6.70
	Four-year college	9.95	3.47	16.98	6.70	23.80	6.90
	All	23.4	6.1	27.0	8.7	30.4	6.30
Life evaluation	Less than high school	6.52	6.80	6.22	6.34	6.16	6.51
	High school	6.60	6.82	6.53	6.73	6.77	7.11
	Four-year college degree	7.13	7.32	7.22	7.36	7.49	7.56
	All	6.77	7.02	6.73	6.94	6.95	7.16
Positive affect	LT high school	0.81	0.77	0.76	0.70	0.77	0.72
smile/enjoy/happy/	High school	0.86	0.84	0.83	0.81	0.84	0.84
not sad	Four-year college	0.88	0.89	0.87	0.87	0.88	0.87
	All	0.86	0.85	0.83	0.82	0.85	0.84
Negative affect	LT high school	0.36	0.39	0.35	0.44	0.23	0.30
anger/worry/	High school	0.32	0.34	0.31	0.34	0.20	0.22
stress	Four-year college	0.30	0.33	0.30	0.31	0.19	0.22
	All	0.32	0.34	0.31	0.34	0.20	0.23
Pain	LT high school	0.30	0.28	0.38	0.47	0.37	0.45
	High school	0.20	0.23	0.26	0.31	0.29	0.32
	Four-year college	0.12	0.13	0.15	0.17	0.20	0.24
	All	0.19	0.20	0.24	0.27	0.27	0.31

2013 rises with age with no sign of a peak in middle age, at least across these coarse age categories. By contrast, women were more likely to commit suicide in middle age than in youth or in old age, matching the age-pattern in life evaluation. Durkheim ([1897] 1951) argued that suicide should rise with age, as did Hamermesh and Soss (1974), though as noted by Cutler, Glaeser, and Norberg (2001), their prediction, though plausible, does not strictly follow from their analysis. That suicide should rise with age is especially likely in the presence of unanticipated negative health events that become harder to reverse with age, leading to the accumulation of irreversible conditions, some of which involve great pain. If so, the puzzle is not with suicide, which rises with age at least for men, but with life evaluation, which fails to fall among the elderly. It is possible that suicide is an impulsive choice that depends, not on the sum of expected future utilities, but on instantaneous utility today. This works for women, but not for men. It is possible that suicide is a forward-looking rational choice for men, but an impulsive decision for women, but this is hardly a principled argument.

Negative affect is lower (i.e., better) in the oldest age group for both men and women—Stone et al. (2010) show that anger and stress decline steadily after young adulthood, and worry does so after middle age—yet neither men's nor women's suicide rates decline monotonically with age. We shall look at age patterns in more detail in section 10.4.

Except among older women, a college degree or better is strongly protective against suicide. Durkheim ([1897] 1951) argued that education would *increase* suicide rates, but the modern literature for the United States is in accord with our findings; see, for example, Phillips et al. (2010) who also cite other studies that reach the same conclusion. The protective effect of a college degree is larger for men than for women, and larger for young than for old; men age twenty-five to thirty-four with a college degree are nearly three times less likely to kill themselves than are men of the same age with a high school diploma but without a college degree. Yet the effect of education is not monotonic; for both men and women, and at all age groups, those without a high school degree are less likely to kill themselves than those with only a high school degree. Once again, this poses problems for the link between SWB and suicide; for the former, more education comes with higher life evaluation, more positive affect, less negative affect, and less physical pain, and this is true across all three education groups, unlike the suicide rate. Higher human capital raises earnings opportunities, so that more educated people have more opportunities for a better life, and more to lose by killing themselves. But only the first of these is consistently seen in the data. Note that while death certificates have information on education, they do not collect income, so with these data, it is not possible to examine whether education works through income, or directly, or both.

It is possible to tabulate these data in many different ways, in particular to consider the relationship between suicide and SWB not only by age, sex, and education, but also by race, by Hispanic status, and by marital status. One economical way to show these patterns is to run descriptive regressions in which suicide rates and SWB are projected on these variables and on selected interactions, and then to examine the two sets of regression coefficients for similarities in sign patterns and in magnitude. We do this as follows: We start from the American Community Surveys (ACS) for 2009 through 2013. From these, we calculate the number of people in each of 2,520 cells defined by (five) years, (two) sexes, (four) marital status categories (never married, married, divorced, and widowed), (three) education levels (less than high school, high school diploma up to some college, four-year college degree or above), (three) race/ethnic categories (non-Hispanic whites, non-Hispanic blacks, and Hispanics), and (seven) age groups (twenty-five to thirty-four, thirty-five to forty-four, forty-five to fifty-four, fifty-five to sixty-four, sixty-five to seventy-four, seventy-five to eighty-four, and eighty-five and over). The ACS gives the numbers of people at risk, and we gather the numbers of suicides in each cell from the microdata files on each death from the CDC. Dividing the suicides by the numbers at risk gives probabilities of death in each cell, and these probabilities are regressed (with the population in each cell as weights) on categorical dummies for each variable, as well as selected interaction terms. Including all interactions gives a fully saturated model that is equivalent to a six-dimensional cross tabulation, which would have obvious difficulties of both overfitting and presentation. Our regressions should be identical to running linear probability models on the ACS data with the mortality data merged in; of course, we can only use as explanatory variables the information that appears on the death certificates as well as in the ACS. (We here use the publicly available microdata, which does not contain any geographical identifiers.)

We process the GHWBI data to match the same categories so that we can run SWB regressions that have exactly the same explanatory variables as the suicide regressions and that can be examined for matching patterns.

Figure 10.1 shows one (out of many) possible regressions. It excludes interactions other than running different regressions for men and women; beyond that, it is hard to find a succinct way of presenting the results. The top panel of the figure is for men, the bottom panel is for women, and the categories are arrayed horizontally. In each case, there is an omitted category (2009, whites, less than high school, never married, ages twenty-five to thirty-four) and the white bars show the coefficients in the suicide regressions. The black bars show the coefficients in the regression for the ladder, though we have changed the signs, so that the two sets of bars should go in the same direction if well-being and suicide match. We have also multiplied the ladder coefficients by ten, so as to put everything on (roughly) the same scale; this factor is the same for men as for women. If suicide and life evaluation match, the black and white bars should be in the same ratio over all categories.

Note first that the black bars are much larger relative to the white bars in the bottom panel for women than in the top panel for men. The suicide scales (on the y axis) are different for men and for women, given the much higher suicide rates among men. But, as we have already seen, the differences in the ladder by sex are small, and this carries over to the patterns in the coefficients of the various categories. For example, the black (ladder) bar for women age eighty-five and older is larger for women than for men, but checking the scales shows that the magnitudes are similar, about eight suicides per thousand, once we examine the scales. This tells us that, even when we allow for all of these categories simultaneously, we cannot match the gender patterns of suicides to the gender patterns in the ladder, because the gender differences in the ladder, overall, and for each category, even when they are in the right direction, are much too small to match the huge differences in suicides, overall, and for each category.

Perhaps there is some fundamental evolved difference between men and women in their propensity to kill themselves, a difference that is not reflected

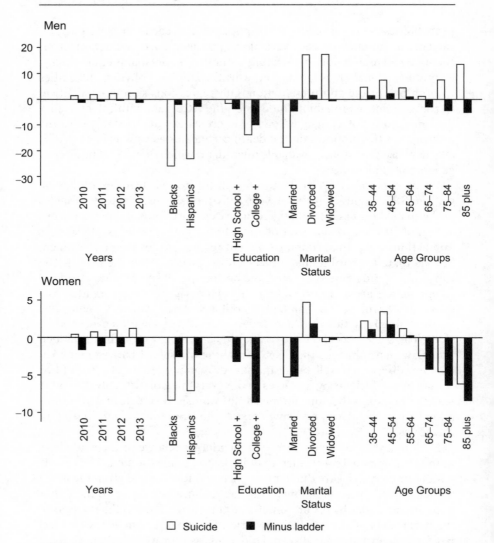

Fig. 10.1   Coefficients of matched variables on suicides and on ladder, 2009–2013, men and women

in their life evaluations or hedonic well-being. Indeed, and with the possible exception of China, women kill themselves less often than men, although women evaluate their lives more highly in only about two-thirds of countries. If so, we should look at each sex separately, looking only horizontally along the upper and lower panels of figure 10.1, without trying to match the top and bottom panels. Starting from the left, the time effects are in the wrong direction for both sexes. Suicides are increasing from 2009 to 2013, for both men and women—even controlling for the other variables—but the ladder is higher after 2009—which might be in part attributed to context effects in the poll in 2009 (Deaton 2012)—and is increasing from 2010 to 2013 for both sexes—which cannot be so explained. Blacks and Hispanics are much less likely to kill themselves than whites, and while both groups have higher ladder scores than whites—this result depends on conditioning by education, and is not true in the raw data—the sizes of the differences are too modest to match the differences in suicide rates, as was the case for the comparison between men and women. Of course, we could rescale the ladder coefficients to better match these differences, but that would make the match even worse for the other categories.

The sign patterns are close to being correct for the education and marital status categories; both education and marriage come with higher life evaluation and lower suicide rates. (There are small sign violations for women with high school degrees and for widows.) But for women, the effects of education on suicide are modest compared with the very large effects of education on life evaluation or, put differently, while the effects of education on the ladder are similar for men and women, it is only among men that education, particularly a college degree, has a substantial effect on suicide. Marriage is consistently protective against suicide, though remarkably, widowhood, while bad for men, is protective for women. Again, the relative magnitudes do not match, with the effects on suicide much more marked than the effects on the ladder. As was the case for race and ethnicity, scaling up the ladder coefficients would exacerbate the differences over years and age groups.

The age-group patterns in figure 10.1 mostly echo the results in table 10.1, albeit with finer groups. For women, the U-shape in the ladder (here shown as an inverted U because of the sign change) matches the pattern of suicides with age while, for men over the age of sixty-five, the patterns do not match, with life evaluation continuing to improve as suicide rates rise. As we shall argue in the next section, it is possible that the dip in life evaluation in middle age is relatively recent, and that it is indeed linked to the rise in suicide in middle age, with both driven by increasing physical and mental distress in middle age.

We do not show more interactions here, but we note that the estimated age profiles differ markedly by race. In particular, for black non-Hispanic men and women, suicide rates fall with age, showing no signs of the peak in middle-age suicide that we see in white men and white women. The ladder for blacks also has no dip in middle age, but *falls* steadily with age so that, once again, there is no match with the suicide rates.

Our results are much less favorable to the match between well-being and suicide than those of Helliwell (2007) and Daly and Wilson (2009). We suspect that these differences are more a matter of interpretation than of reality. Those earlier results also have a substantial number of mismatches, and our tests here, by checking magnitude as well as direction, are more severe.

10.3   Circaseptan Rhythms

Suicides are not equally spread over the days of the week. As most people might guess, and is confirmed in the literature (e.g., McMahon 1983; Maldonado and Kraus 1991), Monday is the peak day for suicides. Figure 10.2 shows averages over the years 2008 through 2013. Suicides fall steadily throughout the week from the Monday high to a low on Saturday, where there are about 950 fewer male suicides and about 200 fewer female suicides each year than on Mondays. From a baseline of around 4,000 (1,000) male (female) suicides each day, these effects are large. Sundays are marginally worse than Saturdays, but the biggest upward jump is between Sunday and Monday. As always, there are fewer female than male suicides, but the weekly patterns are the same; Mondays are bad for both men and women. We do not show similar graphs by age because the circaseptan shape is the same as in figure 10.2 for ten-year age groups (twenty-five to thirty-four, thirty-five to forty-four and so on, up to eighty-five and older). It is worth noting that the pattern holds true even for the highest age groups, so that Mondays are bad even for those who are retired and do not have to go to work.

Deaton (2012, figure 1) shows the corresponding patterns for self-reported well-being and we have checked that these hold over the longer and later 2008 to 2013 period. We do not show these graphs because they are easily summarized. Life evaluation is the same on every day, while affect is better on weekends than in the week, more smiling, enjoyment, happiness, and less sadness, worry, stress, anger, and physical pain. Using the same data, Stone, Schneider, and Harter (2012) show that these patterns hold for all age groups, with minor differences in the shapes across age groups. They also find a very small negative effect of Mondays on positive affect, and a larger but still small positive (negative) effect of Fridays on positive (negative) affect, but these differences between weekdays are small relative to the difference between all weekdays and all weekend days.

The fact that life evaluation is the same for all days of the week is exactly what we would expect of any measure that assesses life as a whole; indeed, its lack of circaseptan rhythm is almost a test of its validity. The same is largely true of lifetime utility in intertemporal choice models, or in the Hamermesh and Soss economic theory of suicide. Note, however, that if today's overall lifetime utility is the (discounted) sum of expected future utilities in each day of the rest of life, and if those future utilities are lower on weekdays, there will be a small (depending on the number of days of life remaining) drop on Mondays as the weekend moves from the future into the past, and an increase over the rest of the week as the weekdays move into the past, but the effect must be small except for those very near the end of life. Beyond that, if life evaluation refers to just the utility of each day, there are no circaseptan effects for expected future utility to work on. These arguments work against

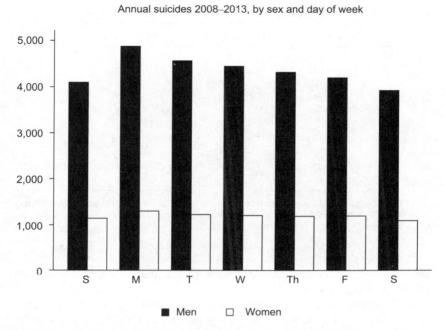

Fig. 10.2   **Circaseptan pattern of suicides: Average numbers of deaths per year**

the claim that suicides are entirely driven by fluctuations in lifetime utility or life evaluation. That suicides have a large impulsive component appears to have a better chance of matching these data.

Even so, the circaseptan pattern of affect does not easily match the suicide patterns in figure 10.2. If we are trying to match affect with suicides day by day, negative affect is only slightly higher on Mondays than on other weekdays, and positive affect is only very slightly lower. And although hedonics are somewhat better on Fridays than on Mondays through Thursdays, there is no steady pattern of improvement over the week to match the steady decline in suicides through the week from the Monday peak.

A possible account can be constructed following Becker and Posner (2004), who postulate that the utility that matters for suicide depends on instantaneous utility relative to the person's past level. Happiness is high at weekends, so the suicide peak on Mondays comes, not just because of the lower happiness on Mondays, but also because of the fall in happiness from Sunday to Monday. Come Tuesday, instantaneous happiness is the same as on Monday, but Sunday now has less weight, and so there is an improvement in suicide-decision utility on Tuesday relative to Monday. If suicide is to go on declining through the week, Sunday's experience must only gradually fade into the background, and if we are to explain why there are more

Table 10.2	Circaseptan patterns of suicide, affect, and life evaluation			
	Ladder	Positive affect	Negative affect	Pain
		Men		
Today	−11,831	−22,410	10,045	28,261
	(1.7)	(12.3)	(8.4)	(5.2)
Yesterday	−5,269	12,821	−6,420	−22,686
	(0.7)	(7.0)	(5.4)	(4.2)
		Women		
Today	−1,107	−4,468	2,129	4,425
	(0.7)	(7.0)	(11.0)	(5.2)
Yesterday	−932	2,356	−1,325	−4,272
	(0.4)	(3.7)	(6.9)	(5.0)

Note: Each column shows a regression of the number of suicide deaths (average for each day for 2008 to 2013) on the SWB measure for that day of the week and for the previous day of the week. Absolute *t*-values are shown in parentheses.

suicides on Sundays than Saturday, we will have to allow some anticipation of Monday on Sunday.

Table 10.2 presents regressions of deaths by suicide against positive affect, negative affect, and the ladder, including both today's and yesterday's value; the data come from 2008 through 2013, though of course we only have seven observations. This procedure can be thought of as two-sample instrumental variable estimation, with day of the week as the instrument for the hedonics and life evaluation. In spite of the small number of observations, the results are remarkably strong and remarkably consistent. The ladder has no apparent effect on suicides, but both positive affect and negative affect do, with all signs in the expected direction, and all attracting very large *t*-values. The coefficient on yesterday's affect is between half and two-thirds of today's affect, consistent with the supposition that suicide-decision utility depends on what happens today relative to what happened yesterday, though yesterday's affect gets less weight. When tomorrow's affect is added to these regressions, it never attracts a significant coefficient. Regressions on today's affect only (excluding yesterday's affect) are significant, but the *t*-values are typically one-fifth of the size of those in the table. We have also run parallel regressions for the components of positive affect (smiling, enjoyment, happiness, and not being sad) and of negative affect (worry, anger, and stress.) All of these show the same patterns of today and (oppositely signed) yesterday, and all have large *t*-values.

The effect sizes in these regressions are substantial. Positive affect has a mean of 0.85 (0.84) for men (women) with a standard deviation over the seven days of 0.016 for both. From the definition of positive affect, this means that 85 percent of men report that, on the previous day, they experienced a lot of happiness, enjoyment, smiling, and not a lot of sadness. A

1 percentage point decrease in positive affect is associated with an additional 224 (45) male (female) suicides, which is muted by a reduction of 128 (24) the next day. For men, the biggest effect is for pain, where a 1 percentage point increase (mean is 22 percent) comes with 282 additional suicides, followed by 227 fewer suicides on the next day. For pain, unlike positive or negative affect (or their components), it is essentially the *change* from the previous day that matters; the coefficients are almost equal and opposite.

Perhaps the most important result of this section is the fact that life evaluation is the same throughout the week, while suicide rates are not. This casts doubt on (at least the completeness of) the economic theory of suicide and also questions the earlier-cited accounts that argue that happiness, invariably measured as life satisfaction, is determined by the same underlying variable as is suicide. If so, there is some unknown determinant that smooths out life evaluation while not smoothing suicide. In contrast to the lack of a link with life evaluation, and in accord with the idea that many suicides are impulsive, we find that positive and negative affects, either singly, or in combinations, are strongly related to the circaseptan pattern of suicides, but only when we recognize that it is not only today's affect that matters, but also the change since yesterday. For pain, which has the strongest effect of all, it is the increase since yesterday that drives suicides.

10.4   Changing Age Patterns

Figures 10.3 (for men) and 10.4 (for women) show suicide rates by age for selected single years between 1979 and 2013. As we have seen, women are much less likely to kill themselves than are men, but the age patterns are also quite different, and perhaps most remarkably, those patterns have seen large changes over the last forty years, especially for women.

Durkheim's view that suicide rates increase with age is borne out—at least in part, and at least for men—by figure 10.3. The suicide rate rises rapidly from ten- to fourteen-year-olds to twenty- to twenty-four-year-olds, and then is stable until the sixties, rising rapidly thereafter. Such a pattern is clearly consistent with the influence of accumulating disability on the probability of suicide. Suicide rates among elderly men rose steadily from 1979 through to the mid-1990s but fell thereafter, first among those age sixty-five to seventy-four, then among those age seventy-five to eighty-four, and finally among those age eighty-five and older, whose suicide rate falls only after 1995. These are possible cohort effects associated with men (but not women) born between 1910 and 1920 who were particularly prone to suicide in old age. Among younger men, suicide rates fell with age until the mid-forties, but only from 1979 to 2000. Since then there is a clear increase in middle age, an increase whose size continues to climb.

Patterns of suicides among women are markedly different. In 1979 and the early 1980s, women were more likely to kill themselves in middle age,

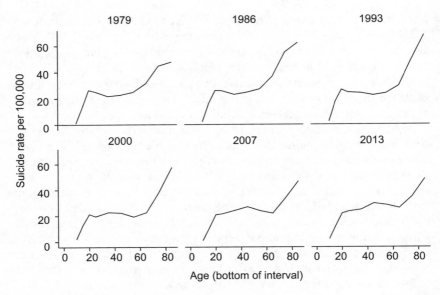

Fig. 10.3   Suicides by age, selected years, men

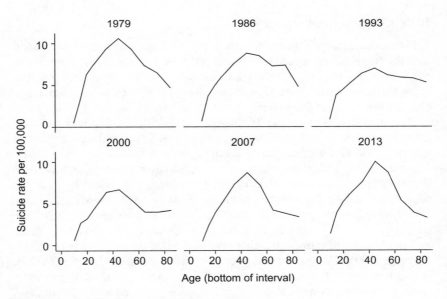

Fig. 10.4   Suicides by age, selected years, women

with the rate peaking in the early forties. This pattern slowly changed as the peak shrank, so that by the early 1990s, suicide rates for women were close to constant after age forty. In recent years, the middle-age peak has reappeared, and by 2013 is almost as high as it was in 1979. These changes are driven by changes in suicide rates in middle age. Suicide rates among elderly women were approximately constant from 1979 to the mid-1990s and, as has been the case for men, have been declining ever since.

The Gallup-Healthways Well-Being Index data started only in 2008, and are therefore not useful for matching to these patterns. As a substitute, the General Social Survey, which has a much coarser well-being question, is available from the early 1970s, though not for every year. The GSS question asks, "Taken all together, how would you say things are these days—would you say that you are very happy, pretty happy, or not too happy?" We have coded this as 3, 2, and 1, and interpret this as a life-satisfaction question, as does the literature; although the word "happy" appears in the question (in contrast to the Gallup ladder), it is offset by the "Taken all together," though it is certainly possible that answers to the question are influenced by the hedonic state of the respondent at the time of interview.

The GSS sample is small, between 1,400 and 2,000 per year, so we have pooled years centered around the years used in figures 10.3 and 10.4—the precise years are marked on the panels in figure 10.5—and we have split those data by sex and by the same age groups as the suicide data. Some of these cells have few observations; for those age fifteen to nineteen, and for those age eighty-five and older, there are cells with around fifty observations. The minimum is for men age eighty-five and older in the first group of years, which has thirty-three observations (there are seventy-four women). For the other age, sex, and year groups, all cells have more than 200 observations, except for men age seventy-five to eighty-four, and women age seventy-five to eighty-four in the first year group, where there are still more than one hundred observations.

Figure 10.5 shows, as expected, that the estimates of life satisfaction are noisy. Given that we do not believe that life evaluation is very different for men and women, or has a different shape over life, putting them on the same graph gives an idea of the margins of error of the estimates. It also allows us to see some fairly clear patterns. Most surprisingly, the U-shape over the life cycle is only apparent in the last two panels—between 2004 and 2014—but not at all before that. Between 1977 and 1988, the GSS measure of life satisfaction rises with age, with a dip among the oldest men and women, something that might be expected given failing health. Subsequently, there are some signs of a middle-age dip in well-being, and of falling well-being after age seventy-five, but recall the small sample sizes for these groups, especially men. These graphs raise the intriguing possibility that the U-shape in life satisfaction is a relatively recent phenomenon in the United States: it

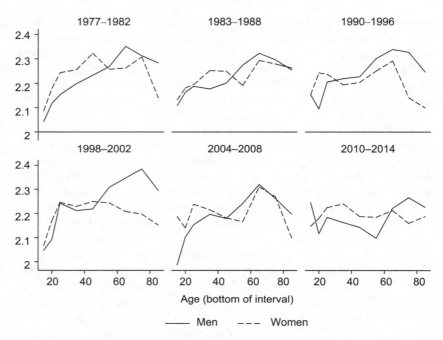

Fig. 10.5   Life satisfaction (GSS) by age, selected periods

is certainly not universal in all countries and so cannot be a fixed biological trait (see Steptoe, Deaton, and Stone 2015).

As was the case in section 10.2, it takes a great deal of imagination to match the well-being patterns to the suicide patterns. Most immediately, there is no clear difference in age profiles of life satisfaction for men and women, in spite of their markedly different life cycle profiles of suicide. In recent years, the increasing dip in well-being for women in middle age matches the increasing rates of suicide in middle age, but this does not work so clearly for men. Indeed, in the early period we have men's well-being and men's suicide rising in parallel through much of the life cycle, except for those age eighty-five and older. Once again, these life satisfaction measures do not line up in any obvious way with the suicide data.

For the years since 2008, we can use the Gallup-Healthways Well-Being Index data to compare the age profiles of SWB with the suicide numbers. The ladder has the U-shape for both men and women, and so cannot be matched with both sets of suicide rates. Much more telling are the Gallup data on pain and on positive affect. For pain, we would expect a steady increase with age, but in fact, there is a peak between ages fifty and sixty when 28 percent of the population report that they experienced a lot of pain yesterday, compared with 15 percent of those in their twenties, and 23 percent among those in their seventies and eighties; there is indeed some increase between the seventies and eighties, as we might have expected. Figure 10.6 shows also that, for men, the middle-age peak increased from 2008 to 2013; the corresponding graphs for women in the bottom panel have similar shapes, but the increase in the middle-age peak is only apparent in 2013. Figure 10.6 shows graphs for positive affect that look like the mirror image of the graphs for pain, attaining their lowest values in middle age.

We do not fully understand these data, nor their relationship with suicide. Other national data in the United States show an epidemic of increasing morbidity and mortality in middle age, at the same time as similar indicators for the elderly are improving. Given this, we suspect that the peak in pain in middle age is both real and recent; indeed, the same factors are possibly implicated in the dips in life evaluation and in positive affect in middle age. If so, the U-shape is not a constant of biology, but is at least in part a response to recent events among middle-aged Americans. The link with suicide is clearly clouded, if only because of the different patterns for men and women. Note again, however, that figure 10.3 shows increasing suicides among middle-aged men in recent years, with a magnitude that is actually two to three times larger than the (apparently much more dramatic) increase among middle-aged women; for men, the peak is less obvious, because there

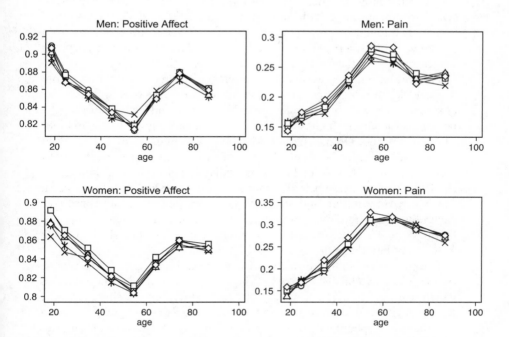

Fig. 10.6   Positive affect and pain by sex and year: 2008 (thick solid line) to 2013 (thin solid line)

are so many more suicides to start with so that the increase does not change the shape of the whole curve.

We currently have no firm explanation for the changing patterns in figures 10.3 and 10.4. We suspect that increasing suicides among both middle-aged men and women in the United States is tied to the recent middle-age epidemic of sickness (mental and physical distress) and death (not only suicides, but accidental poisonings from alcohol, and from prescription and illegal drugs—particularly opioids—as well as a large category of deaths by poisonings where intent is unclear). Whether rising pain is the cause of prescription drug use and misuse or their consequence, or both, is not presently clear. In any case, our best guess is that the patterns of positive affect and of pain in figure 10.6 are real and, when other patterns are allowed for, match the suicide data.

Unless the epidemic is reversed, recent declines in morbidity among the elderly will not persist when the current cohort of middle-aged Americans move into old age.

10.5   Geographies of Suicide

Figure 10.7 shows the state-by-state scatterplot of mean age-adjusted suicide rate against the mean value of the ladder from the GHWBI data. In both cases means are calculated over the years 2008 to 2013. We take men and women together and, in order to avoid possible spurious effects from spatial variations in race and ethnicity, we use data only on non-Hispanic whites, both from the CDC suicide data and from the GHWBI.

The graph itself is somewhat more interesting than the correlation. Note in particular the very large variation in suicide rates even over areas as large as states. The lowest suicide rates are in New Jersey and Massachusetts (9.3 per 100,000), and the highest are in the "suicide belt" of (from low to high) Idaho, Colorado, Utah, Arizona, Montana, Wyoming, New Mexico, and Nevada, all of which have suicide rates of more than 20 per 100,000, with Nevada at 26.2. (Alaska at 19.5 is immediately before Idaho.) Several of the states in the suicide belt are among the top states in life evaluation. In this figure, Hawaii is an outlier in terms of high life evaluation; Hawaiians generally report high life evaluation, but less than half of Hawaii's population is non-Hispanic white, and this minority has substantially higher life evaluation than the majority.

The correlation in figure 10.7 is 0.16, weak but positive, and is similar to that reported by Daly et al. (2011), who interpret it as a "dark contrast" in which relative effects are so strong that high general well-being drives the less fortunate to suicide. Inspired by this, we have redrawn figure 10.7 using the fractions of people whose ladder scores are zero or one (out of ten), less than or equal to two, and less than or equal to three; the correlations of these measures with suicides rates are essentially zero. Once again, we find

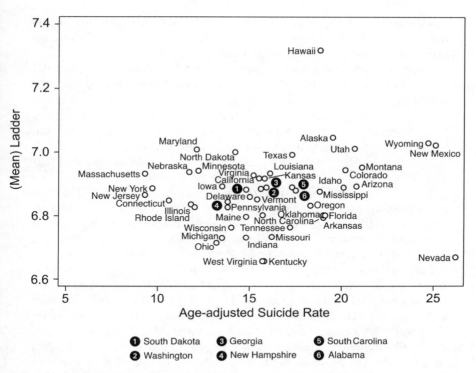

Fig. 10.7   Mean ladder and suicide in the United States, 2008–2013, white non-Hispanics

no obvious univariate relationship between life evaluation and suicide. The correlations between suicide and positive affect and negative affect are also small and perverse. However, and as we shall see repeatedly, there is a much stronger relationship between self-reported physical pain and suicide, where the correlation is 0.39 over the fifty states.

We have also looked at the relationship between suicide and well-being at the county level, which gives us many more data points as well as a wider range of variation. Because suicide is rare, and because many counties have small populations, we need a run of years to get reasonable precision (or indeed any CDC estimates for smaller counties), and the GHWBI data start only in 2008. Previous literature and state-level data suggest that geographical suicides are persistent over time—for example, the suicide belt has been that way for many years—so we have used average county-level age-adjusted mortality rates for non-Hispanic whites for the whole period of ICD10, 1999–2013, and compared it with the GHWBI data from 2008 to 2013. This is not ideal, but will still turn out to be informative, if only because it gives us the ability to look at the correlations between suicide and SWB while controlling for other factors.

We start with the 2,259 counties for which we have age-adjusted suicide rates from the CDC as well as SWB data from the GHWBI. There is an extraordinary range of suicide rates across counties, from 38.2 in Sierra County, NM, and 37 in Nye County, NV, to 5.3 in Holmes County, OH, and 5.4 in Rockland County, NY. Fourteen of the twenty counties with the lowest rates are in New York or New Jersey. If we confine ourselves to the 2,102 counties with at least 100 observations in the GHWBI, the correlation between suicide and the ladder is now negative, −0.12, and between suicide and positive (negative) affect are negative (positive), −0.18 (0.11). The strong positive correlation with physical pain is 0.34, similar to that across the states.

Table 10.3 presents regression results of suicide rates on the SWB measures, physical pain, and a range of other variables suggested in the literature. An immediate question with these regressions is whether the cutoff of 100 for observations in GHWBI is sufficient, so we present regressions with cutoffs of 250, 500, and 1,000. Because the county sample sizes in the GHWBI are almost perfectly correlated with county population sizes, higher cutoffs, while reducing measurement error in the estimated means, also drop smaller-population counties from the analysis. As a result, there is no reason to suppose that, even in the absence of measurement error, the parameters being estimated will be the same. The effects of the cutoff can be illustrated by looking at New Jersey and Montana. With the cutoff of 100 in the first column, twenty-two Montana counties and twenty-one New Jersey counties are included; by the time we reach the cutoff of 1,000 in the last column, there are only three Montana counties left, but seventeen in New Jersey. Even so, the qualitative pattern of results does not change greatly across the table.

All of the regressions include controls for the nine census divisions, with New England as the omitted category. Suicides become more prevalent as we move South and West, with the Mountain dummy picking up much of the suicide belt; there are around nine more suicides per 100,000 in the Mountain division than in New England. With these geographical controls, the ladder has the expected protective effect, but negative affect (anger, stress, and worry) is also, and presumably perversely, protective. Positive affect is not significant, and physical pain, as always, is a strong risk factor. The effect of pain is large; an increase of one standard deviation, 5.9 percentage points (the median is 26 percent), is associated with 0.57 additional suicides per 100,000. As was the case with the age profiles, physical pain appears to be an important correlate of suicide.

Income and income inequality are both estimated to be significantly protective against suicide; we do not show it, but conditional on the log of income, the number of years of education has no effect. We have already noted the protective effect of education in section 10.2, but there we could

Table 10.3 County-level regressions of age-adjusted suicide rate on SWB and other variables

	$n \geq 100$	$n \geq 250$	$n \geq 500$	$n \geq 1000$
Mean population	1.2	1.7	2.60	3.95
Median population	0.48	0.84	1.52	2.63
Number of counties	2,102	1,326	789	431
Ladder	−1.28	−1.42	−3.35	−3.56
	(3.2)	(2.6)	(4.3)	(3.2)
Positive affect	−2.96	−4.43	1.25	15.3
	(0.8)	(0.9)	(0.16)	(1.3)
Negative affect	−11.1	−16.8	−25.0	−20.22
	(3.9)	(4.2)	(4.5)	(2.5)
Pain	9.61	15.5	19.1	33.0
	(5.2)	(5.8)	(5.3)	(6.1)
Log income	−4.24	−3.68	−3.50	−3.28
	(8.8)	(6.5)	(5.4)	(3.9)
S.d. log income	−4.85	−7.89	−5.32	−3.05
	(4.5)	(5.5)	(2.9)	(1.2)
Fraction Catholic	−3.30	−6.65	−9.79	−10.1
	(2.2)	(3.8)	(5.0)	(4.2)
Fraction Protestant	−4.91	−8.23	−10.0	−10.1
	(2.9)	(4.2)	(4.3)	(3.4)
Fraction Jewish	−14.4	−7.50	−8.52	−8.24
	(2.2)	(1.2)	(1.4)	(1.3)
Fraction Mormon	−6.62	−9.99	−12.3	−11.8
	(3.9)	(5.2)	(5.6)	(4.5)
Fraction other Christian	−2.14	−4.27	−7.4	−8.31
	(1.3)	(2.3)	(3.5)	(2.9)
	Census divisions			
Mid-Atlantic	−1.19	−1.12	−0.48	0.01
	(2.4)	(2.6)	(1.1)	(0.0)
East North Central	−0.40	−0.27	0.47	1.00
	(0.9)	(0.7)	(1.1)	(2.0)
West North Central	0.71	0.86	2.15	2.75
	(1.5)	(0.8)	(4.3)	(4.5)
South Atlantic	2.93	3.11	3.87	4.44
	(5.9)	(6.6)	(7.9)	(7.9)
East South Central	2.39	2.26	3.55	4.48
	(4.4)	(4.2)	(6.0)	(5.9)
West South Central	3.77	3.99	4.72	5.43
	(7.4)	(7.9)	(8.9)	(8.5)
Mountain	9.54	9.26	8.89	8.69
	(19)	(19)	(17)	(15)
Pacific	4.34	3.73	4.02	3.40
	(8.8)	(8.3)	(8.9)	(6.2)

Note: Each column is a regression with the county age-adjusted mortality rate as dependent variable. N is the number of observations from the GHWBI surveys in each county. T-values are in parentheses.

not control for income, which may be the mechanism through which education operates. Either way, suicide—like many other causes of death—is less common among those with the higher socioeconomic status that comes with income or education. It is often claimed that local income inequality is itself a cause of mortality, but the results here show the opposite effect for suicide; previous literature has been inconsistent (see Smith and Kawachi 2014).

Religious denominations are often thought to be protective, and all are here estimated to be so; there is no sign here of the often-argued greater propensity of Protestants over Catholics to kill themselves (see Durkheim [1897] 1951; Becker and Woessmann 2015). Belonging to the "other Christian" group, here mostly evangelicals, is always protective, but becomes more so on the right of the table among the larger counties. All religious denominations do better than those in the omitted category, which comprises non-Christians/non-Jews (Jews are included as one of the religious groups), and those who espouse no religion at all. We note the possibility of ecological fallacy; if religion protects individuals, we would expect it to show up in the county aggregates, but the reverse is not true.

We have also added variables constructed from the Behavioral Risk Factor Surveillance Survey (BRFSS), which collected data in 2001, 2003, and 2004 on gun ownership, as well as information on whether an individual is at risk for alcohol abuse; guns are the primary means of committing suicide for men, and alcohol is an important risk factor. The BRFSS is large enough to calculate averages of these measures at the county level, though only for 1,237 counties, which are further reduced by the selection criteria in table 10.3. The fraction owning a gun is not significant conditional on the census division dummies, even though there is substantial county-level variation in gun ownership within divisions. The alcohol abuse variable is, however, highly significant with a coefficient of 19.2 when added to the final regression in the table. The mean of the alcohol abuse variable is 0.05, and ranges from 0 to 0.16.

Our purpose here is not to claim new findings on the spatial correlates of suicide in the United States (for a comprehensive recent analysis see Phillips [2013]). What is new here is the inclusion of the SWB measures; evaluative well-being is modestly protective against suicide, but so is negative affect. The effects of physical pain are what might be expected; the importance of pain and of alcohol in the county cross-section matches their link to changes in suicides over time, particularly among middle-age Americans.

We conclude with a brief examination of international patterns in suicide, using data from the World Health Organization's mortality database. Figure 10.8 shows the scatter plot of suicide rates against mean ladder scores from the Gallup World Poll using data from 2006 to 2010 for both. While there are a few other countries with data, the suicide information does not extend much beyond Europe and Latin America, both of which are included in the figure. The black points are for the rich European and OECD countries, the

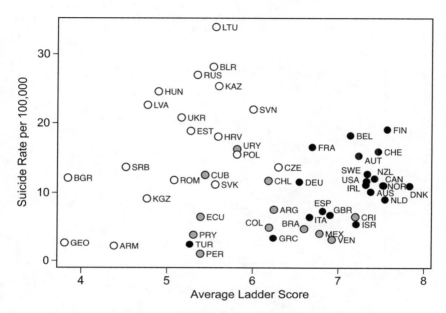

Fig. 10.8   Suicide and life evaluation across countries

gray points are for Latin America, and the white points are for Russia and the former satellites of the former Soviet Union. Note that the United States is not at all exceptional, and is in the middle of the cluster of points on the right. But there are several countries, including France, Belgium, Finland, and Austria, where suicide rates are much higher, though none are as high as the highest of the Eastern European countries, with Belarus, Russia, and Kazakhstan leading the group with rates more than twice as high as in the United States.

Bray and Gunnell (2006) earlier found *positive* relationships between life satisfaction (from the European Values Survey in 1999/2000) and suicide rates for Western European countries, as well as for Eastern European countries, when each group is examined separately, but a *negative* relationship when the two groups are pooled. The Eastern European countries have low life evaluations and high suicide rates. These results are replicated for the Gallup data in figure 10.8. The addition of the Latin American countries groups them firmly with the Western European pattern; they have somewhat lower ladder scores and somewhat lower suicide rates. Our other well-being measures are also related to suicide rates in less than obvious ways. Pain is positively correlated with suicide within the three regions, but not across them. Positive affect is negatively correlated with suicide rates both within and across regions, while negative affect, as was the case in the American counties, is *negatively* correlated with suicides.

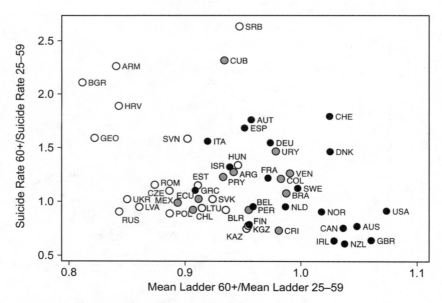

Fig. 10.9   Old versus young, suicide and life evaluation

Durkheim believed that suicide increased with age, as was true in his data. In thirty-one of these fifty-two countries, the suicide rate of those age sixty and over is greater than the suicide rate of those age twenty-five to fifty-nine. For men, the suicides rates for the older group are larger in forty-one countries, and for women in thirty-one countries. As shown in Steptoe, Deaton, and Stone (2015), the U-shape in life evaluation, while evident in the English-speaking rich countries, is not apparent in the rest of Europe nor in Latin America. It is thus reasonable to ask whether international patterns in life evaluation match age patterns in suicide rates. Figure 10.9 plots the ratio of suicide rates of those age sixty and older to those age twenty-five to fifty-nine against the ratios of the mean ladders for the two age groups. This analysis is unaffected by the rescaling of ladder by countries, and is thus robust to cross-country (or cross-region) differences in reporting styles, or at least those that can be represented by rescaling. And indeed, here there is a strong negative link between suicide and life evaluation; in countries where the old are more likely to kill themselves, the old are more likely to have lower life evaluations.

10.6   Discussion and Conclusions

This chapter compares suicide rates with self-reported measures of well-being in the hope that each set of measures might provide insights about the other. We follow Bray and Gunnell (2006) in investigating the possibility that suicide and life satisfaction, or measures of hedonic affect, are markers of population mental health. We do this in a range of contexts, over geographies, over time, over life cycles, and over the days of the week, hunting for insights and tests of theory. We also look at pain, to test whether "yesterday" questions work, because pain is a risk factor for suicide and because pain has strong effects on SWB, thus providing a link.

There is an economic theory of suicide, rooted in intertemporal choice theory, which says that people kill themselves when the utility of being dead exceeds the utility of continuing to live defined as some forward-looking integral. It predicts that higher-utility people are less likely to kill themselves because they have more to lose, and thus suggests that people are more likely to kill themselves as they age. An alternative to the economic theory is that suicide is often an impulsive choice, depending on feelings now, without much thought for the future. One hardly has to subscribe to economists' notions of rationality to agree that for those with accumulating burdens of disease, including worsening pain, suicide can be a rational decision, and indeed the right to medical assistance in committing suicide under such circumstances is legally recognized in a number of countries.

Our findings suggest that, with some exceptions, suicide has little to do with life satisfaction. Correlations between suicide and measured well-being are either absent or inconsistent. Differences in suicides between men and women, between Hispanics, blacks, and whites, between age groups of men or of African Americans, between countries or US states, between calendar years, and between days of the week, do not match differences in life evaluation. Suicide rates in the United States have risen in recent years, though there is no evidence of decreases in SWB. Marriage and education do indeed bring more life satisfaction and less suicide, though the relative sizes of the effects do not match the effects on SWB, even for men and women separately. For example, when we control for age, sex, and race, being married comes with higher life evaluation and lower suicide. For men, and as we should expect, those who are divorced have lower well-being and higher suicide rates, but the magnitude of the effect on suicide is much larger relative to the effect on life evaluation than is the case for marriage. When we look at widowers, there is more suicide, comparable to the suicide associated with divorce, yet widowed men actually show slightly *higher* life evaluation.

Women's suicide rates peak in middle age, men's in old age; yet both men and women show a U-shape in life evaluation. Suicide rates among non-Hispanic blacks fall with age alongside *declines* in life evaluation.

Sixteen percent of suicides happen on Mondays and only 13 percent happen on Saturdays. Yet life evaluation is the same on all days of the week. Monday suicides can be matched to positive affect, or to pain, if "suicide-decision utility" depends on both today's feelings and the change since yesterday. Given that positive affect is not consistently connected to suicide in other contexts, and that pain is, it is possible that the higher pain on Mondays affects both positive affect and suicide, but not overall life satisfaction. These results are also hard to reconcile with an economic theory of suicide that emphasizes the benefits of future (dis)utility versus the (dis)utility of dying unless, for some unknown reason, death itself is less unpleasant on Mondays.

Age patterns of suicide are different for men and for women, and have changed differentially over time. The most important facts about suicide over the last decade is that for white non-Hispanics, both men and women, (a) suicide is rising overall, which is driven by (b) increasing suicide rates in middle age, offset by (c) falling suicide rates among the elderly. The suicide epidemic in middle age is the tip of an iceberg of mortality and morbidity, especially pain, among middle-aged Americans. In the Gallup data, "pain yesterday" is now higher in middle age than in old age. We do not know what is driving this epidemic, but it is showing up in at least some of the SWB indicators, including low positive affect in middle age, and perhaps even as some of the dip in middle-age life evaluation, the presence of which we find little evidence of prior to the last decade. Our tentative hypothesis is that pain is an underlying fundamental cause here, and that it is driving changes in both suicides *and* SWB.

There are very large variations in suicides across states in the United States (by more than a factor of two) and across counties (by more than a factor of seven.) At the county level, but not the state level, suicide rates are lower where life evaluation is higher, but *higher* where negative affect is *lower*, and uncorrelated with positive affect. Pain is strongly correlated with suicide, across both states and counties, and is a significant predictor even conditional on standard predictors, such as income, income inequality, and religious denomination.

Across fifty-two countries in the OECD, Latin America, and Eastern Europe, suicide rates are neither well nor consistently correlated with well-being measures. In a majority of countries, suicides are higher among the elderly, particularly for men. In countries where life evaluation is high in old age relative to middle age, suicides are relatively low in old age, and vice versa. At least some of this is driven by the extreme negative effects of the transition on the elderly in Eastern Europe.

References

Becker, Gary S., and Richard A. Posner. 2004. "Suicide: An Economic Approach." Unpublished Manuscript. http://storage.globalcitizen.net/data/topic/knowledge/uploads/2009051911410705.pdf.
Becker, Sascha O., and Ludger Woessmann. 2015. "Social Cohesion, Religious Belief, and the Effect of Protestantism on Suicide." CESifo Working Paper no.

5288, Center for Economic Studies and IFO Institute for Economic Research. March.

Bray, Isabelle, and David Gunnell. 2006. "Suicide Rates, Life Satisfaction and Happiness as Markers for Population Mental Health." *Social Psychiatry and Psychiatric Epidemiology* 41 (5): 333–37.

Case, Anne, and Christina H. Paxson. 2005. "Sex Differences in Morbidity and Mortality." *Demography* 42 (2): 189–214.

Chen, Joe, Yun Jeong Choi, Kohta Mori, Yasuyuki Sawada, and Saki Sugano. 2010. "Socio-economic Studies on Suicide: A Survey." *Journal of Economic Surveys* 26 (2): 271–306.

Cutler, David M., Edward L. Glaeser, and Karen E. Norberg. 2001. "Explaining the Rise in Youth Suicide." In *Risky Behavior among Youths: An Economic Analysis*, edited by Jonathan Gruber, 219–70. Chicago: University of Chicago Press.

Daly, Mary C., Andrew Oswald, Daniel Wilson, and Stephen Wu. 2011. "Dark Contrasts: The Paradox of High Rates of Suicide in Happy Places." *Journal of Economic Behavior and Organization* 80 (3): 435–42.

Daly, Mary C., and Daniel J. Wilson. 2009. "Happiness, Unhappiness, and Suicide: An Empirical Assessment." *Journal of the European Economic Association* 7 (2–3): 539–49.

Daly, Mary C., Daniel J. Wilson, and Norman J. Johnson. 2013. "Relative Status and Well-Being: Evidence from US Suicide Deaths." *Review of Economics and Statistics* 95 (5): 1480–500.

Deaton, Angus. 2012. "The Financial Crisis and the Wellbeing of Americans." *Oxford Economic Papers* 64 (1): 1–26.

Durkheim, Emile. (1897) 1951. *Suicide: A Study in Sociology*. Translated by John A. Spaulding and George Simpson. New York: The Free Press.

Goldsmith, S. K., T. C. Pelimar, A. M. Kleinman, and W. E. Bunney, eds. 2002. *Reducing Suicide: A National Imperative*. Washington, DC: National Academies Press.

Goudie, Robert J. B., Sach Mukherjee, Jan-Emmanuel de Neve, Andrew Oswald, and Stephen Wu. 2014. "Happiness as a Driver of Risk-Avoiding Behavior: Theory and an Empirical Study of Seatbelt Wearing and Automobile Accidents." *Economica* 81 (324): 674–97.

Hamermesh, Daniel S., and Neal M. Soss. 1974. "An Economic Theory of Suicide." *Journal of Political Economy* 82 (1): 83–98.

Helliwell, John F. 2007. "Well-Being and Social Capital: Does Suicide Pose a Puzzle?" *Social Indicators Research* 81 (3): 455–96.

Koivumaa-Honkanen, Heli, Risto Honkanen, Heimo Viinamäki, Kauko Hiekkilä, Jaakko Kaprio, and Markku Koskenvuo. 2001. "Life Satisfaction and Suicide: A 20-Year Follow-Up Study." *American Journal of Psychiatry* 158 (3): 433–39.

Layard, Richard. 2005. *Happiness: Lessons from a New Science*. London: Allen Lane.

Maldonado, George, and Jess F. Kraus. 1991. "Variation in Suicide Occurrence by Time of Day, Day of the Week, Month, and Lunar Phase." *Suicide and Life-Threatening Behavior* 21 (2): 174–87.

McMahon, Kathleen. 1983. "Short-Term Temporal Cycles in Frequency of Suicide, US 1972–78." *American Journal of Epidemiology* 117 (6): 744–50.

Phillips, Julie A. 2013. "Factors Associated with Temporal and Spatial Patterns in Suicide Rates across US States, 1976–2000." *Demography* 50 (2): 591–614.

Phillips, Julie A., Ashley V. Robin, Colleen N. Nugent, and Ellen L. Idler. 2010. "Understanding Recent Changes in Suicide Rates among the Middle-Aged: Period or Cohort Effects." *Public Health Reports* 125 (5): 680–88.

Robbins, Lionel. 1932. *An Essay on the Nature and Significance of Economic Science*. London: Macmillan.

Smith, Nathan Daniel Lucia, and Ichiro Kawachi. 2014. "State-Level Social Capital and Suicide Mortality in the 50 US States." *Social Science and Medicine* 120 (2): 269–77.

Steptoe, Andrew, Angus Deaton, and Arthur A. Stone. 2015. "Psychological Well-being, Health, and Ageing." *Lancet* 385 (9968): 640–48.

Stone, Arthur A., Stefan Schneider, and James K. Harter. 2012. "Day-of-Week Mood Patterns in the United States: On the Existence of 'Blue Monday', 'Thank God It's Friday' and Weekend Effects." *Journal of Positive Psychology* 7 (4): 306–14.

Stone, Arthur A., Joseph E. Schwartz, Joan E. Broderick, and Angus Deaton. 2010. "A Snapshot of the Age Distribution of Psychological Well-Being in the United States." *Proceedings of the National Academy of Sciences* 107 (22): 9985–90.

United Nations (UN). 2014. Department of Economic and Social Affairs, Population and Development Database 2014. http://www.un.org/en/development/desa/population/publications/development/population-development-database-2014.shtml.

World Health Organization (WHO). *World Mortality Database*. Accessed 2014. http://www.who.int/healthinfo/mortality_data/en/.

Comment   David M. Cutler

Anne Case and Angus Deaton have written a fascinating chapter on the relationship between life satisfaction, suicide, and pain. The chapter is just the tip of the iceberg of an enormous research project looking at measures of life satisfaction over time, across individuals, and across countries. This is a hugely important topic, and Case and Deaton are to be congratulated for taking it on. It is one of the central topics in demography and health today.

The present chapter looks at a piece of the puzzle: What is the relationship between self-reported life satisfaction and suicide? The model that Case and Deaton have in mind is something like figure 10C.1. People differ in their life satisfaction, shown by the solid line in the figure. In a rational model, suicide is chosen when life satisfaction is particularly low and the possibility of improvement is small. Thus, there is a cutoff point s, where people with lower life satisfaction than s commit suicide.

Now imagine that the distribution of life satisfaction shifts to the left, for example, because economic conditions become worse or health deteriorates. For any constant point s, the suicide rate will increase. Indeed it may do so to a great extent, depending on the curvature of the life satisfaction curve at s and the initial prevalence of suicide in the population.

The empirical component of the chapter examines the correlation between

David M. Cutler is Harvard College Professor and the Otto Eckstein Professor of Applied Economics at Harvard University and a research associate of the National Bureau of Economic Research.

For acknowledgments, sources of research support, and disclosure of the author's material financial relationships, if any, please see http://www.nber.org/chapters/c13640.ack.

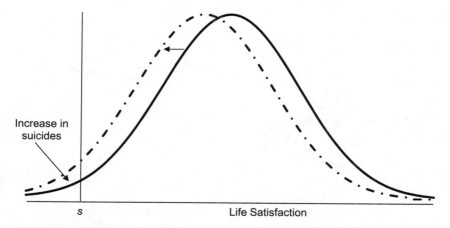

Fig. 10C.1   Life satisfaction and suicide

life satisfaction and suicide across various domains—age, socioeconomic status, time, and the like. The chapter reaches two conclusions. First, life satisfaction and suicide are not highly correlated, indeed the correlation is often of the wrong sign. Second, it is not clear whether life satisfaction or suicide is a better measure of well-being. Suicide seems to reflect temporal factors that one would not expect, such as day of the week, while life satisfaction is measured with difficulty.

These conclusions seem right to me, but I want to expand on a few features of the data and analysis. I will focus mostly on the suicide data, since that is the particularly intriguing part of the chapter.

Measurement

Measuring suicide is not entirely straightforward. Unlike most coding of cause of death, suicide has an intentionality component: Did the person mean to kill themselves? If they did not, the death would be classified as an accidental death, or perhaps a motor vehicle accident. Of course, intention is hard to determine after the fact. Is a death in a single-car crash a suicide or an unfortunate accident? What if the person knew they were at higher risk of death by driving rapidly after drinking, but chose to drive anyway?

These coding issues matter a great deal. Figure 10C.2 shows age-specific mortality from suicide, motor vehicle accidents, and accidental poisoning— largely deaths from heroin or opiate painkillers such as oxycontin. Motor vehicle fatalities and accidental poisoning are roughly comparable in magnitude to suicide through middle age. Thus, small changes in coding can have a large effect on reported suicides. Further, there has been a trend over time to report more suicides and fewer accidental deaths, at least for gun deaths

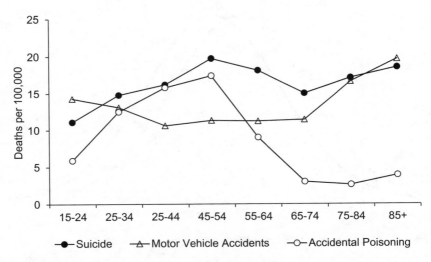

Fig. 10C.2   **Death rates for causes that might be coded as suicides (2013)**

(Cutler, Glaeser, and Norberg 2001). These changes can confound some of the correlations, though it is not obvious that they explain all of the findings.

Socioeconomics and Suicide

One way to consider the relationship between life satisfaction and suicide is to examine very large changes in socioeconomic status and see how they affect suicide. Case and Deaton examine a relatively short time series, where the socioeconomic trends do not vary greatly. I supplement this by examining long-term trends in suicide rates. Socioeconomic status deteriorated rapidly for the elderly in the Great Depression, then increased markedly with the expansion of Social Security and the creation of Medicare and Medicaid in the postwar period. Economic outcomes for younger age individuals, in contrast, have deteriorated over the past few decades. Do suicide rates track these trends?

Figure 10C.3 shows the evolution of suicide rates by age from 1900 to 2010. The results strongly suggest that socioeconomic changes influence suicide. Elderly suicide rates are always above those of younger ages—as first noted by Durkheim ([1897] 1966). Relative to this mean, elderly suicide rates increased substantially in the Great Depression and declined markedly after World War II. In contrast, suicide rates among younger cohorts (fifteen to thirty-four) have increased in the past few decades. At a very broad level, socioeconomic status does influence suicide rates.

That said, significant evidence shows that suicide is not fully rational. Case and Deaton use the intraweek pattern of suicide to suggest nonrationality.

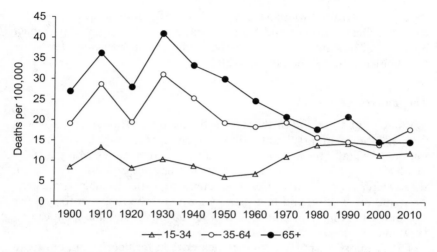

Fig. 10C.3   Suicide rate by age and year
Note: Death rates by ten-year age groups are weighted by population in 1970.

Other data confirm this view. Much of what we know about suicides comes from "psychological autopsies"—interviews with family and friends after a suicide. The most common factor that appears in psychological autopsies is mental illness (Cavanaugh et al. 2003), including depression, bipolar disorder, and anxiety. Seventy percent or more of people who commit suicide have a serious mental illness. It is possible that mental illness acts to focus attention on the present rather than the future ("telescoping"), thus reducing the value of possible future improvements in health.

Beyond mental illness, there are other factors predisposing to suicide that differ by age. As a rough approximation, material circumstances seem to be particularly important for suicide at younger ages. Job, financial, or legal factors are found in about one-third of suicides among people age forty to sixty-four (Hempstead and Phillips 2015). Further, suicide among nonelderly adults increases in recessions (Luo et al. 2011). Interestingly, relative material circumstance (underperformance relative to expectations) may matter more than absolute circumstance, perhaps explaining why blacks and other minority groups have lower suicide rates than whites (Cutler, Glaeser, and Norberg 2011). In older populations, the additional factors often involve pain—typically chronic pain that is not adequately treated—and disability (Conwell, Van Orden, and Caine 2011). Social isolation is another risk factor.

Much of the literature has focused on access to means of suicide. The idea is that suicide is often impulsive, and therefore ready access to guns or possibly harmful prescriptions increases the suicide rate. This certainly seems plausible in light of the high suicide rate in the mountain region of the country—from Wyoming through Arizona. But looking at county data, Case and Deaton do not find evidence that gun availability has an impact on suicide. The same was true in analysis I did of youth suicide a few years ago (Cutler, Glaeser, and Norberg 2011).

The Importance of Pain

What is left at the end of the story is financial hardship and pain—both physical and mental. Mental pain is largely depression; physical pain is musculoskeletal—back pain, arthritis, and related maladies. Many suicides involve one or both of these types of pain. They are troubling in different ways. Depression is readily treatable. There are scales to diagnose depression, and medication and talk therapy have both been shown to improve outcomes. The major question is how to get diagnostic and therapeutic intervention to be used on a wider scale.

The diagnosis of physical pain is clearer than for depression, but treatment is difficult. Opiate medication is a common prescription, but may not be curative, and may actually worsen the problem. Has the rise in opiate medication use actually increased suicide for people with physical pain? Case and Deaton hint at this, but like with many other issues, it will have to await further research.

References

Cavanaugh, J. T. O., A. J. Carson, M. Sharpe, and S. M. Lawrie. 2003. "Psychological Autopsy Studies of Suicide: A Systematic Review." *Psychological Medicine* 33 (3): 395–405.

Conwell, Yeates, Kimberly Van Orden, and Eric D. Caine. 2011. "Suicide in Older Adults." *Psychiatric Clinics of North America* 34 (2): 451–68.

Cutler, David M., Edward L. Glaeser, and Karen E. Norberg. 2001. "Explaining the Rise in Youth Suicide." In *Risky Behavior among Youths: An Economic Analysis*, edited by Jonathan Gruber, 219–70. Chicago: University of Chicago Press.

Durkheim, E. (1897) 1966. *Suicide*. New York: Macmillan.

Hempstead, Katherine A., and Julie A. Phillips. 2015. "Rising Suicide among Adults Aged 40–64: The Role of Job and Financial Circumstances." *American Journal of Preventive Medicine* 48 (5): 491–500.

Luo, F., C. S. Florence, M. Quispe-Agnoli, L. Ouyang, and A. Crosby. 2011. "Impact of Business Cycles on US Suicide Rates, 1928–2007." *American Journal of Public Health* 101:1139–46.

Does Retirement Make You Happy?
A Simultaneous Equations Approach

Raquel Fonseca, Arie Kapteyn, Jinkook Lee, and Gema Zamarro

11.1 Introduction

Continued improvements in life expectancy and fiscal insolvency of public pensions have led to an increase in pension entitlement ages in several countries, but its consequences for subjective well-being are largely unknown.[1] As subjective well-being is known to influence health, if retirement has adverse effects on subjective well-being, it is plausible that the fiscal savings cre-

Raquel Fonseca is professor of economics at the École de Science de la Géstion-Université du Québec à Montréal, a fellow of the Center for Interuniversity Research and Analysis of Organizations (CIRANO), and an adjunct affiliated economist at the RAND Corporation. Arie Kapteyn is professor of economics at the University of Southern California, a research fellow at the Institute for the Study of Labor (IZA) and at Netspar, and a research associate of the National Bureau of Economic Research. Jinkook Lee is professor of economics, senior economist, and director of the Program on Global Aging, Health and Policy at the University of Southern California and an adjunct senior economist at the RAND Corporation. Gema Zamarro is an associate professor and 21st Century Endowed Chair in Teacher Quality in the Department of Education Reform at the University of Arkansas, and adjunct senior economist at the University of Southern California Dornsife Center for Economic and Social Research.

The research reported herein was pursuant to a grant from the US Social Security Administration (SSA), funded as part of the Michigan Retirement Research Consortium (RRC). The findings and conclusions expressed are solely those of the authors and do not represent the views of SSA or any agency of the federal government. The authors also acknowledge support by the National Institute on Aging under grants 2P01AG022481 and 2R01 AG030153. This research is also part of the program of the Industrial Alliance Research Chair on the Economics of Demographic Change. We thank Anne Case and participants in the NBER Conference on the Economics of Aging (The Boulders, Arizona, 2015) for helpful comments. For acknowledgments, sources of research support, and disclosure of the authors' material financial relationships, if any, please see http://www.nber.org/chapters/c13641.ack.

1. An exception is Grip, Lindeboom, and Montizaan (2012), who found a strong and persistent negative effect on psychological well-being from a change in the Dutch civil servants' pension system that affected the pension age eligibility of some cohorts but not of others.

ated by delaying retirement may be at least partly offset by increased health expenditures driven by worsened subjective well-being.

Labor force participation may affect subjective well-being in a number of different ways. Specifically, there is solid evidence that unemployment can adversely affect subjective well-being (e.g., Lucas et al. 2004; Clark and Oswald 1994; Winkelmann and Winkelmann 1998), but some mixed evidence on how retirement might do so.[2] In the United States evidence is mixed, finding both positive (Charles 2004) and negative (Dave, Rashad, and Spasojevic 2008; Szinovacz and Davey 2004) retirement effects. In contrast, consistently positive effects are found in England (Johnston and Lee 2009; Mein et al. 2003) and Finland (Okasanen et al. 2011; Salokangas and Joukamaa 1991), while no effect is found in the Republic of Korea or continental Europe for depression measures (Lee and Smith 2009; Coe and Zamarro 2011), suggesting potential cross-country variations in retirement effects on subjective well-being.[3]

Two other branches of the literature relate retirement and well-being. Recently a number of papers have found that retirement could have positive or negative effects on well-being depending on how the transition to retirement happens. For example Clark and Fawaz (2009), using European and British data sets, find that the type of job in which retirees were employed before retirement affects well-being after retirement. Similarly, Calvo, Haverstick, and Sass (2007) and Bonsang and Klein (2011) find that well-being is affected by whether the individual perceives the transition to retirement as voluntary or not. A different literature relates well-being and aging. Several papers find a U-shaped relationship between life satisfaction and age (see Blanchflower and Oswald 2008; De Ree and Alessie 2011; van Landeghem 2012, among others). Although, De Ree and Alessie (2011) note that age effects cannot be identified without imposing cohort effect assumptions.

In Fonseca et al. (2014), we examined the effect of retirement on subjective well-being within twelve countries, using panel data from the US Health and Retirement Study (HRS) and the Survey of Health, Ageing, and Retirement in Europe (SHARE). In estimating retirement effects, we accounted for potential reverse causation of poor subjective well-being on retirement, using an instrumental variables approach by exploiting variations in public-

---

2. The same mixed results are found in the psychology literature where the debate on how the retirement affects the well-being started a bit earlier than in economics research (see Pinquart and Schindle [2007], and their citations).

3. Several of these studies have tried to circumvent endogeneity problems by using an instrumental variables approach. For example, Charles (2004), Johnson and Lee (2009), and Coe and Zamarro (2011) used pension entitlement age as an instrument; Dave, Rashad, and Spasojevic (2008) used spouse's retirement status; and Lee and Smith (2009) used mandatory retirement policies as instruments. However, up to this point there is no cross-country comparative study of the effect of retirement on an array of well-being measures, while addressing the potential endogeneity of retirement choices.

pension eligibility due to country and cohort-specific retirement ages (early and full entitlement ages). Here, we provide a more comprehensive analysis of the interplay of work/retirement, financial well-being, and subjective well-being.

Financial consequences of retirement complicate the estimation of effects of retirement on subjective well-being as financial circumstances, both in absolute and relative terms (i.e., one's financial means in comparison with others, or in comparison with one's own income before retirement), may influence subjective well-being and, therefore, the effect of retirement is likely to be confounded by the change in income. At the same time, unobservable determinants of income are probably related with unobservable determinants of subjective well-being, making income possibly endogenous if used as a control in subjective well-being regressions. To address these issues, we estimate a simultaneous model, explicitly modeling the interplay of retirement, income, and subjective well-being while still using our instrumental variables approach for retirement decisions based on public-pension eligibility. By estimating the complete system of equations, we are able to get a better understanding of the role of retirement induced through Social Security or pension eligibility in determining the subjective as well as financial well-being of the elderly.

The remainder of the chapter is structured as follows: In section 11.2 the data are described, while in section 11.3 we describe the model we are estimating. Section 11.4 presents and discusses estimation results. To gain further insights in the nature of the estimated relationships, we present some simulations in section 11.5. Section 11.6 considers an alternative specification for the effect of age on retirement as a robustness check. Section 11.7 concludes.

11.2   Data

This chapter makes use of data from HRS and SHARE for a common period of observation (2004–2010). For HRS there are currently eleven waves of data (1992–2012) available. The HRS was designed to cover a wide range of demographics, health, work and retirement, income and assets, as well as family and social networks. SHARE was developed using the HRS model to collect conceptually comparable data across different countries in these key domains. Lee (2007) provides a detailed discussion of the comparability of the surveys. Currently, three waves of SHARE (2004, 2006, and 2010) are available. The first wave of SHARE was collected in 2004 in eleven European countries (Austria, Belgium, Denmark, France, Germany, Greece, Italy, the Netherlands, Spain, Switzerland, and Sweden). The 2008 SHARE wave was devoted to life-history interviews and did not include subjective well-being measures.

All surveys contain several questions that can be used as indicators of sub-

Table 11.1   Data on subjective well-being in HRS and SHARE

Well-being measure	HRS	SHARE
Life satisfaction	Diener scale (2004–2010 Leave Behind Questionnaire, LBQ); a single-item overall life satisfaction (2008–2010 Core interview)	A single-item overall life satisfaction question (2006–2010 Core Interview)
Depressive symptoms	Eight items CESD (1994–2010 Core interview)	Twelve items EURO–D (2004–2010 Core); 8-item CESD questions to a random subsample (2006 Core)

jective and financial well-being. Table 11.1 summarizes the available information and comparability of subjective well-being questions. Although not all surveys include exactly identical questions on subjective well-being, they all include questions that cover comparable domains and harmonized versions of variables can be constructed for cross-country comparison. Comparable measures of total household income can also be constructed. In this respect, the project benefits from ongoing efforts to harmonize aging data sets around the world.[4]

The single-item overall life satisfaction question in SHARE reads as follows:

"On a scale from 0 to 10 where 0 means completely dissatisfied and 10 means completely satisfied, how satisfied are you with your life?" 0 . . . 10

As noted in table 11.1, this question is only available in two waves: 2006 and 2010. The single-item life satisfaction question included in HRS waves 2008 and 2010 reads:

"Please think about your life as a whole. How satisfied are you with it? Are you completely satisfied, very satisfied, somewhat satisfied, not very satisfied, or not at all satisfied?"
1. Completely satisfied
2. Very satisfied
3. Somewhat satisfied
4. Not very satisfied
5. Not at all satisfied
8. Don't know; not ascertained
9. Refused

Although the formulation of the life satisfaction questions in HRS and SHARE is similar, the response scales are not. We have first reverse-coded

4. See http://www.g2aging.org/.

the HRS scale so that it runs from "not at all satisfied" to "completely satisfied." Next we have recoded the SHARE responses as follows: 0, 1, 2 are recoded as 1; 3, 4 are recoded as 2; 5, 6 are recoded as 3; 7, 8 are recoded as 4; and 9, 10 are recoded as 5. After recoding we obtain the following distribution of self-reported life satisfaction by country: (see table 11.2)

The HRS has included an eight-item binary version of the Center for Epidemiologic Studies Depression Scale (CESD) (yes/no/DK/RF) in core interviews from 1994 to 2010. This eight-item measure with binary response categories constitutes a subset of the original twenty-item CESD scale, which uses a four-point Likert scale. Based on the advice of mental health practitioners who compared this modified version of the CESD scale with structured interviews evaluating major depression, a cutoff threshold of 3 (out of 8) is often taken as a clinically important level of psychological distress. Thus, based on this clinical threshold, we created a binary variable of depression. Similarly, for SHARE we created a binary variable based on the recommended clinical threshold for the Euro-D. Table 11.3 presents the prevalence of depression according to the constructed binary measures in the various countries in our sample.

We note that depression is substantially less prevalent in the United States than in the European countries, according to this measure. This suggests that the depression measures might not be strictly comparable. In the analyses that follow we will always include country dummies that hopefully will correct for the lack of comparability.

The key outcome variables considered in this chapter are retirement status, household income, depression, and life satisfaction. Table 11.4 presents the correlations between these four variables by country. Although the correlations are often not very large in absolute value, the signs of the correla-

Table 11.2 **Distribution of life satisfaction by country (%)**

| | Life satisfaction | | | | | |
Country	1	2	3	4	5	Total
Austria	1.3	3.3	15.0	42.3	38.2	100
Belgium	0.4	1.4	10.7	61.0	26.5	100
Denmark	0.3	0.6	6.0	37.0	56.2	100
France	1.3	2.7	20.1	54.6	21.4	100
Germany	0.8	2.6	16.4	47.8	32.5	100
Greece	1.0	2.6	25.3	56.7	14.4	100
Italy	1.9	2.9	18.2	52.0	25.0	100
Netherlands	0.2	0.5	4.6	68.2	26.6	100
Spain	1.5	4.2	18.2	48.4	27.7	100
Sweden	0.5	0.9	7.4	42.3	49.0	100
Switzerland	0.1	1.1	7.2	41.2	50.4	100
United States	0.9	3.1	24.4	46.4	25.3	100
Total	0.8	2.4	17.6	49.2	29.9	100

Table 11.3   Depression by country

| | | Depressed | | |
Country	No	Yes	Total
Austria	81.1	18.9	100
Belgium	75.8	24.3	100
Denmark	84.8	15.2	100
France	68.4	31.6	100
Germany	81.3	18.7	100
Greece	81.5	18.5	100
Italy	69.3	30.7	100
Netherlands	83.0	17.0	100
Spain	68.1	31.9	100
Sweden	82.5	17.5	100
Switzerland	83.7	16.3	100
United States	87.4	12.6	100
Total	82.3	17.7	100

Table 11.4   Correlations between key outcome variables

	Retirement, Log-income	Retirement, depression	Retirement, life satisfaction	Log-income, depression	Log-income, life satisfaction	Depression, life satisfaction
Austria	−0.13	0.09	−0.05	−0.11	0.14	−0.41
Belgium	−0.11	0.04	−0.01	−0.07	0.11	−0.28
Denmark	−0.32	0.01	−0.04	−0.04	0.08	−0.29
France	−0.18	0.05	−0.08	−0.11	0.21	−0.30
Germany	−0.14	0.06	−0.07	−0.07	0.21	−0.32
Greece	−0.28	0.15	−0.15	−0.09	0.22	−0.26
Italy	−0.14	0.09	−0.09	−0.10	0.15	−0.35
Netherlands	−0.24	0.09	−0.04	−0.10	0.11	−0.26
Spain	−0.24	0.17	−0.07	−0.10	0.13	−0.38
Sweden	−0.22	0.08	−0.04	−0.08	0.04	−0.28
Switzerland	−0.16	0.07	−0.04	−0.11	0.13	−0.31
United States	−0.35	0.08	0.02	−0.16	0.13	−0.34
Total	−0.28	0.10	−0.03	−0.15	0.18	−0.31

tions are identical across all countries, with the exception of the correlation between retirement and life satisfaction in the United States, which is slightly positive, whereas in other countries it is negative. We see positive correlations between retirement and depression and between log-income and life satisfaction; we observe negative correlations between retirement and log-income; retirement and life satisfaction; log-income and life satisfaction; and depression and life satisfaction.

Table 11.5 presents descriptive statistics by country. We observe substantial differences in retirement rates across countries, with Italy and Austria

Table 11.5   Descriptive statistics

Country	Retired	Age	Female	Log-household income	Log-household wealth	At least one ADL	Major health condition	Less than high school	High school	Some college
Austria	0.82	66.1	0.56	10.08	11.08	0.07	0.14	0.18	0.61	0.21
Belgium	0.72	65.3	0.51	10.16	12.10	0.09	0.17	0.25	0.50	0.25
Denmark	0.59	64.9	0.54	11.78	13.43	0.06	0.17	0.15	0.49	0.37
France	0.70	65.4	0.55	10.23	12.03	0.09	0.20	0.39	0.40	0.21
Germany	0.67	64.9	0.52	10.20	11.35	0.07	0.19	0.01	0.71	0.28
Greece	0.66	63.9	0.47	9.62	11.66	0.06	0.16	0.48	0.35	0.17
Italy	0.80	65.8	0.49	9.85	11.94	0.08	0.16	0.52	0.41	0.07
Netherlands	0.68	64.3	0.52	10.33	11.51	0.05	0.16	0.14	0.63	0.23
Spain	0.75	66.8	0.49	9.54	11.94	0.10	0.16	0.64	0.28	0.08
Sweden	0.63	66.6	0.53	11.97	13.48	0.06	0.21	0.34	0.43	0.23
Switzerland	0.59	65.5	0.54	11.07	12.64	0.05	0.10	0.17	0.73	0.10
United States	0.62	68.5	0.56	10.62	12.02	0.15	0.43	0.23	0.54	0.23
Total	0.65	66.9	0.54	10.54	12.07	0.11	0.30	0.26	0.52	0.22

having the highest retirement rates and the United States, Switzerland, and Denmark the lowest. Log-income and log-wealth vary substantially across countries. To the extent that this reflects exchange-rate effects, these will be absorbed by additive country dummies in our model. Probably the most striking difference across countries is the high prevalence of major health conditions in the United States in comparison to the European countries, while also the number of ADLs is larger in the United States than in Europe. This may be partly explained by the somewhat higher ages of respondents in the HRS sample.

In the analysis we will use several institutional parameters that vary across countries. Table 11.6 shows replacement rates at full retirement age in the various countries. The replacement rates are net of taxes for a median earner with an uninterrupted career. Obviously individual replacement rates may vary substantially, but for the purpose of international comparison this information is probably about as good as it gets.

Another important institutional variable is the age at which one may be eligible for early or full retirement. Both full and early retirement ages are given in table 11.7. The ages for the United States refer to Social Security claiming ages rather than retirement; sixty-two is the earliest age at which one can claim Social Security. One can claim Social Security at any time between sixty-two and seventy and a half, with an actuarial adjustment for claiming earlier or later than the full retirement age. Receipt of Social Security benefits has no implications for one's ability to be gainfully employed. For comparison purposes we treat the US early claiming age and

Table 11.6   **Replacement rates at full retirement age**

Country	Male_2004	Female_2004	Male_2006	Female_2006	Male_2010	Female_2010
Austria	93.2	84.6	90.3	90.3	89.9	89.9
Belgium	63.1	63.1	63.7	63.7	63.8	63.8
Denmark	54.1	54.1	91.3	91.3	86.9	86.9
France	68.8	68.8	65.7	65.7	60.7	60.7
Germany	71.8	71.8	61.3	61.3	58.5	58.5
Greece	99.9	99.9	110.8	110.8	70.7	70.7
Italy	88.8	88.8	74.8	58.1	92.4	92.4
Netherlands	84.1	84.1	103.2	103.2	100.7	100.7
Spain	88.3	88.3	84.7	84.7	80.1	80.1
Sweden	68.2	68.2	64.1	64.1	53.6	53.6
Switzerland	67.3	68.0	64.5	65.3	65.4	64.4
United States	51	51	44.8	44.8	48.5	48.5

Source: Pensions at a Glance, 2005 (http://stats.oecd.org/Index.aspx?DataSetCode=ELSPENSIONS#).
Note: The replacement rates are net replacement rates (after tax) at the nations' full retirement age for a median earner who entered the labor force at the age of twenty and experienced an uninterrupted career.

Table 11.7   Early and full retirement ages (full retirement ages in parentheses)

Country	2002 Males	2002 Females	2004 Males	2004 Females	2006 Males	2006 Females	2008 Males	2008 Females	2010 Males	2010 Females
Austria	60 (65)	57 (60)	65 (65)	60 (60)	65 (65)	65 (65)	65 (65)	65 (65)	62 (65)	60 (65)
Belgium	60 (65)	60 (65)	60 (65)	60 (65)	60 (65)	60 (65)	60 (65)	60 (65)	60 (65)	60 (65)
Denmark	65 (65)	65 (65)	65 (65)	65 (65)	65 (65)	65 (65)	65 (65)	65 (65)	67 (67)	67 (67)
France	57 (60)	57 (60)	60 (60)	60 (60)	60 (60)	60 (60)	61 (61)	61 (61)	56–60 (65)	56–60 (65)
Germany	63 (65)	63 (65)	63 (65)	63 (65)	63 (65)	63 (65)	63 (67)	63 (67)	63 (67)	63 (67)
Greece	60 (65)	55 (60)	57 (65)	57 (65)	55 (65)	55 (65)	55 (65)	55 (65)	55 (65)	55 (65)
Italy	57 (65)	57 (65)	60 (65)	60 (65)	60 (65)	60 (60)	60 (65)	60 (60)	61 (65)	60 (60)
Netherlands	60 (65)	60 (65)	60 (65)	60 (65)	60 (65)	60 (65)	60 (65)	60 (65)	65 (65)	65 (65)
Spain	60 (65)	60 (65)	60 (65)	60 (65)	60 (65)	60 (65)	60 (65)	60 (65)	61 (65)	61 (65)
Sweden	61 (65)	61 (65)	61 (65)	61 (65)	61 (65)	61 (65)	61 (65)	61 (65)	61 (65)	61 (65)
Switzerland	63 (65)	62 (64)	63 (65)	62 (64)	63 (65)	62 (64)	63 (65)	62 (64)	63 (65)	62 (64)
United States[a]	62 (65)	62 (65)	62 (65+)	62 (65+)	62 (65+)	62 (65+)	62 (65+)	62 (65+)	62 (65+)	62 (65+)

Sources: OECD Pensions at a Glance for several years.

[a]Full retirement age depends on birth year.

full retirement age similarly to the treatment of early and full retirement ages in the European countries.

11.3   Model

We consider a system of four equations. The first equation explains retirement; the second equation models log-income. The third and fourth equations explain depression and life satisfaction. The specifications are as follows:

(1)   **The Labor Supply Equation:** $R_{ict} = \rho_0 + \rho_1 X_{ict} + \rho_2 I_{ict}^L + \rho_{ci} + e_{ict}$

(2)   **The Income Equation:** $\ln Y_{ict} = \gamma_1 X_{ict} + \gamma_2 R_{ict} + \gamma_3 I_{ct}^Y + \gamma_{ci} + \varepsilon_{ict}$

The Subjective Well-Being Equations: For both life satisfaction and depression, we specify linear models of the form:

(3) $SW_{ict} = \alpha_1 \ln Y_{ict} + \alpha_2 X_{ict} + \alpha_3 R_{ict} + \alpha_4 I_{ct}^{SW} + \alpha_{ci} + \upsilon_{ict}$

where Y_{ict} is the logarithm of current per capita household income of an individual i, who lives in country c, at time t, SW_{ict} denotes a given measure of subjective well-being (life satisfaction or depression), and R_{ict} takes the value 1 if the individual is retired at time t and zero otherwise; X_{ict} is the set of individual and household explanatory variables and includes: gender, ethnicity, age, time effects, education, marital status, and health and disability measures; I_{ct}^Y represents institutional variables that may affect the income process such as indices of welfare program generosity or average replacement rates in retirement and unemployment insurance programs; I_{ct}^{SW} denotes institutional variables that may affect subjective well-being directly (e.g., social safety nets), as opposed to indirectly through income $\ln Y_{ict}$; and I_{ict}^L contains a set of indicator variables denoting retirement incentives. In order for these institutional variables to be validly excluded from equations (1) and (2), they must not have a direct effect on well-being. Their effect on well-being is only through the influence on retirement. In particular, we will use dummy variables indicating whether or not an individual is above the full or early retirement age: $I_{ict}^L = 1(\text{age}_{it} \geq \text{Statutory\_retirement\_age}_{ct})$. The inclusion of individual specific constant terms (ρ_{ci}, γ_{ci}, and α_{ci}) is important because it allows us to control for individual unobserved heterogeneity, as well as for time-invariant measurement error in reporting household income or well-being.

Ideally, one would want to estimate dynamic versions of equation (1). Given that we have only two waves of the life satisfaction variable in either survey, estimation of a dynamic panel-data model with individual effects is out of the question. For depression, SHARE has three waves of data (and HRS has more) so a dynamic model can be estimated in principle, but identification would be tenuous. We limit ourselves therefore to static models until the 2012 wave of SHARE becomes available.

A Hausman specification test soundly rejects the random effects assumption of independence of the individual effects of the other right-hand-side variables in equations (1)–(3). So we adhere to a fixed effects assumption, which allows the individual effects to correlate with the explanatory variables in the equations. A straight fixed effects estimation procedure would wipe out all non-time-varying variables, such as country dummies. Due to a result by Mundlak (1978), the estimated coefficients of the time-varying explanatory variables are identical to what would be obtained in a random effects specification, while including the individual means of all time-varying explanatory variables on the right-hand side of the equations. It is easy to see that this also holds if one includes the non-time-varying explanatory variables on the right-hand side. The advantage of this procedure is that one then also obtains estimates of the effects of the non-time-varying variables, such as country dummies, education, and gender.

Several of the right-hand-side variables may not be strictly comparable due to institutional differences, such as education. The same might be true for other variables, such as ADLs and major health conditions, as noted above. We therefore include several interactions of such variables with a dummy for the United States. So the assumption is that these variables are reasonably comparable across European countries, but less so between the United States and Europe. We could, of course, include full interactions of such variables with all country dummies, but we abstain from that, mainly for reasons of parsimony.

11.4 Results

The system is estimated with 2SLS, taking into account random individual effects in a Mundlak-type specification (xtivreg in STATA). Table 11.8 contains the estimation results. Before discussing the estimates, it is worth noting the exclusion restrictions that were imposed to identify the model. The first equation (the retirement equation) is a reduced-form equation and hence no exclusion restrictions are needed. The equation for the logarithm of per capita household income has two endogenous explanatory variables on the right-hand side: retirement status (retired or not) and an interaction between being retired and the pension replacement rate. These two variables are instrumented by all exogenous variables in the model. The excluded variables are whether one is above full or early retirement age and an interaction of these variables with the pension replacement rate. So the assumption is that these variables do not exert a direct effect on household income, but only via the retirement variables.

The equations for being depressed (a binary variable, cf. table 11.3) and life satisfaction (a variable taking on five possible values, cf. table 11.2) have identical structures. Two explanatory variables are endogenous: retirement status and the logarithm of per capita household income. The exclusion restrictions are the same as for the log-household income equation.

As noted, we estimate a Mundlak specification, so that we also have estimated coefficients for the individual means of all time-varying variables. For brevity's sake these coefficients are not reported.

The estimated effects of individual and institutional variables on retirement are largely according to expectation (first column of table 11.8). The probability of being retired decreases with education, but increases with age for most of the relevant age range (the quadratic age relation has a maximum at seventy-six years). Females are more likely to be retired. Major health conditions have a negative effect on the probability of being in the labor force, particularly in the United States. Note that for the interpretation of coefficients for the United States, these have to be added to the overall coefficient. So, for instance, the coefficient of "major health condition" in the retirement equation is 0.008, while the coefficient for "major health condition in the United States" is .040. This means that the effect of a major health condition in the United States is equal to .008 + .040 = .048. Difficulties with activities of daily living reduce the chances of being in the labor force in the United States, but not in Europe. Being eligible for early or full retirement has a strong positive effect on the probability of being retired. The pension-replacement rates appear to have only a limited effect, possibly reflecting the fact that these may be poor proxies of the actual replacement rates faced by individuals. Their effects may also be absorbed by the country dummies. The country dummies generally suggest a higher retirement probability in the European countries than in the regions of the United States. (The Northeast is the reference category). Residents outside the United States are more likely to be retired, presumably because many of these moved to a location outside the United States to spend their retirement years. The time dummies suggest an increase in retirement probability over time, which may reflect the effect of the evolving financial crisis during the observation period.

The income equation (second column in table 11.8) shows a negative effect of retirement on income, which may be compensated by a high pension-replacement rate. For instance, if the pension-replacement rate is 100 percent (as it is in the Netherlands) then the net effect of retirement on income is quite modest. A similar observation can be made with respect to the effect of unemployment. Being unemployed reduces income very substantially, but this can be compensated for by a high income-replacement rate. In this age range income is monotonically decreasing in age (the parabola has a minimum at 164). Since we control for individual effects, we are implicitly also controlling for cohort effects. The effects of health conditions are somewhat difficult to interpret. The ADLs have a negative effect in the United States, but not in Europe, while for the presence of a major health condition the

Table 11.8   **Estimation results**

Variables	Retired	Log HH-income	Depressed	Life satisfaction
Retired		−0.978***	−0.061*	0.179**
		(0.067)	(0.032)	(0.086)
Pension rr * (retired)		0.008***		
		(0.000)		
Unemployed		−0.881***	0.106	−0.596*
		(0.210)	(0.105)	(0.305)
Unemployed * unempl. rr		1.073***	−0.167	0.893*
		(0.350)	(0.175)	(0.511)
Log-household net wealth		0.151***	−0.003*	0.027***
		(0.002)	(0.002)	(0.005)
d2006	0.024***	0.198***	−0.001	−0.149***
	(0.006)	(0.014)	(0.007)	(0.040)
d2008	0.038***	0.349***	0.003	−0.034
	(0.010)	(0.025)	(0.013)	(0.023)
d2010	0.072***	0.420***	0.012	
	(0.016)	(0.039)	(0.020)	
Age	0.049***	−0.154***	−0.016***	−0.064***
	(0.004)	(0.010)	(0.005)	(0.017)
Age^2 divided by 100	−0.032***	0.047***	0.012***	0.029***
	(0.002)	(0.006)	(0.003)	(0.010)
Female	0.022***	−0.158***	0.083***	−0.012
	(0.005)	(0.010)	(0.006)	(0.017)
Married	0.014	0.257***	−0.081***	0.258***
	(0.010)	(0.024)	(0.013)	(0.039)
Married and female	0.011	0.182***	0.016	0.078
	(0.013)	(0.030)	(0.016)	(0.050)
College	−0.097***	0.363***	−0.088***	0.205***
	(0.005)	(0.012)	(0.010)	(0.023)
College in United States	−0.012	0.292***	−0.034***	−0.109***
	(0.008)	(0.016)	(0.011)	(0.027)
High school	−0.021***	0.147***	−0.056***	0.135***
	(0.004)	(0.008)	(0.005)	(0.013)
High school in United States	−0.019***	0.130***	−0.022***	−0.110***
	(0.007)	(0.013)	(0.008)	(0.020)
ADL	−0.142***	0.291***	0.014	0.115***
	(0.011)	(0.024)	(0.015)	(0.042)
ADL in United States	0.175***	−0.249***	0.057***	−0.225***
	(0.010)	(0.021)	(0.013)	(0.036)
Major health condition	0.008	−0.073***	0.079***	−0.071***
	(0.006)	(0.015)	(0.007)	(0.020)
Major health condition in United States	0.040***	0.207***	−0.058***	−0.058*
	(0.008)	(0.020)	(0.011)	(0.033)
Austria	0.185***	−0.547***	0.091***	0.086*
	(0.013)	(0.030)	(0.016)	(0.048)
Belgium	0.204***	−0.519***	0.160***	0.022
	(0.010)	(0.024)	(0.016)	(0.045)
Denmark	0.099***	0.864***	−0.018	0.531***
	(0.011)	(0.023)	(0.023)	(0.053)

(*continued*)

Table 11.8   (continued)

Variables	Retired	Log HH-income	Depressed	Life satisfaction
France	0.126***	−0.387***	0.207***	−0.141***
	(0.010)	(0.022)	(0.014)	(0.041)
Germany	0.151***	−0.463***	0.097***	−0.003
	(0.011)	(0.023)	(0.015)	(0.044)
Greece	0.107***	−1.264***	0.137***	−0.297***
	(0.012)	(0.028)	(0.023)	(0.065)
Italy	0.169***	−0.840***	0.234***	−0.198***
	(0.011)	(0.025)	(0.019)	(0.053)
Netherlands	0.181***	−0.490***	0.079***	0.122***
	(0.011)	(0.026)	(0.014)	(0.041)
Spain	0.134***	−1.124***	0.252***	−0.197***
	(0.011)	(0.025)	(0.023)	(0.062)
Sweden	0.058***	1.135***	−0.017	0.472***
	(0.010)	(0.020)	(0.026)	(0.057)
Switzerland	0.065***	0.363***	0.032**	0.393***
	(0.012)	(0.023)	(0.015)	(0.038)
Midwest	0.034	−0.057	0.000	0.105
	(0.027)	(0.064)	(0.033)	(0.115)
South	0.049**	−0.065	−0.005	0.085
	(0.021)	(0.050)	(0.026)	(0.090)
West	−0.001	−0.177***	0.032	0.123
	(0.025)	(0.060)	(0.031)	(0.098)
Residing outside United States	0.346***	−0.008	0.102	−0.243
	(0.107)	(0.256)	(0.150)	(0.784)
Above full ret. age	0.103***			
	(0.014)			
Above early ret. age	0.154***			
	(0.014)			
Pension rr * (above full ret. age)	0.000			
	(0.000)			
Pension rr * (above early ret. age)	−0.001***			
	(0.000)			
Log-household income			0.011	−0.016
			(0.008)	(0.016)
Constant	−3.726***	10.777***	−0.379	5.371***
	(0.101)	(0.354)	(0.295)	(0.727)
Observations	120,775	120,775	116,254	63,661
Number of groups	52,028	52,028	51,006	40,429

Note: Standard errors in parentheses.
***Significant at the 1 percent level.
**Significant at the 5 percent level.
*Significant at the 10 percent level.

pattern is reversed. Caution needs to be exercised when interpreting country dummies as these are affected by exchange rates (except for the comparison of countries within the euro zone: Austria, Belgium, France, Germany, Greece, Italy, the Netherlands, and Spain).

For the purpose of this chapter, the final two columns in table 11.8 are of the most interest. It appears that being retired both reduces the likelihood of depression (though only significantly so at the 10 percent level) and improves life satisfaction. This is in contrast with the findings in table 11.4, where we found that in the raw data retirement was negatively related to life satisfaction in all countries (with the sole exception of the United States), while retirement was positively related to depression in all countries. Generally the coefficients in the last two columns of table 11.8 have opposite signs. For instance, unemployment increases the likelihood of depression, while it reduces life satisfaction. Note, however, that these effects are mitigated very substantially in the case of a high unemployment-replacement rate. Being married, having a higher education, and having more wealth all increase life satisfaction and reduce the likelihood of depression. On the other hand, having a major health condition or experiencing difficulties with activities of daily living reduce life satisfaction and increase the likelihood of depression.

Notably, household income does not appear to have an appreciable effect on either depression or life satisfaction, once we control for all the other explanatory variables. This is also in marked contrast with the raw correlations relations reported in table 11.4.

11.5 Simulations

To obtain a better understanding of the quantitative importance of the estimation results we use the estimated system to simulate the effects of some counterfactual policies. To have a valid benchmark to compare the simulations with we first simulate outcomes for the dependent variables within sample and compare with the values observed in the data. The results of this exercise are presented in table 11.9.

The second simulation investigates the effect of setting pension-replacement rates to 100 percent in all countries. The results of this simulation are presented in table 11.10.

In contrast, the third simulation investigates the effect of setting pension-replacement rates to 40 percent in all countries. The results of this simulation are presented in table 11.11.

The fourth and final simulation considers the effect of raising early retirement age to sixty-seven and full retirement age to seventy. Results are given in table 11.12.

Table 11.9 shows that the model does a reasonable job of reproducing sample statistics, with the exception of log-income, which seems to be systematically overpredicted.

Table 11.9   Predicted and observed outcome variables

Country	Retirement predicted	Retirement observed	Log-income predicted	Log-income, observed	Depression predicted	Depression observed	Life satisfaction predicted	Life satisfaction observed
Austria	0.82	0.82	10.48	10.08	0.19	0.19	4.11	4.13
Observations	3,365	3,365	3,365	3,365	3,337	3,337	1,839	1,839
Belgium	0.72	0.72	10.65	10.16	0.25	0.24	4.11	4.12
Observations	8,066	8,066	8,066	8,066	8,046	8,046	4,838	4,838
Denmark	0.59	0.59	11.05	11.78	0.14	0.15	4.50	4.48
Observations	5,257	5,257	5,257	5,257	5,225	5,225	3,857	3,857
France	0.70	0.70	10.64	10.23	0.32	0.32	3.91	3.92
Observations	7,010	7,010	7,010	7,010	6,908	6,908	4,244	4,244
Germany	0.66	0.67	10.59	10.2	0.19	0.19	4.08	4.09
Observations	6,170	6,170	6,170	6,170	6,149	6,149	3,529	3,529
Greece	0.66	0.66	10.89	9.62	0.20	0.19	3.79	3.81
Observations	4,395	4,395	4,395	4,395	4,395	4,395	2,400	2,400
Italy	0.80	0.80	10.72	9.85	0.32	0.31	3.93	3.96
Observations	6,088	6,088	6,088	6,088	6,055	6,055	4,161	4,161
Netherlands	0.68	0.68	10.88	10.33	0.18	0.17	4.20	4.20
Observations	6,522	6,522	6,522	6,522	6,501	6,501	4,007	4,007
Spain	0.75	0.75	10.63	9.54	0.33	0.32	3.94	3.97
Observations	4,587	4,587	4,587	4,587	4,537	4,537	2,940	2,940
Sweden	0.63	0.63	10.78	11.97	0.16	0.17	4.40	4.38
Observations	6,784	6,784	6,784	6,784	6,762	6,762	4,080	4,080
Switzerland	0.59	0.59	10.8	11.07	0.16	0.16	4.41	4.41
Observations	3,108	3,108	3,108	3,108	3,102	3,102	2,257	2,257
United States	0.62	0.62	10.33	10.62	0.13	0.13	3.92	3.92
Observations	59,423	59,423	59,423	59,423	55,237	55,237	25,509	25,509
Total	0.66	0.65	10.54	10.54	0.18	0.18	4.05	4.05
Observations	120,775	120,775	120,775	120,775	116,254	116,254	63,661	63,661

Table 11.10   Simulated outcomes with 100 percent replacement rates

Country	Retirement simulated	Retirement predicted	Log-income simulated	Log-income, predicted	Depression simulated	Depression predicted	Life satisfaction simulated	Life satisfaction predicted
Austria	0.81	0.82	10.56	10.48	0.20	0.19	4.11	4.11
Belgium	0.71	0.72	10.87	10.65	0.25	0.25	4.11	4.11
Denmark	0.58	0.59	11.15	11.05	0.15	0.14	4.49	4.50
France	0.68	0.70	10.85	10.64	0.33	0.32	3.9	3.91
Germany	0.65	0.66	10.79	10.59	0.19	0.19	4.07	4.08
Greece	0.67	0.66	10.86	10.89	0.20	0.20	3.79	3.79
Italy	0.79	0.80	10.84	10.72	0.32	0.32	3.92	3.93
Netherlands	0.68	0.68	10.91	10.88	0.18	0.18	4.20	4.20
Spain	0.75	0.75	10.74	10.63	0.33	0.33	3.94	3.94
Sweden	0.62	0.63	10.98	10.78	0.16	0.16	4.39	4.40
Switzerland	0.58	0.59	10.97	10.8	0.16	0.16	4.40	4.41
United States	0.60	0.62	10.60	10.33	0.13	0.13	3.91	3.92
Total	0.64	0.66	10.74	10.54	0.18	0.18	4.04	4.05

Table 11.11   Simulated outcomes with 40 percent replacement rates

Country	Retirement simulated	Retirement predicted	log–income simulated	log–income predicted	Depression simulated	Depression predicted	Life satisfaction simulated	Life satisfaction predicted
Austria	0.84	0.82	10.13	10.48	0.19	0.19	4.12	4.11
Belgium	0.73	0.72	10.50	10.65	0.25	0.25	4.12	4.11
Denmark	0.60	0.59	10.84	11.05	0.14	0.14	4.50	4.50
France	0.71	0.70	10.48	10.64	0.32	0.32	3.91	3.91
Germany	0.67	0.66	10.45	10.59	0.18	0.19	4.08	4.08
Greece	0.69	0.66	10.51	10.89	0.19	0.20	3.80	3.79
Italy	0.82	0.80	10.43	10.72	0.31	0.32	3.93	3.93
Netherlands	0.69	0.68	10.56	10.88	0.17	0.18	4.20	4.20
Spain	0.77	0.75	10.34	10.63	0.33	0.33	3.95	3.94
Sweden	0.64	0.63	10.66	10.78	0.16	0.16	4.40	4.40
Switzerland	0.60	0.59	10.67	10.80	0.16	0.16	4.41	4.41
United States	0.62	0.62	10.28	10.33	0.12	0.13	3.92	3.92
Total	0.66	0.66	10.4	10.54	0.18	0.18	4.05	4.05

Table 11.12   Simulated outcomes: Full retirement age is seventy; early retirement age is sixty-seven

Country	Retirement simulated	Retirement predicted	Log-income simulated	Log-income predicted	Depression simulated	Depression predicted	Life satisfaction simulated	Life satisfaction predicted
Austria	0.75	0.82	10.50	10.48	0.20	0.19	4.10	4.11
Belgium	0.68	0.72	10.66	10.65	0.25	0.25	4.10	4.11
Denmark	0.56	0.59	11.06	11.05	0.15	0.14	4.49	4.50
France	0.62	0.70	10.67	10.64	0.33	0.32	3.89	3.91
Germany	0.62	0.66	10.61	10.59	0.19	0.19	4.07	4.08
Greece	0.62	0.66	10.90	10.89	0.20	0.20	3.78	3.79
Italy	0.73	0.80	10.74	10.72	0.32	0.32	3.91	3.93
Netherlands	0.66	0.68	10.89	10.88	0.18	0.18	4.19	4.20
Spain	0.71	0.75	10.65	10.63	0.33	0.33	3.93	3.94
Sweden	0.58	0.63	10.8	10.78	0.17	0.16	4.39	4.40
Switzerland	0.56	0.59	10.82	10.8	0.16	0.16	4.40	4.41
United States	0.58	0.62	10.35	10.33	0.13	0.13	3.92	3.92
Total	0.61	0.66	10.56	10.54	0.18	0.18	4.04	4.05

The simulations in tables 11.10 and 11.11 show only small effects of changes in replacement rates. In view of the small estimates of the coefficient estimates of the replacement variables, this is not surprising. Incomes, which are directly affected by replacement rates, show most sensitivity to the level of replacement rates: high replacement rates lead to high incomes and low replacement rates lead to low incomes.

Table 11.12 shows the effects of increasing full and early retirement ages. The effects of changing eligibility ages on retirement is considerably larger than the effects of changing replacement rates, although it should be observed that the change in retirement ages simulated here is quite dramatic. As one would expect, the effects are largest in the countries where currently eligibility ages are low, such as Austria, France, and Italy. To obtain more insight in the incidence of the effects, we break down the results by age in tables 13–16. For each country, the first row presents the simulated counterfactuals, while the second row presents the predicted in-sample values. The effects on retirement are large in the age range fifty-five to sixty-nine in

Table 11.13	Simulated retirement by age							
Country		< = 54	55–59	60–64	65–69	70–74	> = 75	Total
Austria	Simulated	0.27	0.49	0.65	0.78	1.03	1.08	0.75
	Predicted	0.27	0.54	0.8	0.95	1.03	1.08	0.82
Belgium	Simulated	0.27	0.43	0.57	0.75	1.01	1.07	0.68
	Predicted	0.27	0.43	0.67	0.92	1.01	1.07	0.72
Denmark	Simulated	0.14	0.30	0.46	0.65	0.92	0.98	0.56
	Predicted	0.14	0.30	0.46	0.82	0.92	0.98	0.59
France	Simulated	0.19	0.36	0.51	0.69	0.94	1.01	0.62
	Predicted	0.19	0.44	0.74	0.86	0.94	1.01	0.70
Germany	Simulated	0.22	0.37	0.52	0.70	0.95	1.01	0.62
	Predicted	0.22	0.37	0.56	0.87	0.95	1.01	0.66
Greece	Simulated	0.17	0.38	0.59	0.76	1.00	1.06	0.62
	Predicted	0.17	0.40	0.70	0.92	1.00	1.06	0.66
Italy	Simulated	0.25	0.45	0.63	0.77	1.02	1.07	0.73
	Predicted	0.25	0.49	0.78	0.94	1.02	1.07	0.80
Netherlands	Simulated	0.25	0.40	0.56	0.77	1.04	1.09	0.66
	Predicted	0.25	0.40	0.56	0.94	1.04	1.09	0.68
Spain	Simulated	0.21	0.39	0.60	0.75	0.99	1.05	0.71
	Predicted	0.21	0.39	0.69	0.92	0.99	1.05	0.75
Sweden	Simulated	0.13	0.29	0.43	0.61	0.87	0.93	0.58
	Predicted	0.13	0.29	0.51	0.78	0.87	0.93	0.63
Switzerland	Simulated	0.13	0.29	0.44	0.62	0.87	0.93	0.56
	Predicted	0.13	0.29	0.50	0.79	0.87	0.93	0.59
United States	Simulated	0.08	0.23	0.37	0.55	0.81	0.89	0.58
	Predicted	0.08	0.23	0.44	0.7	0.81	0.89	0.62
Total	Simulated	0.16	0.31	0.46	0.63	0.88	0.94	0.61
	Predicted	0.16	0.32	0.55	0.79	0.88	0.94	0.66

Table 11.14   **Simulated log-income by age**

Country		< = 54	55–59	60–64	65–69	70–74	> = 75	Total
Austria	Simulated	11.95	11.44	10.93	10.43	9.88	9.04	10.50
	Predicted	11.95	11.43	10.89	10.39	9.88	9.04	10.48
Belgium	Simulated	12.08	11.57	11.06	10.45	9.87	9.09	10.66
	Predicted	12.08	11.57	11.01	10.38	9.87	9.09	10.65
Denmark	Simulated	12.48	11.91	11.41	10.85	10.22	9.38	11.06
	Predicted	12.48	11.91	11.41	10.8	10.22	9.38	11.05
France	Simulated	12.09	11.60	11.08	10.49	9.91	9.11	10.67
	Predicted	12.09	11.56	10.99	10.42	9.91	9.11	10.64
Germany	Simulated	11.93	11.52	10.94	10.37	9.86	9.02	10.61
	Predicted	11.93	11.52	10.93	10.30	9.86	9.02	10.59
Greece	Simulated	12.13	11.64	11.09	10.52	10.06	9.28	10.9
	Predicted	12.13	11.64	11.08	10.50	10.06	9.28	10.89
Italy	Simulated	12.15	11.64	11.12	10.60	10.08	9.38	10.74
	Predicted	12.15	11.62	11.07	10.55	10.08	9.38	10.72
Netherlands	Simulated	12.14	11.67	11.17	10.61	10.05	9.26	10.89
	Predicted	12.14	11.67	11.17	10.58	10.05	9.26	10.88
Spain	Simulated	12.13	11.67	11.11	10.61	10.07	9.35	10.65
	Predicted	12.13	11.67	11.08	10.57	10.07	9.35	10.63
Sweden	Simulated	12.37	11.86	11.36	10.78	10.15	9.27	10.80
	Predicted	12.37	11.86	11.32	10.71	10.15	9.27	10.78
Switzerland	Simulated	12.22	11.75	11.24	10.67	10.06	9.24	10.82
	Predicted	12.22	11.75	11.22	10.6	10.06	9.24	10.80
United States	Simulated	12.05	11.59	11.05	10.47	9.91	9.10	10.35
	Predicted	12.05	11.59	11.01	10.39	9.91	9.10	10.33
Total	Simulated	12.12	11.63	11.10	10.52	9.96	9.15	10.56
	Predicted	12.12	11.63	11.07	10.45	9.96	9.15	10.54

countries like Austria, Belgium, and France. In the remaining countries the effects show up at somewhat later ages. As one would expect, the effects on income are most noticeable in these same age ranges, but now the size of the effect also depends on replacement rates. For instance, in the Netherlands, the effect is quite modest.

The effect on depression is generally modest. We note a slight uptick in France and Italy in the age group sixty to sixty-four. Similarly, the effect on life satisfaction is most visible in the sixty to sixty-nine age range in France and Italy. The effects are most visible in the United States in the age range sixty-five to sixty-nine.

11.6   An Alternative Age Specification

Our specification for the effect of age on the four outcomes of interest has been quadratic in all four equations. To investigate if this rather sparse parameterization of the age effects drives some of our results, the appendix

Table 11.15   Simulated depression rates by age

Country		< = 54	55–59	60–64	65–69	70–74	> = 75	Total
Austria	Simulated	0.18	0.19	0.19	0.19	0.19	0.24	0.20
	Predicted	0.18	0.19	0.18	0.18	0.19	0.24	0.19
Belgium	Simulated	0.24	0.24	0.24	0.25	0.25	0.28	0.25
	Predicted	0.24	0.24	0.24	0.24	0.25	0.28	0.25
Denmark	Simulated	0.14	0.14	0.14	0.13	0.14	0.18	0.15
	Predicted	0.14	0.14	0.14	0.12	0.14	0.18	0.14
France	Simulated	0.31	0.30	0.32	0.33	0.32	0.37	0.33
	Predicted	0.31	0.30	0.30	0.32	0.32	0.37	0.32
Germany	Simulated	0.19	0.18	0.18	0.18	0.17	0.22	0.19
	Predicted	0.19	0.18	0.18	0.17	0.17	0.22	0.19
Greece	Simulated	0.19	0.18	0.19	0.20	0.21	0.25	0.20
	Predicted	0.19	0.18	0.18	0.19	0.21	0.25	0.20
Italy	Simulated	0.31	0.31	0.32	0.32	0.33	0.36	0.32
	Predicted	0.31	0.30	0.30	0.30	0.33	0.36	0.32
Netherlands	Simulated	0.18	0.17	0.17	0.17	0.18	0.2	0.18
	Predicted	0.18	0.17	0.17	0.16	0.18	0.2	0.18
Spain	Simulated	0.34	0.32	0.33	0.33	0.32	0.36	0.33
	Predicted	0.34	0.32	0.32	0.32	0.32	0.36	0.33
Sweden	Simulated	0.16	0.15	0.15	0.16	0.16	0.21	0.17
	Predicted	0.16	0.15	0.14	0.15	0.16	0.21	0.16
Switzerland	Simulated	0.17	0.16	0.15	0.16	0.16	0.18	0.16
	Predicted	0.17	0.16	0.15	0.15	0.16	0.18	0.16
United States	Simulated	0.14	0.13	0.13	0.12	0.11	0.14	0.13
	Predicted	0.14	0.13	0.12	0.11	0.11	0.14	0.13
Total	Simulated	0.20	0.18	0.18	0.17	0.17	0.19	0.18
	Predicted	0.20	0.18	0.17	0.16	0.17	0.19	0.18

presents estimation and simulation results for a specification in which the quadratic age function is replaced by forty age dummies (for ages fifty-one through ninety). Figure 11A.1 plots the estimated age dummies, while table 11A.1 presents the estimates of the remaining parameters. The graphs confirm that the likelihood of being retired increases with age, while income falls with age (this may partly be a cohort effect). Life satisfaction shows a slight increase with age. The graph with depression suggests that depression also increases somewhat with age, but inspection of the estimated coefficients reveals that these effects are not significant.

Comparing table 11A.1 with table 11.8 shows that the sizes of the estimated coefficients are affected by the more flexible age specification, but qualitatively conclusions don't change. Virtually all estimates have the same sign in table 11.8 and in table 11A.1. The most noteworthy change is that, whereas in table 11.9 retirement has a marginally significant (at the 10 percent level) negative effect on the prevalence of depression and a significant (at the 5 percent level) positive on life satisfaction, these effects are insignificant in table 11A.1, although the signs remain the same.

Table 11.16   **Simulated life satisfaction by age**

Country		< = 54	55–59	60–64	65–69	70–74	> = 75	Total
Austria	Simulated	4.14	4.11	4.10	4.11	4.13	4.05	4.10
	Predicted	4.14	4.12	4.13	4.14	4.13	4.05	4.11
Belgium	Simulated	4.10	4.10	4.10	4.09	4.13	4.10	4.10
	Predicted	4.10	4.10	4.12	4.12	4.13	4.10	4.11
Denmark	Simulated	4.50	4.49	4.49	4.50	4.51	4.48	4.49
	Predicted	4.50	4.49	4.49	4.53	4.51	4.48	4.50
France	Simulated	3.91	3.91	3.89	3.88	3.92	3.87	3.89
	Predicted	3.91	3.93	3.93	3.91	3.92	3.87	3.91
Germany	Simulated	4.06	4.06	4.06	4.07	4.13	4.06	4.07
	Predicted	4.06	4.06	4.07	4.10	4.13	4.06	4.08
Greece	Simulated	3.81	3.80	3.79	3.75	3.77	3.73	3.78
	Predicted	3.81	3.80	3.81	3.78	3.77	3.73	3.79
Italy	Simulated	3.96	3.94	3.91	3.91	3.91	3.89	3.91
	Predicted	3.96	3.95	3.94	3.94	3.91	3.89	3.93
Netherlands	Simulated	4.18	4.19	4.19	4.20	4.20	4.18	4.19
	Predicted	4.18	4.19	4.19	4.23	4.20	4.18	4.2
Spain	Simulated	3.92	3.92	3.92	3.93	3.95	3.95	3.93
	Predicted	3.92	3.92	3.93	3.96	3.95	3.95	3.94
Sweden	Simulated	4.41	4.41	4.40	4.40	4.39	4.35	4.39
	Predicted	4.41	4.41	4.42	4.43	4.39	4.35	4.40
Switzerland	Simulated	4.39	4.40	4.40	4.40	4.42	4.40	4.40
	Predicted	4.39	4.40	4.41	4.43	4.42	4.40	4.41
United States	Simulated	3.84	3.85	3.88	3.91	3.95	3.95	3.92
	Predicted	3.84	3.85	3.89	3.94	3.95	3.95	3.92
Total	Simulated	4.07	4.03	4.04	4.04	4.04	4.03	4.04
	Predicted	4.07	4.03	4.06	4.06	4.04	4.03	4.05

Tables 11A.2–11A.9 repeat the simulation exercise of tables 11.9–11.16. Comparing table 11.9 with table 11A.2 shows that the model with forty age dummies provides a somewhat better fit than the model with a quadratic age specification, as one would expect. The simulation results presented in tables 11A.3–11A.9 are qualitatively very similar to the results presented in tables 11.10–11.16. Also, in the specification with age dummies effects are generally small. The exercise with a substantial increase in early and full retirement ages shows the biggest effect in both cases, in particular for the age bracket sixty to sixty-nine.

11.7   Concluding Remarks

We have estimated a simultaneous system of equations explaining the joint determination of retirement, income, depression, and life satisfaction. The system accounts for unobserved individual heterogeneity, by including fixed effects. Statistical tests show that omitting these would lead to serious misspecification. To identify causal effects we have used variation in institutions across countries that influence retirement decisions and household incomes.

In the raw data, being retired is positively correlated with the risk of depression and negatively correlated with life satisfaction. Once we account for endogeneity of retirement these relations change sign. In the most flexible specification with forty age dummies, the effect of retirement on either depression or life satisfaction is insignificant. Interestingly, income does not appear to play much of a role in the determination of depression or life satisfaction, once other factors are accounted for. This also contrasts with the correlations in the raw data, which suggested that a higher income leads to higher life satisfaction and to fewer depressive symptoms.

As one would expect, household wealth, being married, and educational attainment are all positively related to life satisfaction and reduce the probability of depression. Health conditions and difficulties with activities of daily living increase the probability of depression and reduce life satisfaction.

The fairly weak effects of retirement on life satisfaction and depression suggest that, at least as far as these variables are concerned, gradual increases in retirement ages will have only moderate effects. We should note, however, that the effects estimated here are average effects. Plausibly, the effects of retirement will vary across subgroups, so to inform policy an analysis of the heterogeneity of effects across different socioeconomic strata is called for.

Appendix

Specification with Age Dummies

Table 11A.1   **Estimation results**

Variables	Retired	Log HH-income	Depressed	Life satisfaction
Retired		−2.448***	−0.013	0.230
		(0.153)	(0.064)	(0.147)
Pension rr * (retired)		0.007***		
		(0.001)		
Unemployed		−1.342***	0.123	−0.576*
		(0.261)	(0.107)	(0.299)
Unemployed * unempl. rr		0.836*	−0.165	0.889*
		(0.430)	(0.175)	(0.499)
Log-household net wealth		0.150***	−0.003*	0.027***
		(0.003)	(0.002)	(0.004)
d2006	0.026***	0.247***	−0.004	−0.150***
	(0.006)	(0.018)	(0.007)	(0.039)
d2008	0.041***	0.433***	−0.002	−0.034
	(0.010)	(0.032)	(0.014)	(0.022)
d2010	0.073***	0.567***	0.005	
	(0.016)	(0.049)	(0.021)	
Female	0.023***	−0.162***	0.086***	−0.006
	(0.005)	(0.010)	(0.007)	(0.017)
Married	0.011	0.272***	−0.082***	0.246***
	(0.010)	(0.030)	(0.013)	(0.039)
Married and female	0.013	0.206***	0.015	0.078
	(0.013)	(0.037)	(0.016)	(0.049)
College	−0.098***	0.360***	−0.095***	0.191***
	(0.005)	(0.013)	(0.010)	(0.024)
College in United States	−0.010	0.288***	−0.038***	−0.108***
	(0.008)	(0.015)	(0.011)	(0.028)
High school	−0.021***	0.144***	−0.058***	0.132***
	(0.004)	(0.009)	(0.005)	(0.014)
High school in United States	−0.019***	0.127***	−0.025***	−0.112***
	(0.007)	(0.013)	(0.008)	(0.020)
ADL	−0.138***	0.349***	0.001	0.086*
	(0.011)	(0.028)	(0.016)	(0.044)
ADL in United States	0.172***	−0.251***	0.069***	−0.196***
	(0.010)	(0.023)	(0.015)	(0.038)
Major health condition	0.008	−0.064***	0.079***	−0.069***
	(0.006)	(0.018)	(0.007)	(0.020)
Major health condition in United States	0.040***	0.270***	−0.060***	−0.056*
	(0.008)	(0.026)	(0.011)	(0.033)
Austria	0.182***	−0.575***	0.105***	0.132**
	(0.013)	(0.031)	(0.018)	(0.053)
Belgium	0.210***	−0.533***	0.173***	0.064
	(0.010)	(0.026)	(0.018)	(0.049)
Denmark	0.082***	0.828***	−0.024	0.553***
	(0.011)	(0.024)	(0.024)	(0.054)

(*continued*)

Table 11A.1 (continued)

Variables	Retired	Log HH-income	Depressed	Life satisfaction
France	0.137***	−0.403***	0.217***	−0.106**
	(0.010)	(0.024)	(0.015)	(0.044)
Germany	0.142***	−0.476***	0.106***	0.029
	(0.011)	(0.024)	(0.016)	(0.047)
Greece	0.100***	−1.288***	0.154***	−0.260***
	(0.012)	(0.029)	(0.025)	(0.068)
Italy	0.169***	−0.866***	0.250***	−0.157***
	(0.011)	(0.027)	(0.021)	(0.057)
Netherlands	0.162***	−0.515***	0.089***	0.158***
	(0.011)	(0.027)	(0.015)	(0.044)
Spain	0.132***	−1.148***	0.269***	−0.161**
	(0.011)	(0.026)	(0.024)	(0.065)
Sweden	0.058***	1.104***	−0.027	0.489***
	(0.010)	(0.020)	(0.026)	(0.058)
Switzerland	0.058***	0.349***	0.030*	0.412***
	(0.012)	(0.023)	(0.015)	(0.039)
Midwest	0.038	0.000	−0.001	0.115
	(0.027)	(0.079)	(0.033)	(0.113)
South	0.048**	0.003	−0.006	0.090
	(0.021)	(0.061)	(0.026)	(0.088)
West	−0.003	−0.180**	0.033	0.131
	(0.025)	(0.074)	(0.031)	(0.097)
Residing outside United States	0.367***	0.558*	0.078	−0.323
	(0.106)	(0.319)	(0.152)	(0.813)
Above full ret. age	0.176***			
	(0.016)			
Above early ret. age	0.003			
	(0.017)			
Pension rr * (above full ret. age)	−0.001***			
	(0.000)			
Pension rr * (above early ret. age)	0.001**			
	(0.000)			
Log-household income			0.013	−0.017
			(0.008)	(0.015)
Constant	0.052***	9.103***	−0.467**	4.808***
	(0.015)	(0.036)	(0.182)	(0.442)
Observations	120,775	120,775	116,254	63,661
R-squared				
Number of groups	52,028	52,028	51,006	40,429
Individual effects	RE	RE	RE	RE

Note: Standard errors in parentheses.
***Significant at the 1 percent level.
**Significant at the 5 percent level.
*Significant at the 10 percent level.

Table 11A.2   Predicted and observed outcome variables

Country	Retirement predicted	Retirement observed	Log-income predicted	Log-income observed	Depression predicted	Depression observed	Life satisfaction predicted	Life satisfaction observed
Austria	0.82	0.82	10.15	10.08	0.19	0.19	4.12	4.13
Observations	3,365	3,365	3,365	3,365	3,337	3,337	1,839	1,839
Belgium	0.72	0.72	10.44	10.16	0.25	0.24	4.11	4.12
Observations	8,066	8,066	8,066	8,066	8,046	8,046	4,838	4,838
Denmark	0.59	0.59	11.05	11.78	0.14	0.15	4.5	4.48
Observations	5,257	5,257	5,257	5,257	5,225	5,225	3,857	3,857
France	0.7	0.7	10.49	10.23	0.32	0.32	3.91	3.92
Observations	7,010	7,010	7,010	7,010	6,908	6,908	4,244	4,244
Germany	0.66	0.67	10.49	10.2	0.19	0.19	4.08	4.09
Observations	6,170	6,170	6,170	6,170	6,149	6,149	3,529	3,529
Greece	0.66	0.66	10.73	9.62	0.2	0.19	3.79	3.81
Observations	4,395	4,395	4,395	4,395	4,395	4,395	2,400	2,400
Italy	0.8	0.8	10.45	9.85	0.31	0.31	3.93	3.96
Observations	6,088	6,088	6,088	6,088	6,055	6,055	4,161	4,161
Netherlands	0.68	0.68	10.73	10.33	0.17	0.17	4.2	4.2
Observations	6,522	6,522	6,522	6,522	6,501	6,501	4,007	4,007
Spain	0.75	0.75	10.42	9.54	0.33	0.32	3.94	3.97
Observations	4,587	4,587	4,587	4,587	4,537	4,537	2,940	2,940
Sweden	0.63	0.63	10.77	11.97	0.16	0.17	4.4	4.38
Observations	6,784	6,784	6,784	6,784	6,762	6,762	4,080	4,080
Switzerland	0.59	0.59	10.83	11.07	0.16	0.16	4.41	4.41
Observations	3,108	3,108	3,108	3,108	3,102	3,102	2,257	2,257
United States	0.62	0.62	10.47	10.62	0.13	0.13	3.92	3.92
Observations	59,423	59,423	59,423	59,423	55,237	55,237	25,509	25,509
Total	0.66	0.65	10.53	10.54	0.18	0.18	4.05	4.05
Observations	120,775	120,775	120,775	120,775	116,254	116,254	63,661	63,661

Table 11A.3   Simulated outcomes with 100 percent replacement rates

Country	Retirement simulated	Retirement predicted	Log-income simulated	Log-income predicted	Depression simulated	Depression predicted	Life satisfaction simulated	Life satisfaction predicted
Austria	0.82	0.82	10.22	10.15	0.19	0.19	4.12	4.12
Belgium	0.72	0.72	10.64	10.44	0.25	0.25	4.11	4.11
Denmark	0.59	0.59	11.14	11.05	0.14	0.14	4.5	4.5
France	0.69	0.7	10.68	10.49	0.32	0.32	3.9	3.91
Germany	0.66	0.66	10.67	10.49	0.19	0.19	4.07	4.08
Greece	0.66	0.66	10.7	10.73	0.2	0.2	3.79	3.79
Italy	0.8	0.8	10.56	10.45	0.32	0.31	3.93	3.93
Netherlands	0.68	0.68	10.75	10.73	0.18	0.17	4.2	4.2
Spain	0.75	0.75	10.51	10.42	0.33	0.33	3.94	3.94
Sweden	0.63	0.63	10.95	10.77	0.16	0.16	4.4	4.4
Switzerland	0.59	0.59	10.99	10.83	0.16	0.16	4.4	4.41
United States	0.61	0.62	10.72	10.47	0.13	0.13	3.91	3.92
Total	0.65	0.66	10.72	10.53	0.18	0.18	4.04	4.05

Table 11A.4   Simulated outcomes with 40 percent replacement rates

Country	Retirement simulated	Retirement predicted	Log-income simulated	Log-income predicted	Depression simulated	Depression predicted	Life satisfaction simulated	Life satisfaction predicted
Austria	0.83	0.82	9.84	10.15	0.19	0.19	4.12	4.12
Belgium	0.72	0.72	10.31	10.44	0.25	0.25	4.12	4.11
Denmark	0.6	0.59	10.86	11.05	0.14	0.14	4.5	4.5
France	0.7	0.7	10.36	10.49	0.32	0.32	3.91	3.91
Germany	0.67	0.66	10.37	10.49	0.18	0.19	4.08	4.08
Greece	0.67	0.66	10.38	10.73	0.2	0.2	3.8	3.79
Italy	0.8	0.8	10.2	10.45	0.31	0.31	3.93	3.93
Netherlands	0.69	0.68	10.43	10.73	0.17	0.17	4.21	4.2
Spain	0.76	0.75	10.17	10.42	0.33	0.33	3.95	3.94
Sweden	0.63	0.63	10.66	10.77	0.16	0.16	4.4	4.4
Switzerland	0.6	0.59	10.71	10.83	0.16	0.16	4.41	4.41
United States	0.62	0.62	10.43	10.47	0.13	0.13	3.92	3.92
Total	0.66	0.66	10.41	10.53	0.18	0.18	4.05	4.05

Table 11A.5   Simulated outcomes: Full retirement age is seventy and early retirement age is sixty-seven

Country	Retirement simulated	Retirement predicted	Log-income simulated	Log-income predicted	Depression simulated	Depression predicted	Life satisfaction simulated	Life satisfaction predicted
Austria	0.77	0.82	10.24	10.15	0.19	0.19	4.1	4.12
Belgium	0.7	0.72	10.49	10.44	0.25	0.25	4.11	4.11
Denmark	0.57	0.59	11.09	11.05	0.14	0.14	4.49	4.5
France	0.65	0.7	10.59	10.49	0.32	0.32	3.9	3.91
Germany	0.64	0.66	10.55	10.49	0.19	0.19	4.07	4.08
Greece	0.63	0.66	10.78	10.73	0.2	0.2	3.78	3.79
Italy	0.75	0.8	10.54	10.45	0.32	0.31	3.92	3.93
Netherlands	0.66	0.68	10.76	10.73	0.18	0.17	4.19	4.2
Spain	0.73	0.75	10.47	10.42	0.33	0.33	3.93	3.94
Sweden	0.6	0.63	10.83	10.77	0.16	0.16	4.39	4.4
Switzerland	0.57	0.59	10.89	10.83	0.16	0.16	4.4	4.41
United States	0.59	0.62	10.53	10.47	0.13	0.13	3.91	3.92
Total	0.63	0.66	10.59	10.53	0.18	0.18	4.04	4.05

Table 11A.6 **Simulated retirement by age**

Country		< = 54	55–59	60–64	65–69	70–74	> = 75	Total
Austria	Simulated	0.27	0.45	0.74	0.85	1.02	1.07	0.77
	Predicted	0.27	0.48	0.84	0.97	1.02	1.07	0.82
Belgium	Simulated	0.28	0.4	0.64	0.8	1	1.06	0.7
	Predicted	0.28	0.4	0.67	0.94	1	1.06	0.72
Denmark	Simulated	0.14	0.26	0.54	0.71	0.9	0.95	0.57
	Predicted	0.14	0.26	0.54	0.83	0.9	0.95	0.59
France	Simulated	0.2	0.33	0.62	0.76	0.95	1.01	0.65
	Predicted	0.2	0.36	0.78	0.89	0.95	1.01	0.7
Germany	Simulated	0.22	0.33	0.6	0.74	0.93	0.99	0.64
	Predicted	0.22	0.33	0.61	0.88	0.93	0.99	0.66
Greece	Simulated	0.17	0.34	0.68	0.83	0.98	1.05	0.63
	Predicted	0.17	0.36	0.76	0.94	0.98	1.05	0.66
Italy	Simulated	0.27	0.42	0.72	0.84	1.01	1.06	0.75
	Predicted	0.27	0.44	0.82	0.96	1.01	1.06	0.8
Netherlands	Simulated	0.24	0.36	0.63	0.83	1.01	1.06	0.66
	Predicted	0.24	0.36	0.63	0.94	1.01	1.06	0.68
Spain	Simulated	0.22	0.36	0.67	0.81	0.98	1.03	0.73
	Predicted	0.22	0.36	0.72	0.93	0.98	1.03	0.75
Sweden	Simulated	0.14	0.26	0.5	0.66	0.86	0.93	0.6
	Predicted	0.14	0.26	0.53	0.8	0.86	0.93	0.63
Switzerland	Simulated	0.14	0.26	0.52	0.67	0.86	0.91	0.57
	Predicted	0.14	0.26	0.55	0.8	0.86	0.91	0.59
United States	Simulated	0.09	0.2	0.44	0.58	0.8	0.88	0.59
	Predicted	0.09	0.2	0.46	0.71	0.8	0.88	0.62
Total	Simulated	0.17	0.28	0.54	0.67	0.87	0.94	0.63
	Predicted	0.17	0.29	0.58	0.8	0.87	0.94	0.66

Table 11A.7 **Simulated log-income by age**

Country		< = 54	55–59	60–64	65–69	70–74	> = 75	Total
Austria	Simulated	12.13	11.34	10.65	10.24	9.48	8.47	10.24
	Predicted	12.13	11.29	10.46	10.03	9.48	8.47	10.15
Belgium	Simulated	12.24	11.55	10.91	10.37	9.53	8.58	10.49
	Predicted	12.24	11.55	10.84	10.1	9.53	8.58	10.44
Denmark	Simulated	12.89	12.11	11.46	10.92	10.04	9.02	11.09
	Predicted	12.89	12.11	11.46	10.69	10.04	9.02	11.05
France	Simulated	12.4	11.7	10.98	10.46	9.64	8.67	10.59
	Predicted	12.4	11.64	10.67	10.2	9.64	8.67	10.49
Germany	Simulated	12.17	11.62	10.86	10.37	9.64	8.63	10.55
	Predicted	12.17	11.62	10.83	10.11	9.64	8.63	10.49
Greece	Simulated	12.49	11.71	10.87	10.33	9.66	8.71	10.78
	Predicted	12.49	11.68	10.74	10.16	9.66	8.71	10.73
Italy	Simulated	12.37	11.63	10.89	10.46	9.71	8.88	10.54
	Predicted	12.37	11.59	10.7	10.23	9.71	8.88	10.45
Netherlands	Simulated	12.39	11.73	11.06	10.47	9.67	8.72	10.76
	Predicted	12.39	11.73	11.06	10.27	9.67	8.72	10.73
Spain	Simulated	12.39	11.73	10.91	10.52	9.75	8.87	10.47
	Predicted	12.39	11.73	10.82	10.3	9.75	8.87	10.42
Sweden	Simulated	12.76	12.09	11.44	10.92	10.04	8.96	10.83
	Predicted	12.76	12.09	11.38	10.65	10.04	8.96	10.77
Switzerland	Simulated	12.65	12.01	11.31	10.82	9.96	8.95	10.89
	Predicted	12.65	12.01	11.26	10.55	9.96	8.95	10.83
United States	Simulated	12.59	12	11.32	10.82	9.98	8.96	10.53
	Predicted	12.59	12	11.28	10.56	9.98	8.96	10.47
Total	Simulated	12.49	11.85	11.17	10.69	9.87	8.88	10.59
	Predicted	12.49	11.84	11.09	10.43	9.87	8.88	10.53

Table 11A.8 **Simulated depression rates by age**

Country		< = 54	55–59	60–64	65–69	70–74	> = 75	Total
Austria	Simulated	0.19	0.19	0.16	0.17	0.19	0.25	0.19
	Predicted	0.19	0.19	0.16	0.17	0.19	0.25	0.19
Belgium	Simulated	0.26	0.24	0.22	0.24	0.24	0.29	0.25
	Predicted	0.26	0.24	0.22	0.23	0.24	0.29	0.25
Denmark	Simulated	0.16	0.15	0.13	0.12	0.12	0.17	0.14
	Predicted	0.16	0.15	0.13	0.11	0.12	0.17	0.14
France	Simulated	0.32	0.31	0.3	0.31	0.32	0.37	0.32
	Predicted	0.32	0.31	0.29	0.3	0.32	0.37	0.32
Germany	Simulated	0.21	0.2	0.17	0.17	0.17	0.22	0.19
	Predicted	0.21	0.2	0.17	0.16	0.17	0.22	0.19
Greece	Simulated	0.2	0.18	0.17	0.19	0.2	0.25	0.2
	Predicted	0.2	0.18	0.17	0.19	0.2	0.25	0.2
Italy	Simulated	0.32	0.3	0.29	0.3	0.33	0.36	0.32
	Predicted	0.32	0.3	0.29	0.3	0.33	0.36	0.31
Netherlands	Simulated	0.2	0.17	0.15	0.16	0.17	0.2	0.18
	Predicted	0.2	0.17	0.15	0.15	0.17	0.2	0.17
Spain	Simulated	0.34	0.33	0.31	0.32	0.32	0.36	0.33
	Predicted	0.34	0.33	0.31	0.31	0.32	0.36	0.33
Sweden	Simulated	0.17	0.16	0.14	0.14	0.15	0.2	0.16
	Predicted	0.17	0.16	0.14	0.14	0.15	0.2	0.16
Switzerland	Simulated	0.18	0.17	0.15	0.15	0.15	0.18	0.16
	Predicted	0.18	0.17	0.15	0.15	0.15	0.18	0.16
United States	Simulated	0.15	0.14	0.13	0.12	0.11	0.13	0.13
	Predicted	0.15	0.14	0.12	0.12	0.11	0.13	0.13
Total	Simulated	0.21	0.19	0.17	0.16	0.16	0.19	0.18
	Predicted	0.21	0.19	0.17	0.16	0.16	0.19	0.18

Table 11A.9 **Simulated life satisfaction by age**

Country		< = 54	55–59	60–64	65–69	70–74	> = 75	Total
Austria	Simulated	4.15	4.08	4.1	4.12	4.14	4.07	4.1
	Predicted	4.15	4.09	4.13	4.15	4.14	4.07	4.12
Belgium	Simulated	4.12	4.09	4.1	4.09	4.14	4.12	4.11
	Predicted	4.12	4.09	4.11	4.13	4.14	4.12	4.11
Denmark	Simulated	4.51	4.49	4.51	4.5	4.49	4.47	4.49
	Predicted	4.51	4.49	4.51	4.53	4.49	4.47	4.5
France	Simulated	3.93	3.9	3.89	3.87	3.91	3.88	3.9
	Predicted	3.93	3.91	3.93	3.91	3.91	3.88	3.91
Germany	Simulated	4.07	4.06	4.08	4.06	4.11	4.05	4.07
	Predicted	4.07	4.06	4.08	4.1	4.11	4.05	4.08
Greece	Simulated	3.8	3.76	3.82	3.78	3.78	3.74	3.78
	Predicted	3.8	3.77	3.85	3.8	3.78	3.74	3.79
Italy	Simulated	3.97	3.91	3.91	3.91	3.92	3.9	3.92
	Predicted	3.97	3.92	3.94	3.94	3.92	3.9	3.93
Netherlands	Simulated	4.2	4.17	4.2	4.2	4.2	4.19	4.19
	Predicted	4.2	4.17	4.2	4.23	4.2	4.19	4.2
Spain	Simulated	3.91	3.9	3.93	3.94	3.96	3.95	3.93
	Predicted	3.91	3.9	3.95	3.97	3.96	3.95	3.94
Sweden	Simulated	4.43	4.42	4.44	4.39	4.37	4.34	4.39
	Predicted	4.43	4.42	4.44	4.42	4.37	4.34	4.4
Switzerland	Simulated	4.39	4.4	4.43	4.4	4.4	4.38	4.4
	Predicted	4.39	4.4	4.44	4.43	4.4	4.38	4.41
United States	Simulated	3.83	3.81	3.89	3.92	3.97	3.94	3.91
	Predicted	3.83	3.81	3.89	3.96	3.97	3.94	3.92
Total	Simulated	4.07	4.01	4.05	4.04	4.05	4.03	4.04
	Predicted	4.07	4.01	4.07	4.07	4.05	4.03	4.05

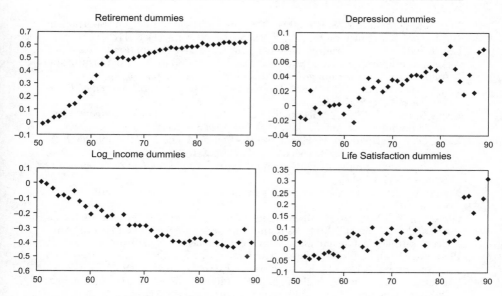

Fig. 11A.1   Estimated age dummies

References

Blanchflower, D. G., and A. J. Oswald. 2008. "Is Well-Being U-shaped over the Life Cycle?" *Social Science and Medicine* 66 (8): 1733–49.

Bonsang, E., and T. J. Klein. 2011. "Retirement and Subjective Well-Being." IZA Discussion Paper no. 5536, Institute for the Study of Labor.

Calvo, E., Kelly Haverstick, and Steven A. Sass. 2007. "What Makes Retirees Happier: A Gradual or 'Cold Turkey' Retirement." CRR Working Paper no. 2007-18, Center for Retirement Research at Boston College.

Charles, K. K. 2004. "Is Retirement Depressing? Labor Force Inactivity and Psychological Well-Being in Later Life." *Research in Labor Economics* 23:269–99.

Clark, A. E., and Y. Fawaz. 2009. "Valuing Jobs via Retirement: European Evidence." *National Institute Economic Review* 209:88–103.

Clark, A., and A. J. Oswald. 1994. "Unhappiness and Unemployment." *Economic Journal* 104:648–59.

Coe, N. B., and G. Zamarro. 2011. "Retirement Effects on Health in Europe." *Journal of Health Economics* 30:77–86.

Dave, D., I. Rashad, and J. Spasojevic. 2008. "The Effects of Retirement on Physical and Mental Health Outcomes." *Southern Economic Journal* 75:497–523.

De Ree, J., and R. Alessie. 2011. "Life Satisfaction and Age: Dealing with Underidentification in Age-Period-Cohort Models." *Social Science and Medicine* 73 (1): 177–82.

Fonseca, R., A. Kapteyn, J. Lee, and G. Zamarro. 2014. "A Longitudinal Study of Well-Being of Older Europeans: Does Retirement Matter?" *Journal of Population Aging* 7:21–41.

Grip, A., M. Lindeboom, and R. Montizaan. 2012. "Shattered Dreams: The Effects of Changing the Pension System Late in the Game." *Economic Journal* 122:1–25.

Johnston, D. W., and W. S. Lee. 2009. "Retiring to the Good Life? The Short-Term Effects of Retirement on Health." *Economics Letters* 103 (1): 8–11.

Lee, J. 2007. "Harmonization of Ageing Surveys and Cross-national Studies of Ageing." Report, Behavioral and Social Research Program, National Institute on Aging. http://www.nia.nih.gov/sites/default/files/meeting-report_5.pdf.

Lee, J., and J. Smith. 2009. "Work, Retirement, and Depression." *Journal of Population and Aging* 2:57–71.

Lucas, R. E., A. E. Clark, Y. Georgellis, and E. Diener. 2004. "Unemployment Alters the Setpoint for Life Satisfaction." *Psychological Science* 15 (1): 8–13.

Mein, G., P. Martikainen, H. Hemingway, S. Stansfeld, and M. Marmot. 2003. "Is Retirement Good or Bad for Mental and Physical Health Functioning? Whitehall II Longitudinal Study of Civil Servants." *Journal of Epidemiology and Community Health* 57 (1): 46–49.

Mundlak, Y. 1978. "On the Pooling of Time Series and Cross Section Data." *Econometrica* 46:69–85.

Okasanen, T., J. Vahtera, H. Westerlund, J. Pentti, N. Sjösten, M. Virtanen, I. Kawachi, and M. Kivimäki. 2011. "Is Retirement Beneficial for Mental Health? Antidepressant Use before and after Retirement." *Epidemiology* 22 (4): 560–62.

Pinquart, M., and I. Schindle. 2007. "Changes of Life Satisfaction in the Transition to Retirement: A Latent-Class Approach." *Psychology and Aging* 22 (3): 442–55.

Salokangas, R. K., and M. Joukamaa. 1991. "Physical and Mental Health Changes in Retirement Age." *Psychotherapy and Phychosomatics* 55 (2–4): 100–07.

Szinovacz, M. E., and A. Davey. 2004. "Retirement Transitions and Spouse Disability: Effects on Depressive Symptoms." *Journal of Gerontology B: Psychology* 59 (6): S333–42.

van Landeghem, B. 2012. "A Test for the Convexity of Human Well-Being over the Life Cycle: Longitudinal Evidence from a 20-Year Panel." *Journal of Economic Behavior and Organization* 81 (2): 571–82.

Winkelmann, L., and R. Winkelmann. 1998. "Why are the Unemployed So Unhappy? Evidence from Panel Data." *Economica* 65:1–15.

Comment   Anne Case

This is an interesting chapter on an important topic. At a fundamental level, the question of whether retirement makes people happy (or, more specifically here, increases their reported life satisfaction) would appear to be unanswerable with observational data, and is much like trying to quantify whether having children makes one happy. If people who want children have children, and those who do not choose away from parenthood, then in expectation people in both groups are happier than they would be in the alternative state. And so it should be with respect to retirement.

Anne Case is the Alexander Stewart 1886 Professor of Economics and Public Affairs and professor of economics and public affairs at the Woodrow Wilson School of Public and International Affairs and the Economics Department at Princeton University and a research associate of the National Bureau of Economic Research.

For acknowledgments, sources of research support, and disclosure of the author's material financial relationships, if any, please see http://www.nber.org/chapters/c13642.ack.

But working people reflecting on retirement may have a difficult time forming expectations: they face a multidimensional problem, one in which information gaps and uncertainty about future states of the world can leave decision making overwhelming. For many people, work is an important component in self-definition, and an important pillar in self-worth. They may have little idea how they will define themselves after retirement. Individuals may not know (or it may be unknowable) how days and social interactions will be structured; how health will evolve, and the speed at which it will decline; and whether savings will be adequate to buffer themselves, and possibly their children and grandchildren, in later years. Many ordinary least squares estimates of the impact of retirement on well-being implicitly assume people stumble into retirement (or not), perhaps for some of the reasons stated above, and in this way sidestep the issue of the joint endogeneity of life satisfaction and retirement.

To overcome obstacles caused by the joint determination of income, life satisfaction, and the decision to retire, Fonseca et al. develop and estimate a simultaneous equation system in which retirement, income, and life satisfaction are jointly determined. To identify the impact of retirement on well-being, the authors use country-year statutory early and full-retirement ages, and those age cutoffs interacted with pension generosity, as instruments for retirement, and country-year generosity in average pension replacement rates and those of the unemployment insurance system as instruments for household income. Their results, presented in table 11.8, suggest that retirement is negatively associated with depression and positively associated with life satisfaction.

These results may offer some comfort to those in the throes of making retirement decisions. However, many questions about how the authors arrive at these results remain. In their simultaneous equations model, the authors control for a host of household and individual characteristics that may affect retirement, income, and well-being. These include household net wealth, and individuals' sex, marital status, and education. But household net wealth must be determined by household income, as well as being a determinant of it. This question of joint determination of income and wealth would seem especially acute in the authors' specification, which includes individual-level fixed effects (so that the coefficient on log-household net wealth is being identified off of deviations in household income from its mean over the sample period relative to deviations in household net wealth from its mean). Endogeneity of any one right-side variable will render all coefficients biased and inconsistent, so this is more than an academic concern. A similar problem arises in the inclusion of measures of health and disability as right-hand-side controls. Disability and the presence of a major health condition may cause incomes to fall, but it is also the case that lower income is thought to be a major determinant in individuals' health status. Depression is likely to manifest in lower health status, and more difficulties with activities of daily living, in addition to difficulties with ADLs leading to higher depression. Again, the endogeneity of right-side variables is a concern here.

A second set of concerns involves functional form. The authors' individual and household level controls may have different effects when a person is retired or is still working. The impact of retirement on life satisfaction may be different if one is better educated or if one is married, for example. Such nuances are not allowed for here. Perhaps more importantly, the authors include a quadratic term in age in all of their equations—to capture any curvature in the underlying relationship between age and retirement, income, and well-being. Restricting the underlying relationships in this way frees the authors to use indicators that an individual is above early or full-retirement age as instruments for retirement in their well-being equations. If the underlying relationship is not well captured by the quadratic term in age, then using indicators that a person is above (say) sixty, and eligible for early retirement benefits, or above (say) age sixty-five and eligible for full retirement benefits as instruments may be problematic.

I have on hand recent data for white non-Hispanic respondents from the National Health Interview Survey (NHIS) that allows me to plot the relationship between a respondent's age and a marker for serious mental distress in the United States from 2010 to 2013. The mental distress indicator is constructed using the Kessler 6 questionnaire, which has been included in the annual NHIS survey since 1997. Individuals are asked how often they have felt sad, nervous, restless, hopeless, "everything was an effort," and worthless. Scoring answers as 1 = all of the time, 2 = most of the time, 3 = some of the time, 4 = little of the time, and 5 = none of the time, and adding the scores on the six questions together, I use an aggregate score of 18 or lower as a marker for "serious mental distress."[1] The relationship between age and the Kessler-6 indicator is shown as the solid line in figure 11C.1. The fraction of individuals at risk for serious mental distress increases from age fifty into the late fifties, and then begins to fall with age, to approximately age seventy-two, above which age it flattens out. That an equation including only a quadratic in age would not capture this pattern well can be seen by examining the dashed line in figure 11C.1, which is the age pattern one would estimate using age and age squared as explanatory variables. Adding to such an equation an indicator for age greater than sixty, and an indicator for age greater than sixty-five, would improve the fit of the predicted age-distress relationship, with the indicators lowering the estimated distress for individuals above those ages. In the current chapter, that lowering is attributed to retirement. However, the fall in distress began much earlier—in the late fifties—and falls smoothly through age seventy-two, suggesting something else may be driving the decline in reports of distress. (I have replicated figure 11C.1 using only individuals who are currently working, and find a similar

1. For details on this measure, see http://www.hcp.med.harvard.edu/ncs/k6_scales.php.

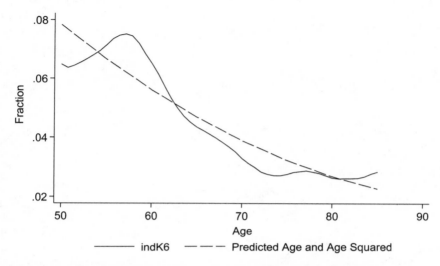

Fig. 11C.1 Fraction with Kessler 6 score ≤ 18, white non-Hispanics, NHIS

pattern throughout the age range studied here.) Understanding the underlying age pattern is important for the present chapter, as identification relies
on statutory retirement ages as instruments.

In sum, this chapter contributes to what we know (and do not know)
about whether retirement leads to happiness. I am certain it will stimulate
more research on this important topic.

Contributors

Philip Armour
RAND Corporation
1776 Main Street
PO Box 2138
Santa Monica, CA 90401–3208

Abhijit Banerjee
Department of Economics, E52–540
Massachusetts Institute of Technology
77 Massachusetts Avenue
Cambridge, MA 02139

James Banks
Arthur Lewis Building-3.020
School of Social Sciences
The University of Manchester
Manchester M13 9PL England

Sharon Barnhardt
CESS Nuffield–FLAME University
Lavale, Pune 412115 India

John Beshears
Harvard Business School
Baker Library 439
Soldiers Field
Boston, MA 02163

Jay Bhattacharya
117 Encina Commons
CHP/PCOR
Stanford University
Stanford, CA 94305–6019

Richard Blundell
University College London
Department of Economics
Gower Street
London WC1E 6BT England

Anne Case
Woodrow Wilson School of Public
    and International Affairs
367 Wallace Hall
Princeton University
Princeton, NJ 08544

Amitabh Chandra
John F. Kennedy School of
    Government
Harvard University
79 John F. Kennedy Street
Cambridge, MA 02138

Michael Chernew
Harvard Medical School
Department of Health Care Policy
180 Longwood Avenue
Boston, MA 02115

James J. Choi
Yale School of Management
165 Whitney Avenue
PO Box 208200
New Haven, CT 06520–8200

David M. Cutler
Department of Economics
Harvard University
1875 Cambridge Street
Cambridge, MA 02138

Angus Deaton
Woodrow Wilson School
361 Wallace Hall
Princeton University
Princeton, NJ 08544–1013

Esther Duflo
Department of Economics, E52–544
Massachusetts Institute of Technology
77 Massachusetts Avenue
Cambridge, MA 02139

Raquel Fonseca
Université du Québec à Montréal
Département des sciences économiques
315, rue Sainte-Catherine Est
Montréal (Québec), H2X 3X2 Canada

Kaushik Ghosh
National Bureau of Economic
    Research
1050 Massachusetts Avenue
Cambridge, MA 02138

Florian Heiss
University of Duesseldorf
LS Statistics and Econometrics
Universitaetsstrasse 1, Geb. 24.31
40225 Düsseldorf Germany

Tyler Hoppenfeld
Evidence for Policy Design
Harvard University
79 John F. Kennedy Street
Cambridge, MA 02138

Michael D. Hurd
RAND Corporation
1776 Main Street
PO Box 2138
Santa Monica, CA 90407

Joshua Hurwitz
National Bureau of Economic
    Research
1050 Massachusetts Avenue
Cambridge, MA 02138

Hidehiko Ichimura
Graduate School of Economics
University of Tokyo
Hongo 7–3–1
Tokyo 113–0033 Japan

Arie Kapteyn
University of Southern California
Center for Economic and Social
    Research
635 Downey Way Suite 312
Los Angeles, CA 90089–3332

David Laibson
Department of Economics
Littauer M-12
Harvard University
Cambridge, MA 02138

Mary Beth Landrum
Harvard Medical School
Department of Health Care Policy
180 Longwood Avenue
Boston, MA 02115–5899

Jinkook Lee
Center for Economic and Social
    Research
University of Southern California
635 Downey Way
Los Angeles, CA 90089–3332

Thomas MaCurdy
Department of Economics
Stanford University
Stanford, CA 94305–6072

Brigitte C. Madrian
Harvard Kennedy School
79 John F. Kennedy Street
Cambridge, MA 02138

Daniel McFadden
Sol Price School of Public Policy
University of Southern California
University Gateway 101C
Los Angeles, CA 90089

Zoë Oldfield
Institute for Fiscal Studies
7 Ridgemount Street
London, WC1 7AE England

James M. Poterba
Department of Economics, E52–444
Massachusetts Institute of Technology
77 Massachusetts Avenue
Cambridge, MA 02139

Susann Rohwedder
RAND Corporation
1776 Main Street
PO Box 2138
Santa Monica, CA 90407

Jonathan Skinner
Department of Economics
6106 Rockefeller Hall
Dartmouth College
Hanover, NH 03755

James P. Smith
RAND Corporation
1776 Main Street
PO Box 2138
Santa Monica, CA 90407–2138

Steven F. Venti
Department of Economics
6106 Rockefeller Center
Dartmouth College
Hanover, NH 03755

David R. Weir
Population Studies Center
University of Michigan
426 Thompson Street
Ann Arbor, MI 48104

Joachim Winter
Department of Economics
LMU Munich
Ludwigstr. 33
D-80539 Munich Germany

David A. Wise
Kennedy School of Government
Harvard University
79 John F. Kennedy Street
Cambridge, MA 02138

Richard Woodbury
National Bureau of Economic
    Research
1050 Massachusetts Avenue
Cambridge, MA 02138

Amelie Wuppermann
Department of Economics
LMU Munich
Ludwigstr. 33
D-80539 Munich Germany

Gema Zamarro
219B Graduate Education Building
College of Education and Health
    Professions
University of Arkansas
Fayetteville, AR 72701

Yaoyao Zhu
Department of Economics
University of Southern California
3620 S. Vermont Avenue, KAP Hall
    300
Los Angeles, CA 90089–0253

Author Index

Subject Index